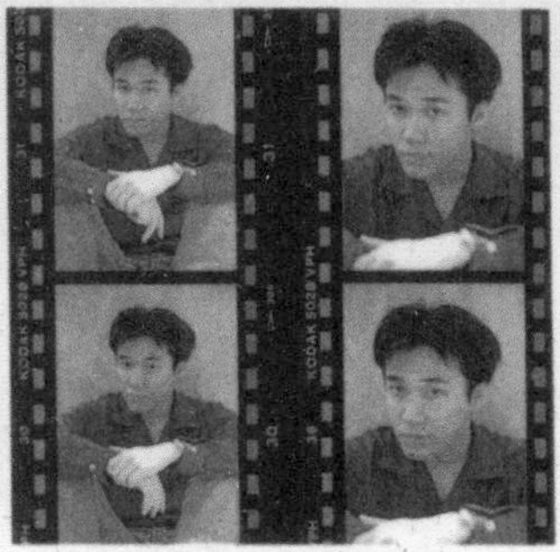

井上雄彦

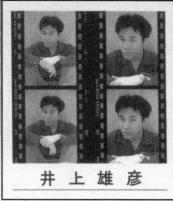

Takehiko Inoue

I WANT A DOG.

I'VE ALWAYS LOVED ANIMALS. WHEN I WAS A KID, I WAS SO ATTACHED TO A NEIGHBOR'S DOG THAT I RENAMED HIM "KORO" AND PRETENDED HE WAS MINE WHEN WE PLAYED. THESE DAYS, I'M OBSESSED WITH A HUSKY NAMED "GINJI" WHO BELONGS TO MY NEIGHBOR. WHEN I CALL HIM, GINJI POKES HIS GIANT HEAD UP OVER OUR FENCE (A FENCE THAT COMES UP TO MY SHOULDERS!) AND STARES ME RIGHT IN THE EYE.

I LIKE BIG DOGS.

Takehiko Inoue's *Slam Dunk* is one of the most popular manga of all time, having sold over 100 million copies worldwide. He followed that series up with two titles lauded by critics and fans alike—*Vagabond*, a fictional account of the life of Miyamoto Musashi, and *Real*, a manga about wheelchair basketball.

SLAM DUNK
Vol. 8: Basketball

SHONEN JUMP Manga Edition

STORY AND ART BY TAKEHIKO INOUE

English Adaptation/Kelly Sue DeConnick
Translation/Joe Yamazaki
Touch-up Art & Lettering/James Gaubatz
Cover & Graphic Design/Sean Lee
Editor/Kit Fox

VP, Production/Alvin Lu
VP, Sales & Product Marketing/Gonzalo Ferreyra
VP, Creative/Linda Espinosa
Publisher/Hyoe Narita

Printed in the U.S.A.

Published by VIZ Media, LLC
P.O. Box 77010
San Francisco, CA 94107

10 9 8 7 6 5 4 3 2 1
First printing, February 2010

www.viz.com

THE WORLD'S
MOST POPULAR MANGA

www.shonenjump.com

STORY AND ART BY

TAKEHIKO INOUE

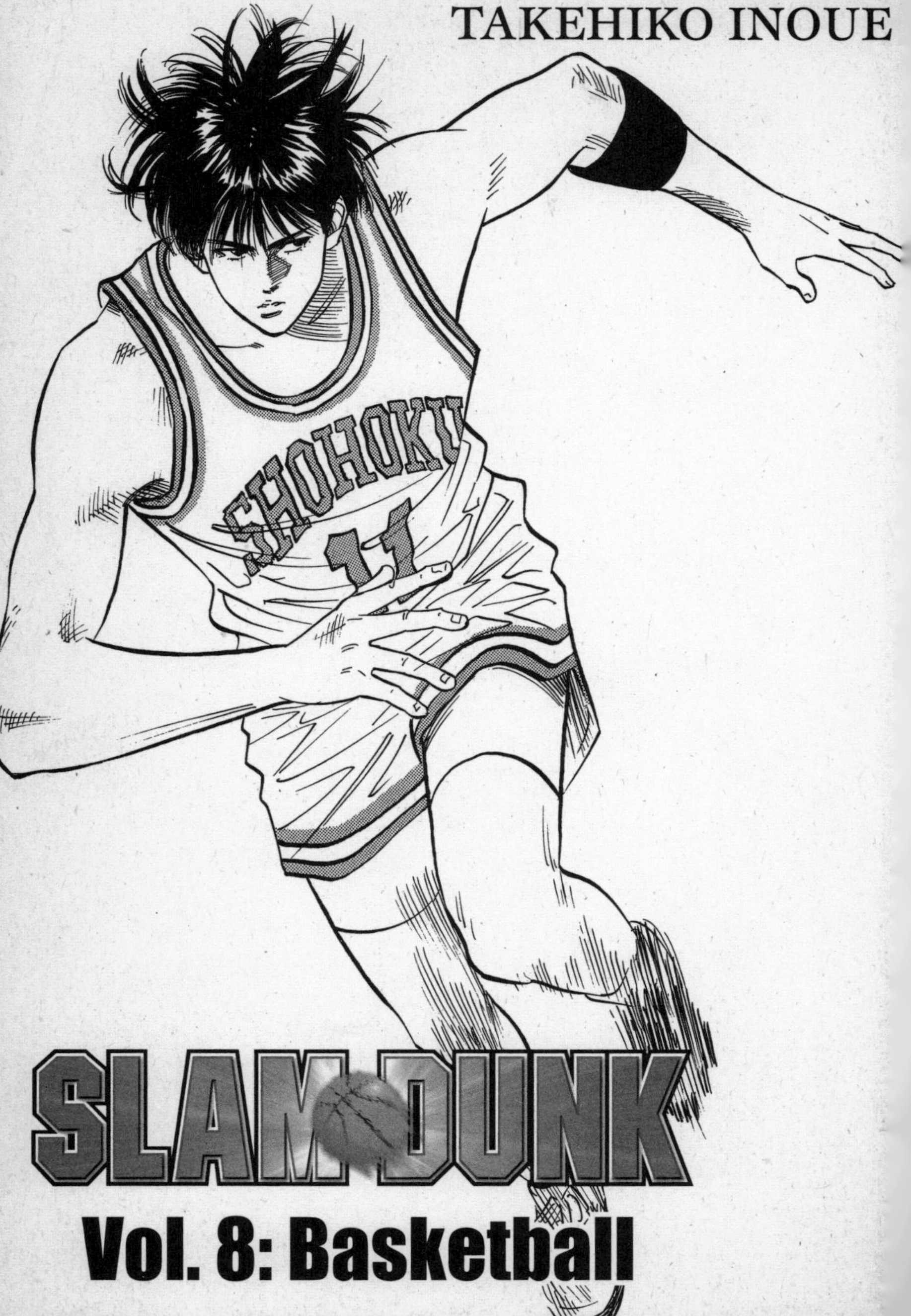
SHOHOKU
11

SLAM DUNK

Vol. 8: Basketball

Character Introduction

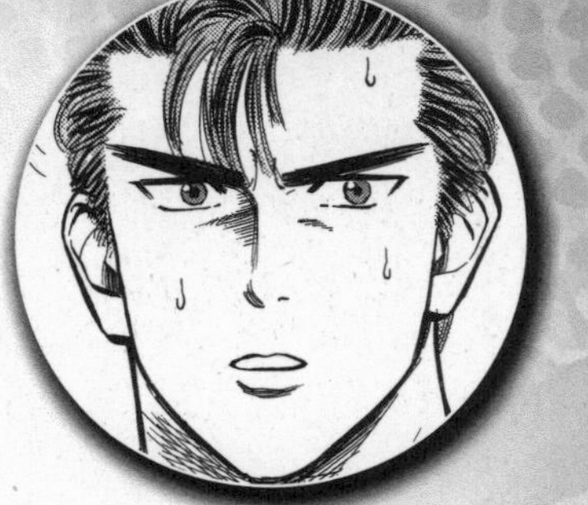

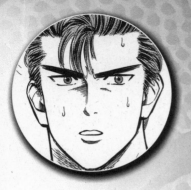

Hanamichi Sakuragi
A first-year at Shohoku High School, Sakuragi is in love with Haruko Akagi.

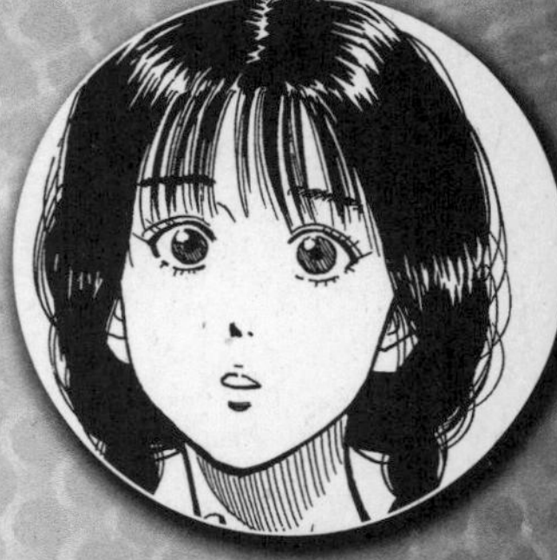

Haruko Akagi
Also a first-year at Shohoku, Takenori Akagi's little sister has a crush on Kaede Rukawa.

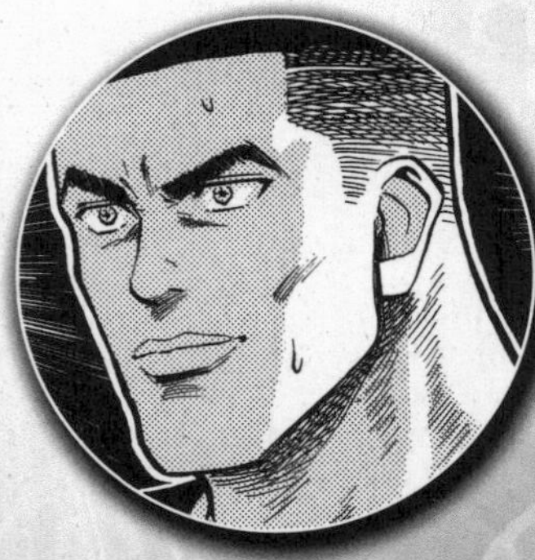

Takenori Akagi
A third-year and the basketball team's captain, Akagi has an intense passion for his sport.

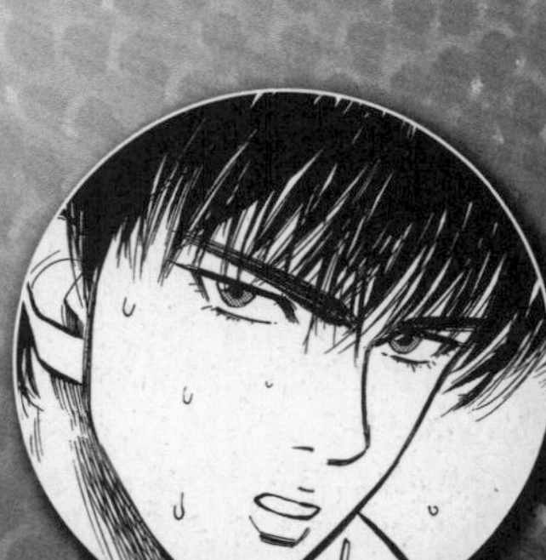

Kaede Rukawa
The object of Haruko's affection (and that of many of Shohoku's female students!), this first-year has been a star player since junior high.

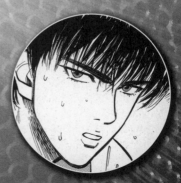

Sakuragi's Friends

Ohkusu Mito Takamiya Noma

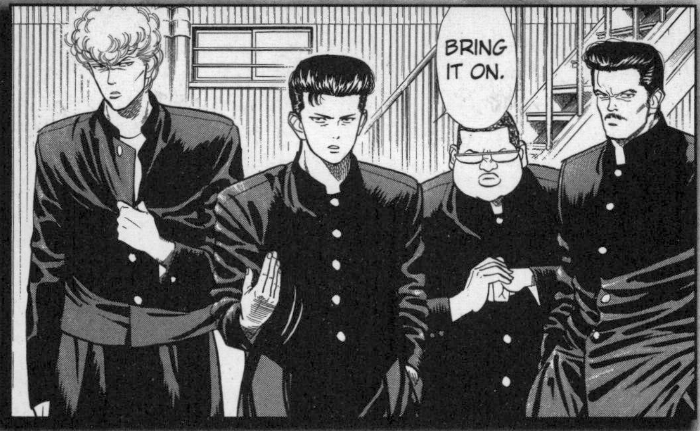
BRING IT ON.

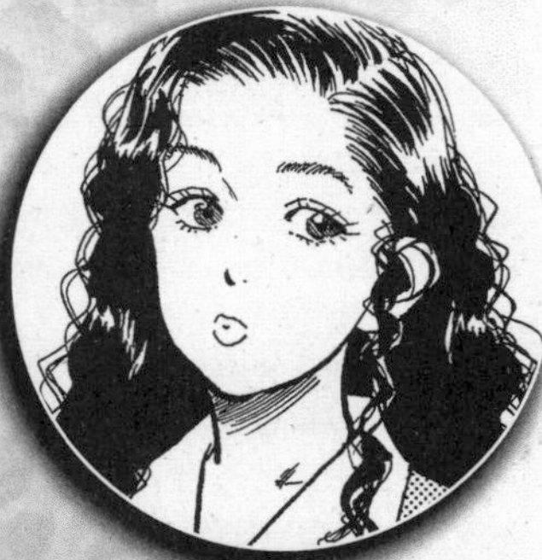

Ayako

Basketball Team Manager

Our Story Thus Far

Hanamichi Sakuragi is rejected by close to 50 girls during his three years in junior high. In high school, he joins the basketball team in order to get closer to his beloved Haruko, whose brother is the team captain. However, the endless fundamental drills do not suit his personality, and he and Captain Akagi frequently butt heads.

During their exhibition game against one the prefecture's top teams, Shohoku makes a good showing and actually leads at one point, but a lapse in concentration costs them the game.

Back at school, rumor has it that Ryota Miyagi has been released from the hospital, where he was recovering from a fight, and will be returning to the team. Just what Shohoku needs—another problem child!

Vol. 8: Basketball

Table of Contents

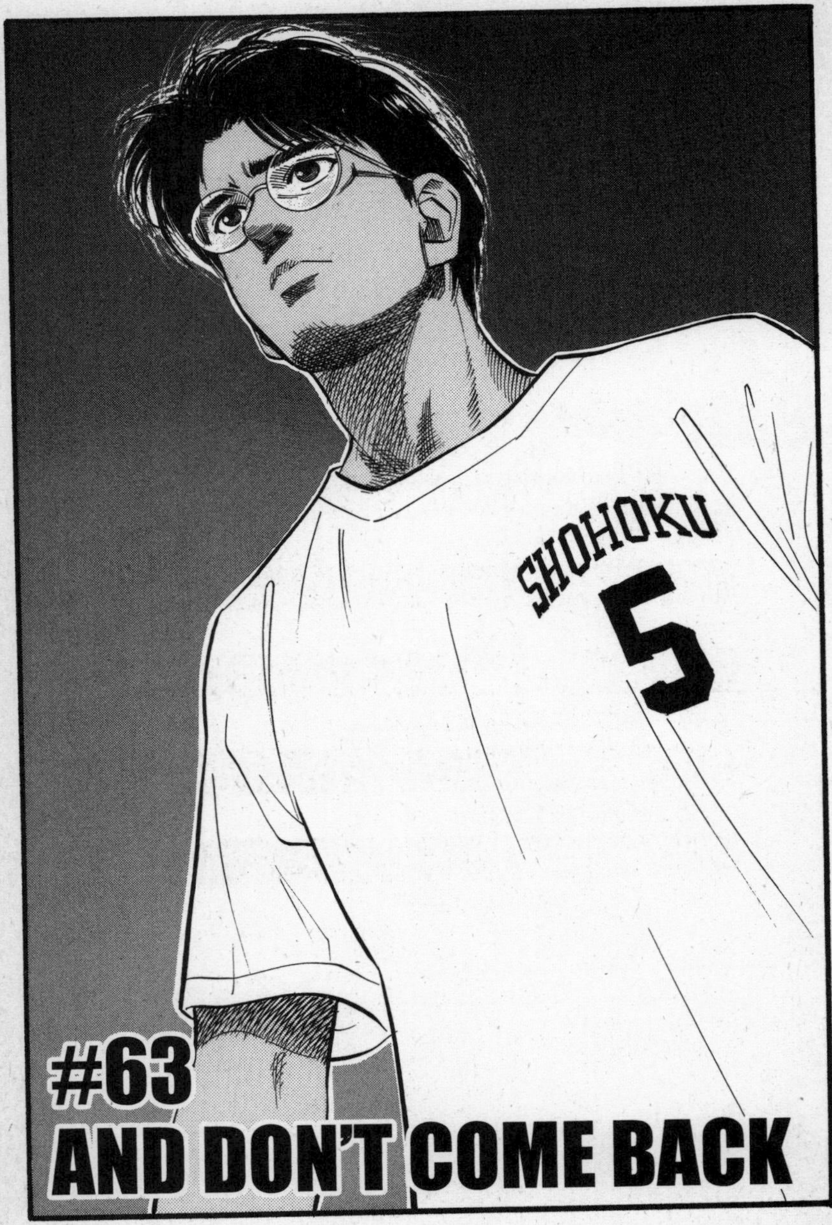
SHOHOKU
5
#63
AND DON'T COME BACK

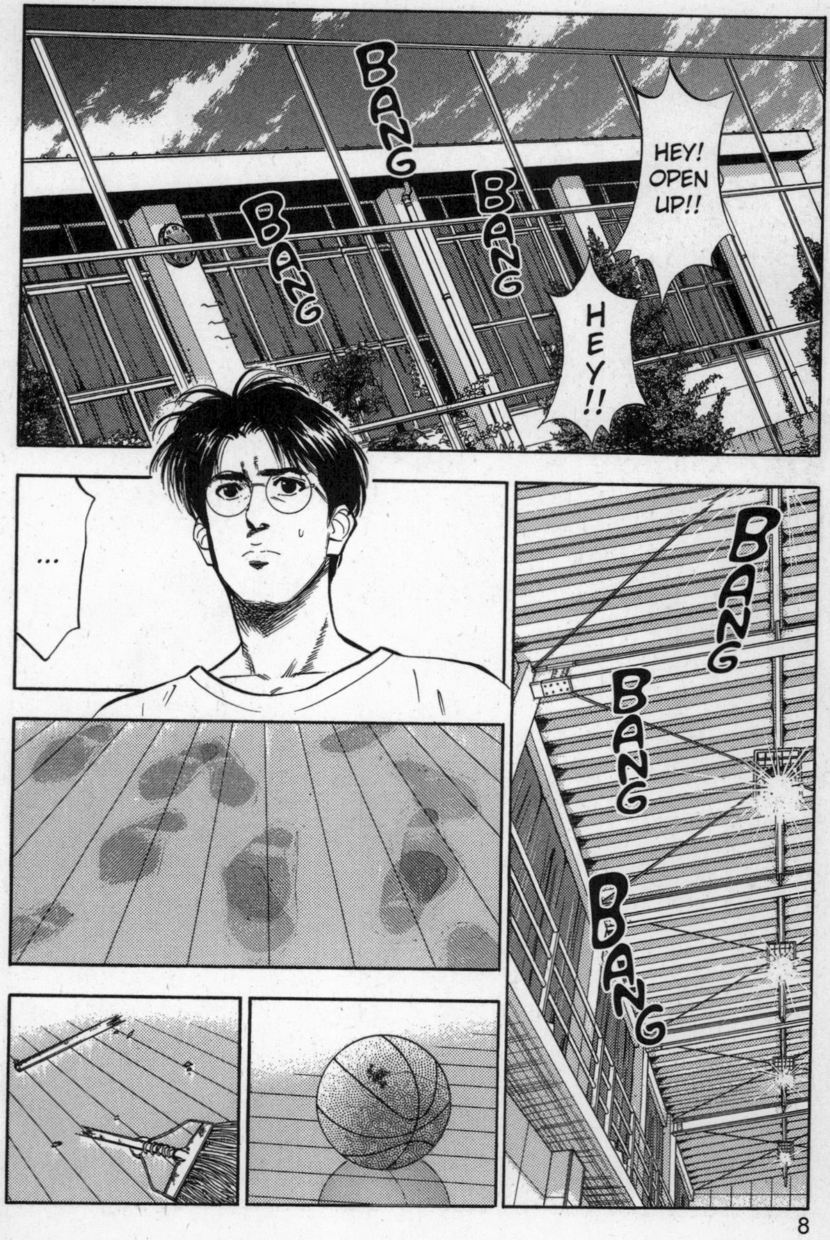
HEY! OPEN UP!!
HEY!!
BANG BANG
BANG BANG
BANG BANG BANG
...

READ THIS WAY

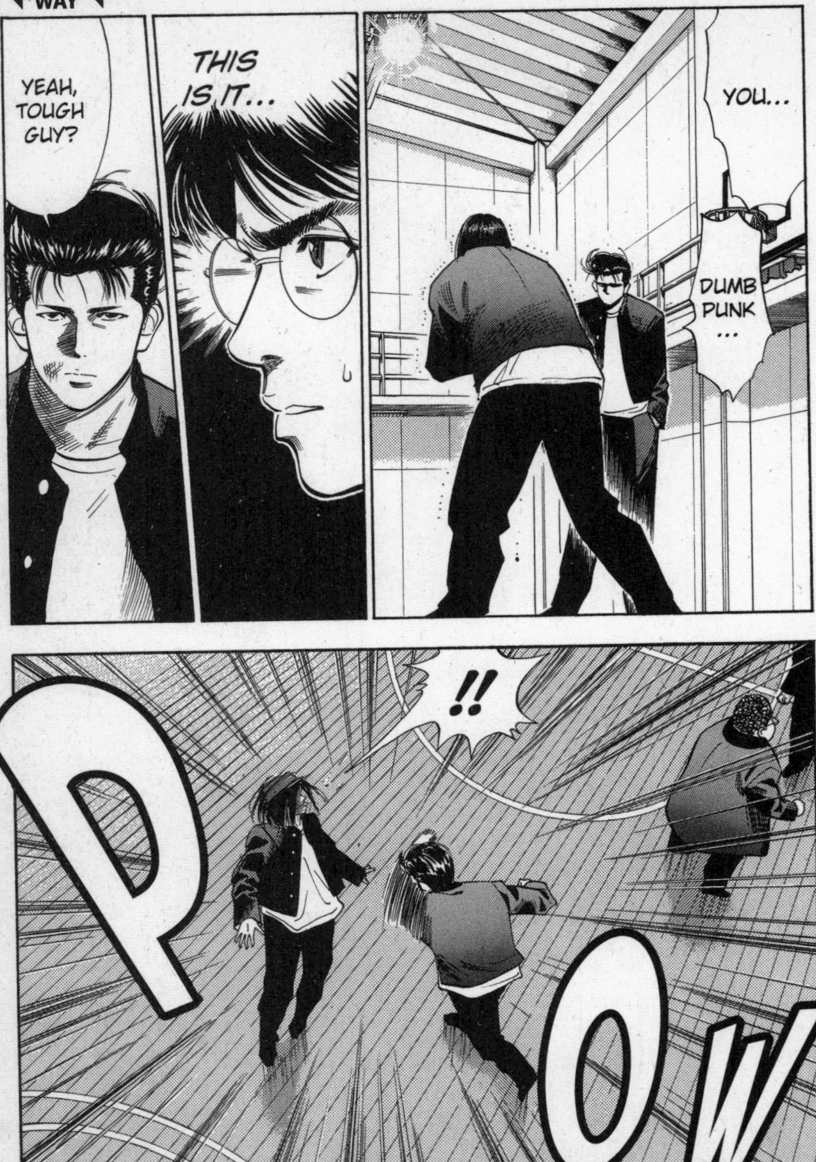
YOU...
DUMB PUNK ...
THIS IS IT...
YEAH, TOUGH GUY?
!!
POW

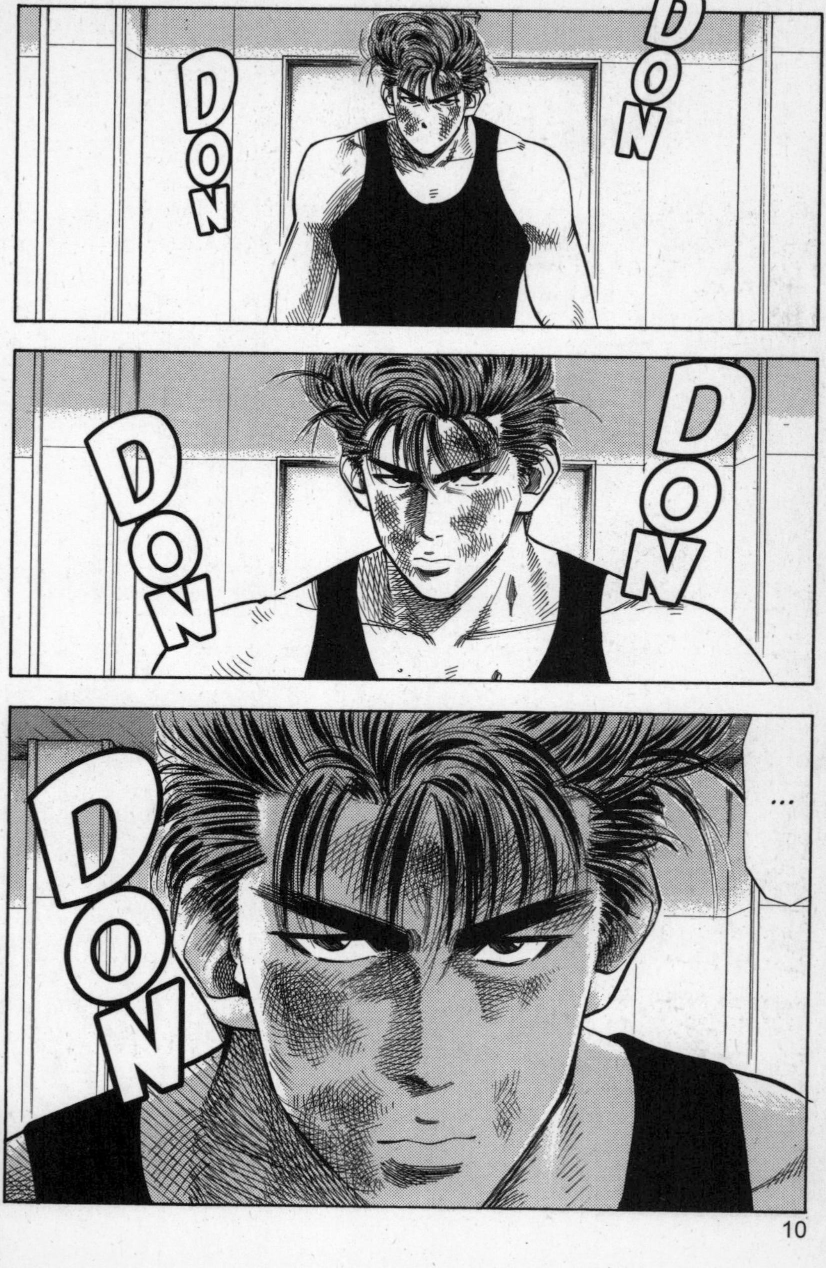
DON
DON
DON
DON
...
DON

READ THIS WAY

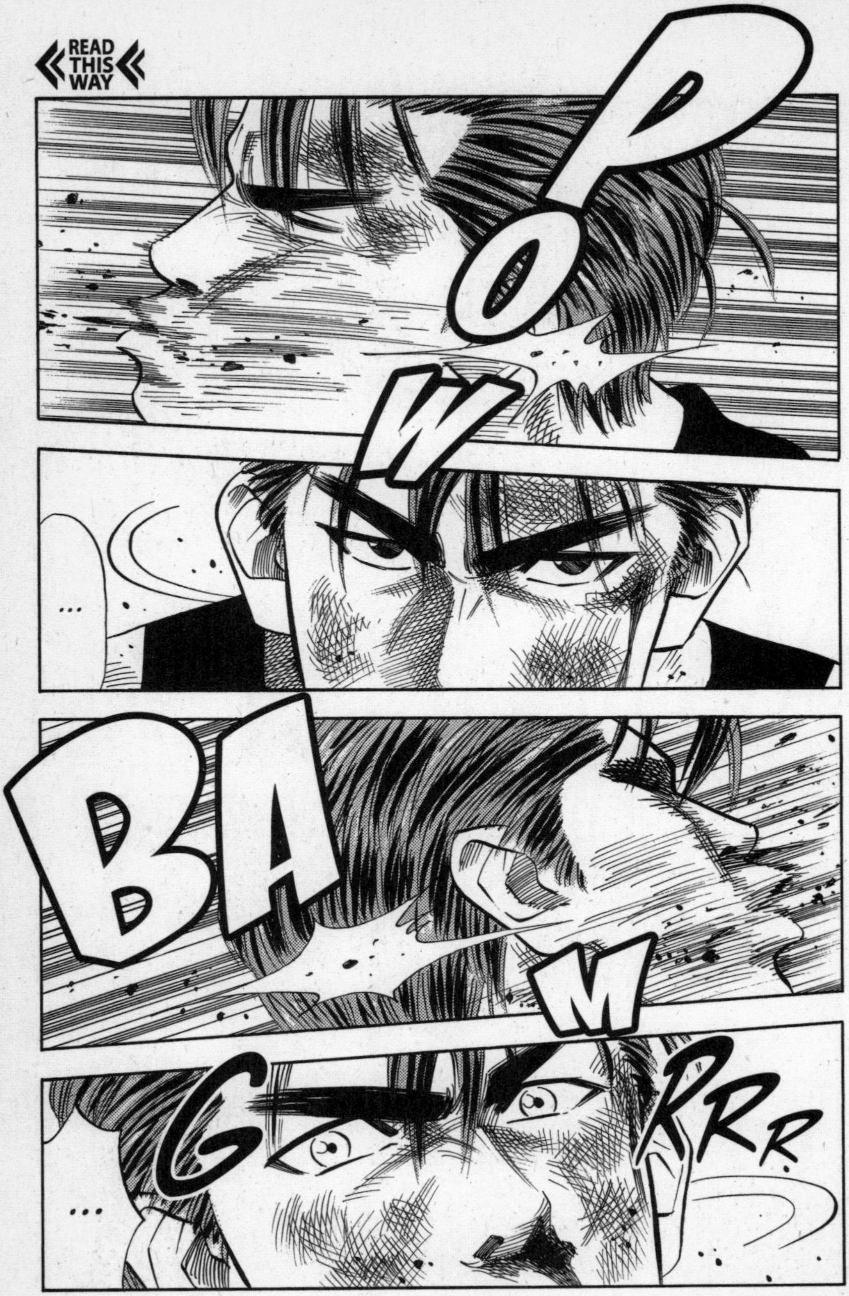
POW
...
BAM
GRRR
...

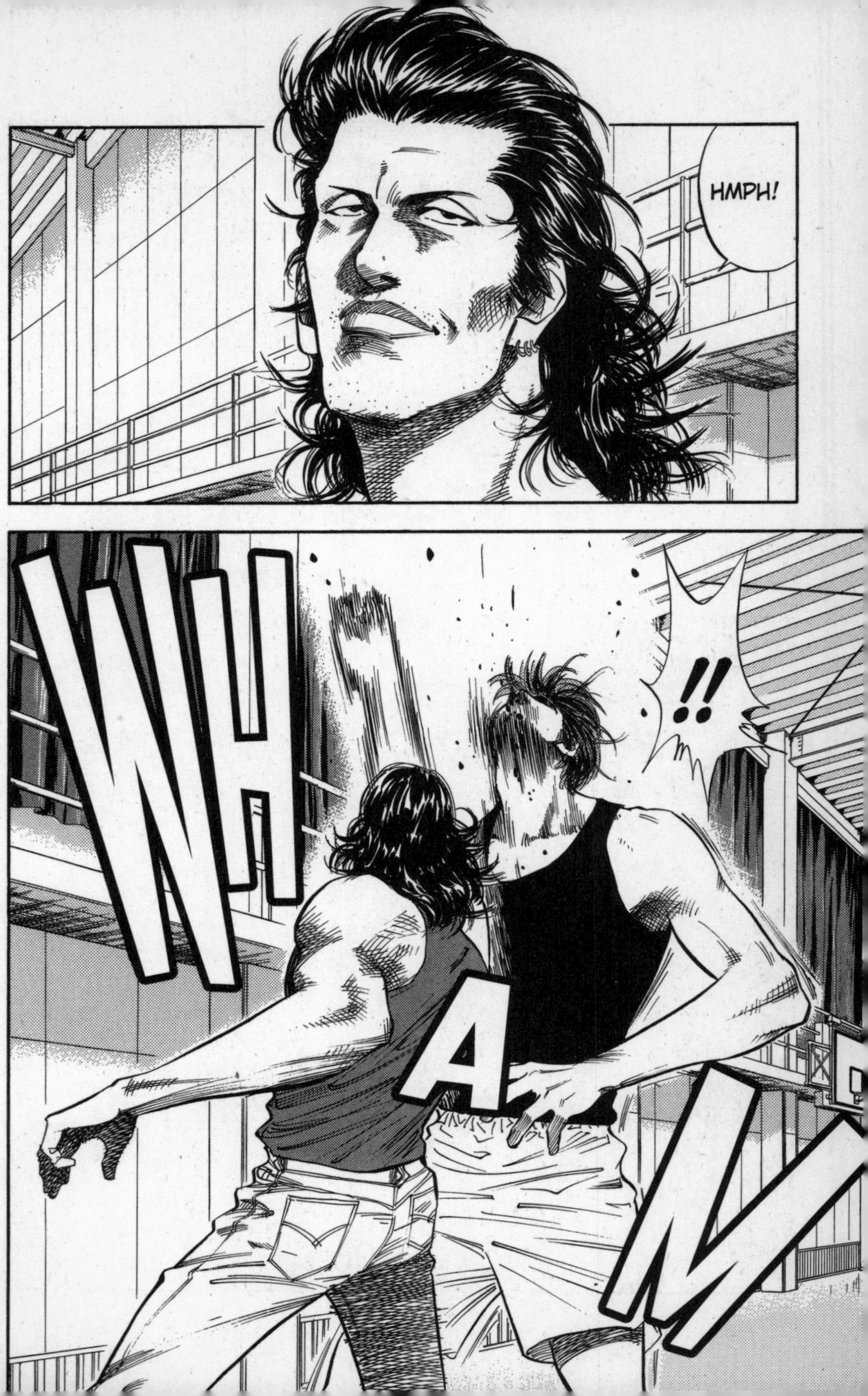
HMPH!
WHAM
!!

READ THIS WAY

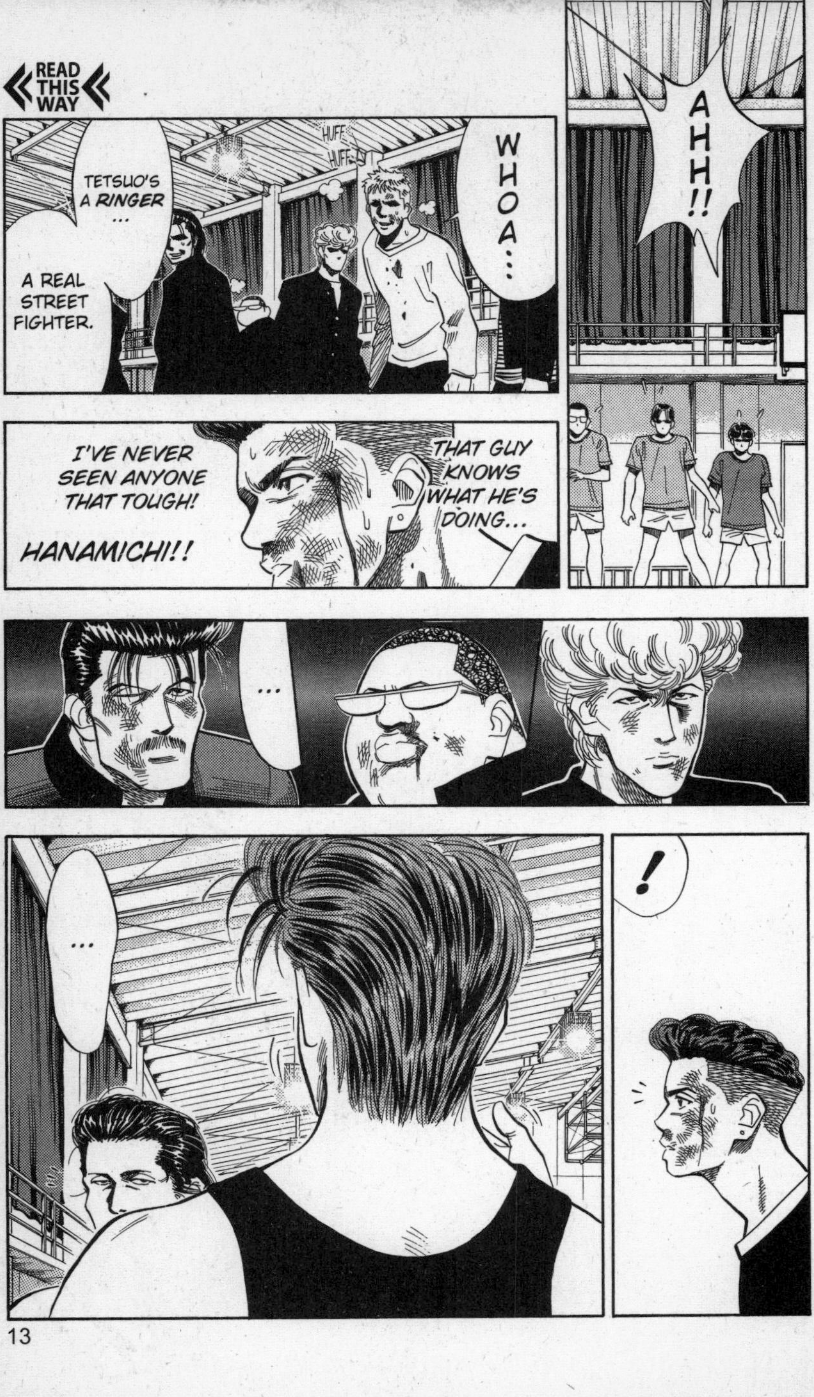

AHH!!
WHOA...
TETSUO'S A RINGER ...
A REAL STREET FIGHTER.
HUFF HUFF
THAT GUY KNOWS WHAT HE'S DOING...
I'VE NEVER SEEN ANYONE THAT TOUGH!
HANAMICHI!!
...
!
...

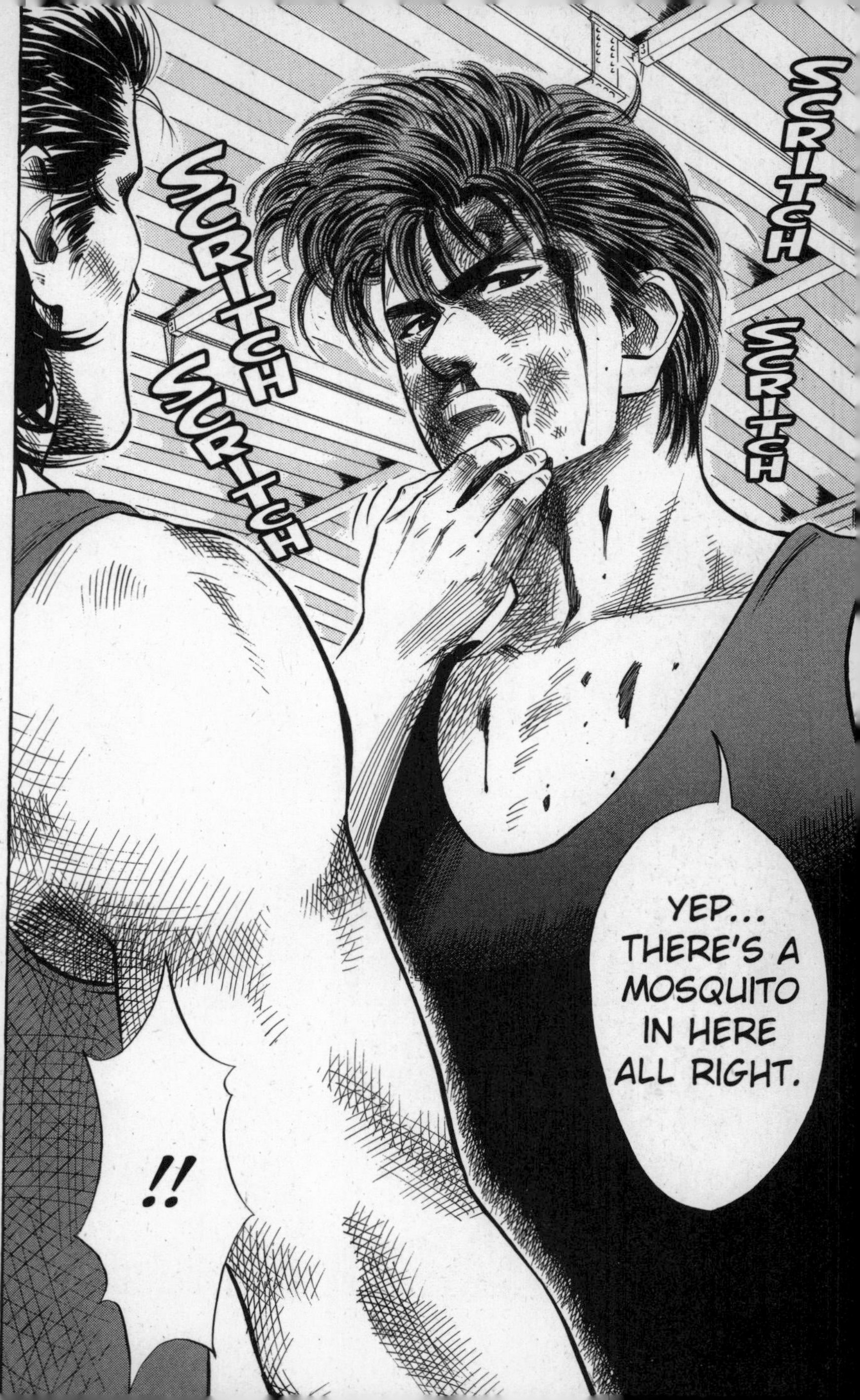
SCRITCH
SCRITCH
SCRITCH
SCRITCH
YEP... THERE'S A MOSQUITO IN HERE ALL RIGHT.
!!

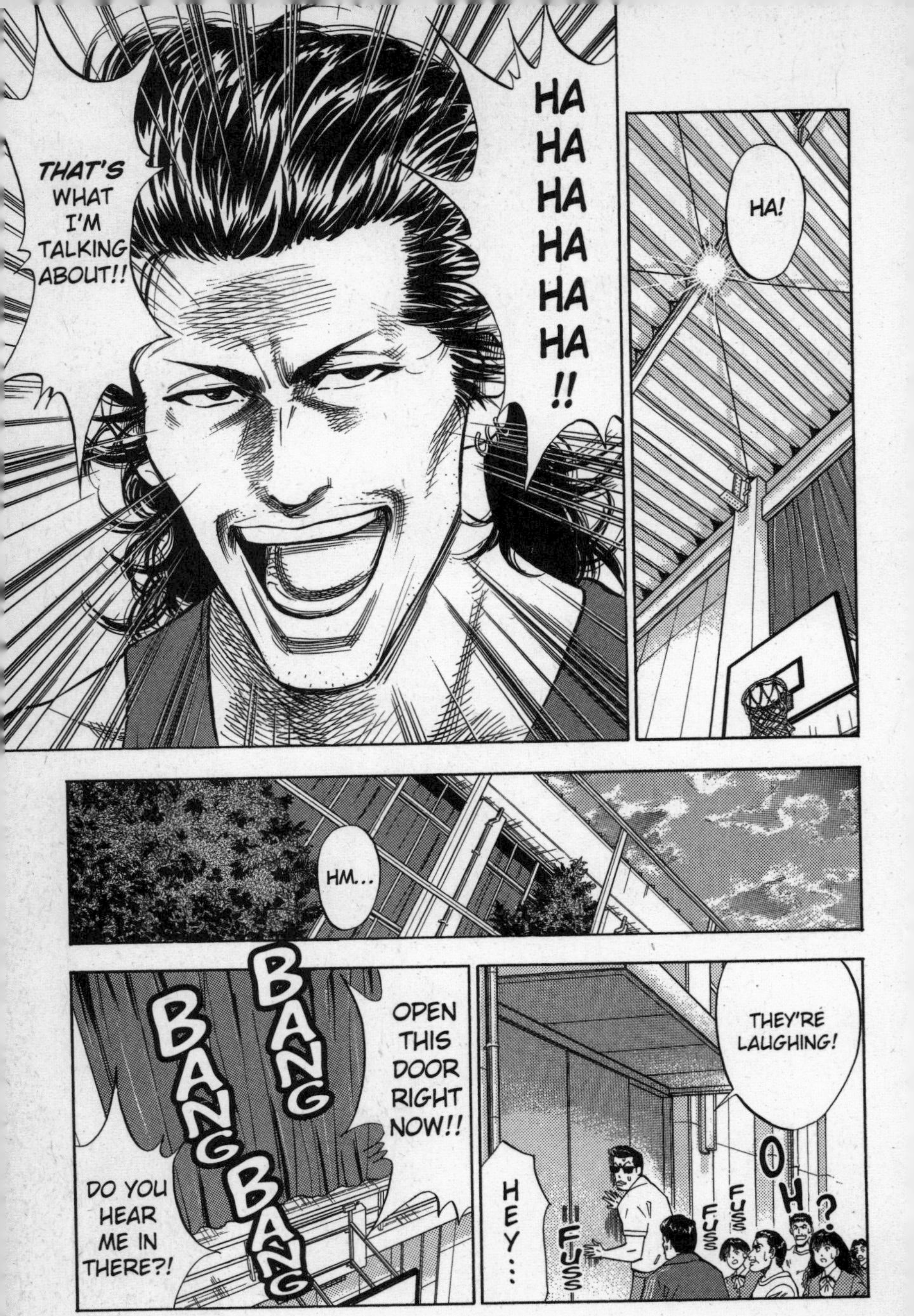
HA!
HA HA HA HA HA HA!!
THAT'S WHAT I'M TALKING ABOUT!!
HM...
THEY'RE LAUGHING!
OH?
FUSS FUSS
FUSS
HEY...
BANG
OPEN THIS DOOR RIGHT NOW!!
BANG BANG BANG
DO YOU HEAR ME IN THERE?!

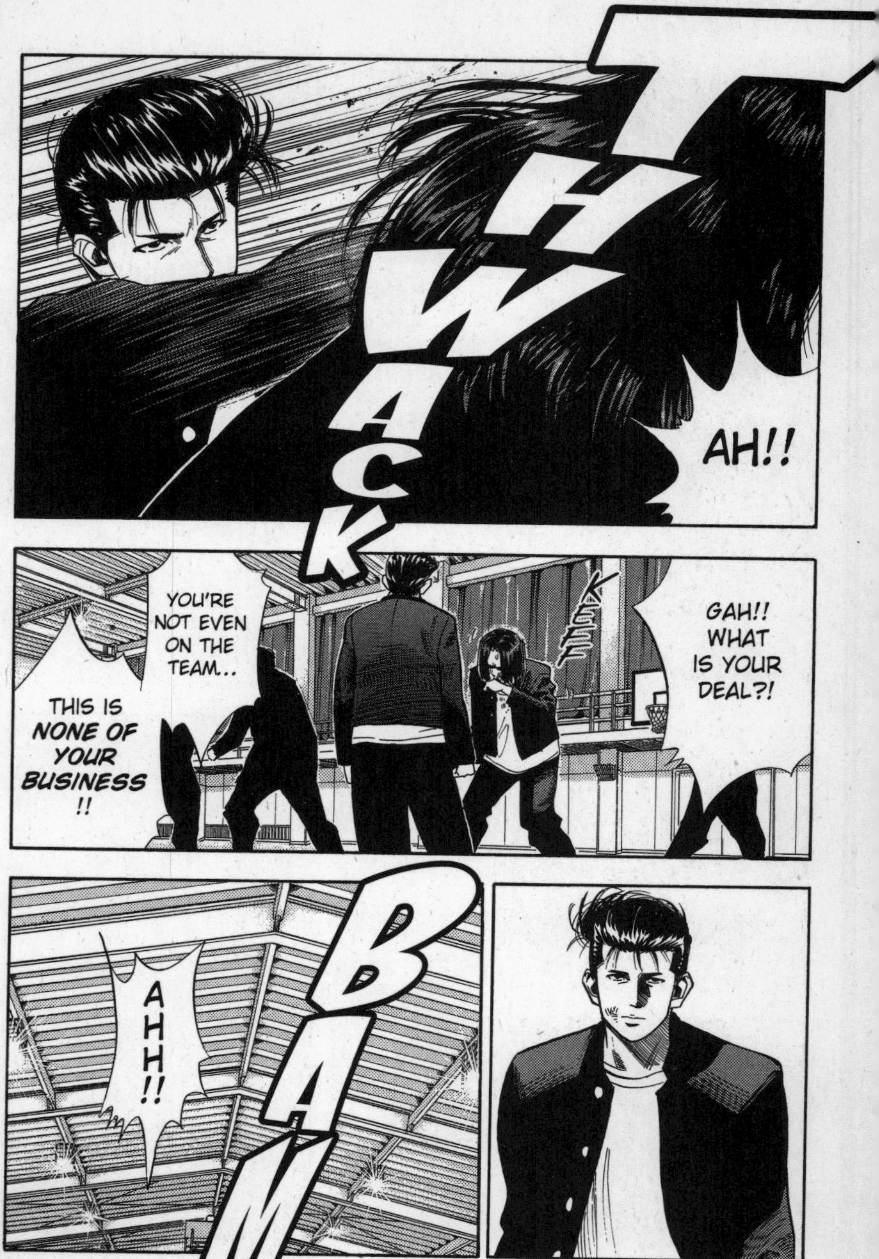
THWACK
AH!!
GAH!! WHAT IS YOUR DEAL?!
KEFF
YOU'RE NOT EVEN ON THE TEAM...
THIS IS NONE OF YOUR BUSINESS!!
AHH!!
BAM

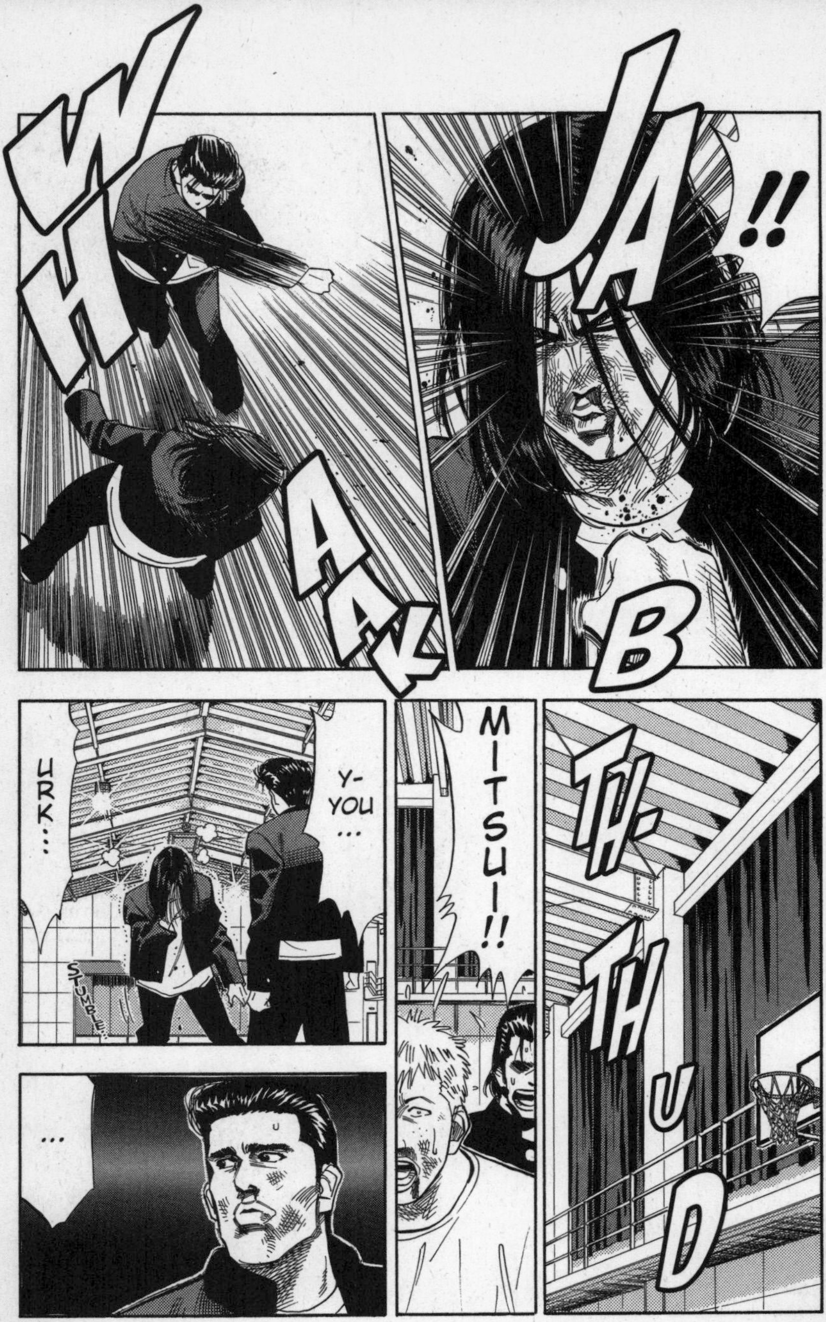

JA!!
B
WH
AAK
TH-
THUD
MITSUI!!
Y-YOU...
URK...
STUMBLE...
...

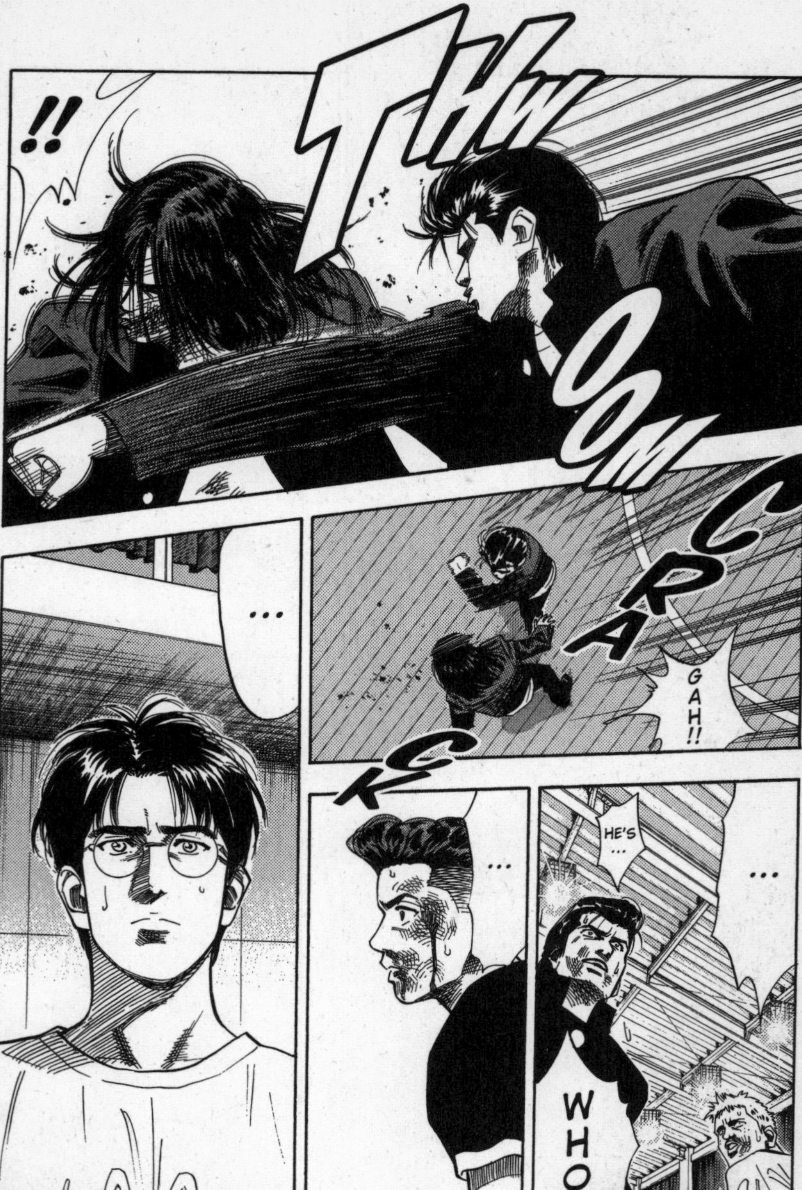
THWOOOM
!!
CRACK
GAH!!
HE'S ...
...
WHOA!!
...
...

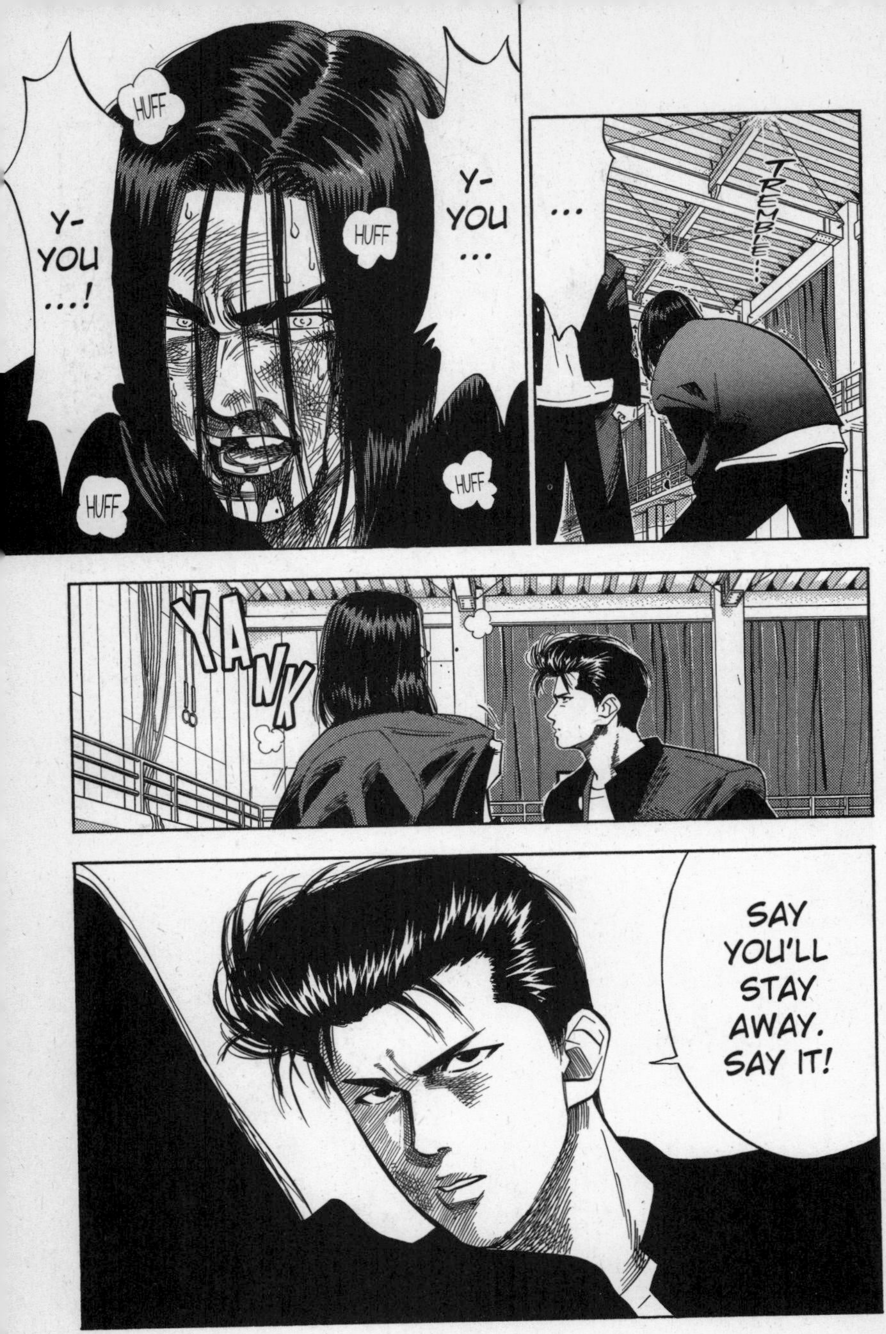
...
TREMBLE...
HUFF
Y- YOU ...
HUFF
Y- YOU ...!
HUFF
HUFF
YANK
SAY YOU'LL STAY AWAY. SAY IT!

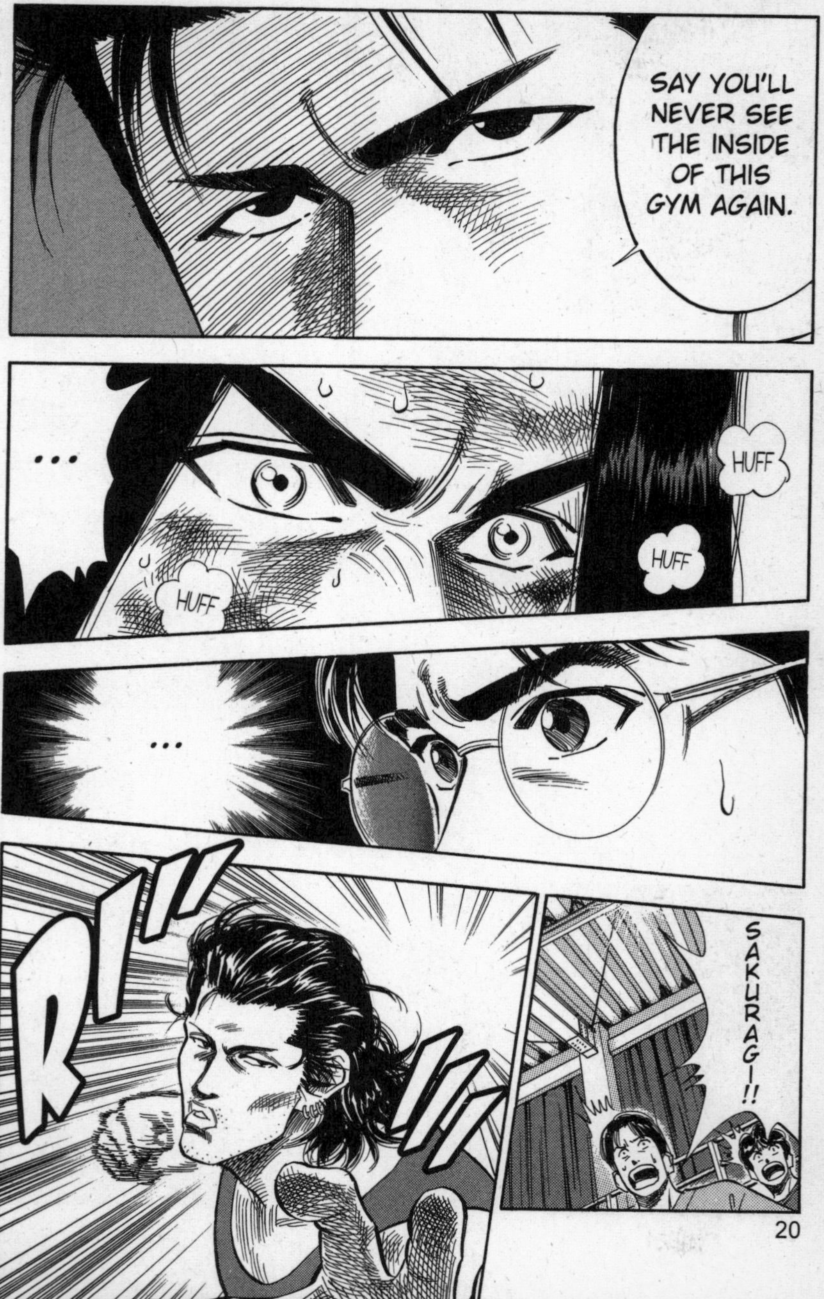

SAY YOU'LL NEVER SEE THE INSIDE OF THIS GYM AGAIN.
HUFF
HUFF
HUFF
...
...
SAKURAGI!!
RI''

READ THIS WAY

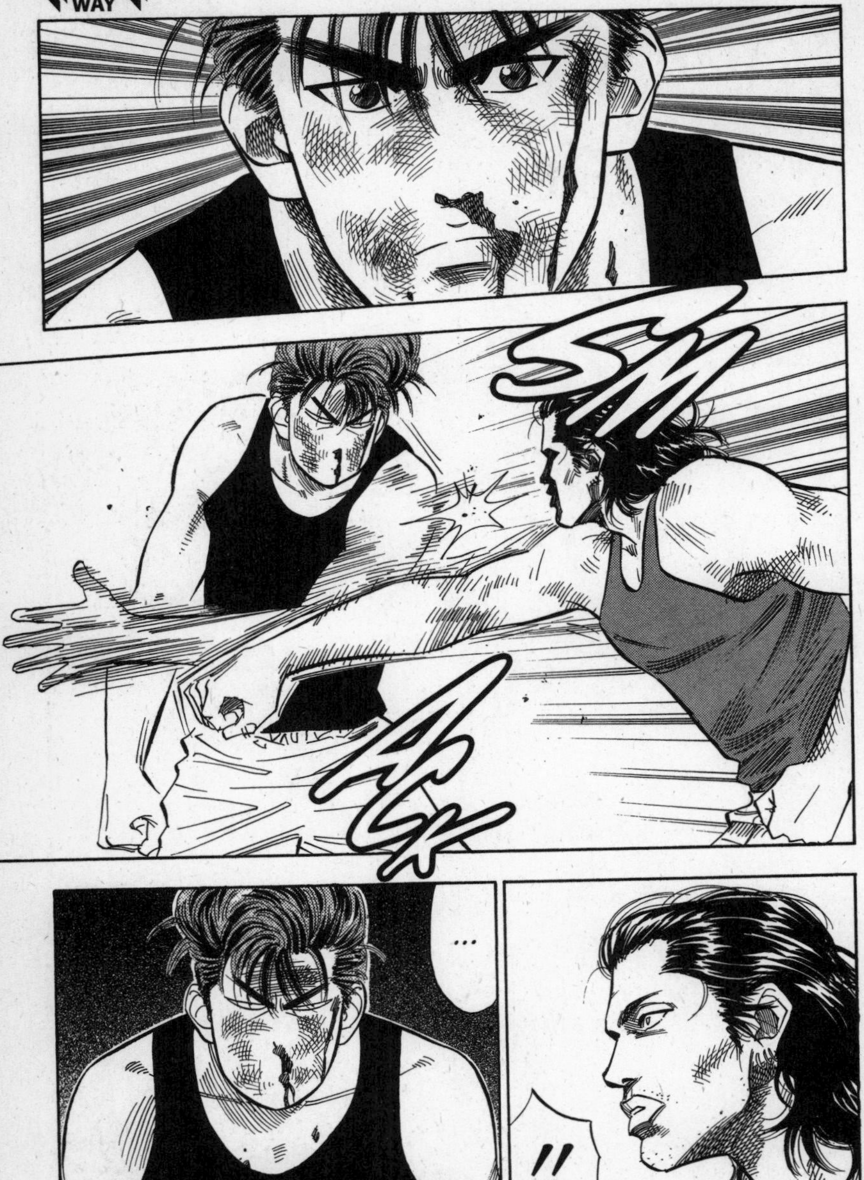
SMACK
!!
...

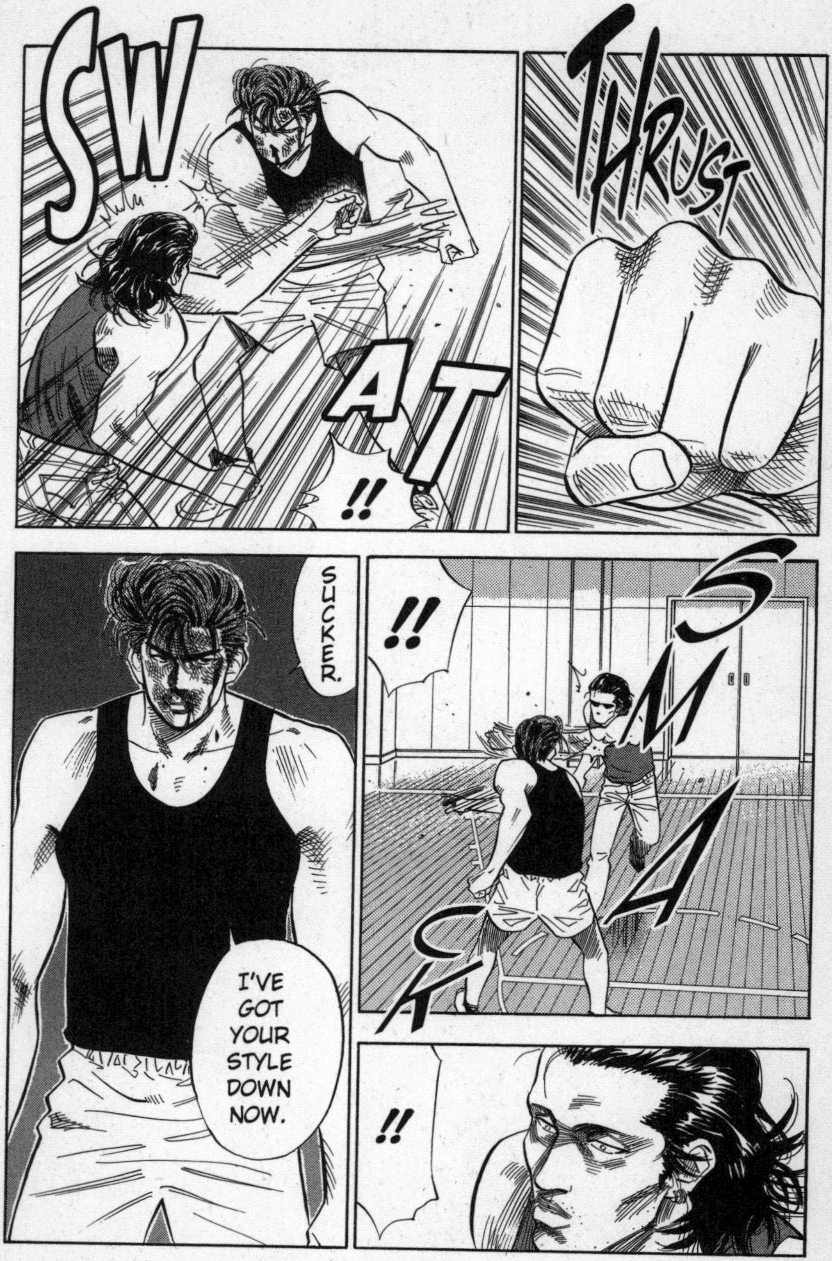
THRUST
SWAT
!!
SMACK
!!
!!
SUCKER.
I'VE GOT YOUR STYLE DOWN NOW.

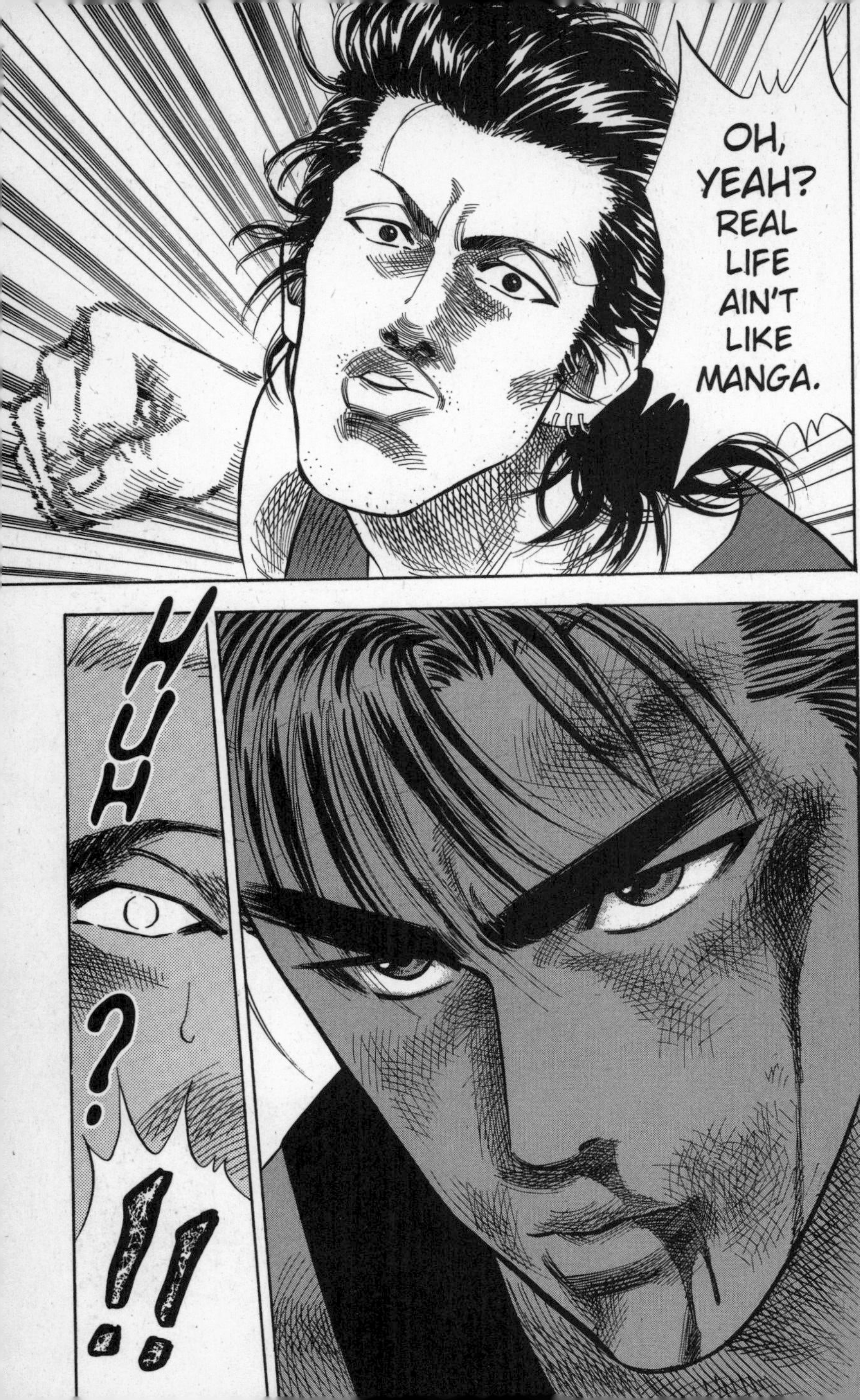
OH, YEAH? REAL LIFE AIN'T LIKE MANGA.
HUH ?!!

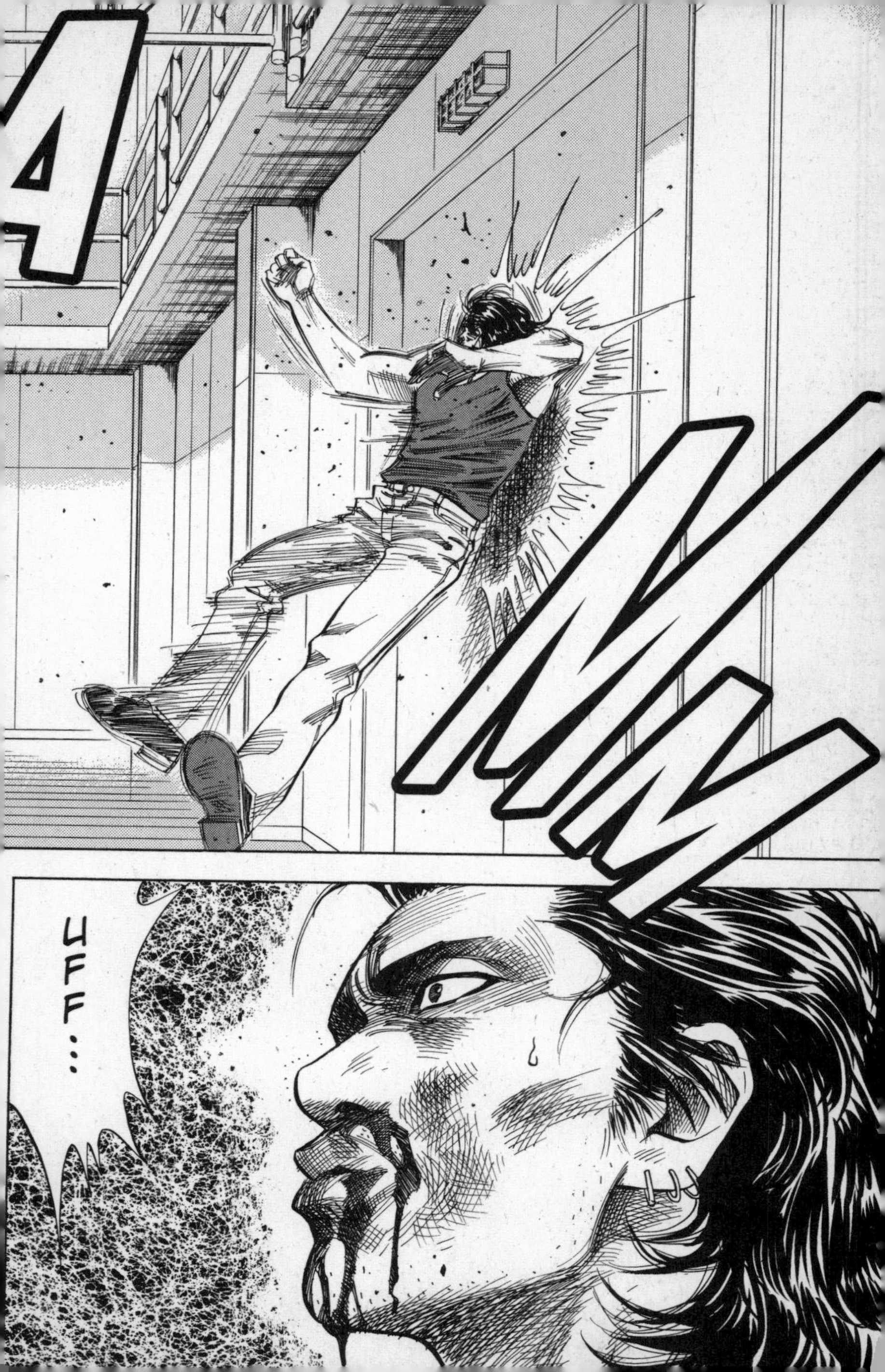
UFF...

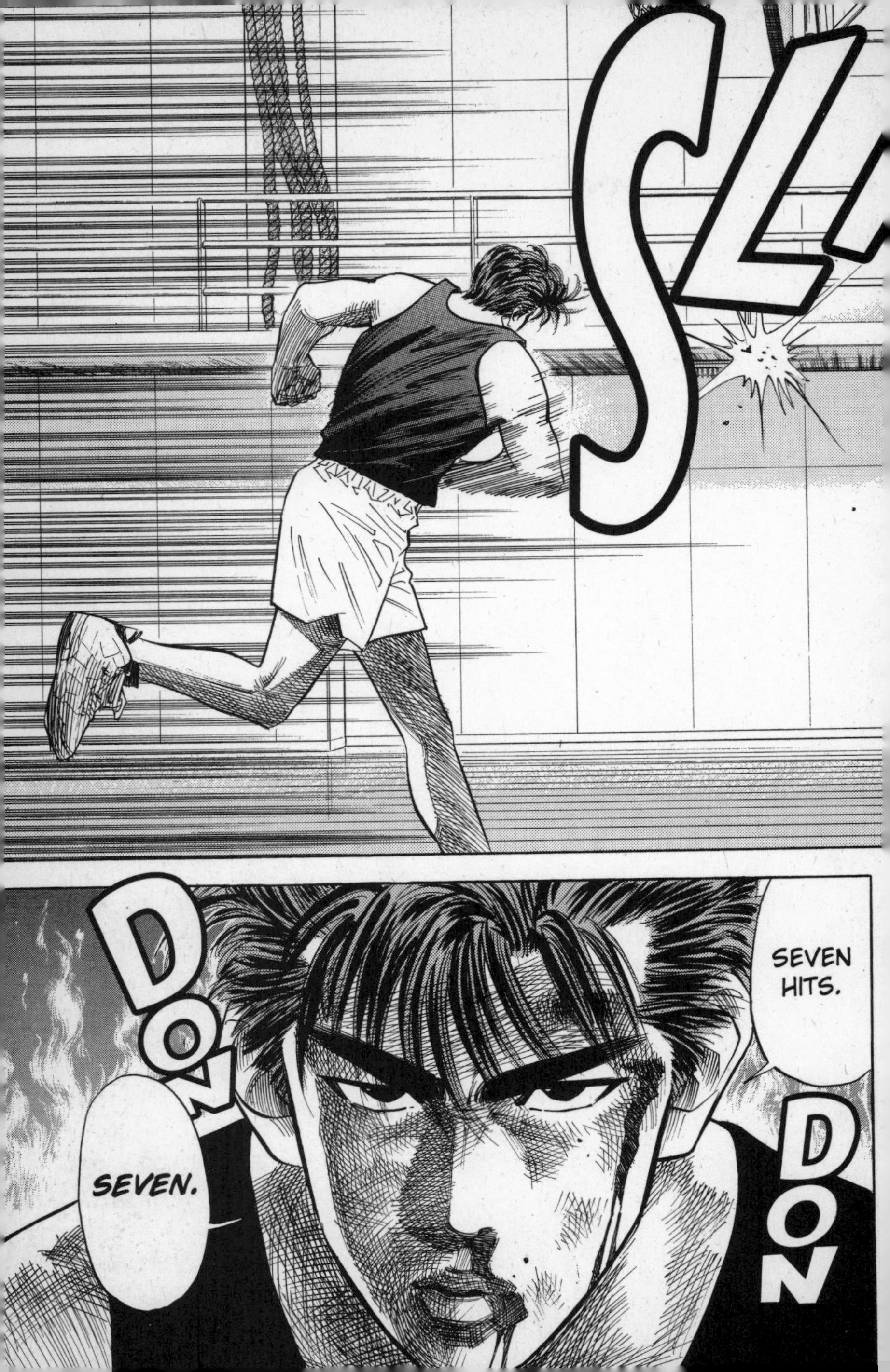
SEVEN HITS.
DON
SEVEN.
DON

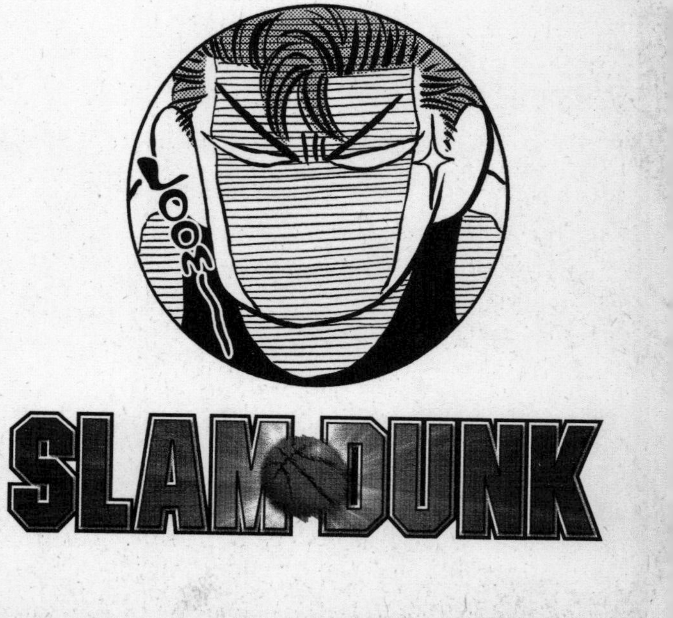
VOOM

SLAM DUNK

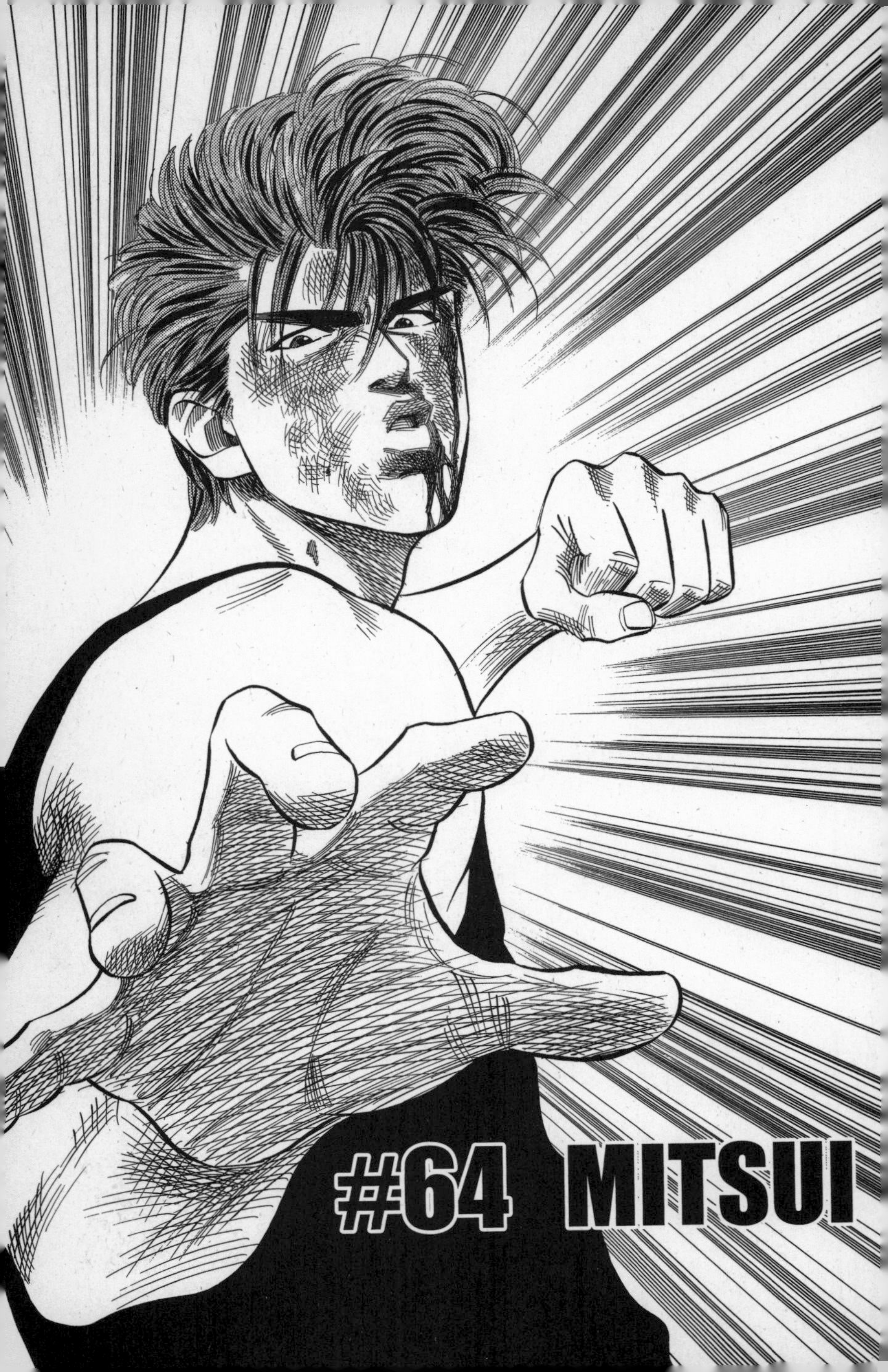
#64 MITSUI

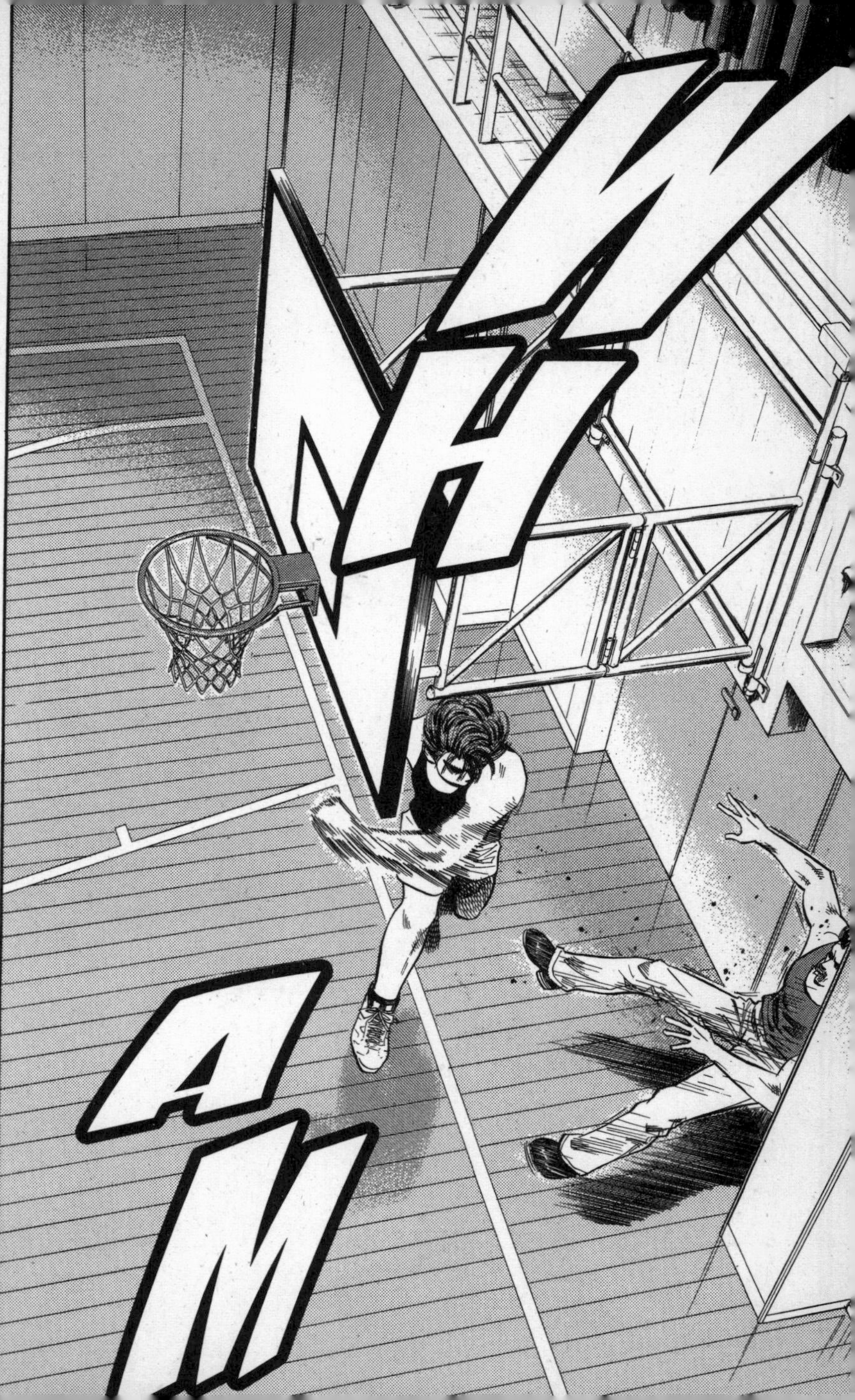
WHAM

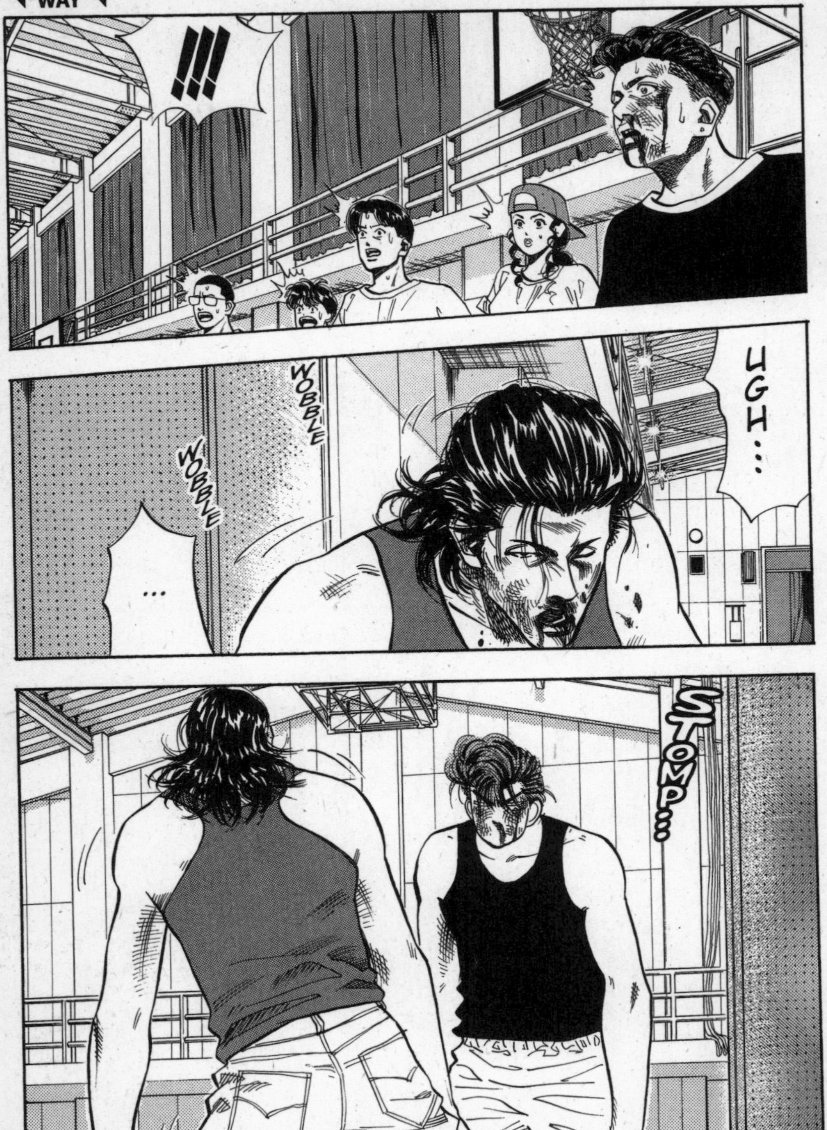
!!!
UGH...
WOBBLE
WOBBLE
...
STOMP...

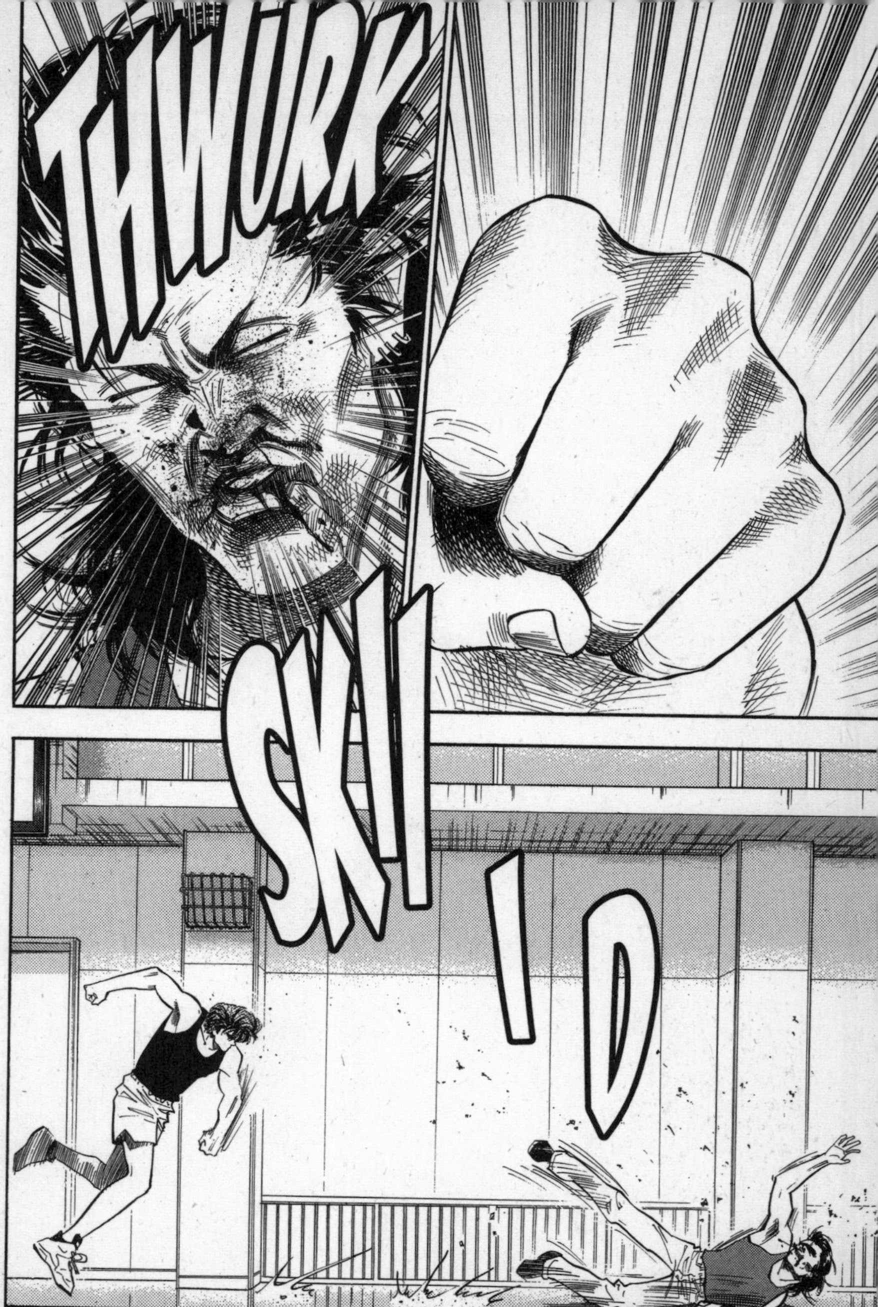
THWURK
SKIID

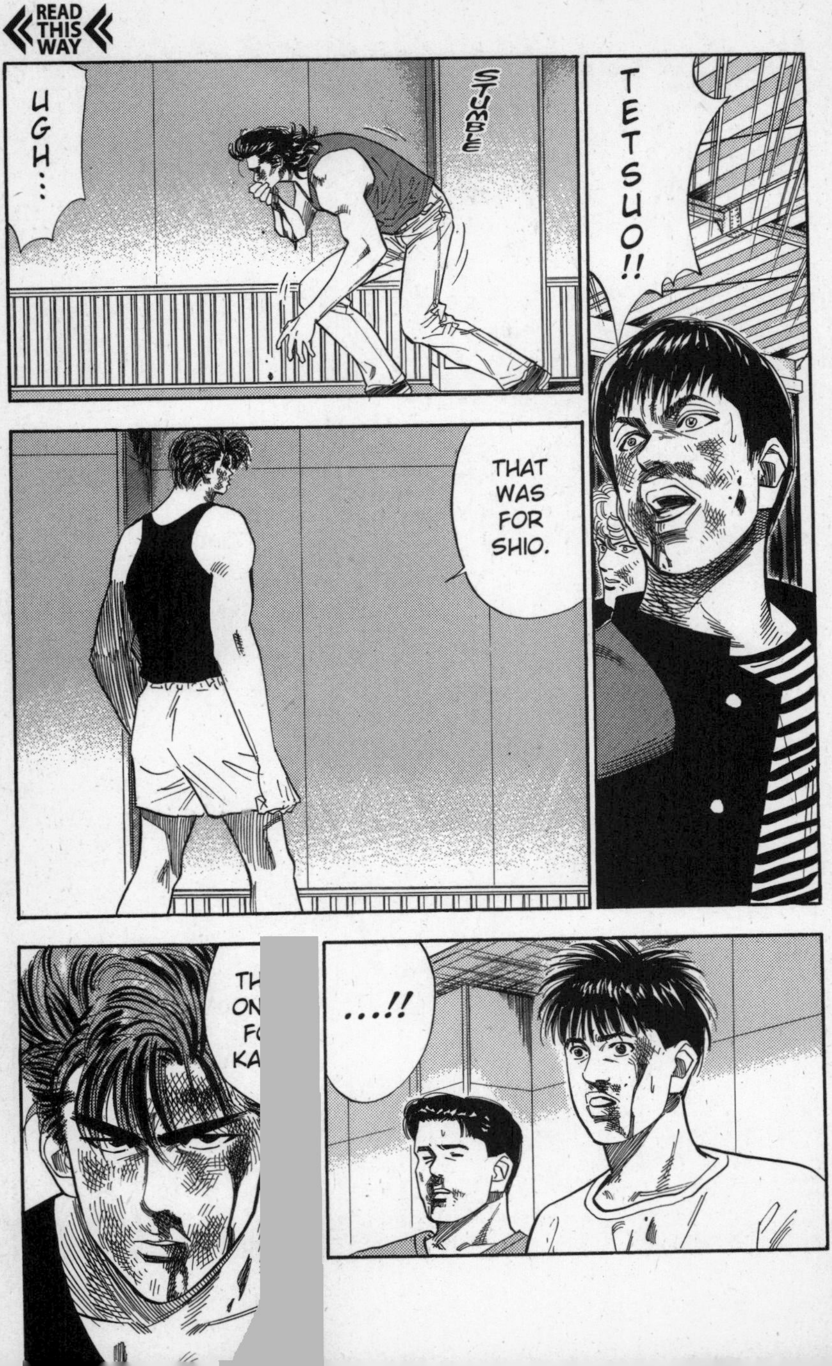
READ THIS WAY
TETSUO!!
STUMBLE
UGH...
THAT WAS FOR SHIO.
...!!

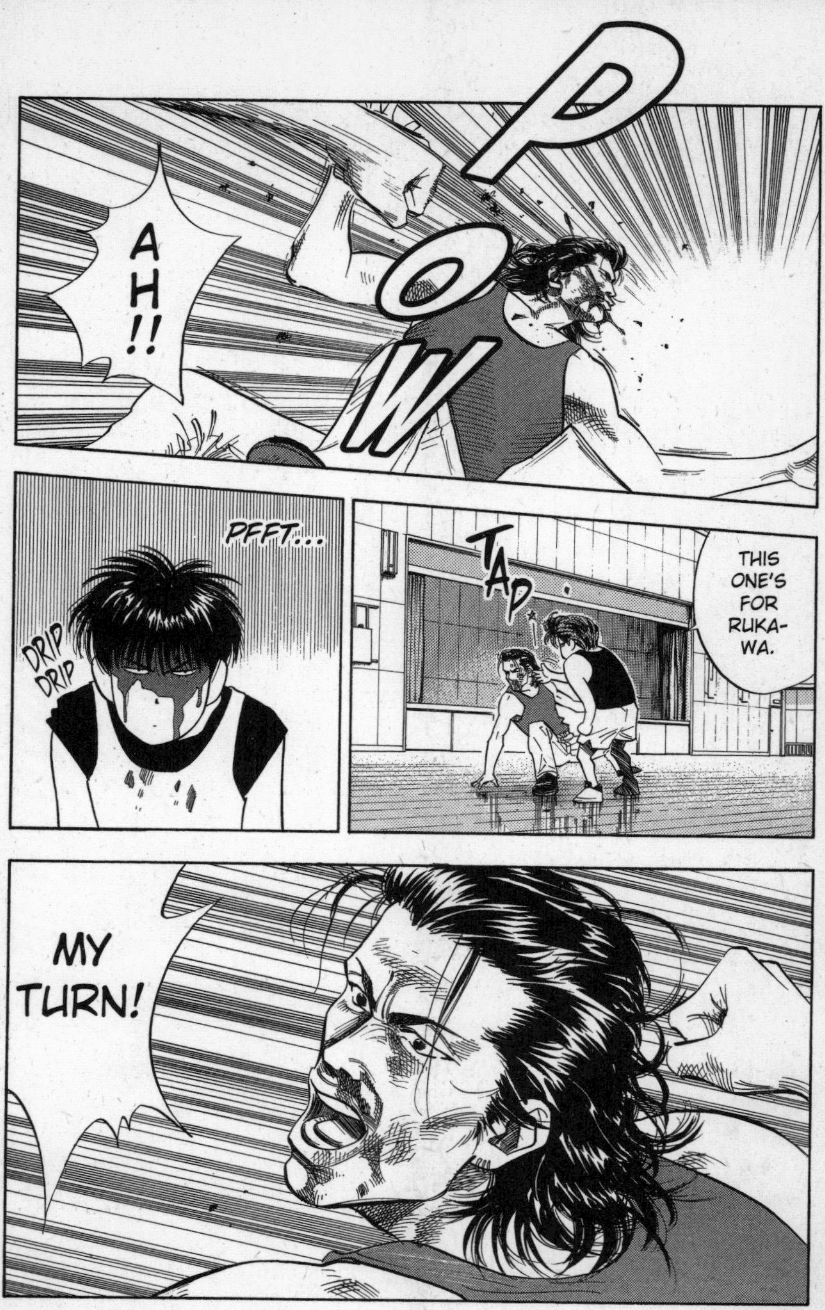
POW
AH!!
TAP
THIS ONE'S FOR RUKA-WA.
PFFT...
DRIP DRIP
MY TURN!

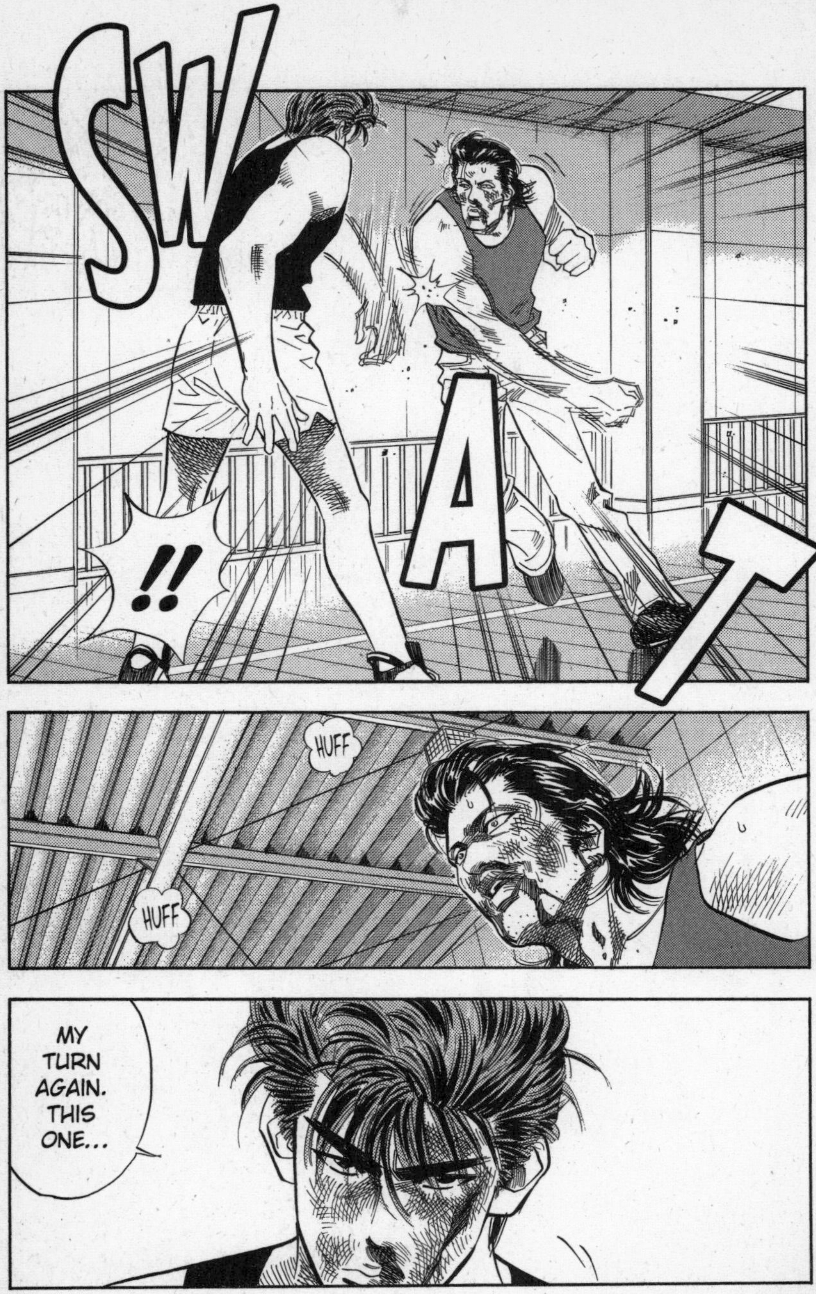
SWAT
!!
HUFF
HUFF
MY TURN AGAIN. THIS ONE...

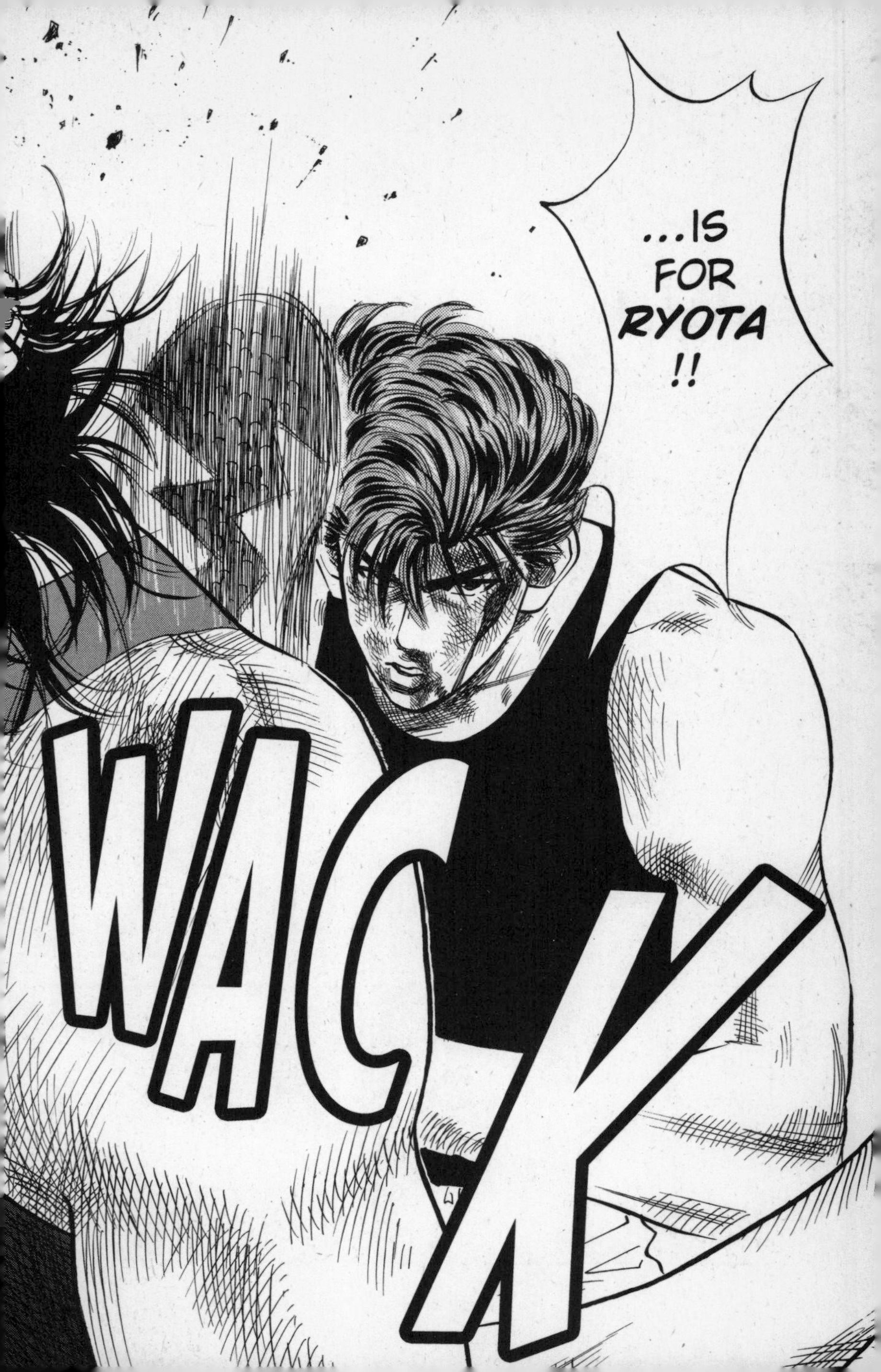
...IS FOR RYOTA !!
WACK

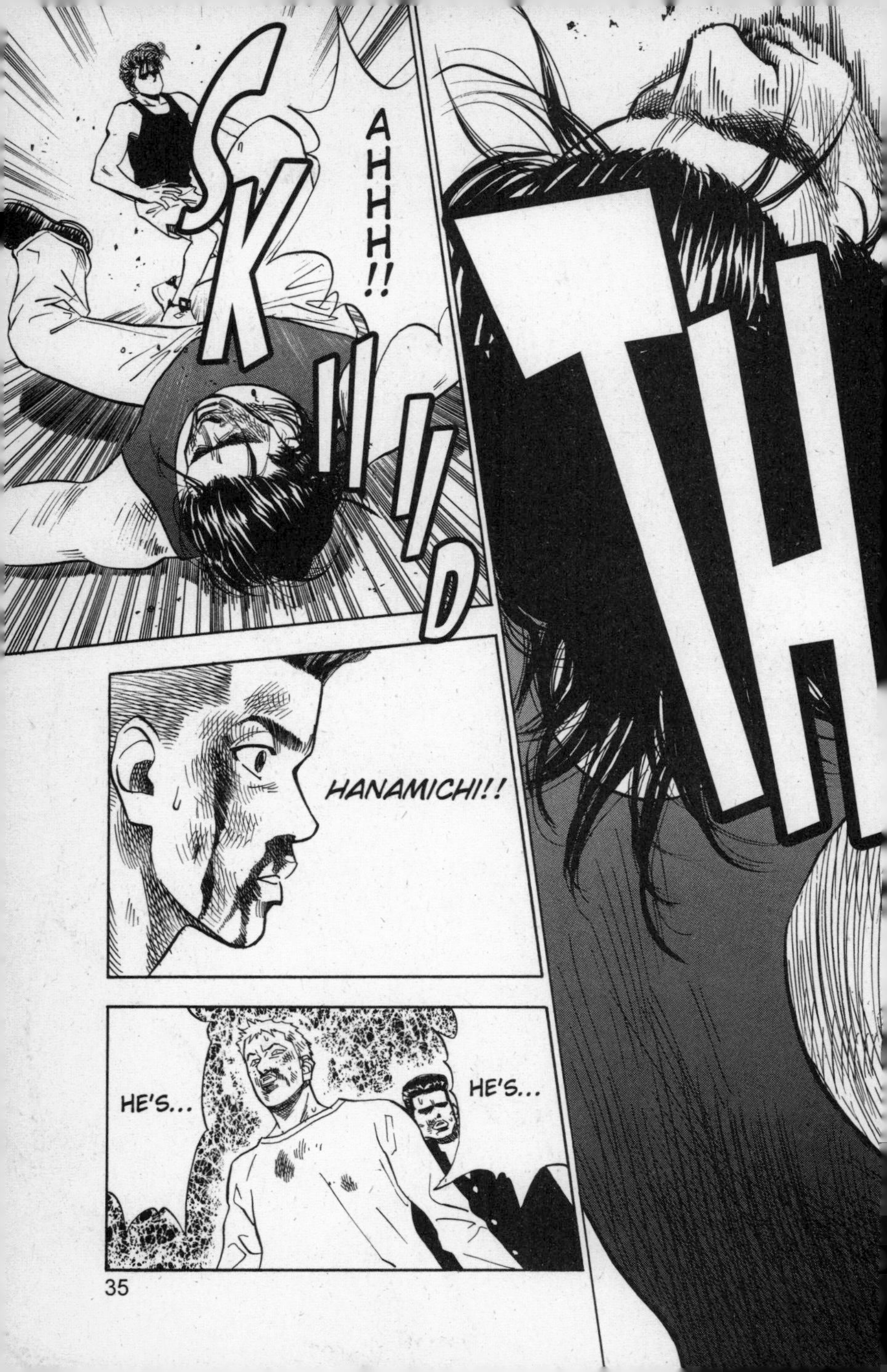
AHHHH!!
SKIIID
HANAMICHI!!
HE'S...
HE'S...

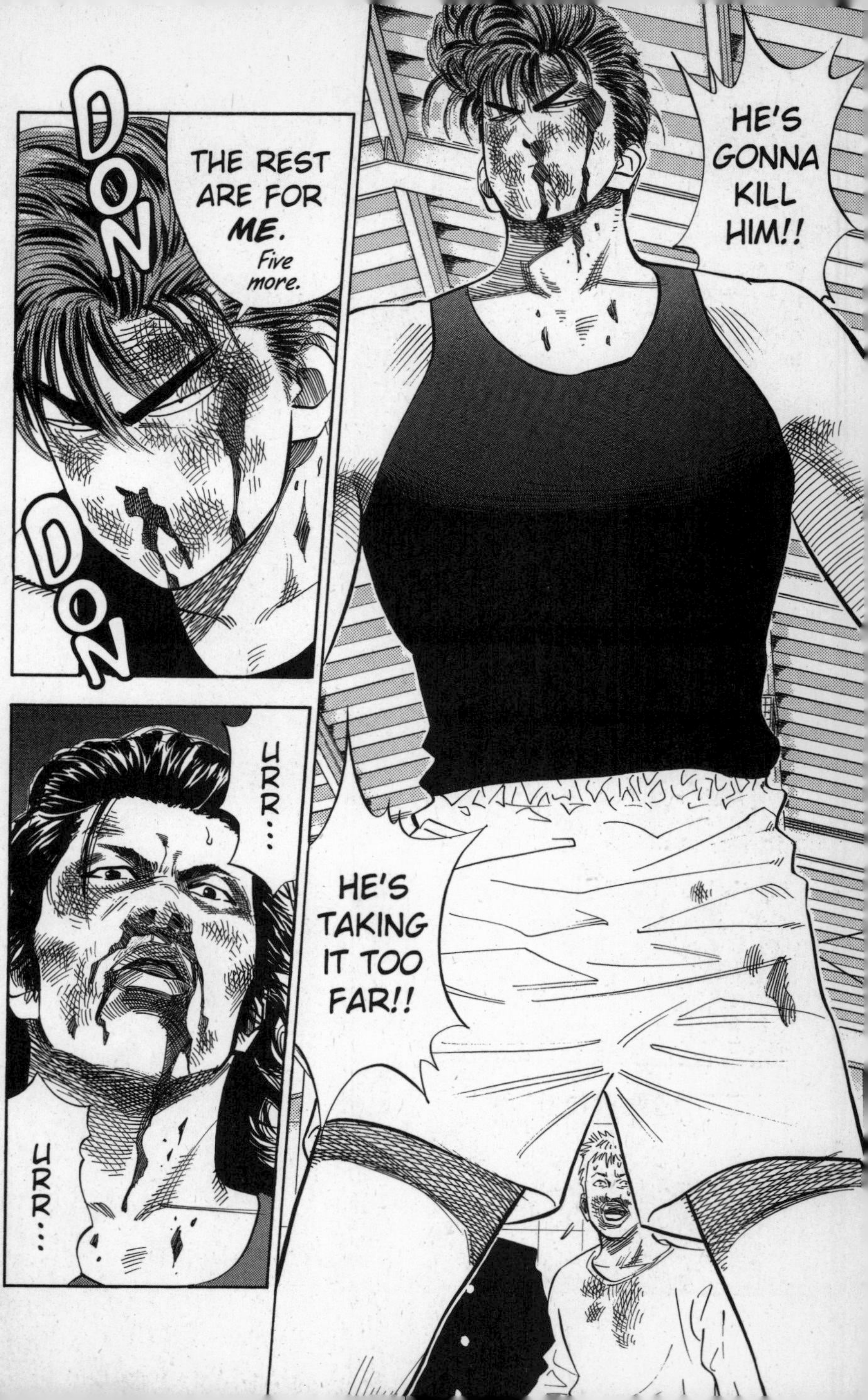
HE'S GONNA KILL HIM!!
HE'S TAKING IT TOO FAR!!
DON
THE REST ARE FOR **ME.**
Five more.
DON
URR...
URR...

READ THIS WAY

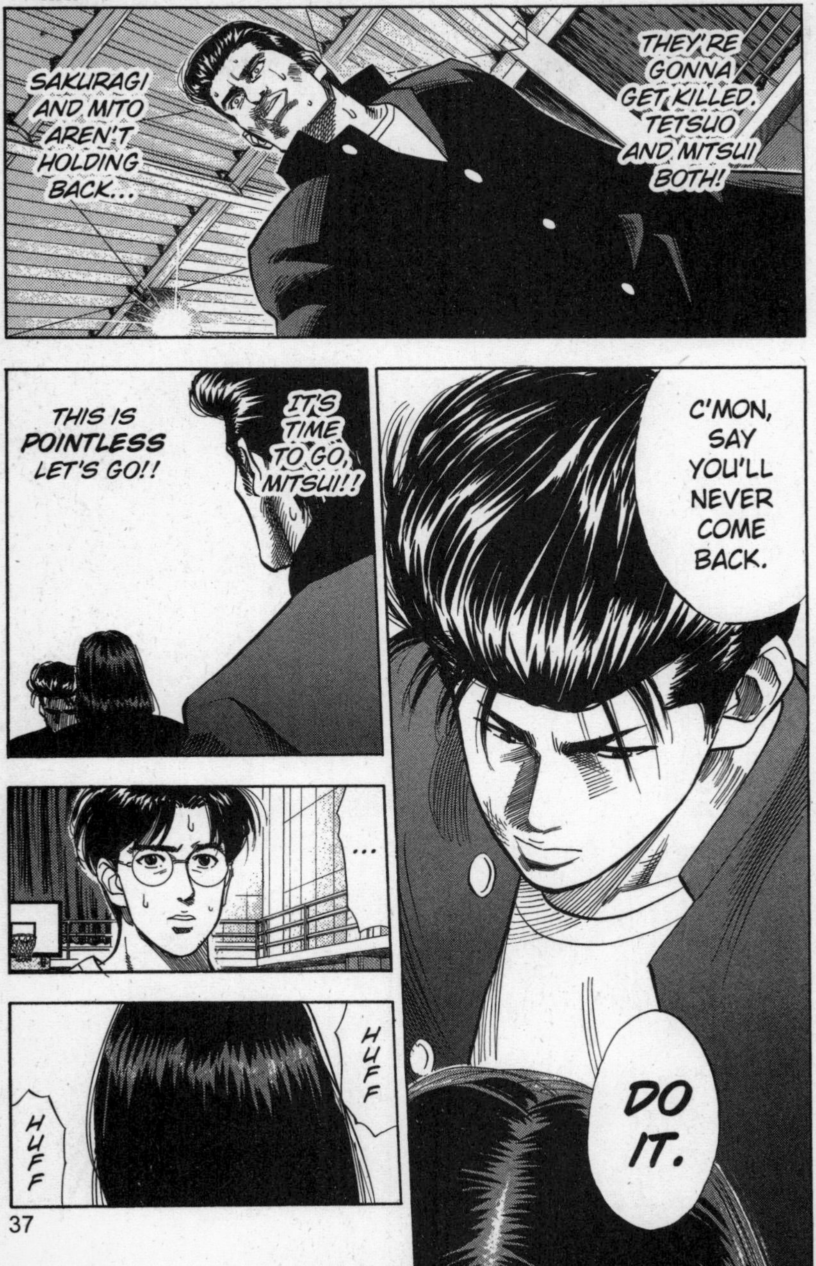

THEY'RE GONNA GET KILLED. TETSUO AND MITSUI BOTH!
SAKURAGI AND MITO AREN'T HOLDING BACK...
C'MON, SAY YOU'LL NEVER COME BACK.
DO IT.
IT'S TIME TO GO, MITSUI!!
THIS IS POINTLESS LET'S GO!!
...
HUFF
HUFF

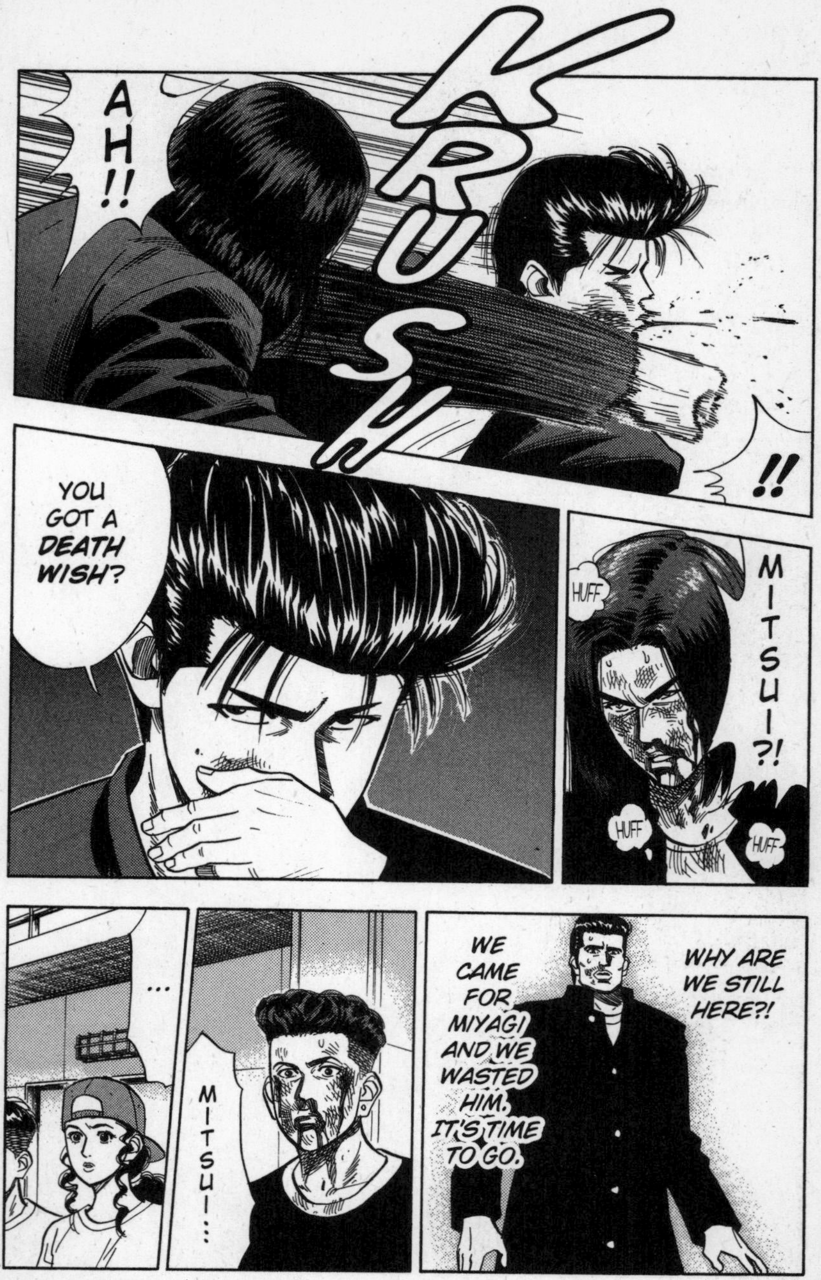
KRUSH
AH!!
!!
MITSUI?!
HUFF
HUFF
HUFF
YOU GOT A DEATH WISH?
WHY ARE WE STILL HERE?!
WE CAME FOR MIYAGI AND WE WASTED HIM. IT'S TIME TO GO.
MITSUI...
...

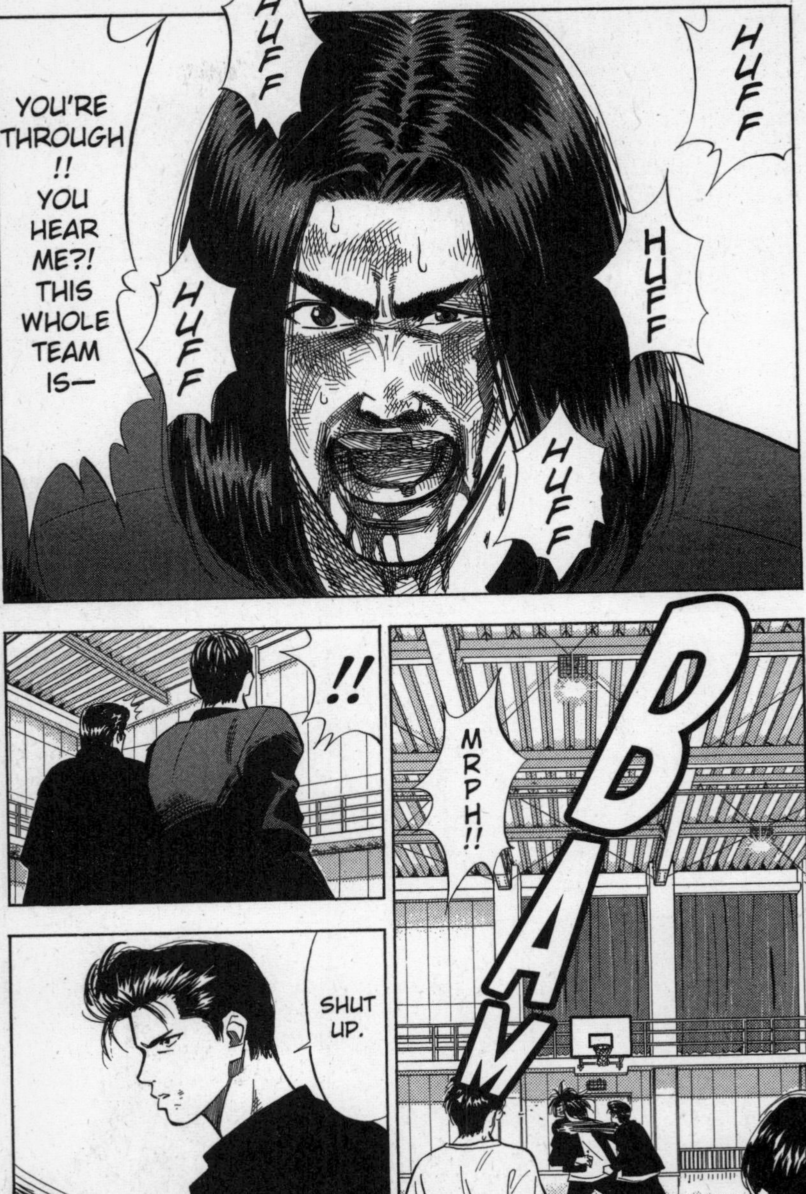
HUFF
HUFF
HUFF
HUFF
HUFF
YOU'RE THROUGH!! YOU HEAR ME?! THIS WHOLE TEAM IS—
MRPH!!
BAM
!!
SHUT UP.

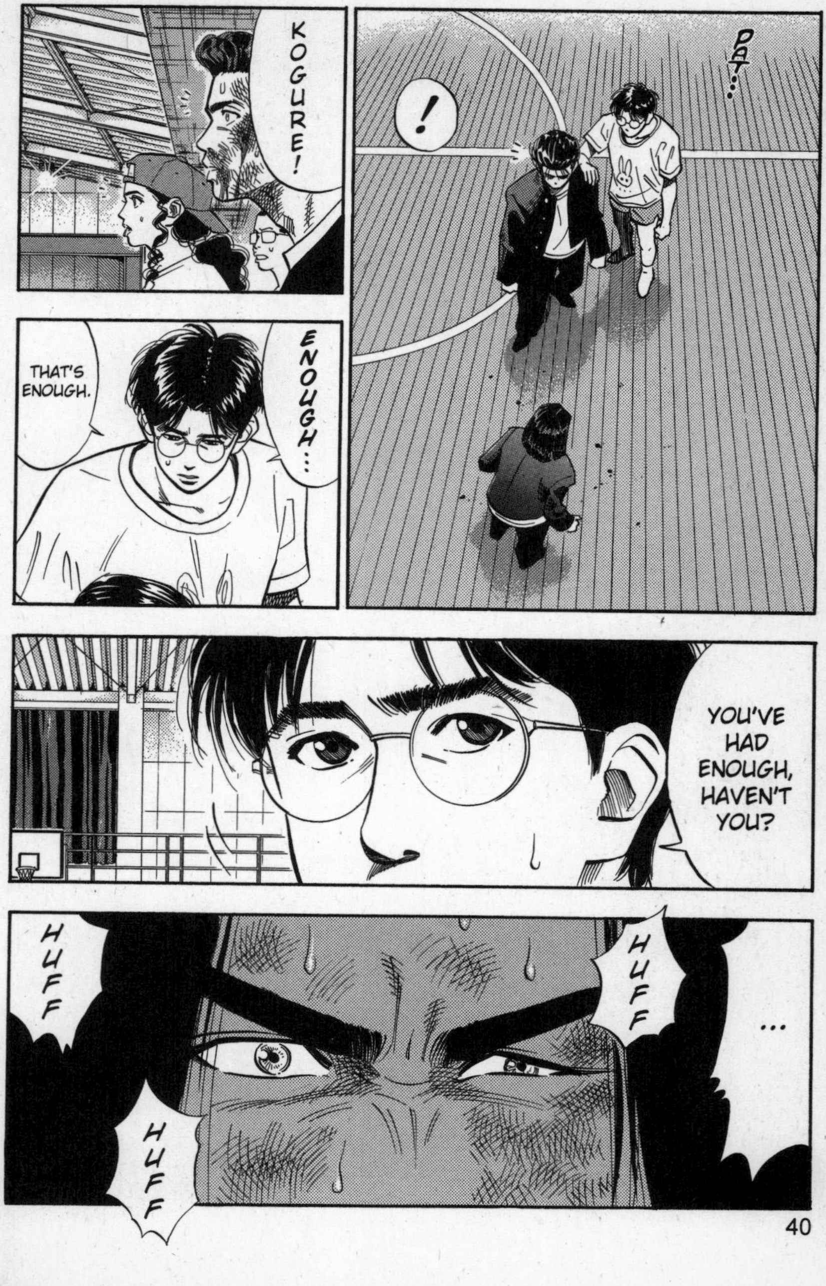
PAT...
!
KOGURE!
ENOUGH...
THAT'S ENOUGH.
YOU'VE HAD ENOUGH, HAVEN'T YOU?
HUFF HUFF
...
HUFF HUFF
HUFF HUFF

READ THIS WAY

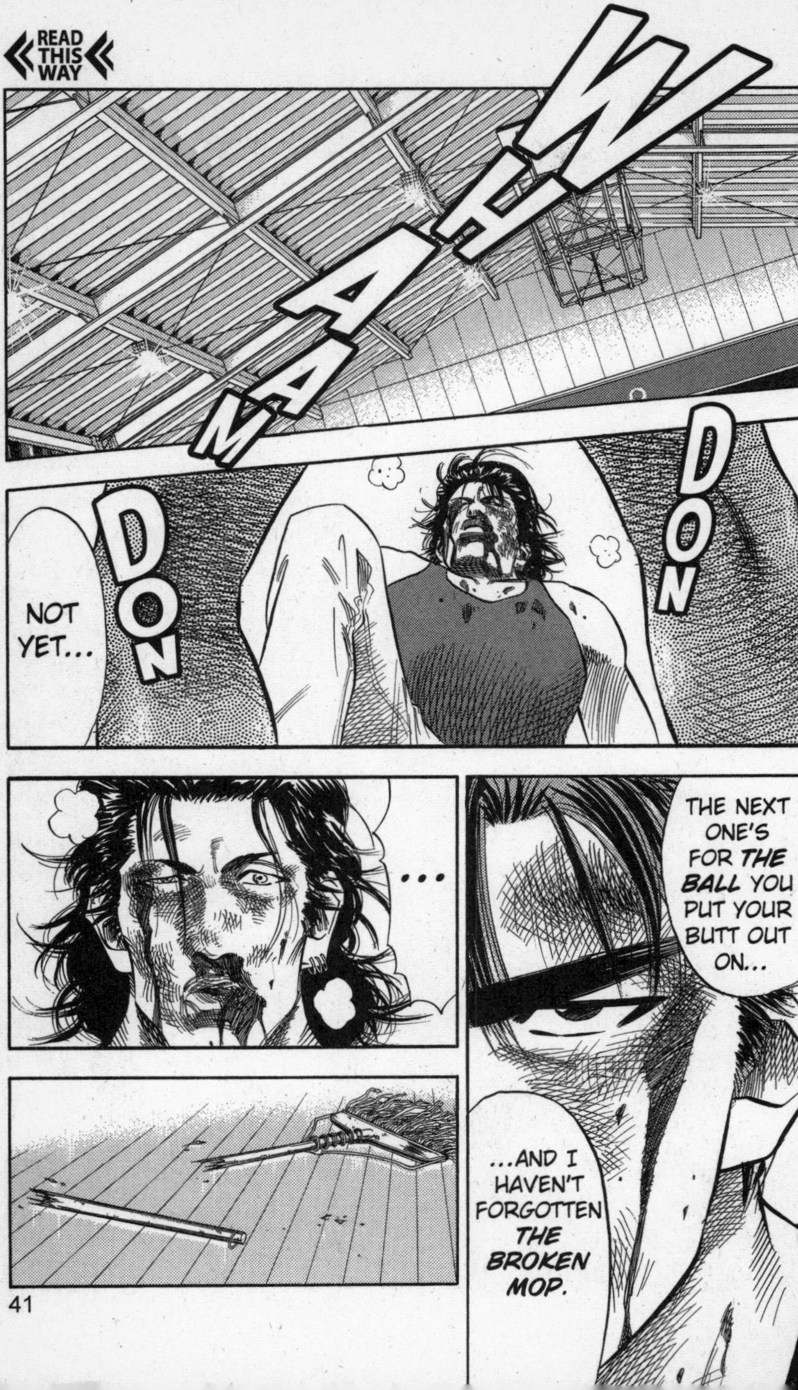
WHAM
DON
DON
NOT YET...
THE NEXT ONE'S FOR ***THE BALL*** YOU PUT YOUR BUTT OUT ON...
...AND I HAVEN'T FORGOTTEN ***THE BROKEN MOP.***
...

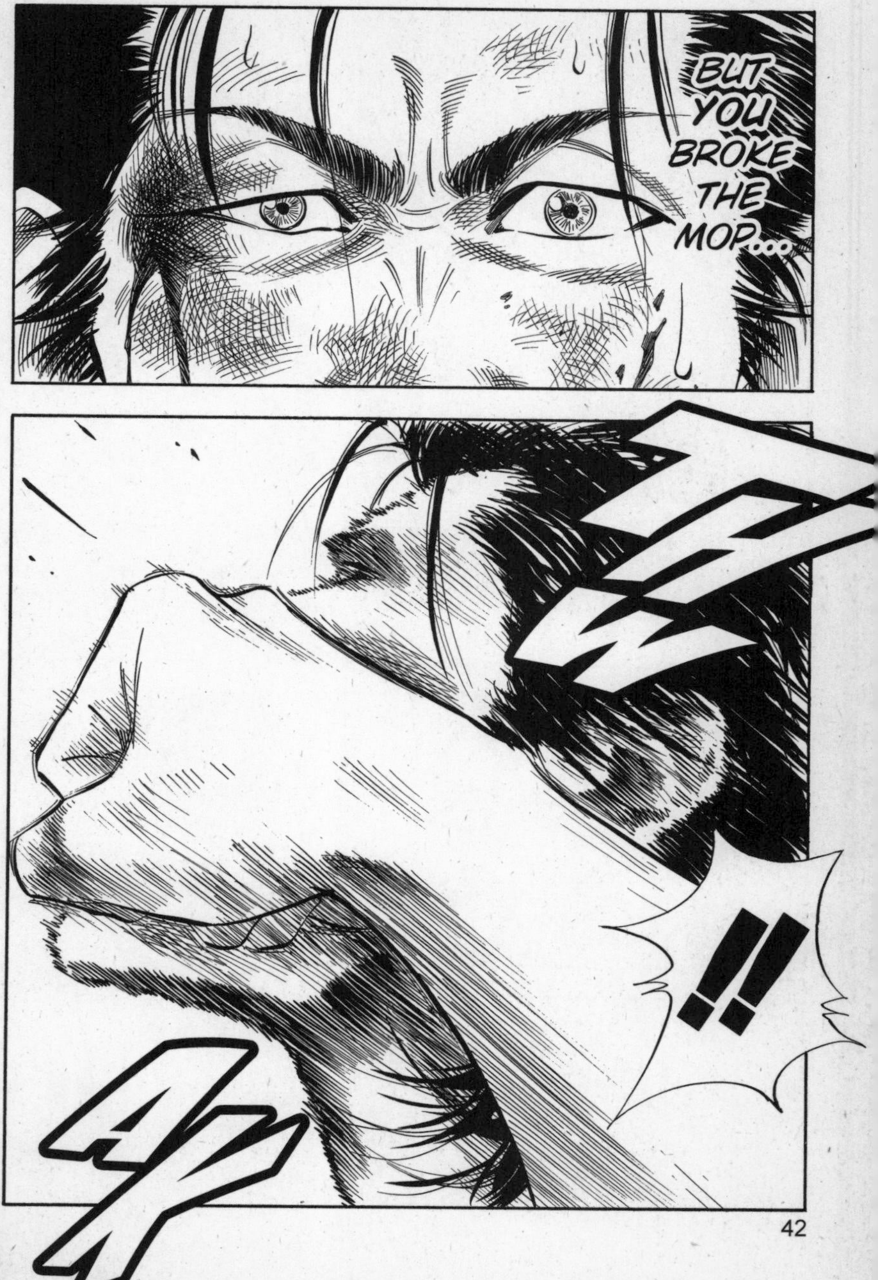
BUT YOU BROKE THE MOP...
!!

READ THIS WAY

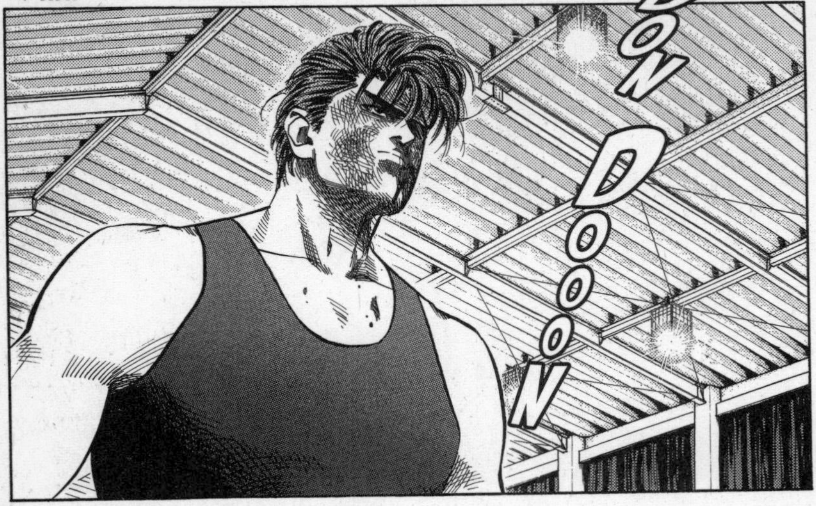
DON
DOOOON

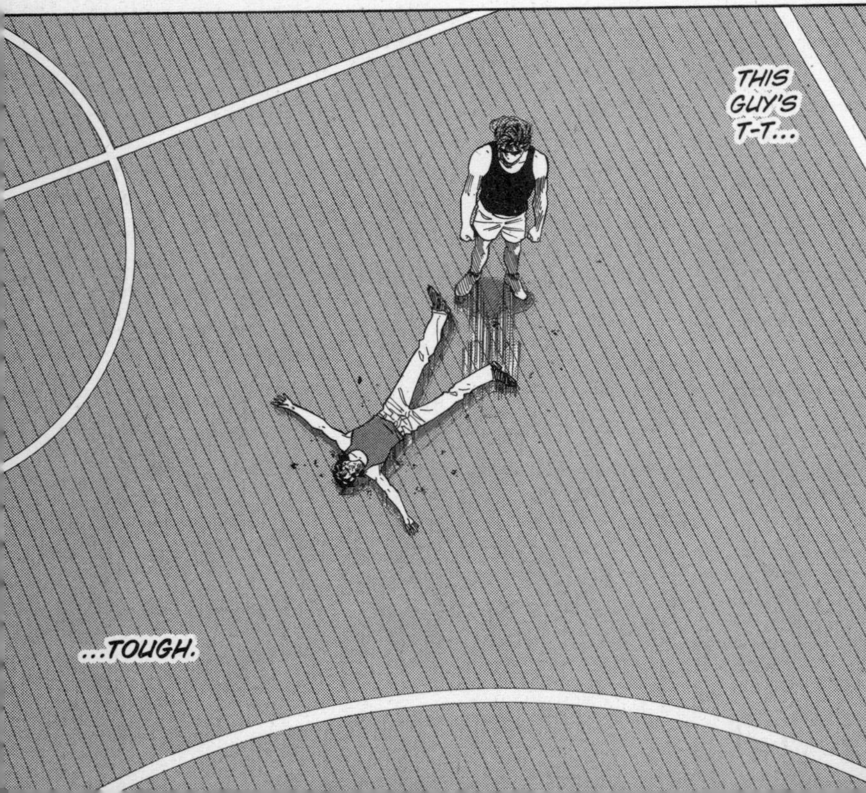
THIS GUY'S T-T...
...TOUGH.

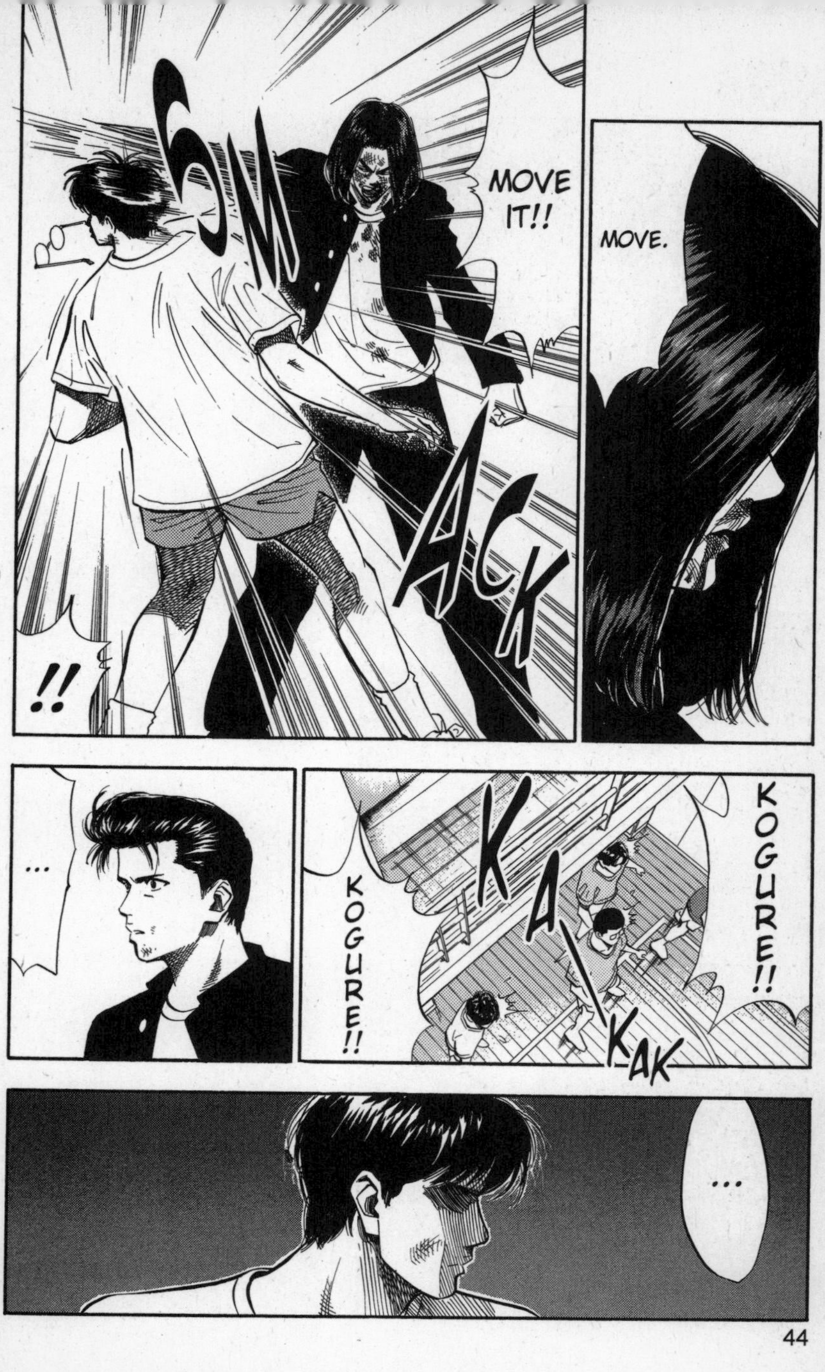
MOVE.
MOVE IT!!
ACK
!!
KOGURE!!
KA
KAK
KOGURE!!
...
...

READ THIS WAY

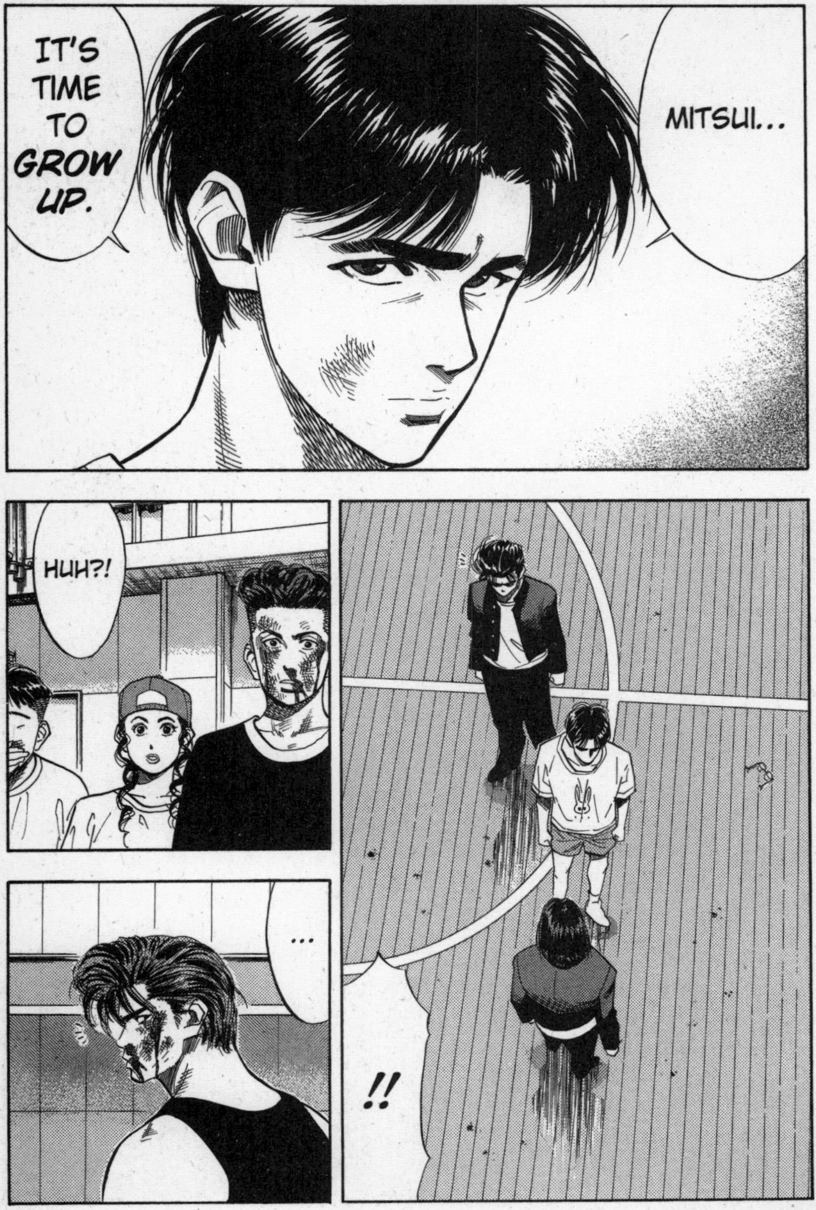
MITSUI...
IT'S TIME TO GROW UP.
!!
HUH?!
...

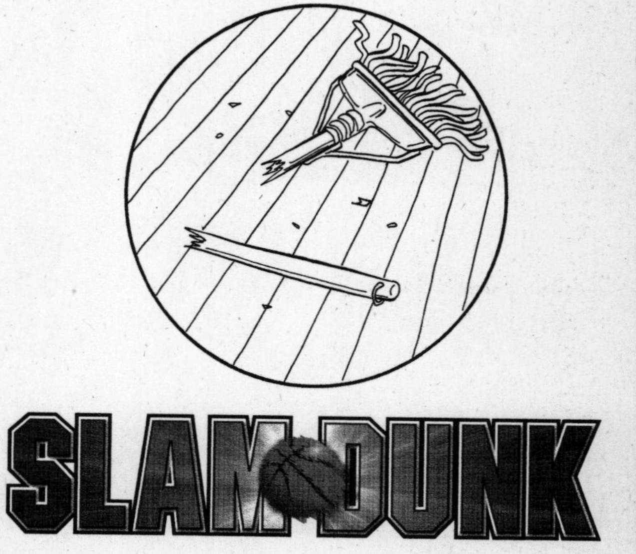

SLAM DUNK

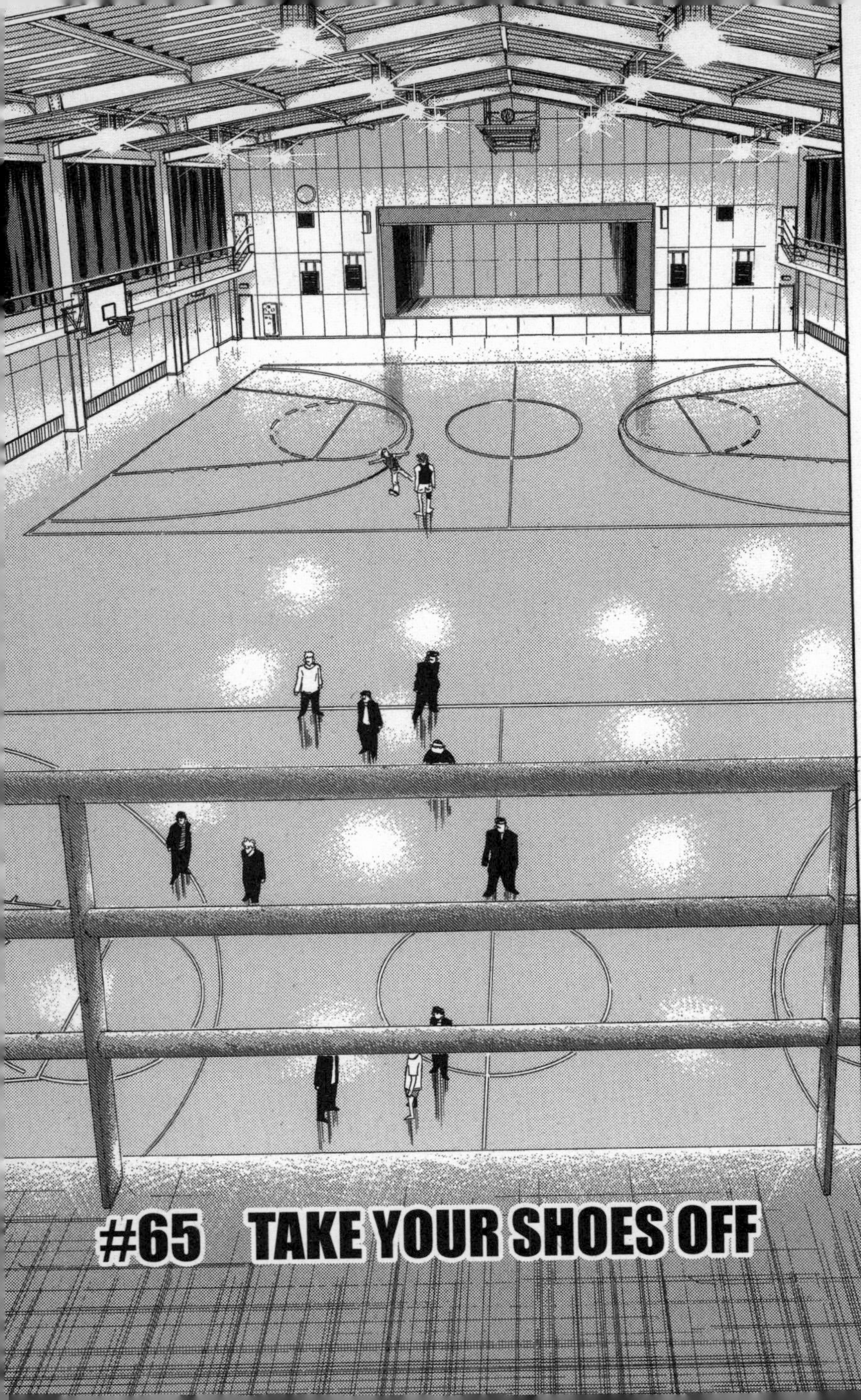
#65 TAKE YOUR SHOES OFF

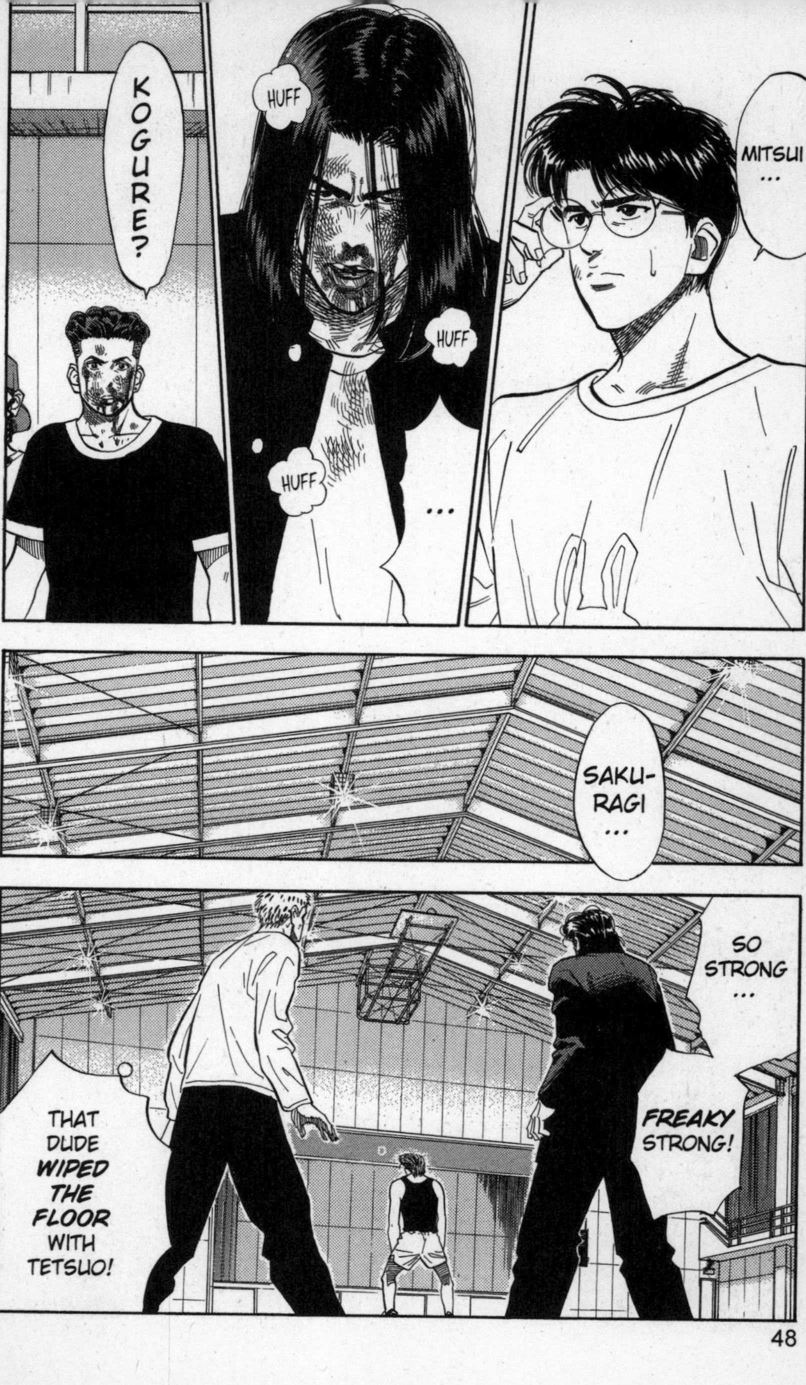
MITSUI ...
HUFF
HUFF
HUFF
...
KOGURE?
SAKU-RAGI ...
SO STRONG ...
FREAKY STRONG!
THAT DUDE WIPED THE FLOOR WITH TETSUO!

READ THIS WAY

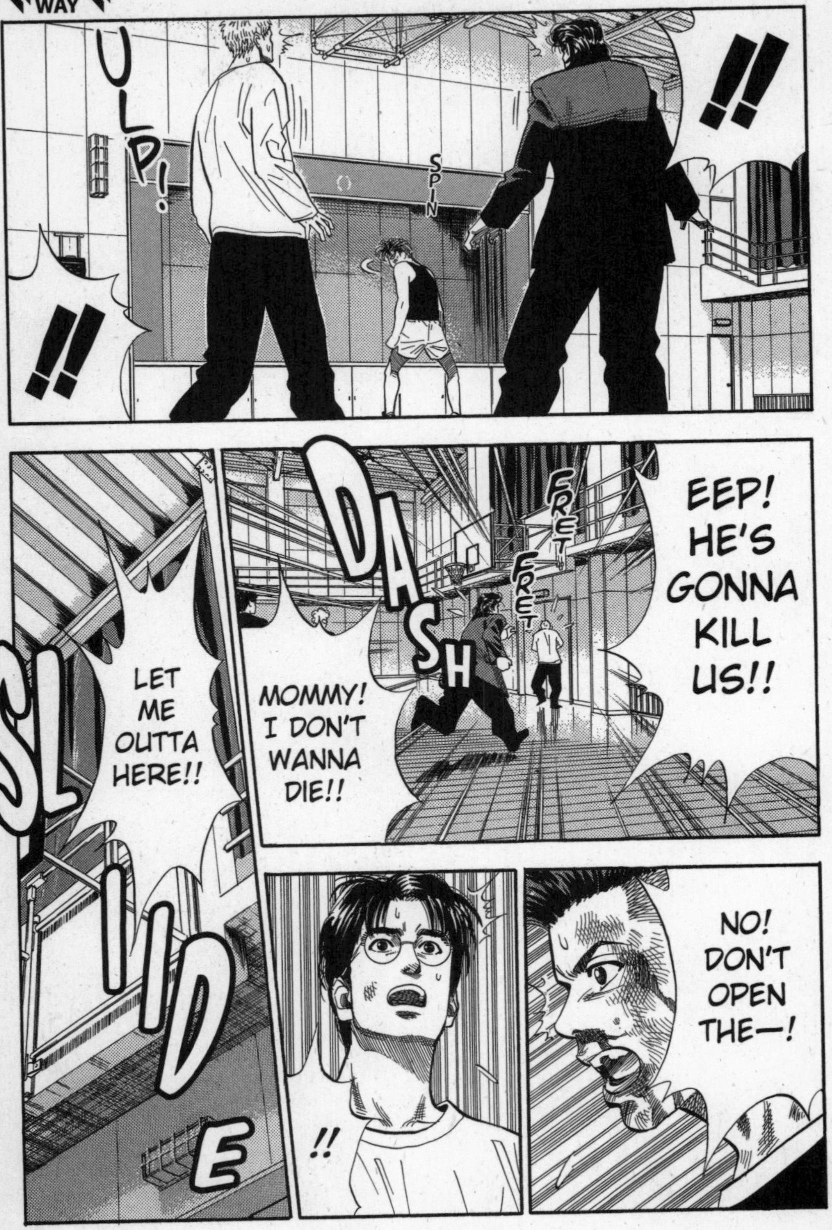
!!
SPIN
ULP!
!!
EEP! HE'S GONNA KILL US!!
FRET FRET
DASH
MOMMY! I DON'T WANNA DIE!!
NO! DON'T OPEN THE—!
!!
LET ME OUTTA HERE!!
SLIIDE

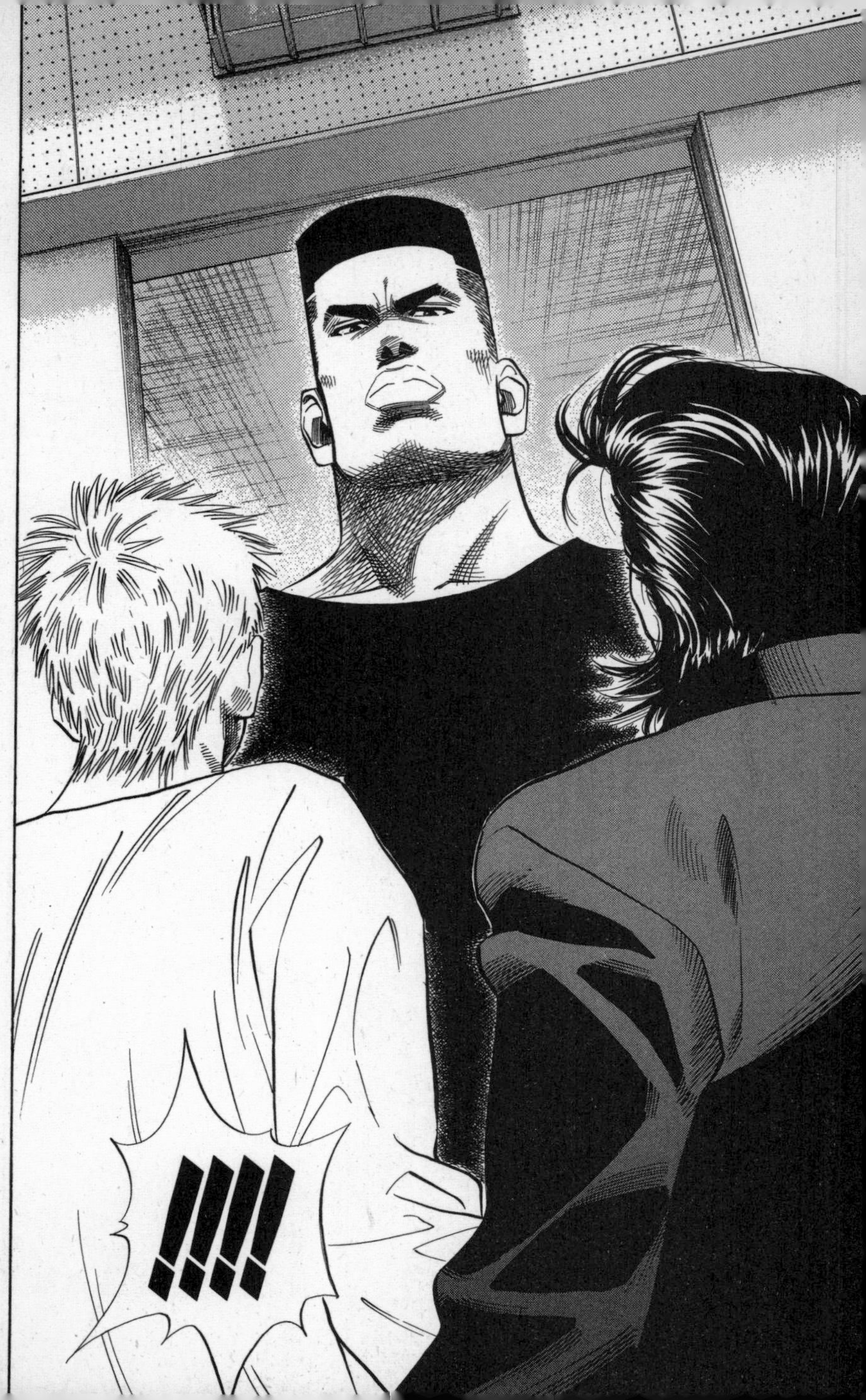
!!!!

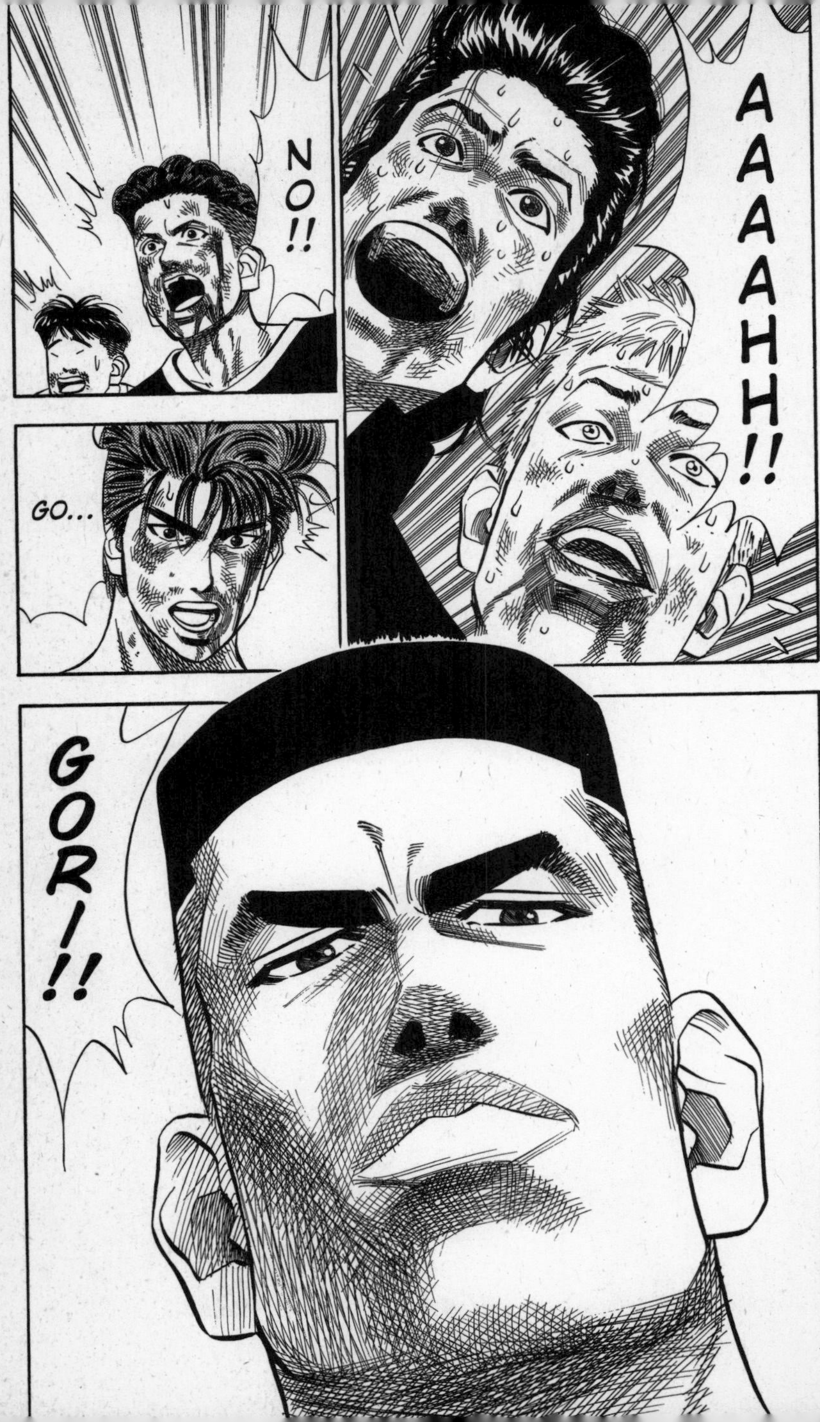
AAAAHH!!
NO!!
GO...
GORI!!

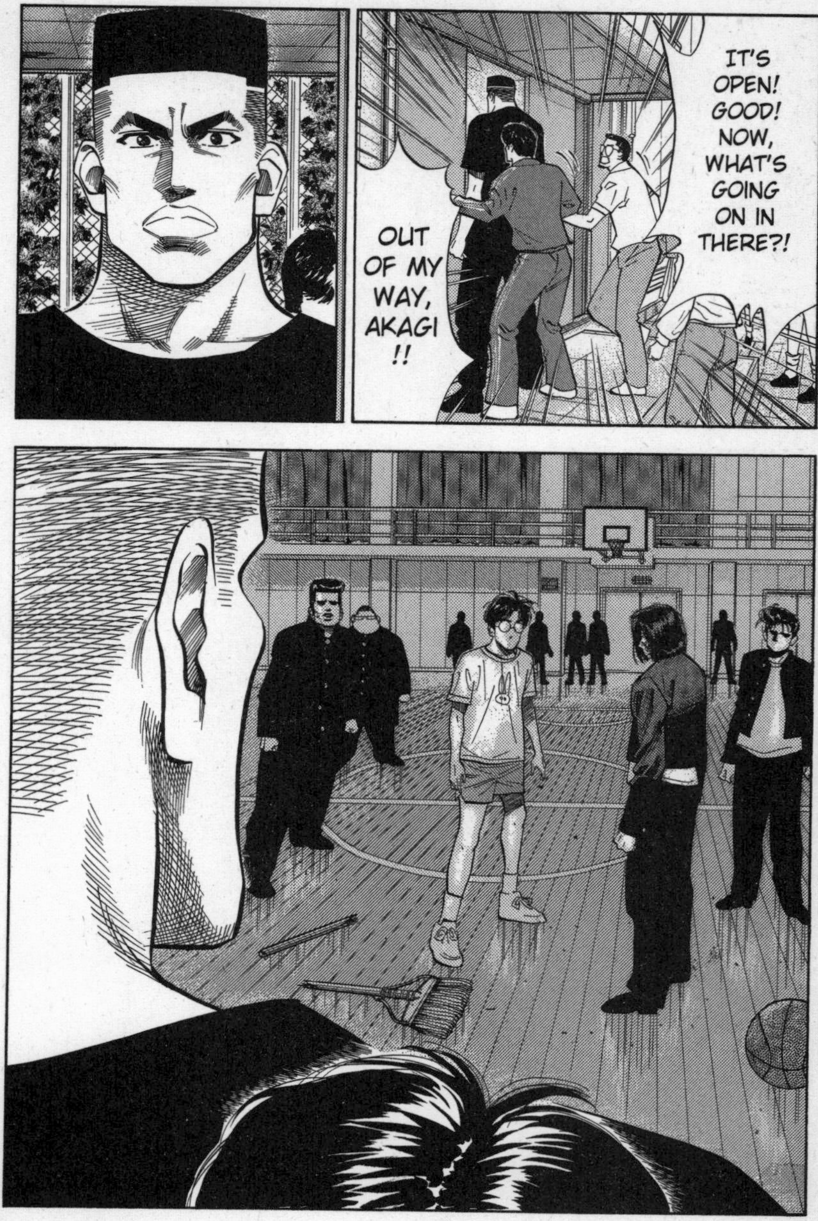
IT'S OPEN! GOOD! NOW, WHAT'S GOING ON IN THERE?!
OUT OF MY WAY, AKAGI!!

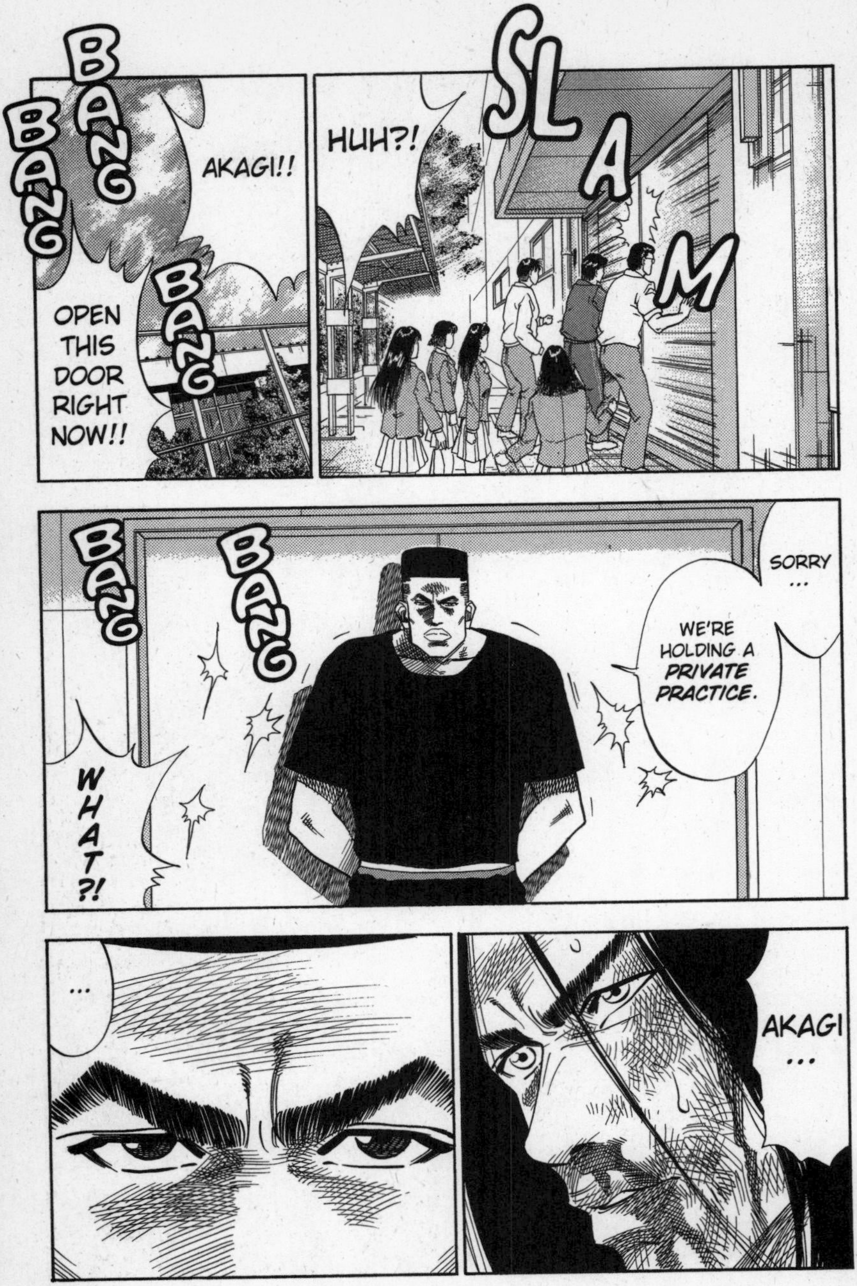
SLAM
HUH?!
BANG
BANG
AKAGI!!
OPEN THIS DOOR RIGHT NOW!!
BANG
SORRY...
WE'RE HOLDING A *PRIVATE PRACTICE*.
BANG
BANG
WHAT?!
AKAGI...
...

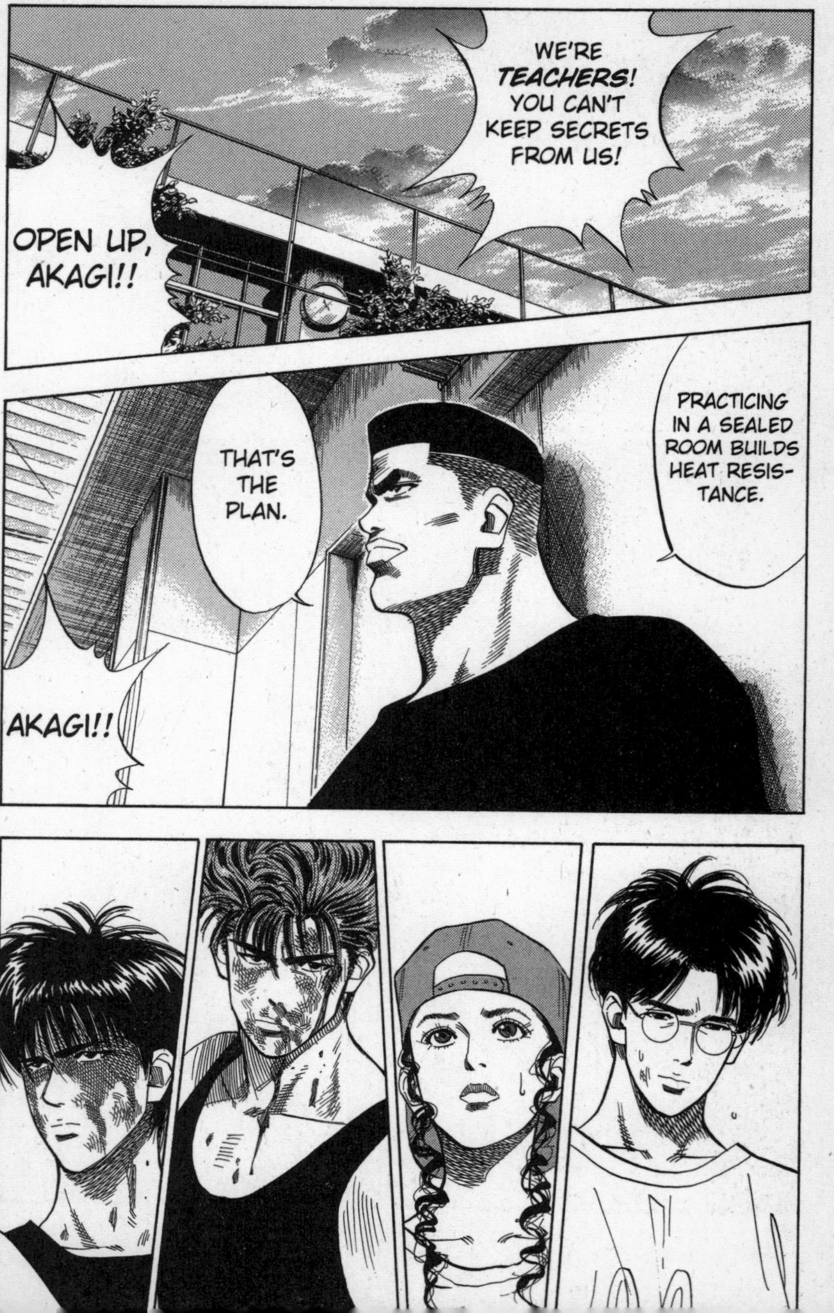
WE'RE *TEACHERS*! YOU CAN'T KEEP SECRETS FROM US!
OPEN UP, AKAGI!!
PRACTICING IN A SEALED ROOM BUILDS HEAT RESIS-TANCE.
THAT'S THE PLAN.
AKAGI!!

READ THIS WAY

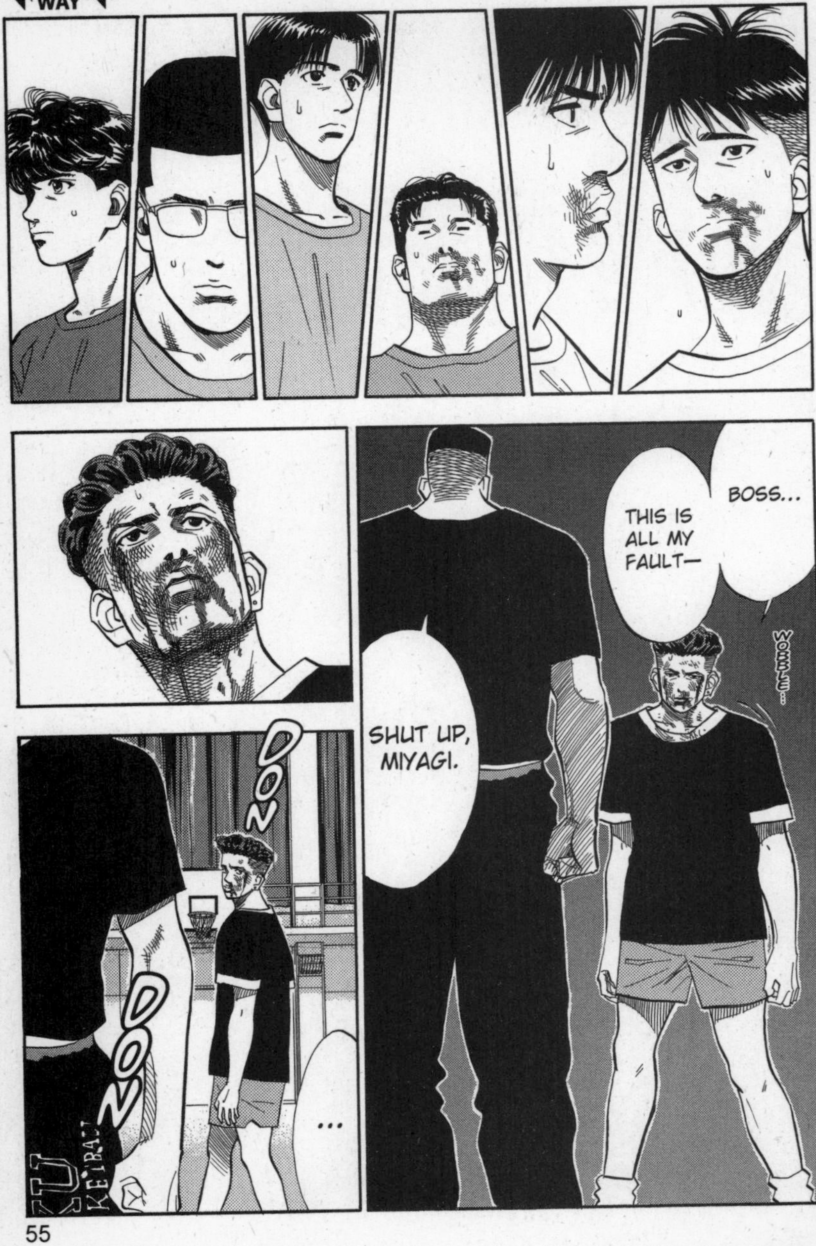
BOSS...
THIS IS ALL MY FAULT—
WOBBLE...
SHUT UP, MIYAGI.
DON
DON
...

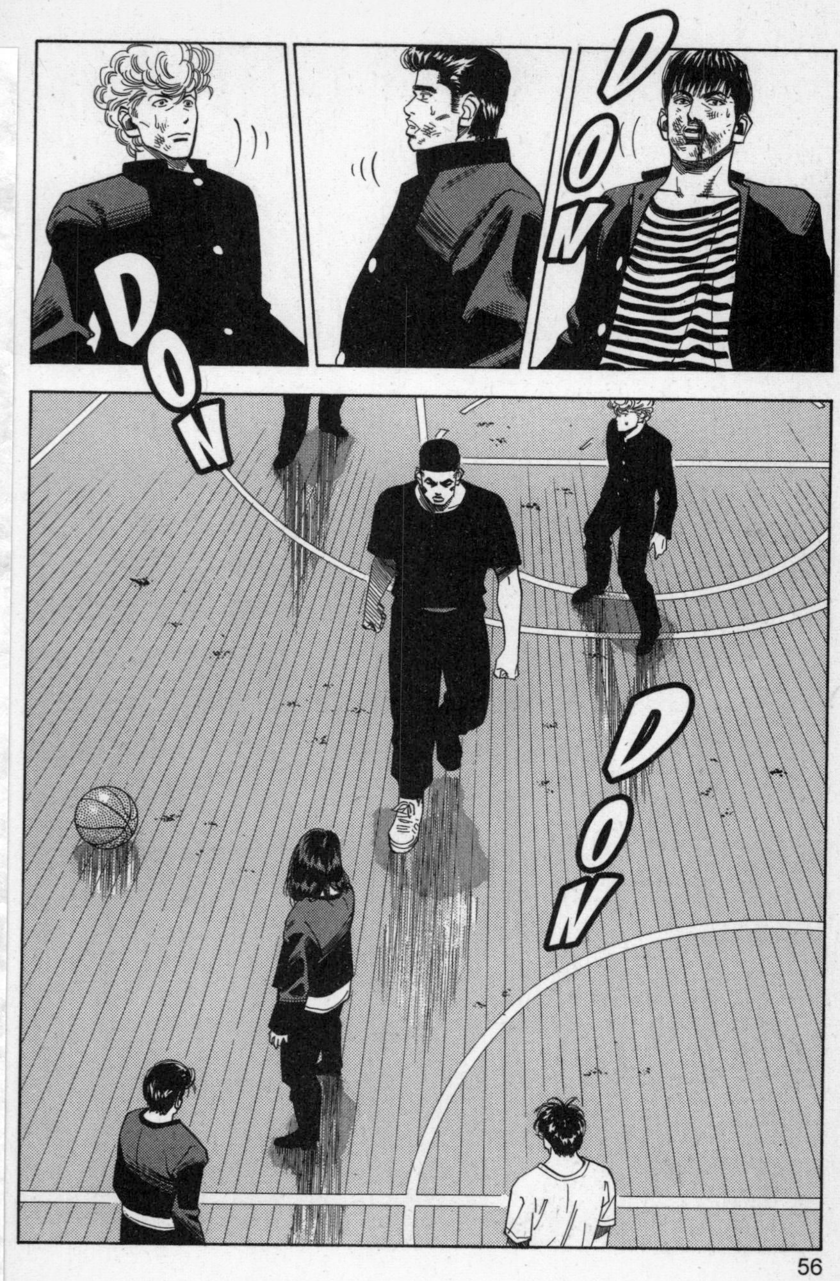
DON
DON
DON

READ THIS WAY

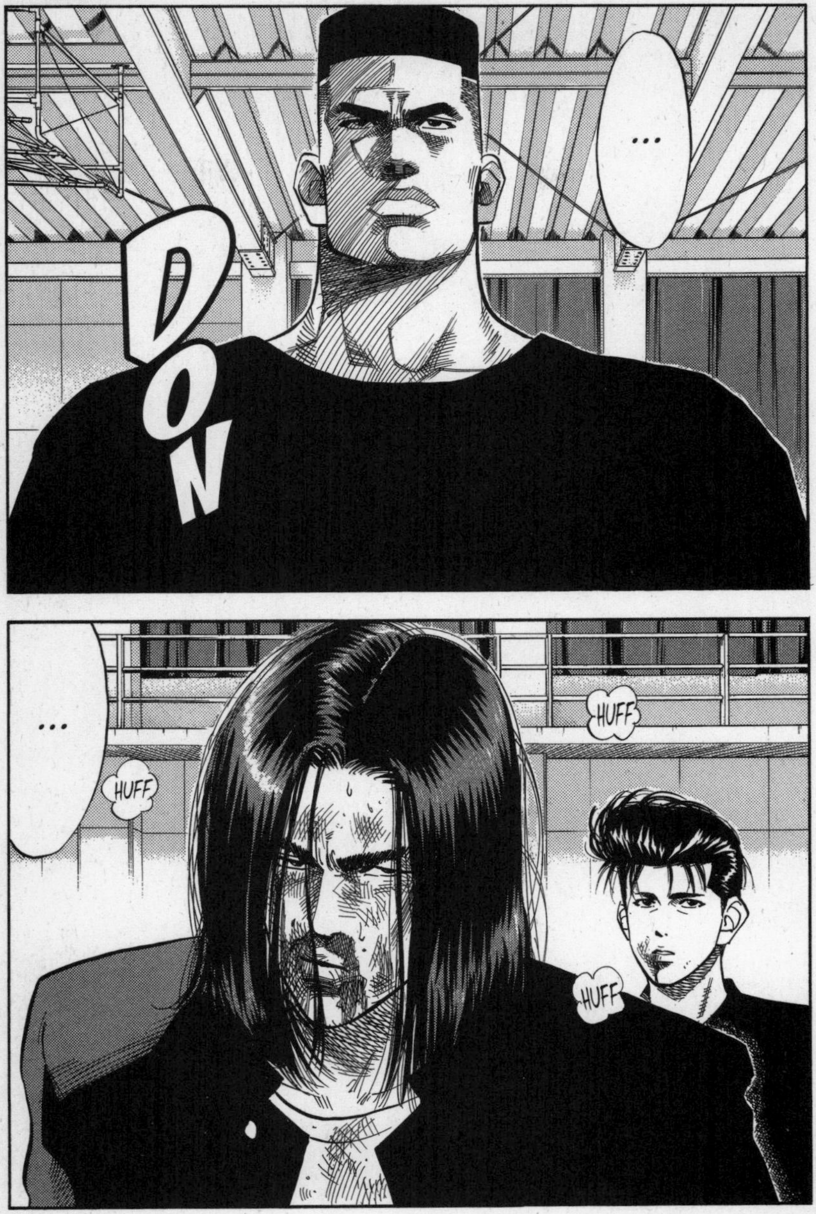

...
DON
HUFF
HUFF
...
HUFF

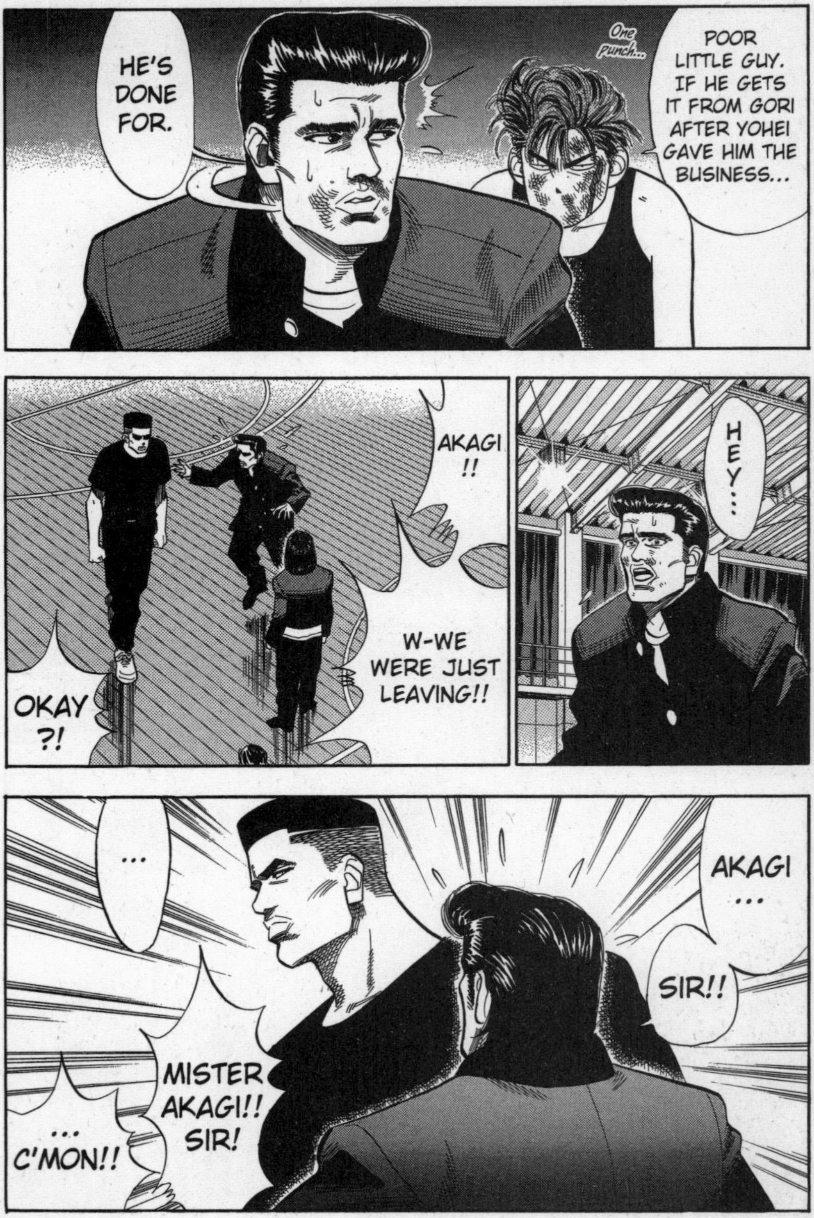
One punch...
POOR LITTLE GUY. IF HE GETS IT FROM GORI AFTER YOHEI GAVE HIM THE BUSINESS...
HE'S DONE FOR.
HEY...
AKAGI!!
W-WE WERE JUST LEAVING!!
OKAY?!
AKAGI...
SIR!!
...
MISTER AKAGI!! SIR!
...C'MON!!

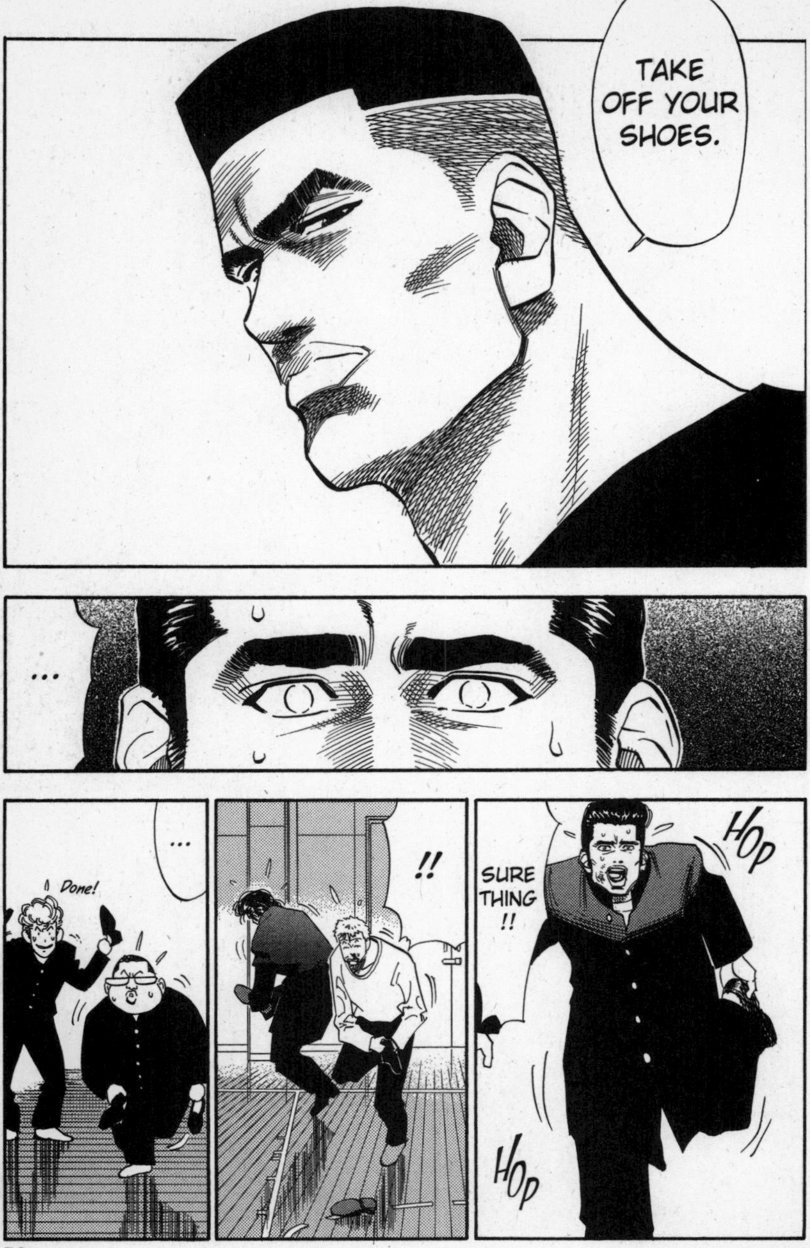
TAKE OFF YOUR SHOES.
...
HOP
SURE THING !!
HOP
!!
...
Done!

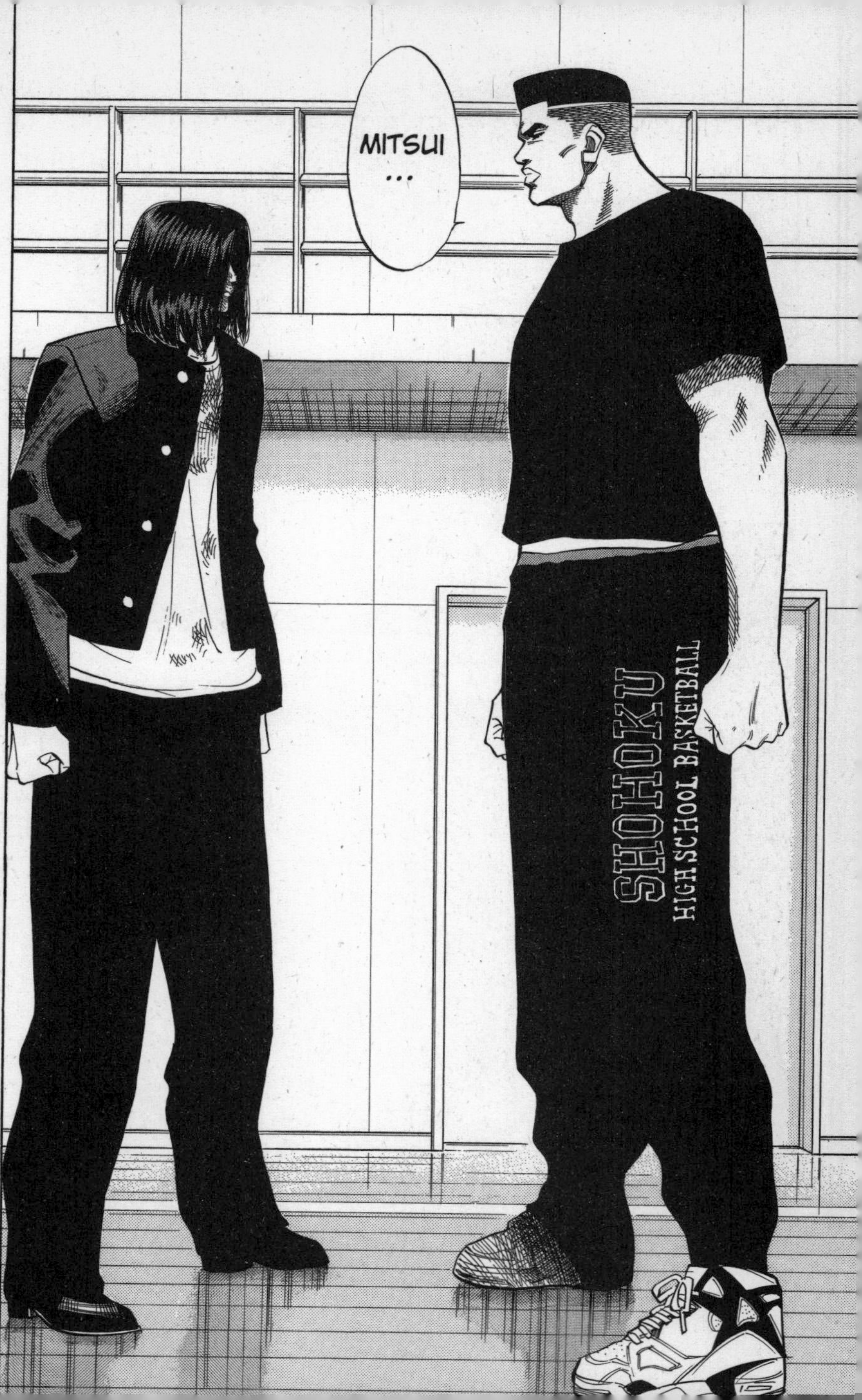
MITSUI ...
SHOHOKU
HIGH SCHOOL BASKETBALL

READ THIS WAY

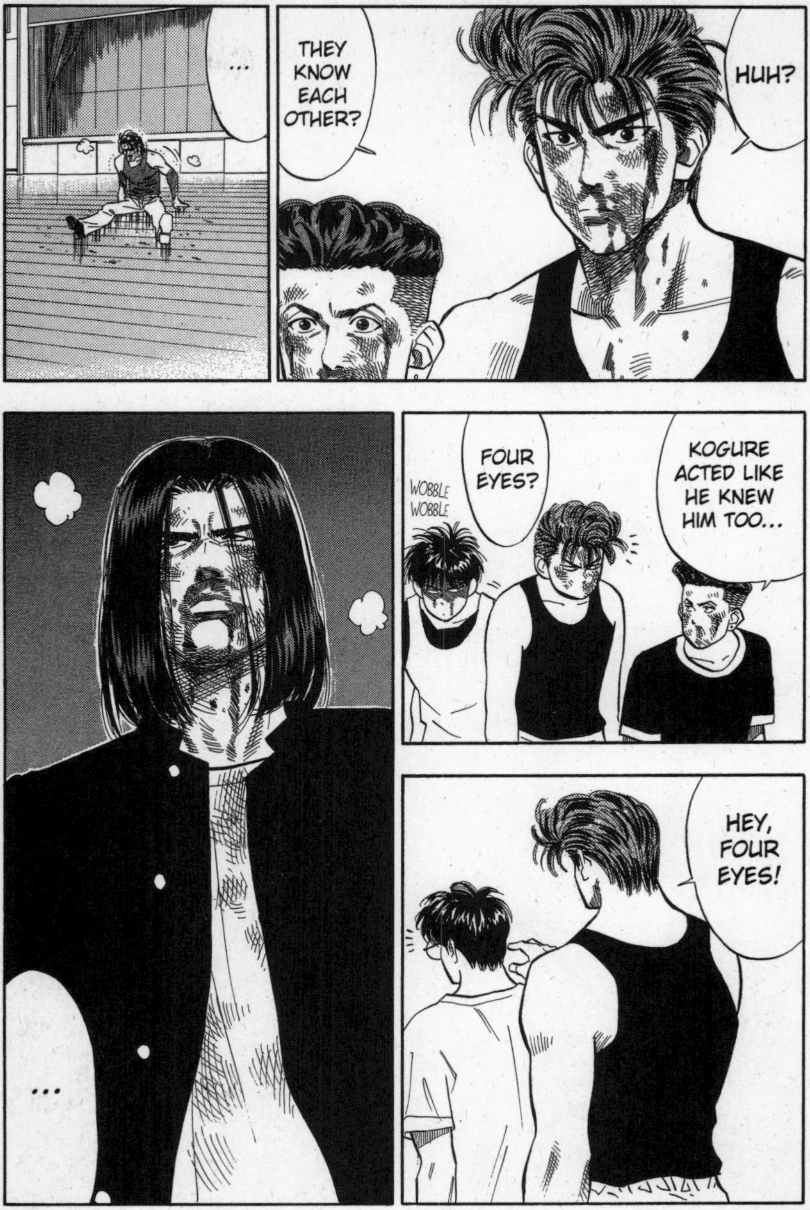
HUH?
THEY KNOW EACH OTHER?
...
KOGURE ACTED LIKE HE KNEW HIM TOO...
FOUR EYES?
WOBBLE WOBBLE
HEY, FOUR EYES!
...

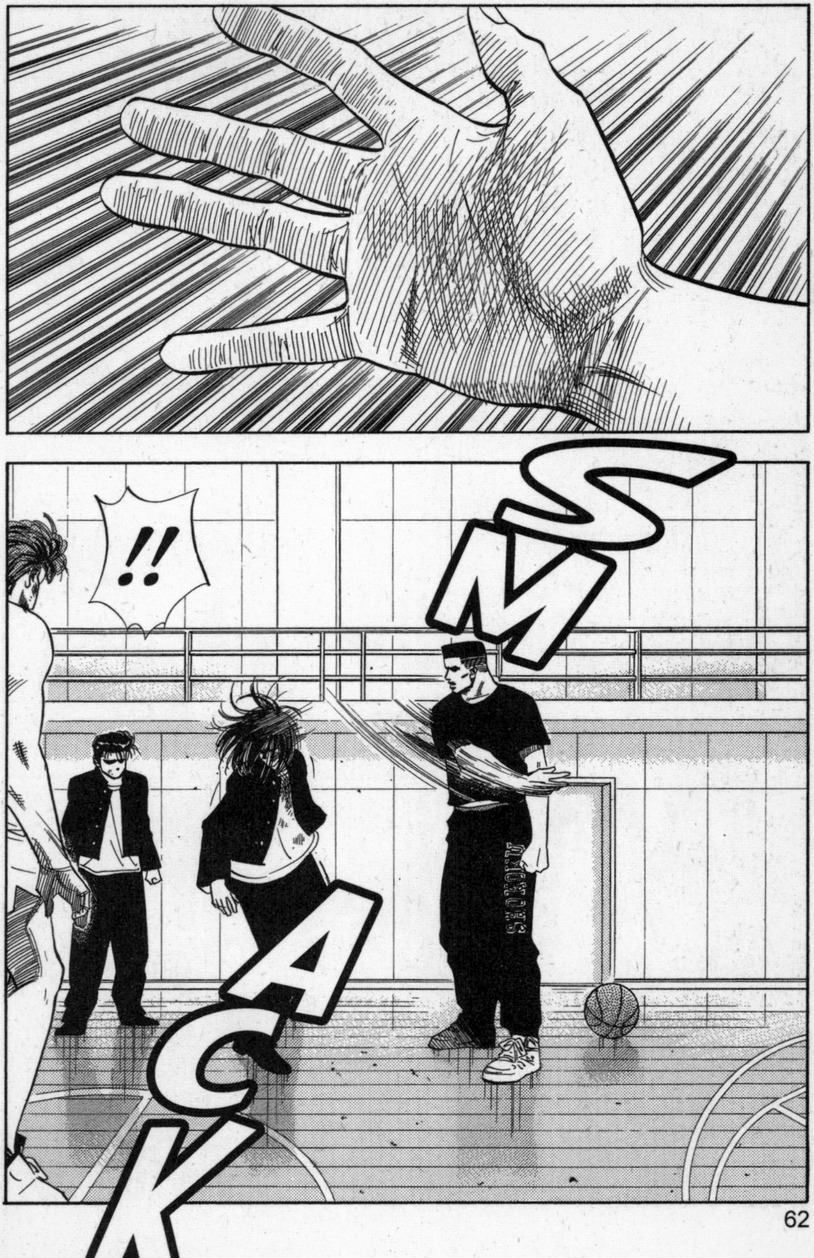
SMACK
!!

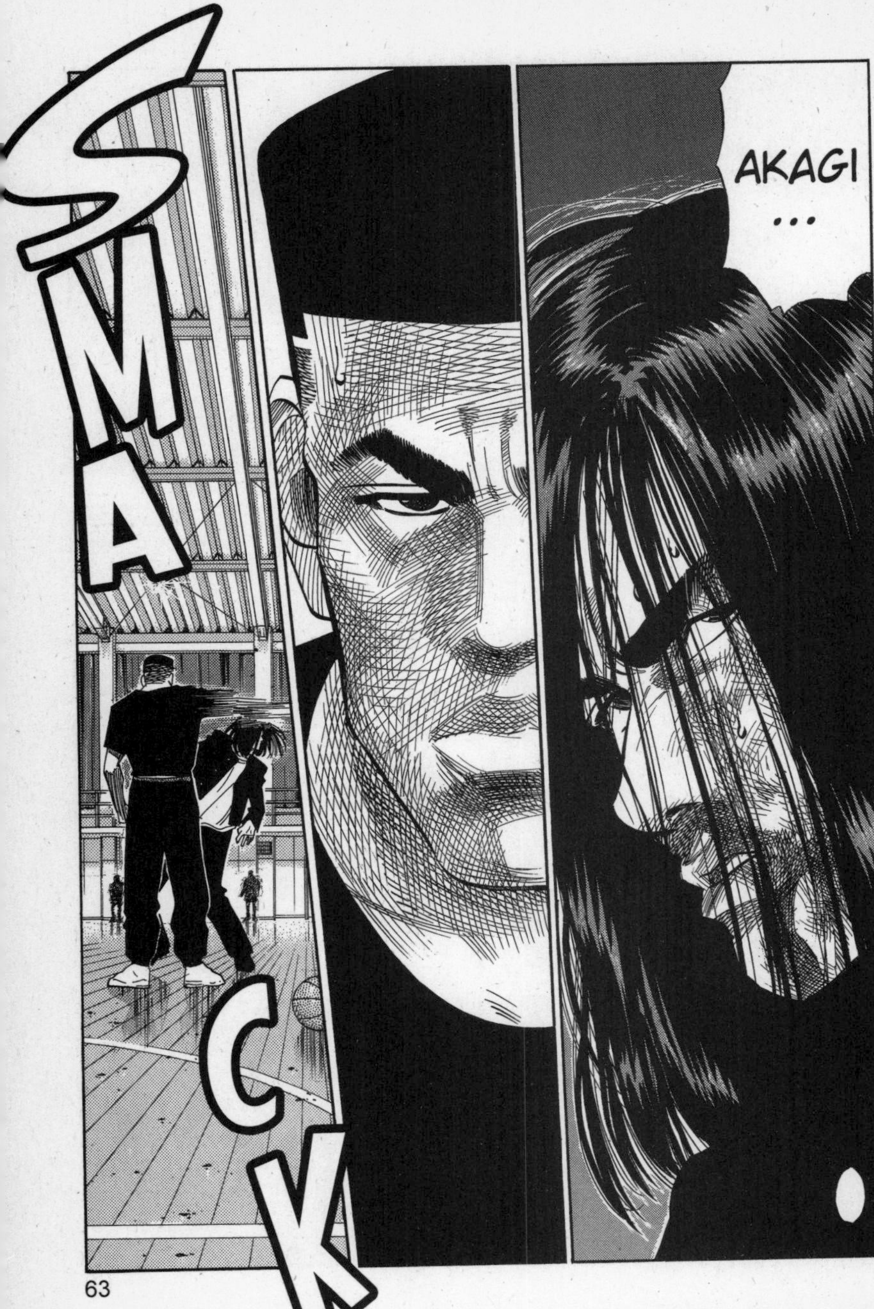
AKAGI
...
SMACK

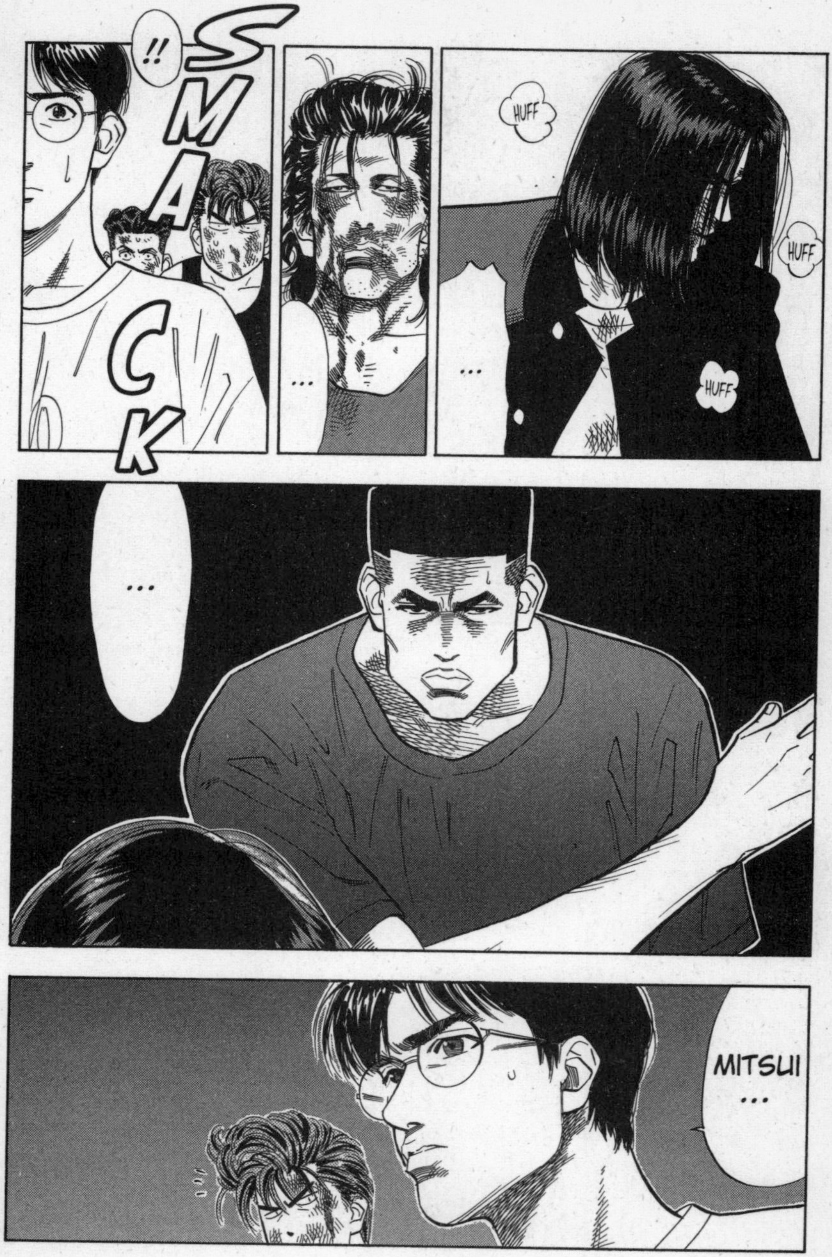
HUFF
HUFF
HUFF
...
...
!!
SMACK
...
MITSUI ...

READ THIS WAY

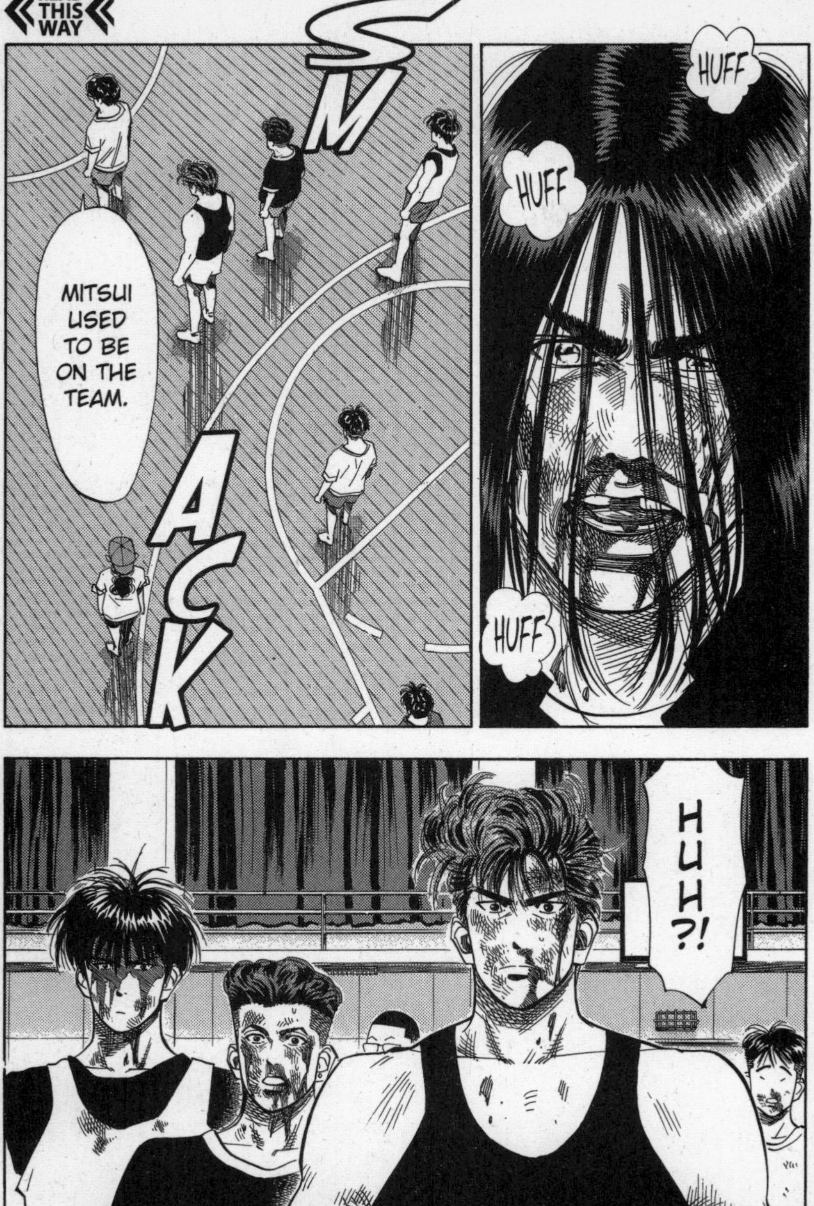
HUFF
HUFF
HUFF
SMACK
MITSUI USED TO BE ON THE TEAM.
HUH?!

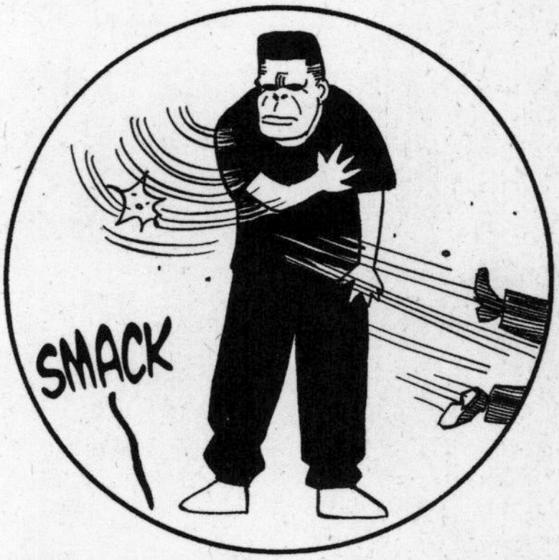
SMACK

SLAM DUNK

#66 MVP

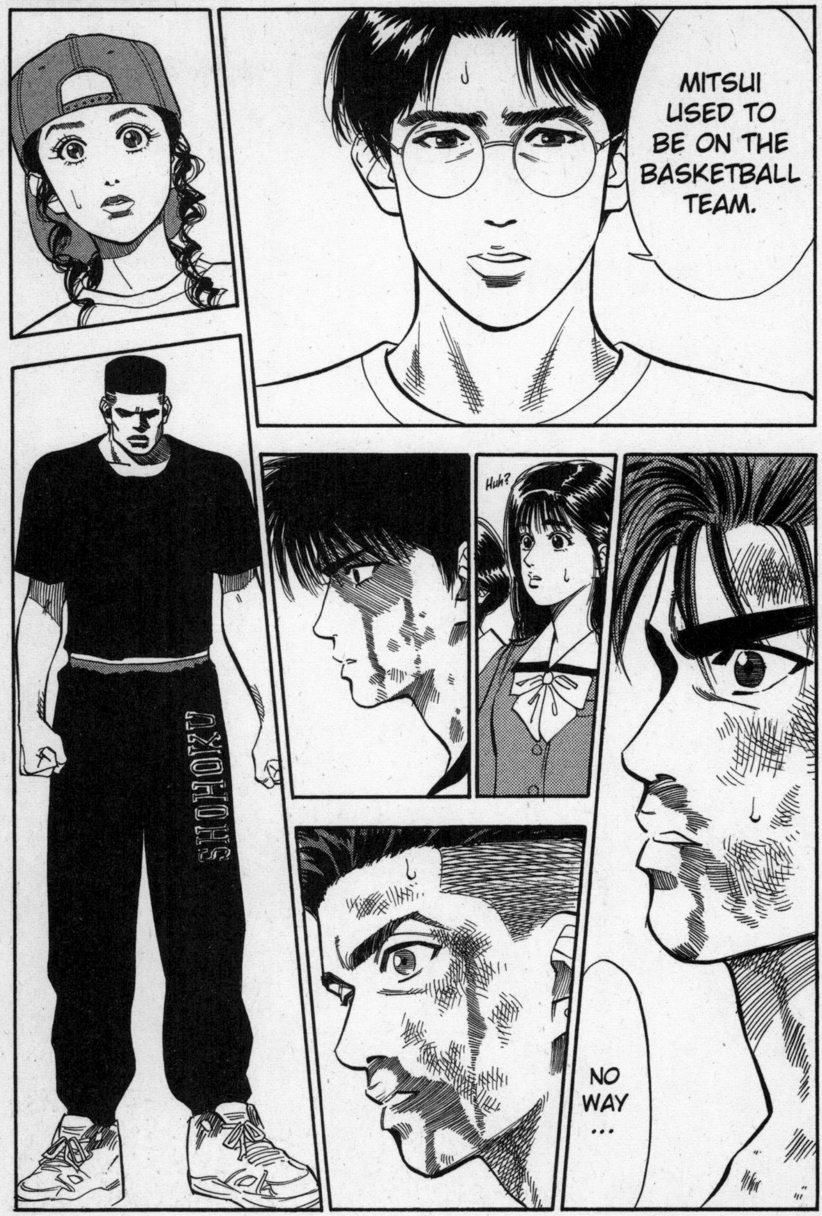
MITSUI USED TO BE ON THE BASKETBALL TEAM.
Huh?
NO WAY ...

#66 MVP

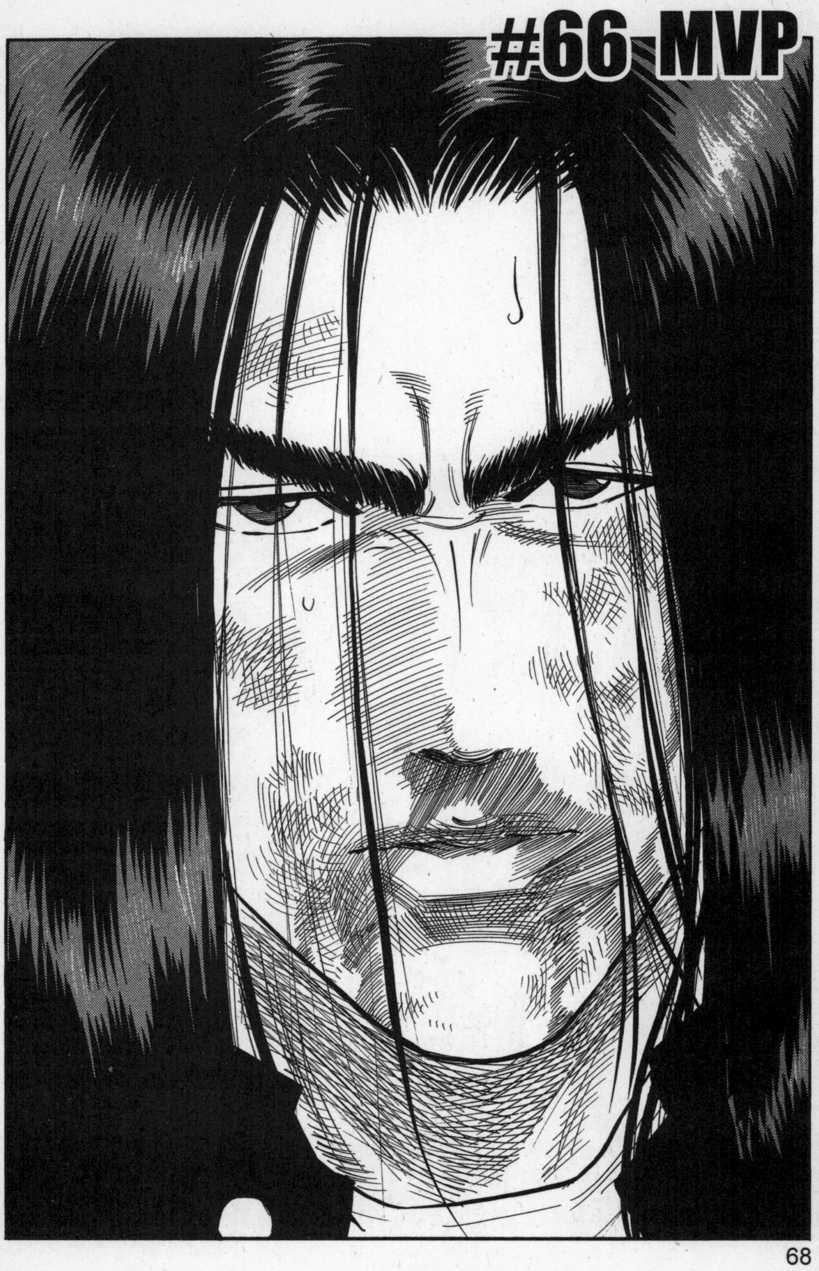

READ THIS WAY

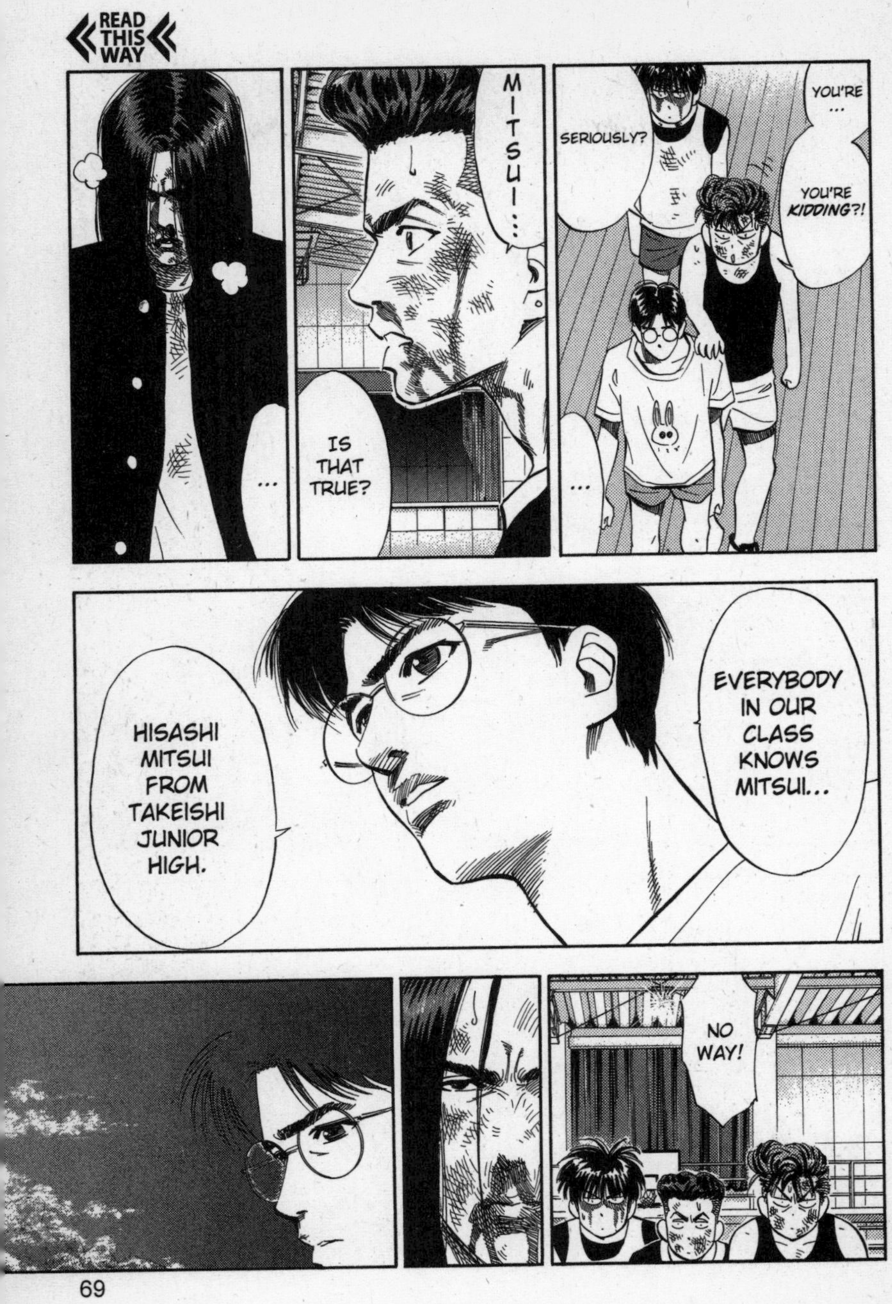

YOU'RE ...
YOU'RE *KIDDING*?!
SERIOUSLY?
...
MITSUI...
IS THAT TRUE?
...
EVERYBODY IN OUR CLASS KNOWS MITSUI...
HISASHI MITSUI FROM TAKEISHI JUNIOR HIGH.
NO WAY!

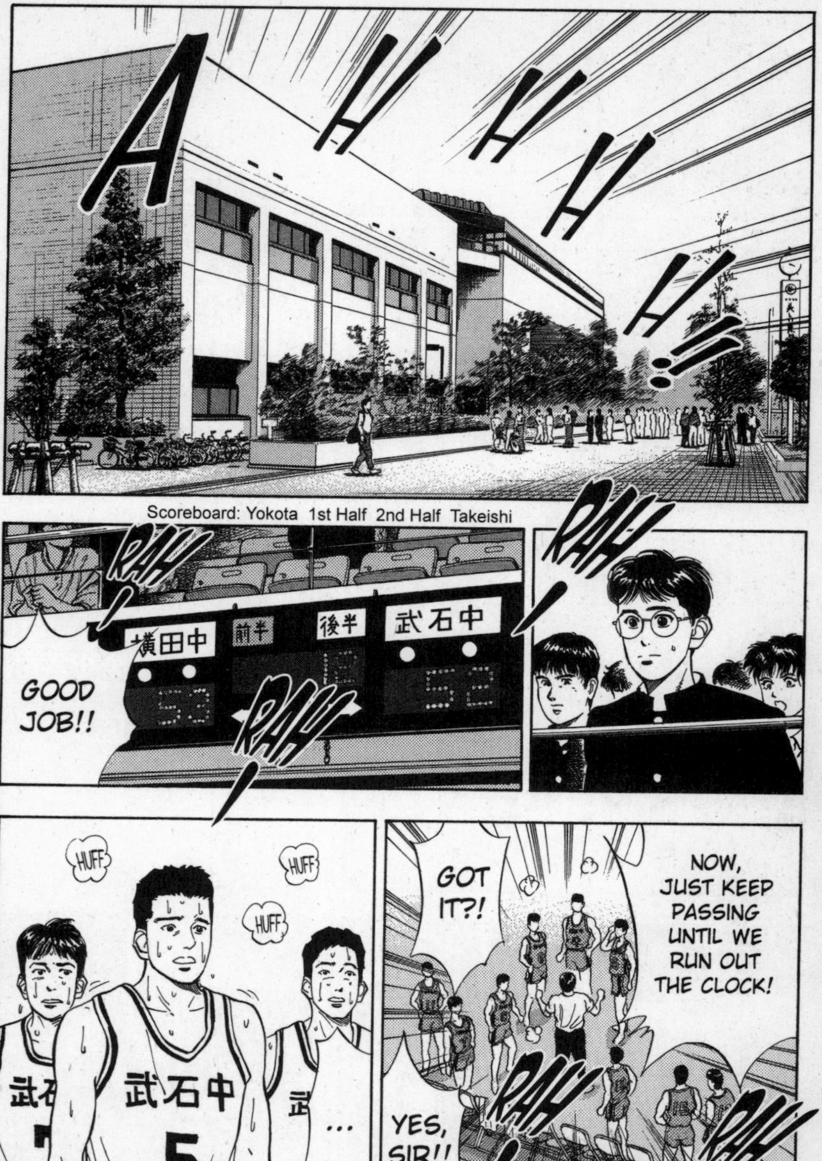
AHHHH!!
RAH
Scoreboard: Yokota 1st Half 2nd Half Takeishi
横田中 前半 後半 武石中
RAH
GOOD JOB!!
RAH
NOW, JUST KEEP PASSING UNTIL WE RUN OUT THE CLOCK!
GOT IT?!
YES, SIR!!
RAH
RAH
HUFF
HUFF
HUFF
武石中
5
...

READ THIS WAY

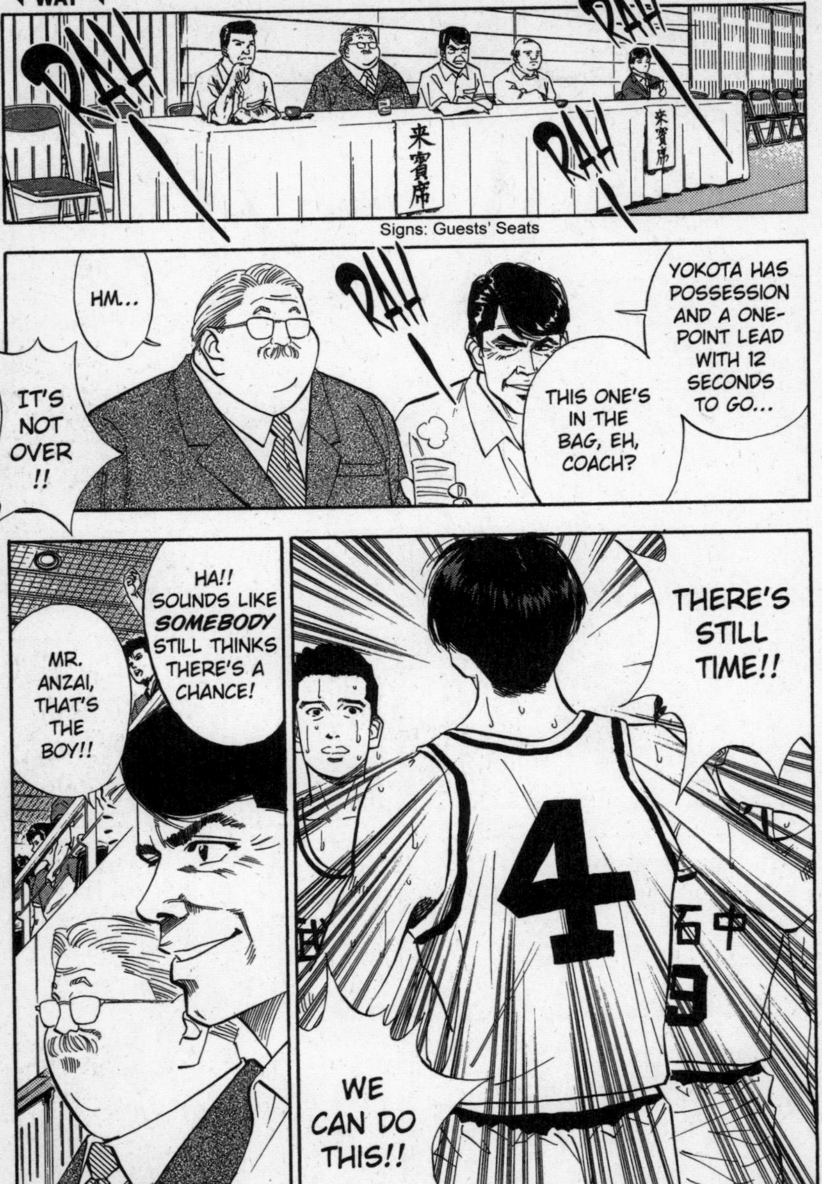
RAH!
RAH!
RAH!
來賓席
來賓席
YOKOTA HAS POSSESSION AND A ONE-POINT LEAD WITH 12 SECONDS TO GO...
RAH!
THIS ONE'S IN THE BAG, EH, COACH?
HM...
IT'S NOT OVER!!
THERE'S STILL TIME!!
WE CAN DO THIS!!
HA!! SOUNDS LIKE *SOMEBODY* STILL THINKS THERE'S A CHANCE!
MR. ANZAI, THAT'S THE BOY!!

Signs: Guests' Seats

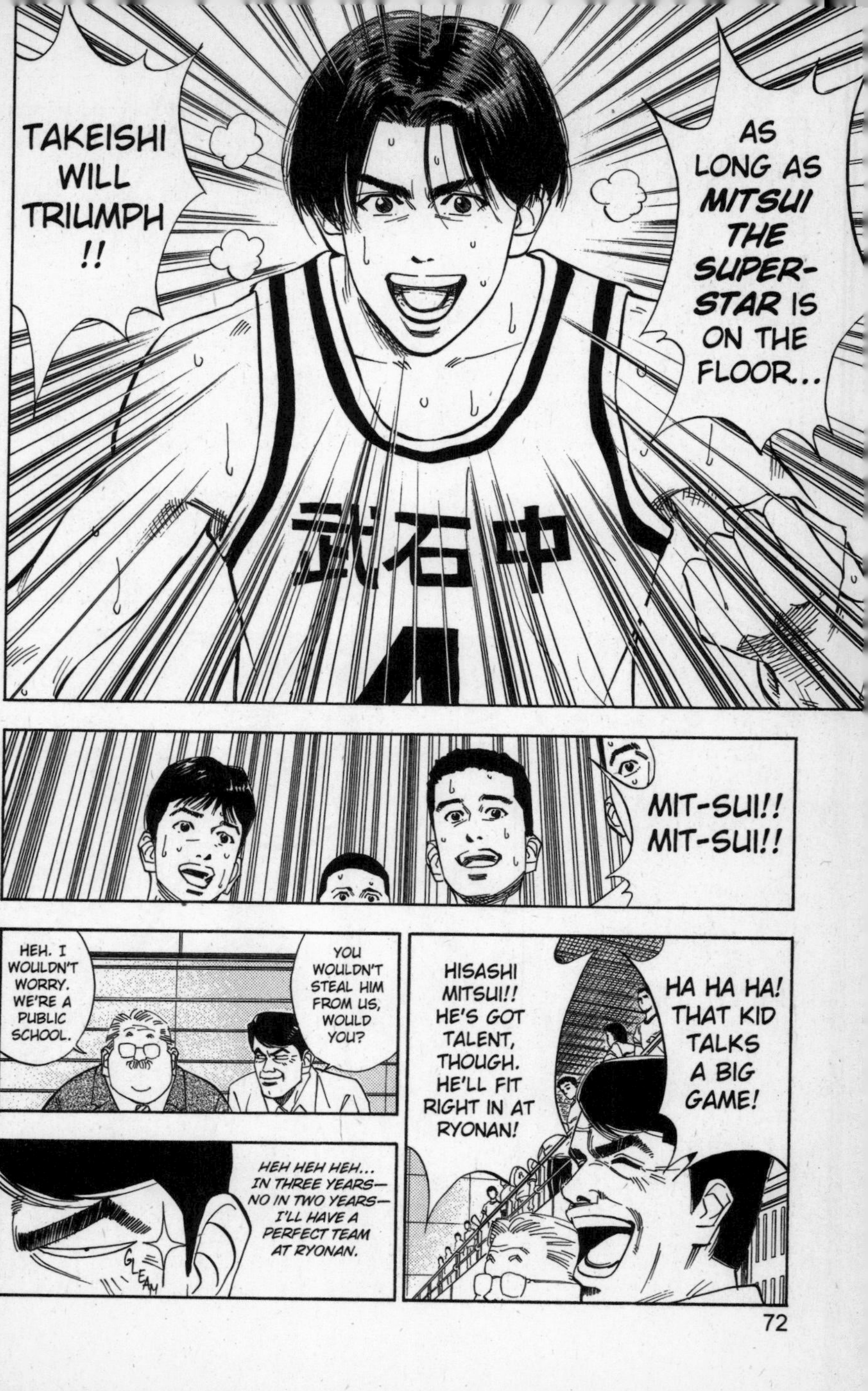
AS LONG AS MITSUI THE SUPER-STAR IS ON THE FLOOR...
TAKEISHI WILL TRIUMPH!!
武石中
MIT-SUI!! MIT-SUI!!
HA HA HA! THAT KID TALKS A BIG GAME!
HISASHI MITSUI!! HE'S GOT TALENT, THOUGH. HE'LL FIT RIGHT IN AT RYONAN!
YOU WOULDN'T STEAL HIM FROM US, WOULD YOU?
HEH. I WOULDN'T WORRY. WE'RE A PUBLIC SCHOOL.
HEH HEH HEH... IN THREE YEARS— NO IN TWO YEARS— I'LL HAVE A PERFECT TEAM AT RYONAN.
GLEAM

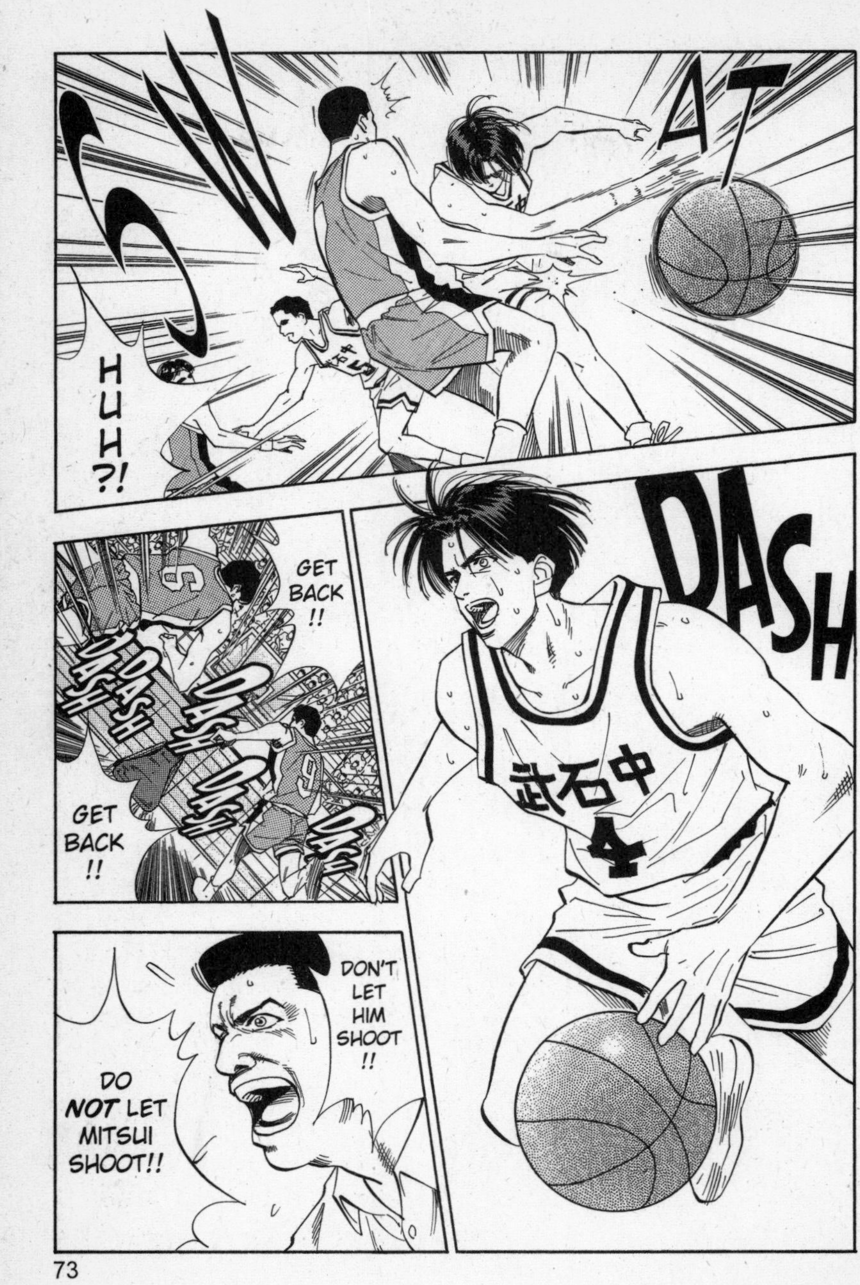
SWAT
HUH?!
DASH
GET BACK!!
DASH
DASH DASH
DASH DASH
GET BACK!!
DON'T LET HIM SHOOT!!
DO *NOT* LET MITSUI SHOOT!!

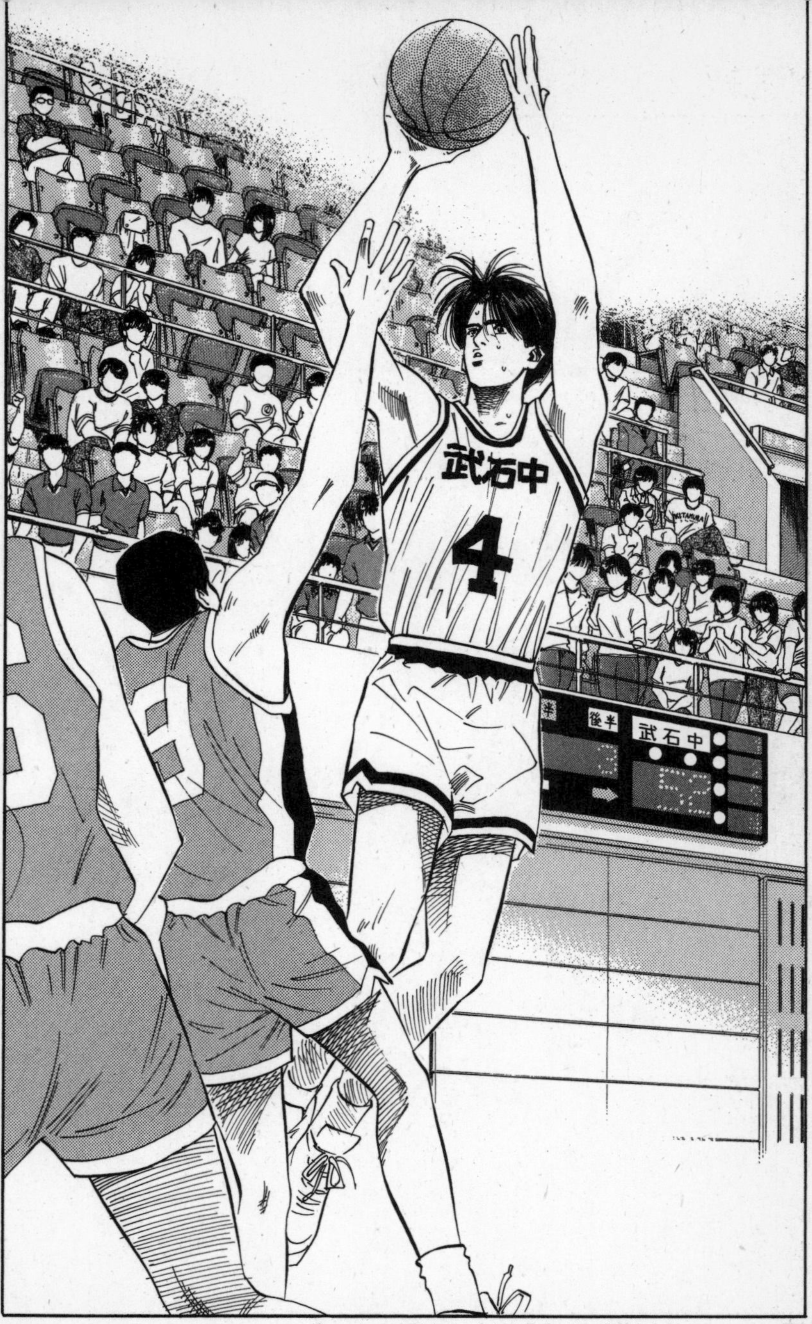
武石中
4
後半
武石中

Scoreboard: Yokota 1st Half 2nd Half Takeishi

READ THIS WAY

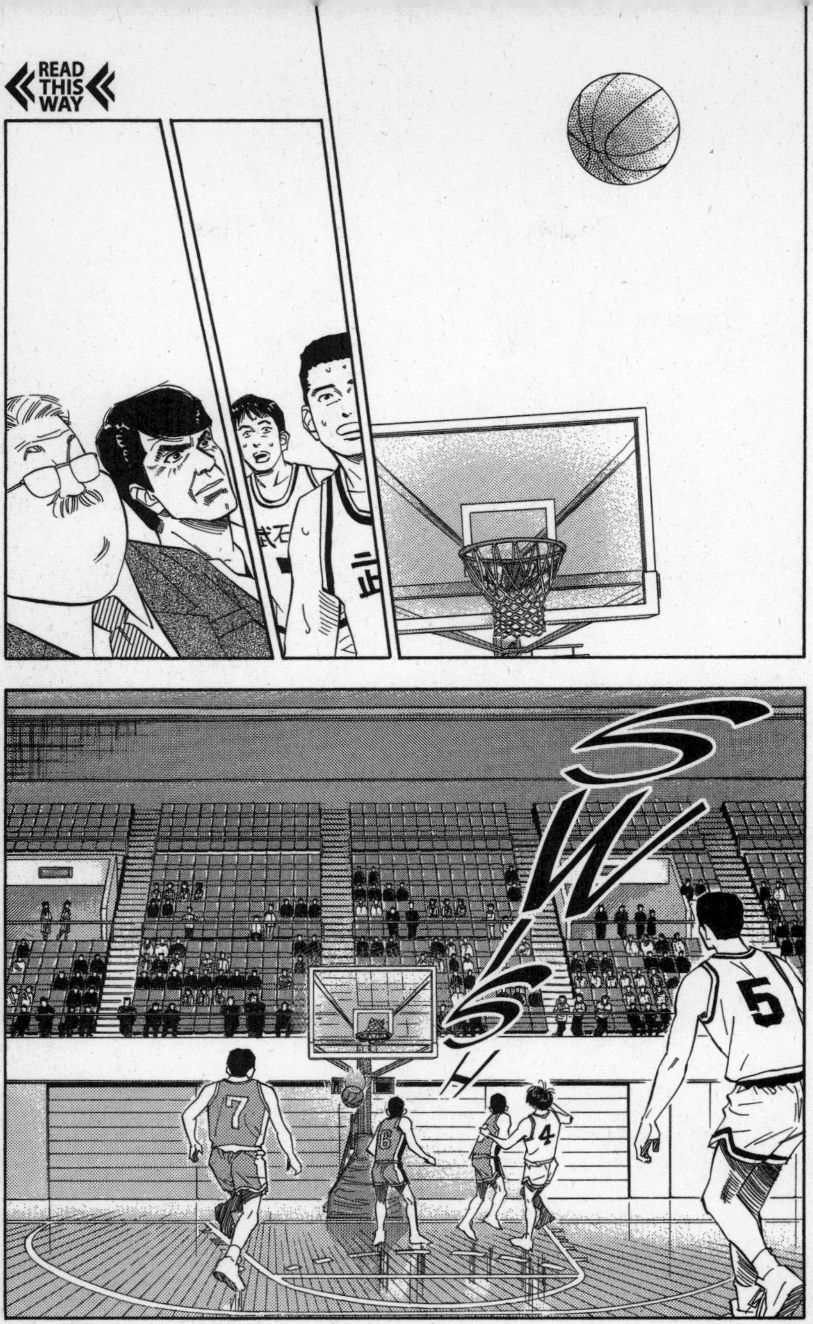
SWISH

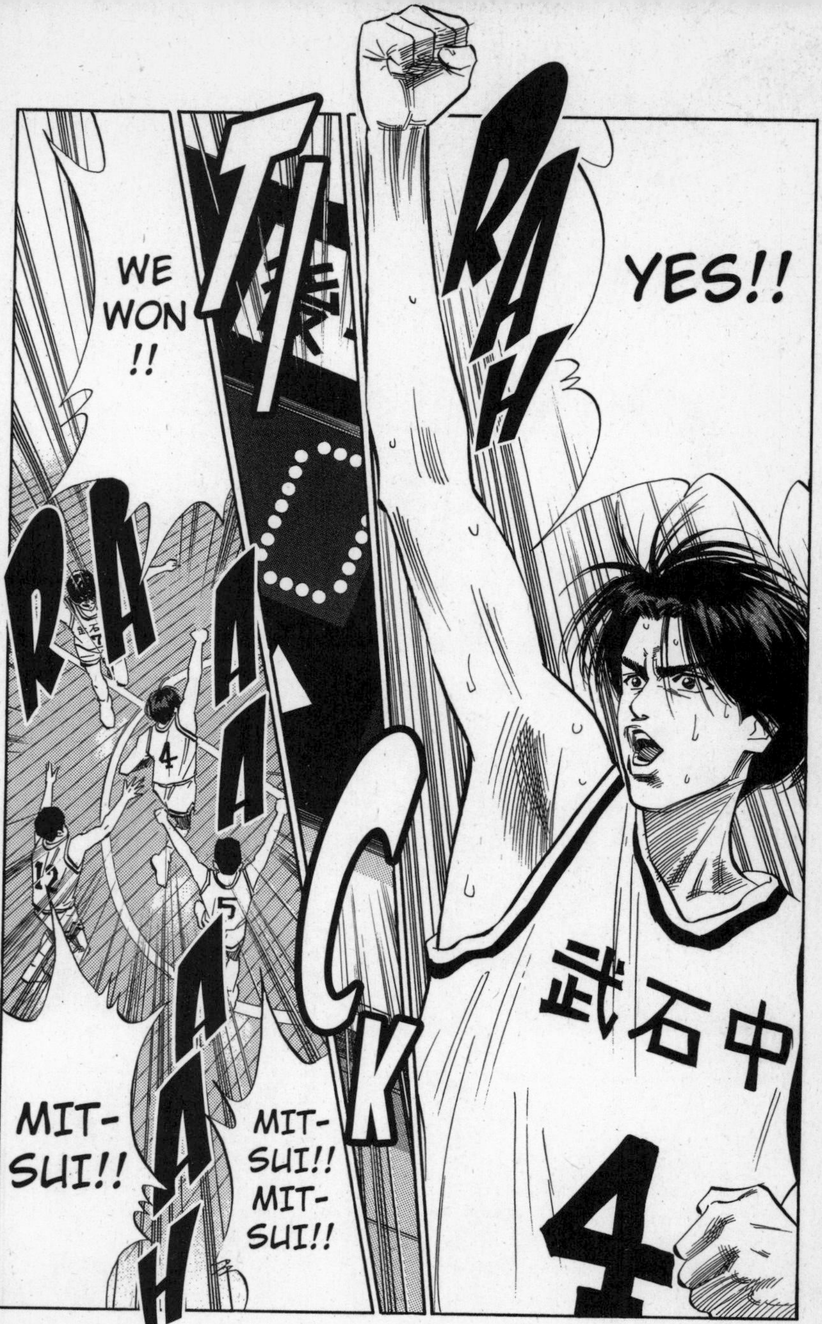
YES!!
WE WON!!
MIT-SUI!!
MIT-SUI!! MIT-SUI!!
武石中
4

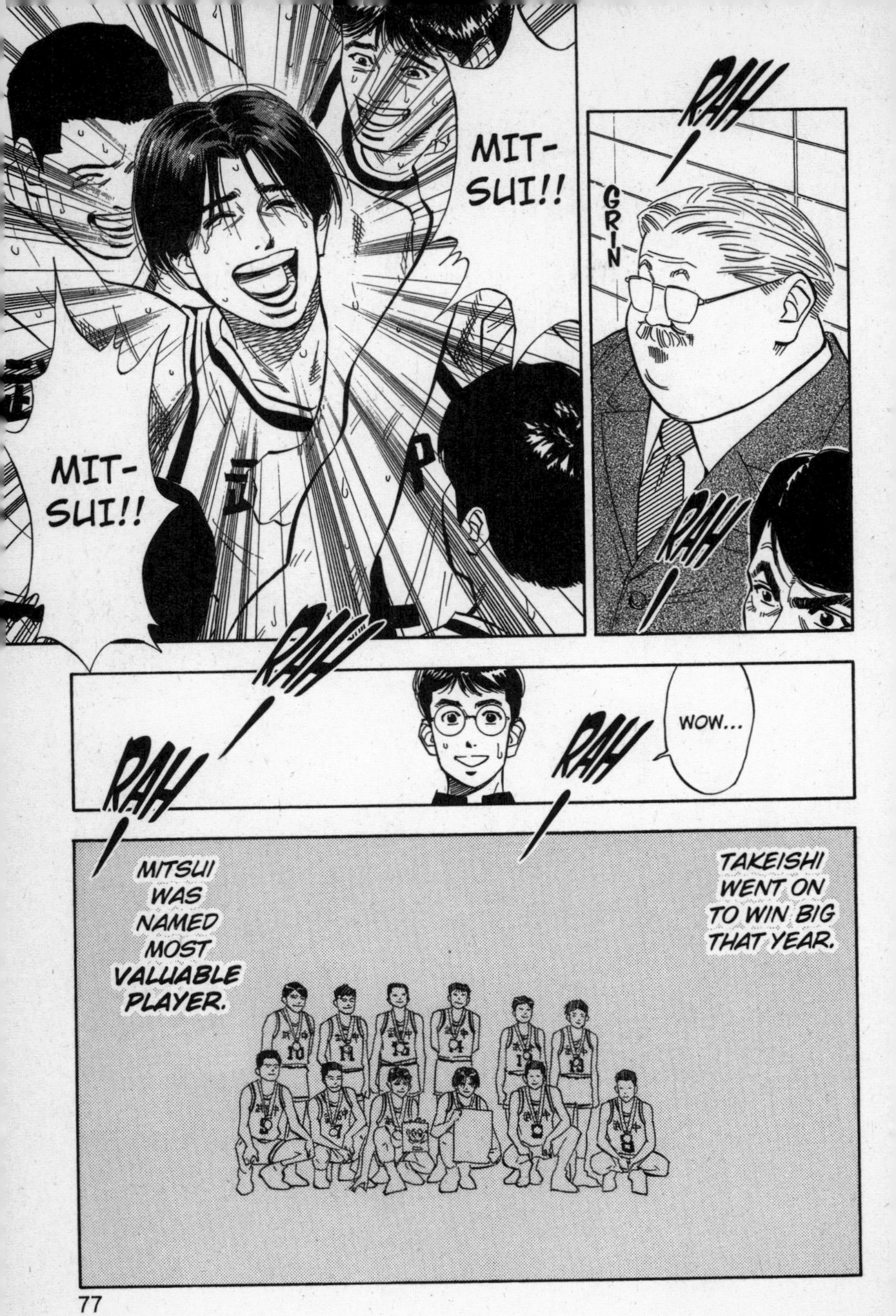
RAH
GRIN
RAH
MIT-SUI!!
MIT-SUI!!
RAH
RAH
WOW...
RAH
TAKEISHI WENT ON TO WIN BIG THAT YEAR.
MITSUI WAS NAMED MOST VALUABLE PLAYER.

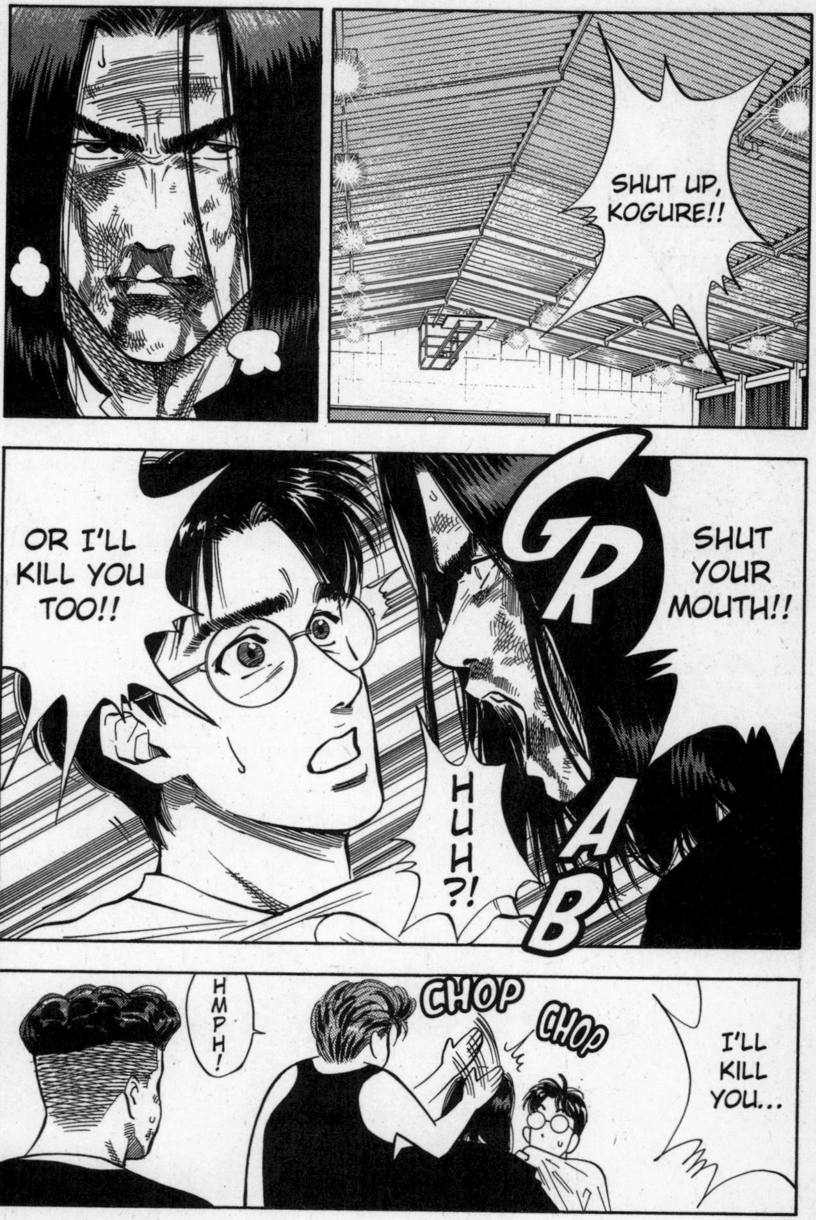
SHUT UP, KOGURE!!
SHUT YOUR MOUTH!!
GRAB
OR I'LL KILL YOU TOO!!
HUH?!
I'LL KILL YOU...
CHOP
CHOP
HMPH!

READ THIS WAY

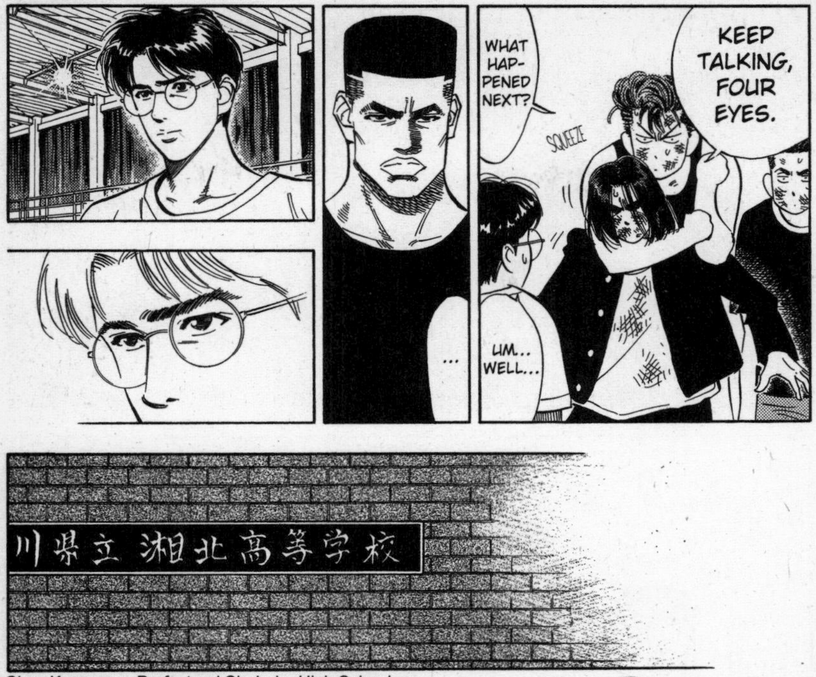
KEEP TALKING, FOUR EYES.
WHAT HAP-PENED NEXT?
SQUEEZE
UM.. WELL...
...
川県立 湘北高等学校

Sign: Kanagawa Prefectural Shohoku High School

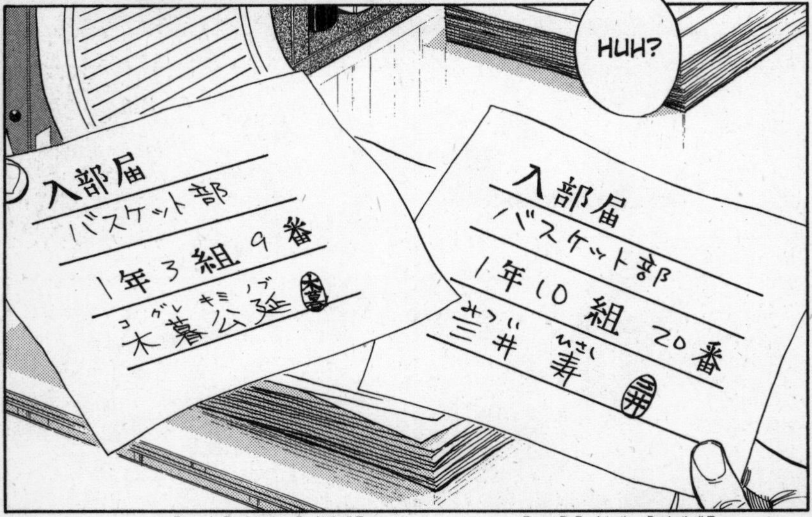
HUH?
入部届
バスケット部
1年10組 20番
みつい ひさし
三井 寿
入部届
バスケット部
1年3組 9番
コグレ キミノブ
木暮公延

Paper L: Registration, Basketball Team
Year 1 Class 3 Number 9, Kiminobu Kogure (Seal) Kogure

Paper R: Registration, Basketball Team
Year 1 Class 10 Number 20, Hisashi Mitsui (Seal) Mitsui

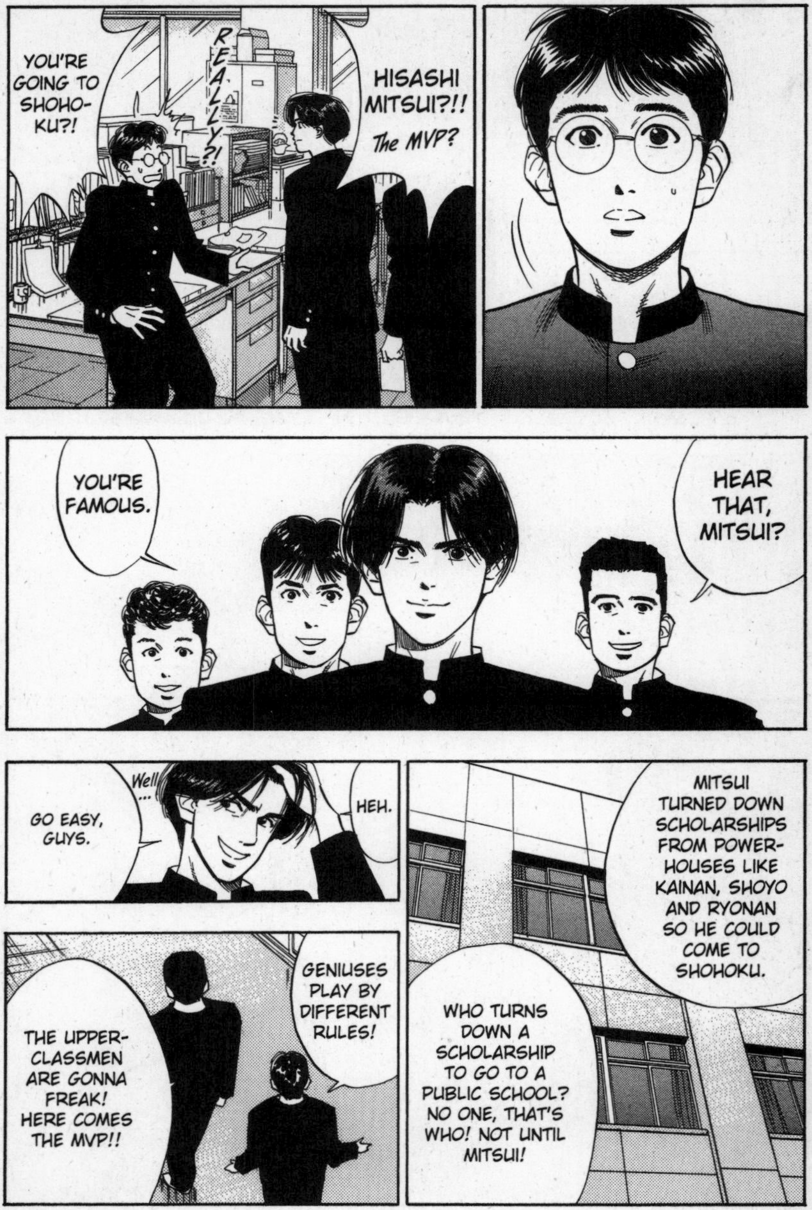
HISASHI MITSUI?!! The MVP?
REALLY?!
YOU'RE GOING TO SHOHOKU?!
HEAR THAT, MITSUI?
YOU'RE FAMOUS.
MITSUI TURNED DOWN SCHOLARSHIPS FROM POWERHOUSES LIKE KAINAN, SHOYO AND RYONAN SO HE COULD COME TO SHOHOKU.
WHO TURNS DOWN A SCHOLARSHIP TO GO TO A PUBLIC SCHOOL? NO ONE, THAT'S WHO! NOT UNTIL MITSUI!
HEH.
Well...
GO EASY, GUYS.
GENIUSES PLAY BY DIFFERENT RULES!
THE UPPERCLASSMEN ARE GONNA FREAK! HERE COMES THE MVP!!

READ THIS WAY

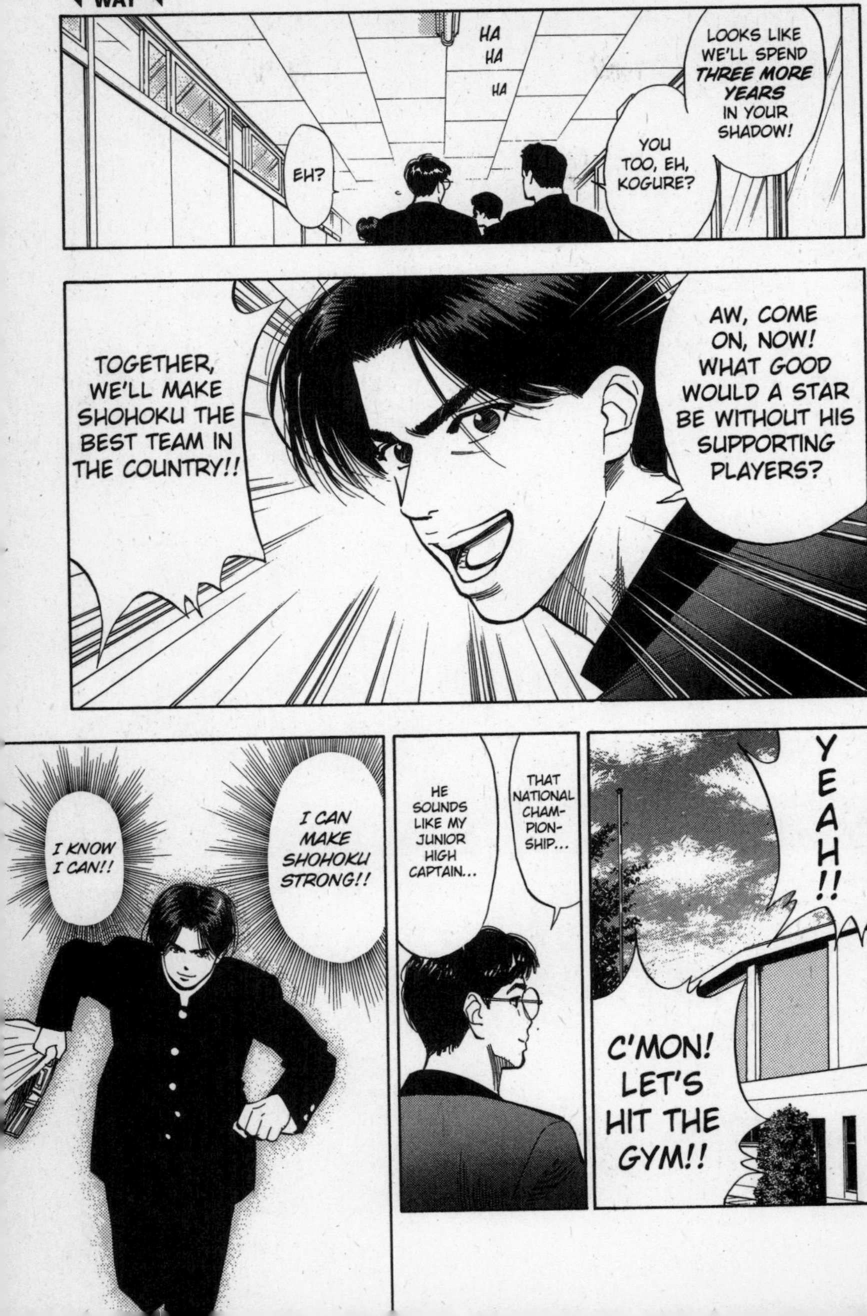
LOOKS LIKE WE'LL SPEND THREE MORE YEARS IN YOUR SHADOW!
YOU TOO, EH, KOGURE?
HA HA HA
EH?
AW, COME ON, NOW! WHAT GOOD WOULD A STAR BE WITHOUT HIS SUPPORTING PLAYERS?
TOGETHER, WE'LL MAKE SHOHOKU THE BEST TEAM IN THE COUNTRY!!
YEAH!!
C'MON! LET'S HIT THE GYM!!
THAT NATIONAL CHAMP-PION-SHIP...
HE SOUNDS LIKE MY JUNIOR HIGH CAPTAIN...
I CAN MAKE SHOHOKU STRONG!!
I KNOW I CAN!!

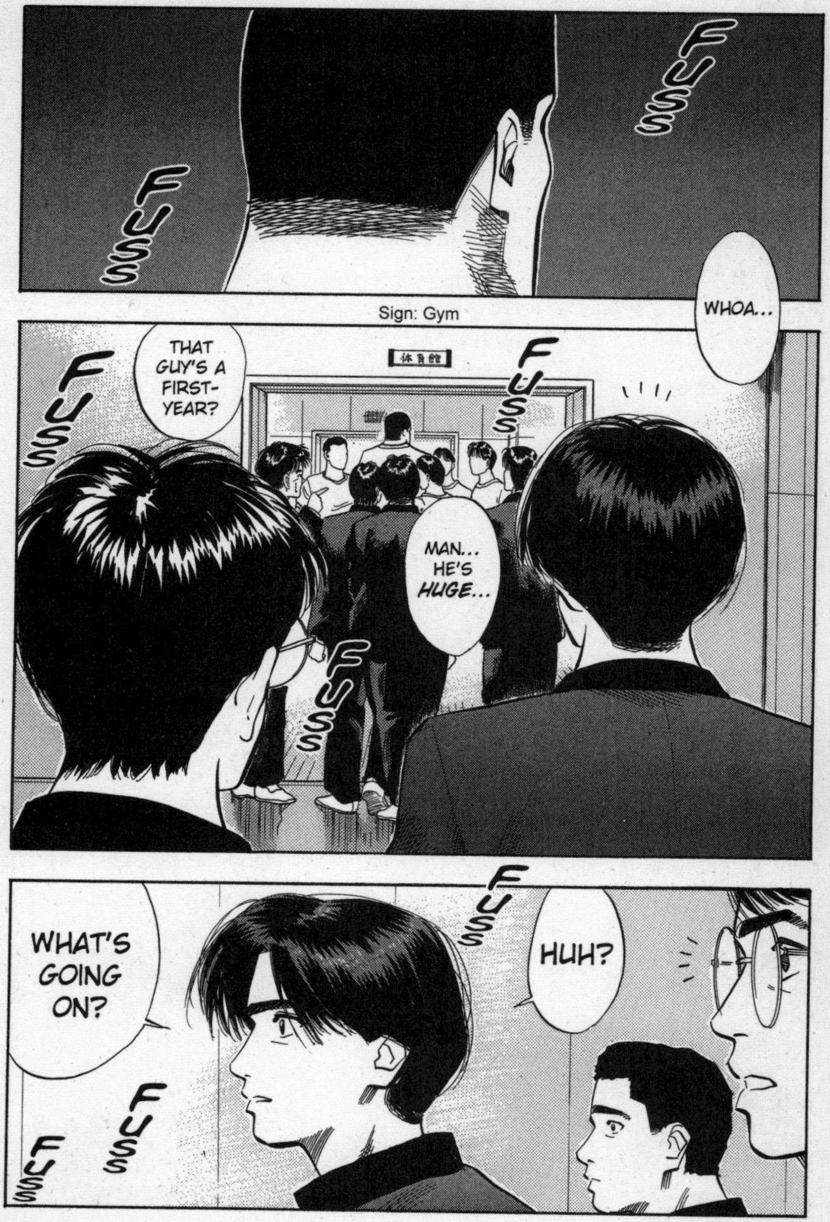
FUSS
FUSS
Sign: Gym
WHOA...
FUSS
THAT GUY'S A FIRST-YEAR?
FUSS
MAN... HE'S HUGE...
FUSS
FUSS
HUH?
WHAT'S GOING ON?
FUSS
FUSS

DUDE. CAN YOU DUNK?

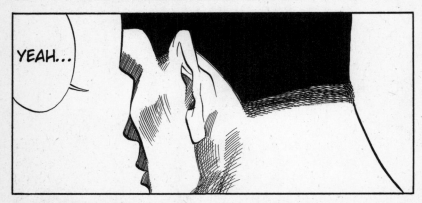

YEAH...

MURMUR

MURMUR

MURMUR

MURMUR

MURMUR

POP

...

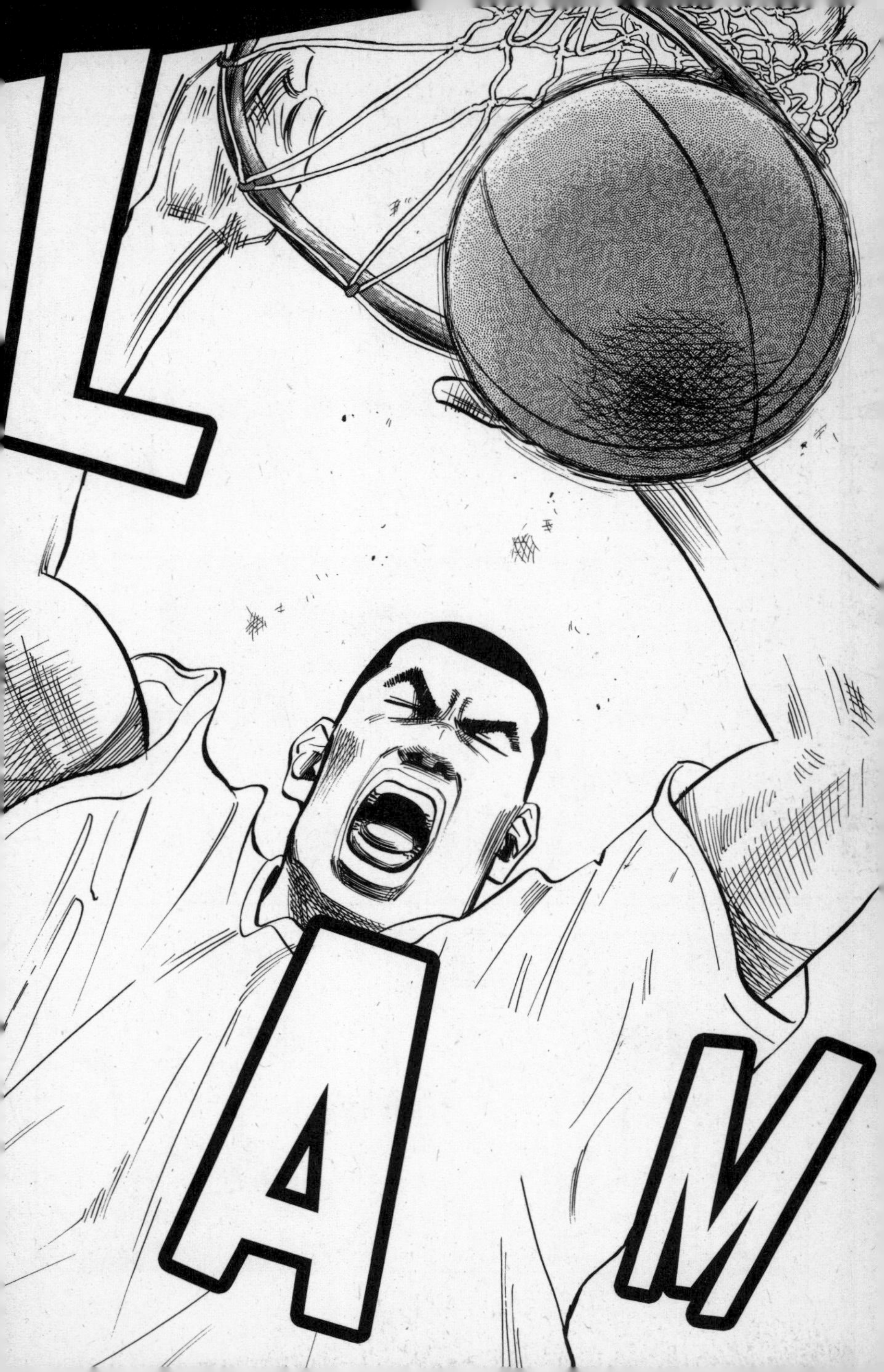
LAM

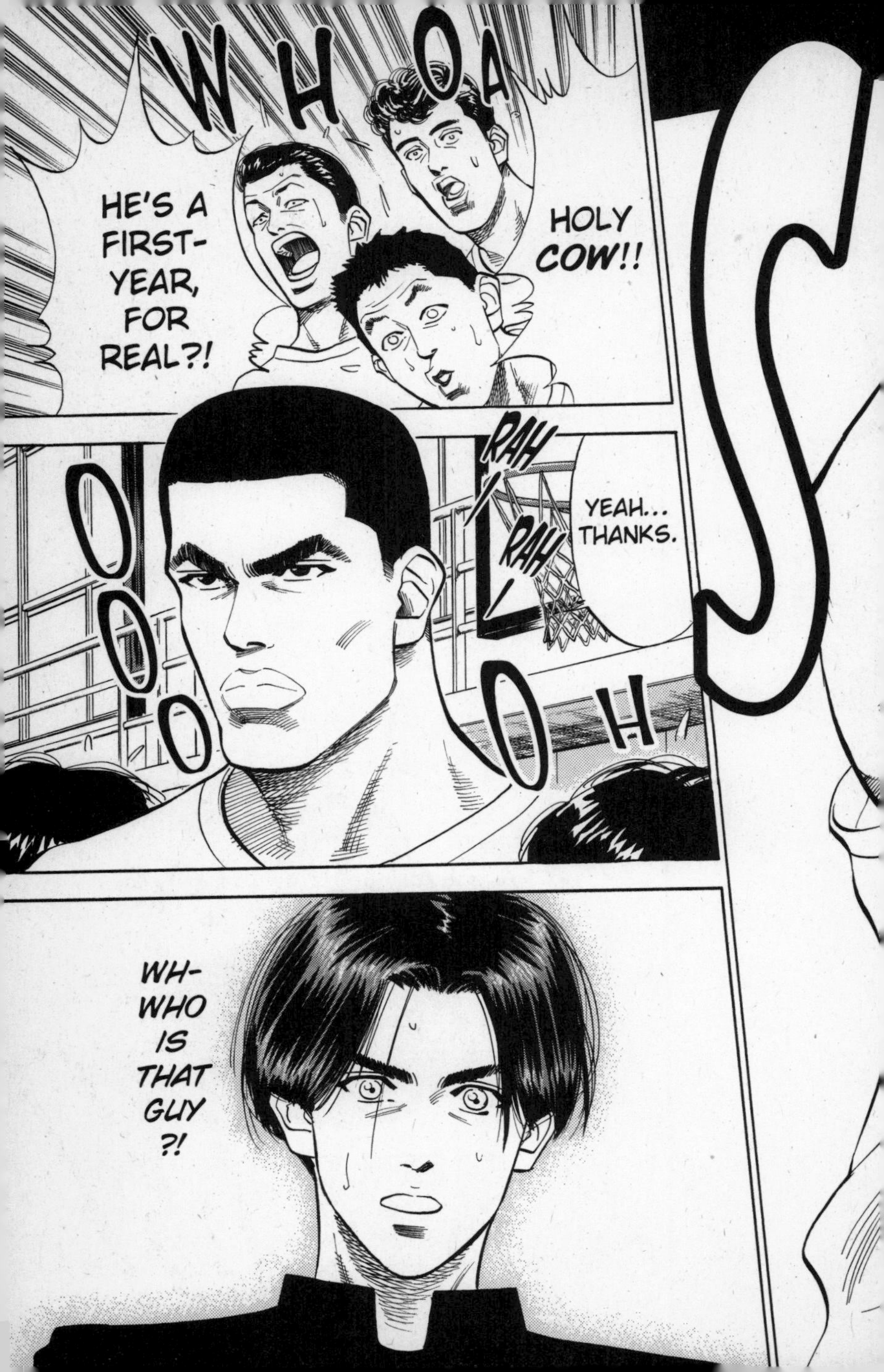
WHOA
HOLY COW!!
HE'S A FIRST-YEAR, FOR REAL?!
YEAH... THANKS.
RAH RAH
OOOOOOH
WH-WHO IS THAT GUY?!

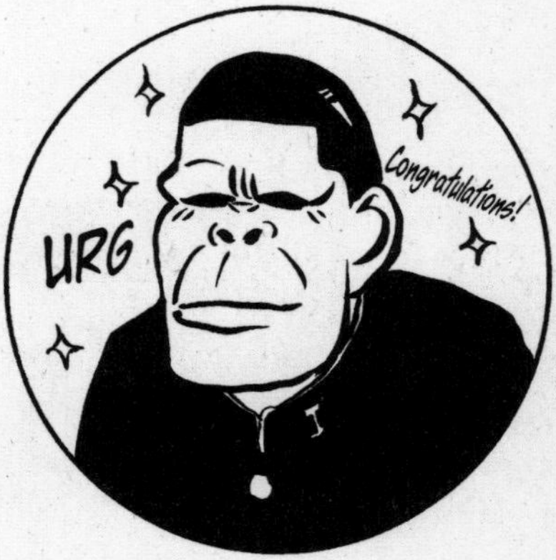
URG
Congratulations!

SLAM DUNK

#67 A NATIONAL TITLE

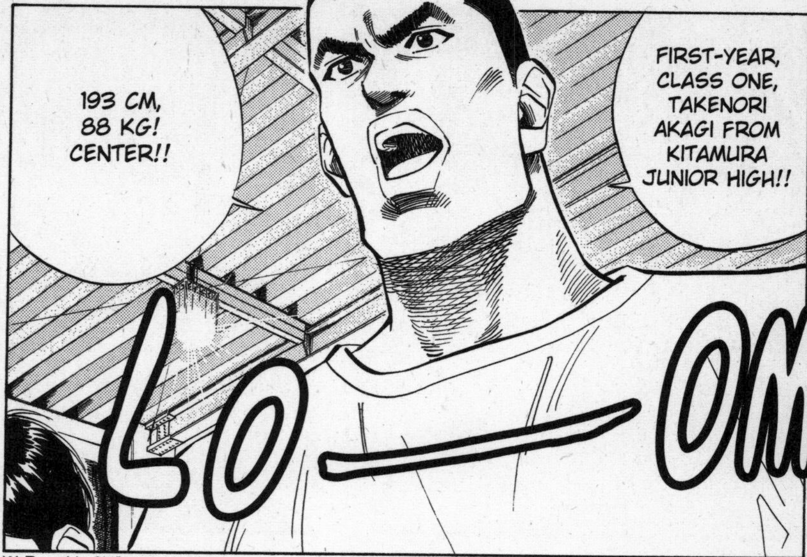
FIRST-YEAR, CLASS ONE, TAKENORI AKAGI FROM KITAMURA JUNIOR HIGH!!
193 CM, 88 KG! CENTER!!
LO—OM

※ Roughly 6'4" and 194 lbs.

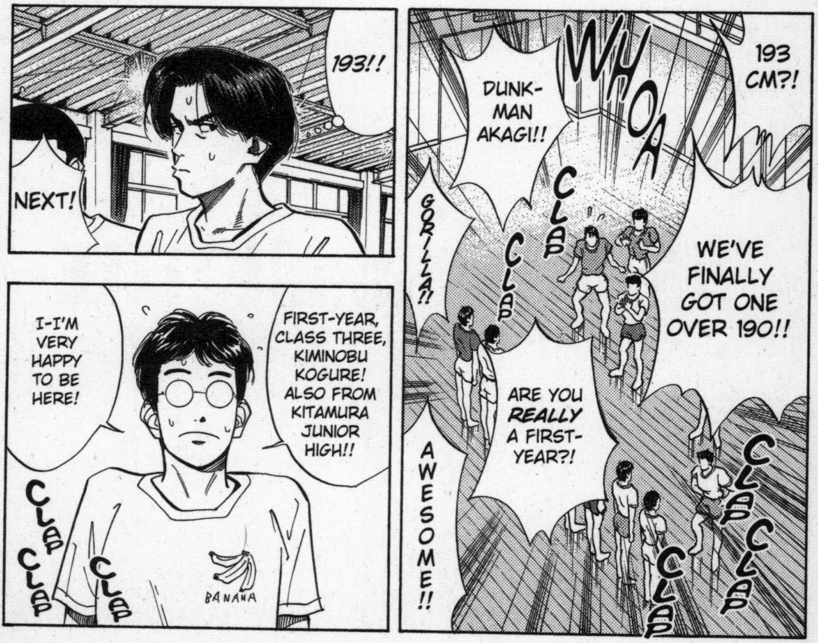
193 CM?!
WHOA
DUNK-MAN AKAGI!!
CLAP
CLAP
GORILLA!!
WE'VE FINALLY GOT ONE OVER 190!!
ARE YOU *REALLY* A FIRST-YEAR?!
CLAP
CLAP
CLAP
CLAP
AWESOME!!
193!!
NEXT!
FIRST-YEAR, CLASS THREE, KIMINOBU KOGURE! ALSO FROM KITAMURA JUNIOR HIGH!!
I-I'M VERY HAPPY TO BE HERE!
CLAP
CLAP
CLAP
CLAP
BANANA

READ THIS WAY

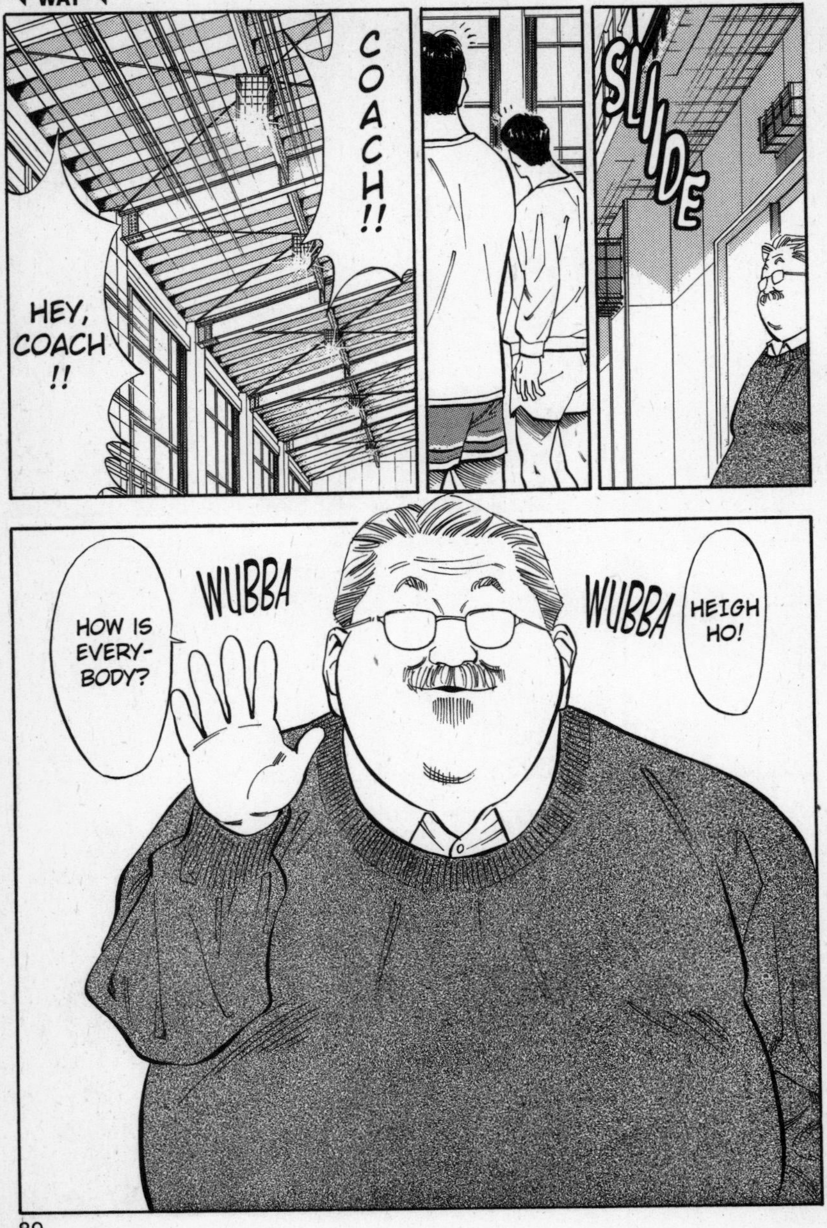
SLIDE
COACH!!
HEY, COACH!!
HEIGH HO!
WUBBA
WUBBA
HOW IS EVERY-BODY?

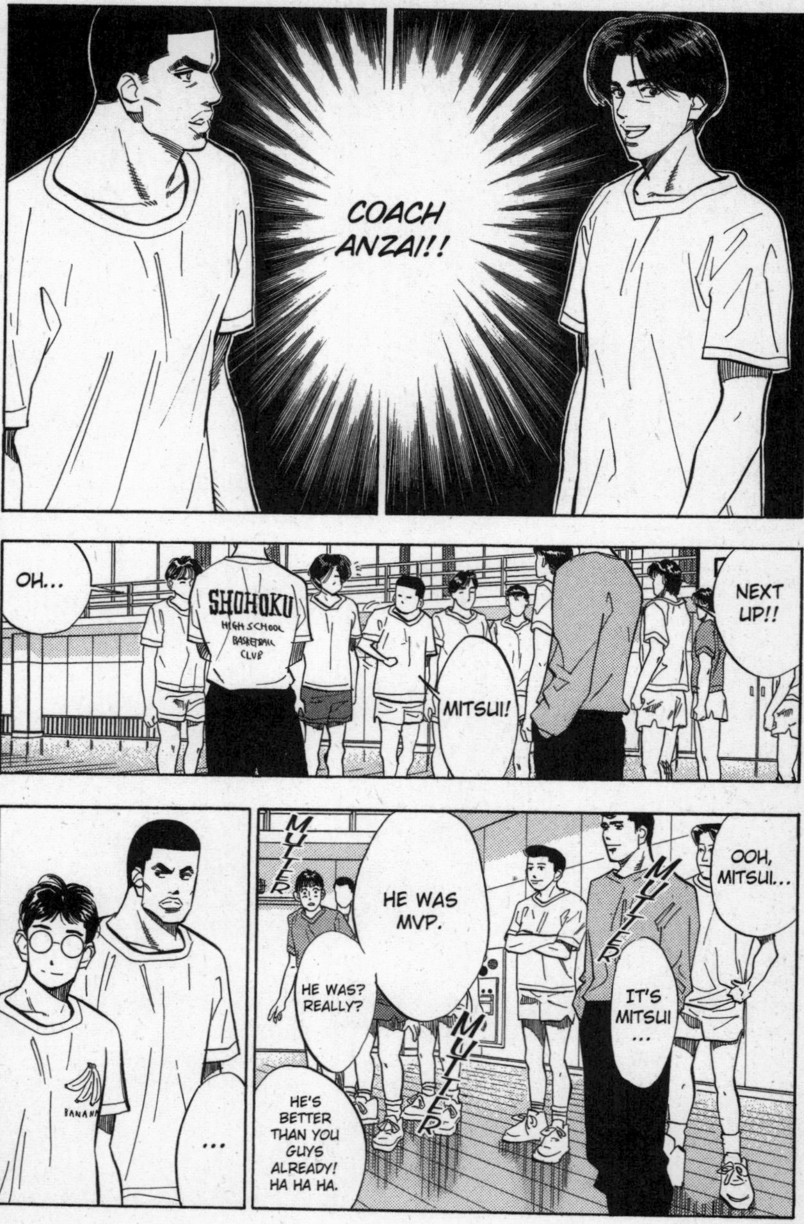
COACH ANZAI!!
NEXT UP!!
MITSUI!
OH...
OOH, MITSUI...
MUTTER
IT'S MITSUI ...
HE WAS MVP.
MUTTER
MUTTER
HE WAS? REALLY?
HE'S BETTER THAN YOU GUYS ALREADY! HA HA HA.
SHOHOKU HIGH SCHOOL BASKETBALL CLUB
...

READ THIS WAY

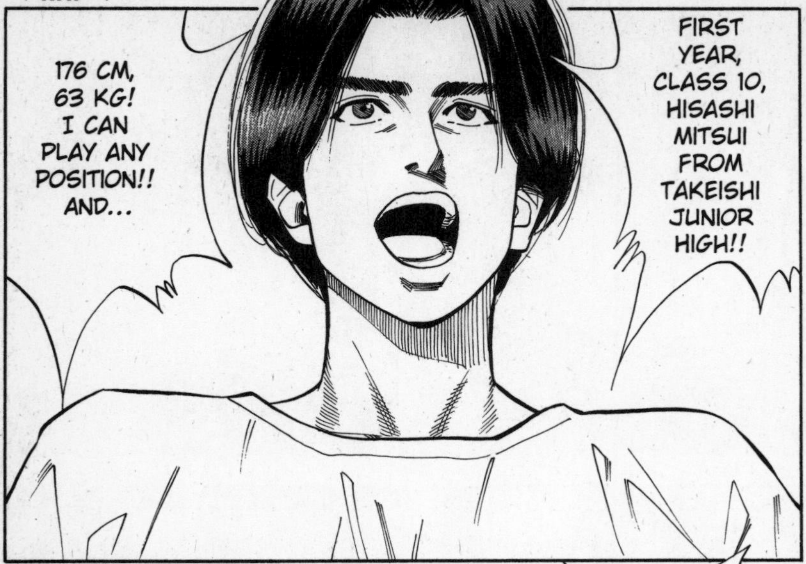
FIRST YEAR, CLASS 10, HISASHI MITSUI FROM TAKEISHI JUNIOR HIGH!!
176 CM, 63 KG! I CAN PLAY ANY POSITION!! AND...

※ Roughly 5'9" and 139 lbs.

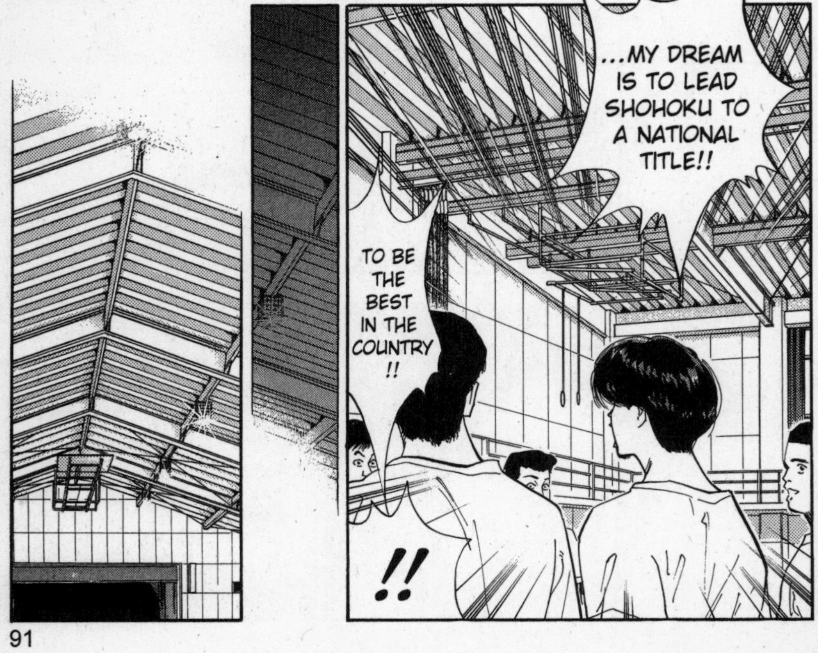
...MY DREAM IS TO LEAD SHOHOKU TO A NATIONAL TITLE!!
TO BE THE BEST IN THE COUNTRY!!
!!

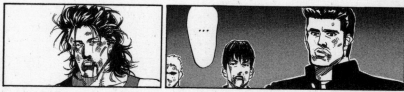

NATIONALS...

NATIONAL CHAMPIONS...

READ THIS WAY

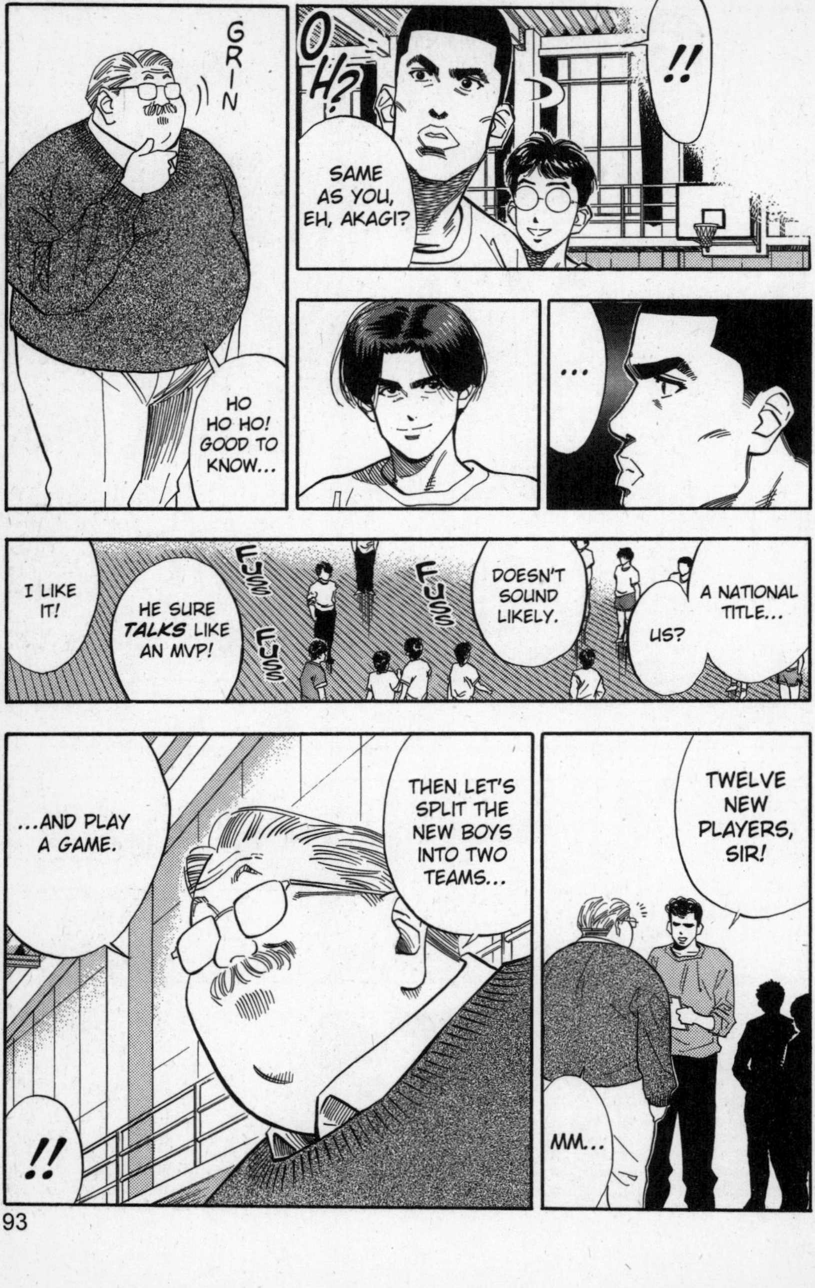
!!
OH?
SAME AS YOU, EH, AKAGI?
...
GRIN
HO HO HO! GOOD TO KNOW...
A NATIONAL TITLE...
US?
FUSS
DOESN'T SOUND LIKELY.
FUSS
FUSS
HE SURE *TALKS* LIKE AN MVP!
I LIKE IT!
TWELVE NEW PLAYERS, SIR!
MM...
THEN LET'S SPLIT THE NEW BOYS INTO TWO TEAMS...
...AND PLAY A GAME.
!!

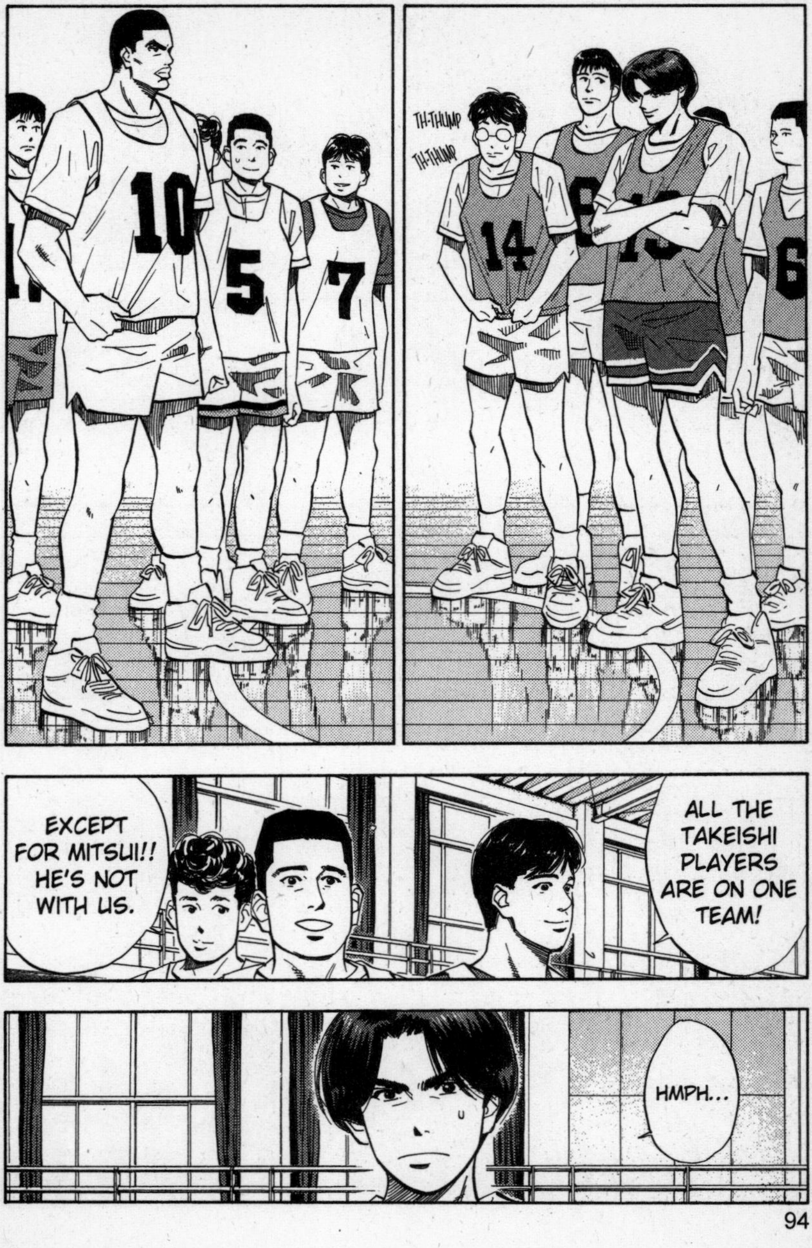
TH-THUMP
TH-THUMP
ALL THE TAKEISHI PLAYERS ARE ON ONE TEAM!
EXCEPT FOR MITSUI!! HE'S NOT WITH US.
HMPH...

READ THIS WAY

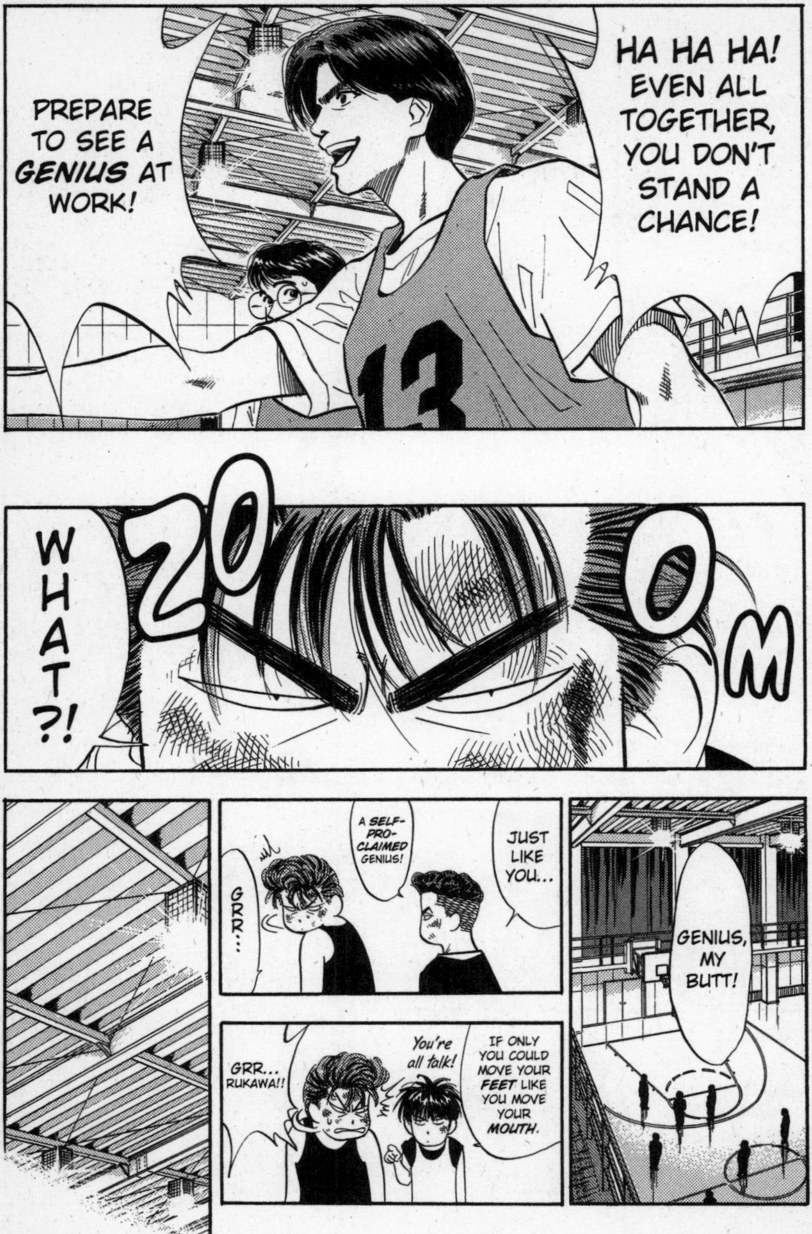
HA HA HA! EVEN ALL TOGETHER, YOU DON'T STAND A CHANCE!
PREPARE TO SEE A *GENIUS* AT WORK!
ZOOOM
WHAT?!
GENIUS, MY BUTT!
JUST LIKE YOU...
A *SELF-PROCLAIMED* GENIUS!
GRR...
IF ONLY YOU COULD MOVE YOUR *FEET* LIKE YOU MOVE YOUR *MOUTH*.
You're all talk!
GRR... RUKAWA!!

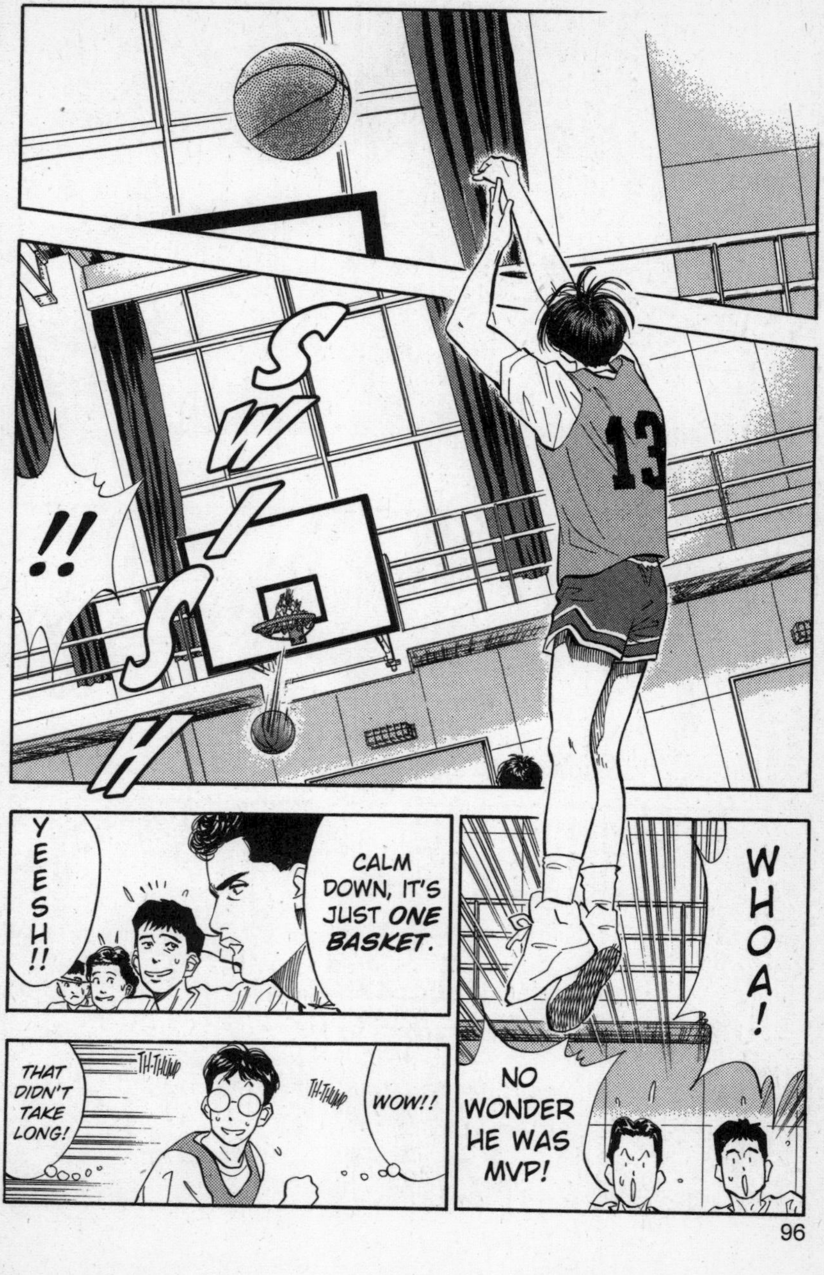
SWISH
!!
WHOA!
NO WONDER HE WAS MVP!
CALM DOWN, IT'S JUST ONE BASKET.
YEESH!!
WOW!!
TH-THUMP
TH-THUMP
THAT DIDN'T TAKE LONG!

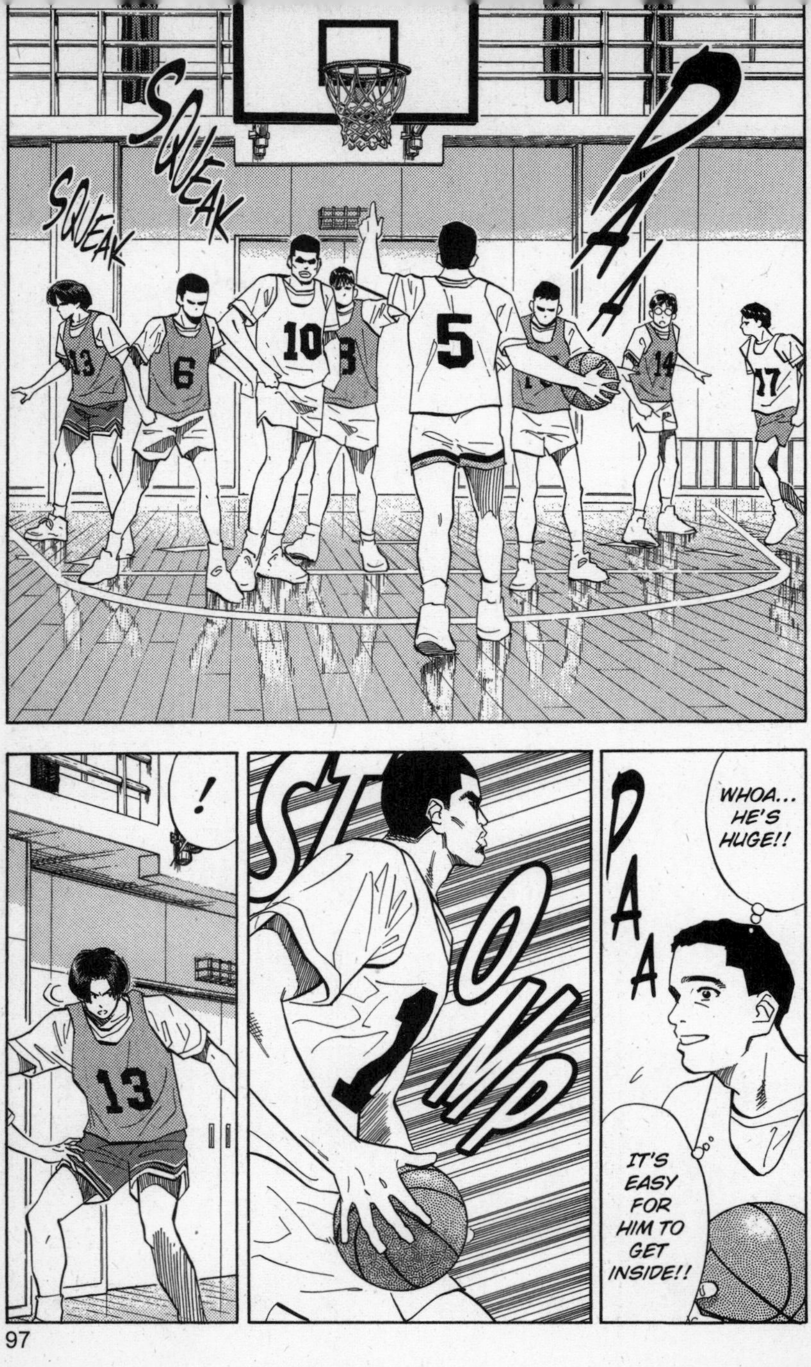
PAAA
SQUEAK
SQUEAK
PAA
WHOA... HE'S HUGE!!
IT'S EASY FOR HIM TO GET INSIDE!!
STOMP
!

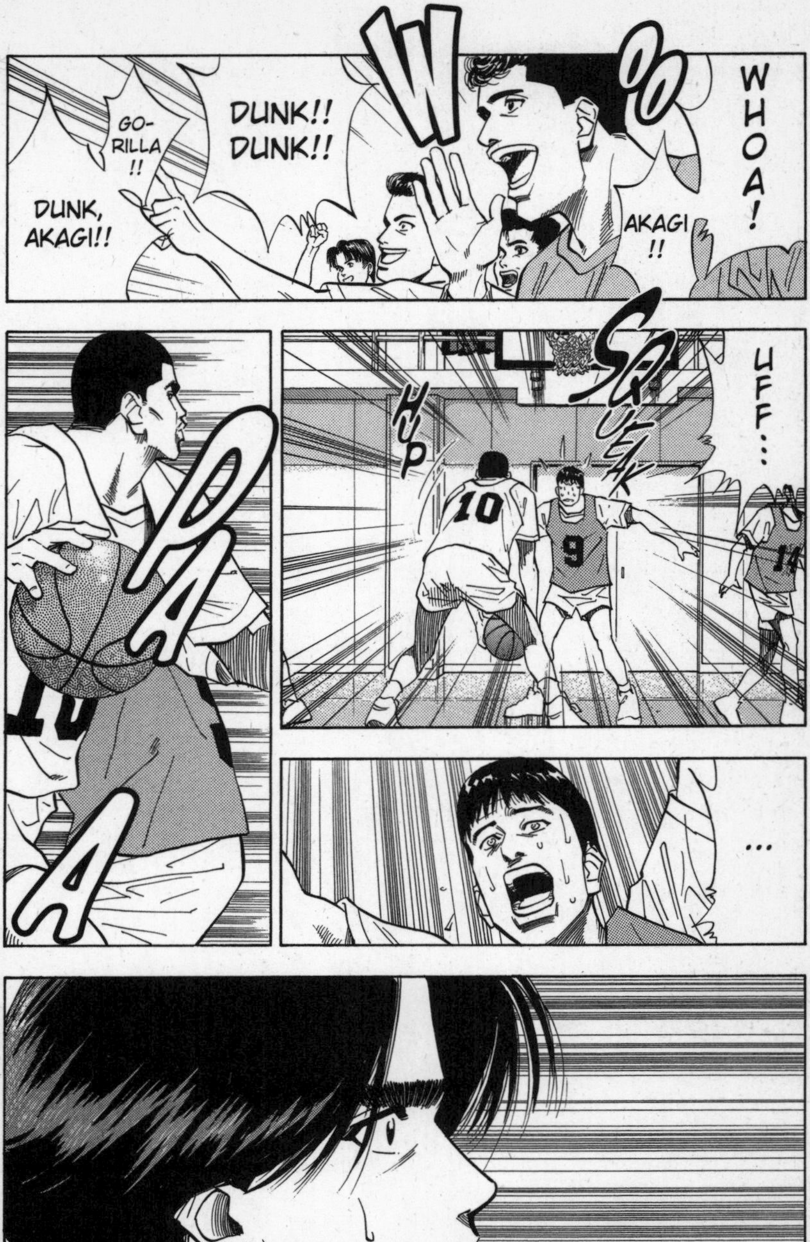
WHOA!
WOO
AKAGI!!
DUNK!! DUNK!!
GO-RILLA!!
DUNK, AKAGI!!
UFF...
SQUEAK
HUP
PA
A
...

READ THIS WAY

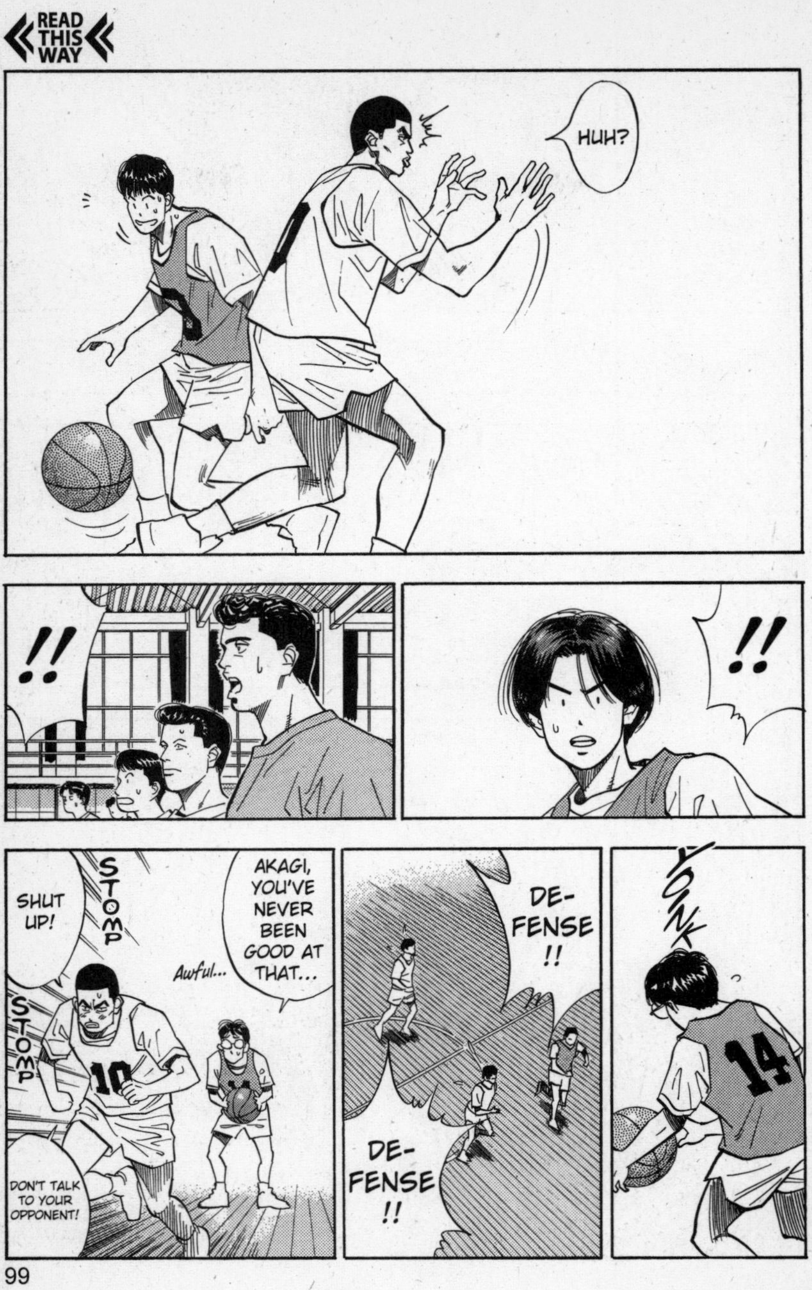
HUH?
!!
!!
YONK
DE-FENSE!!
DE-FENSE!!
AKAGI, YOU'VE NEVER BEEN GOOD AT THAT...
STOMP
SHUT UP!
Awful...
STOMP
DON'T TALK TO YOUR OPPONENT!

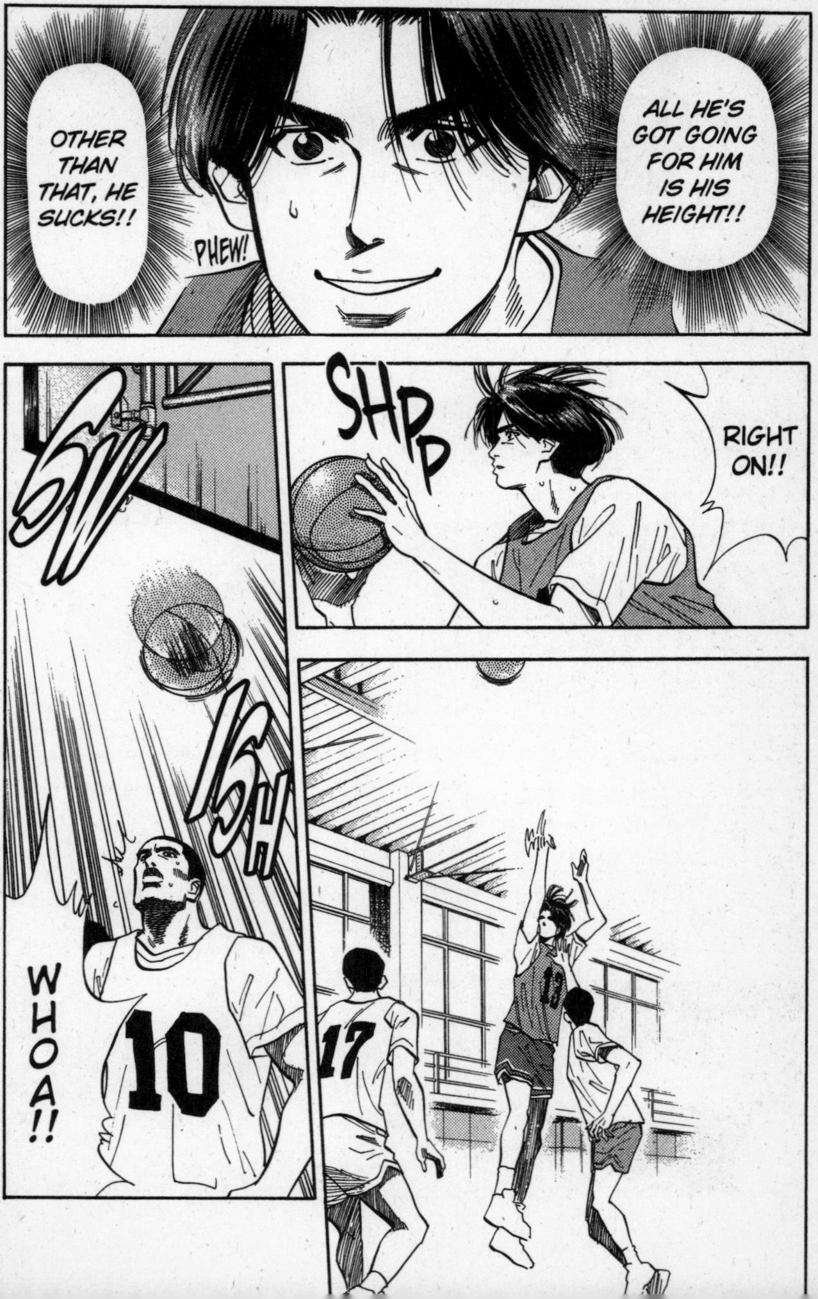
ALL HE'S GOT GOING FOR HIM IS HIS HEIGHT!!
PHEW!
OTHER THAN THAT, HE SUCKS!!
SHPP
RIGHT ON!!
SWISH
WHOA!!

READ THIS WAY

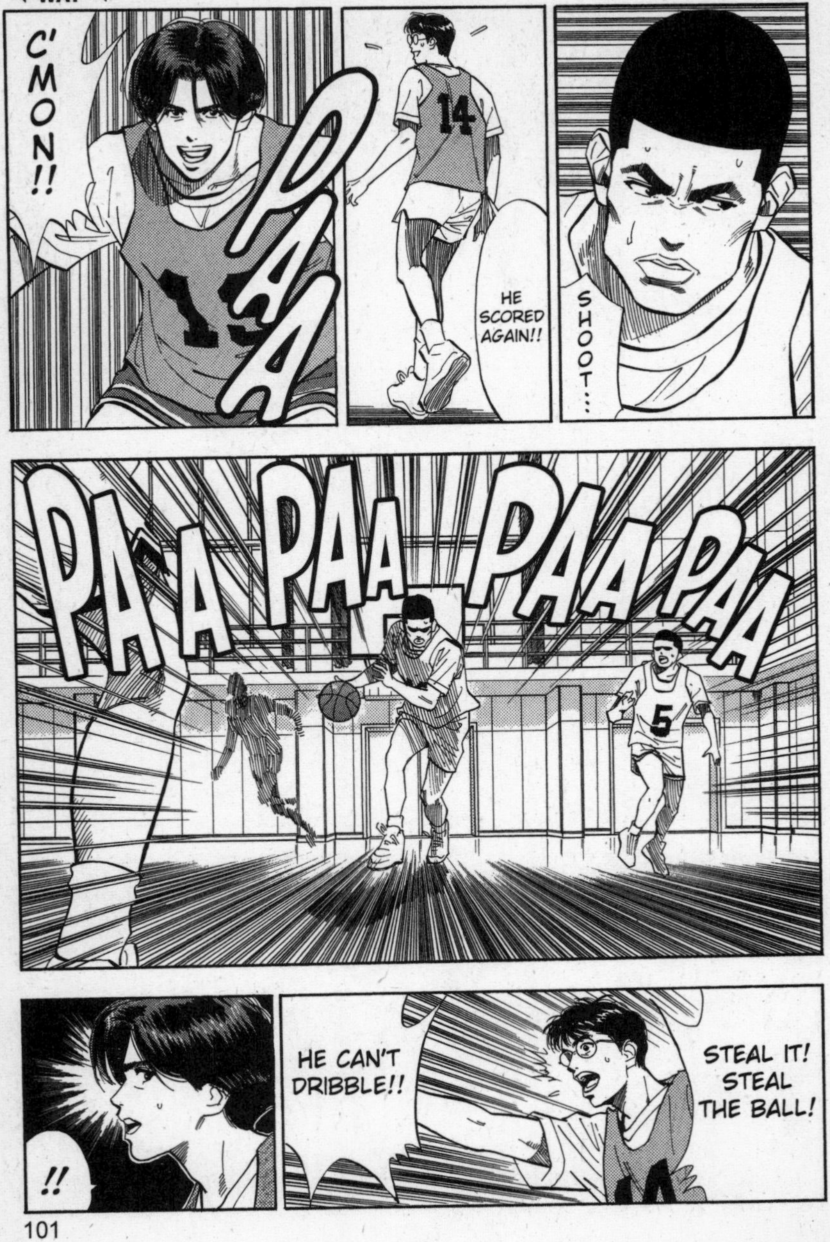
SHOOT...
HE SCORED AGAIN!!
C'MON!!
PAAA
PA A PAA PAA PAA
STEAL IT! STEAL THE BALL!
HE CAN'T DRIBBLE!!
!!

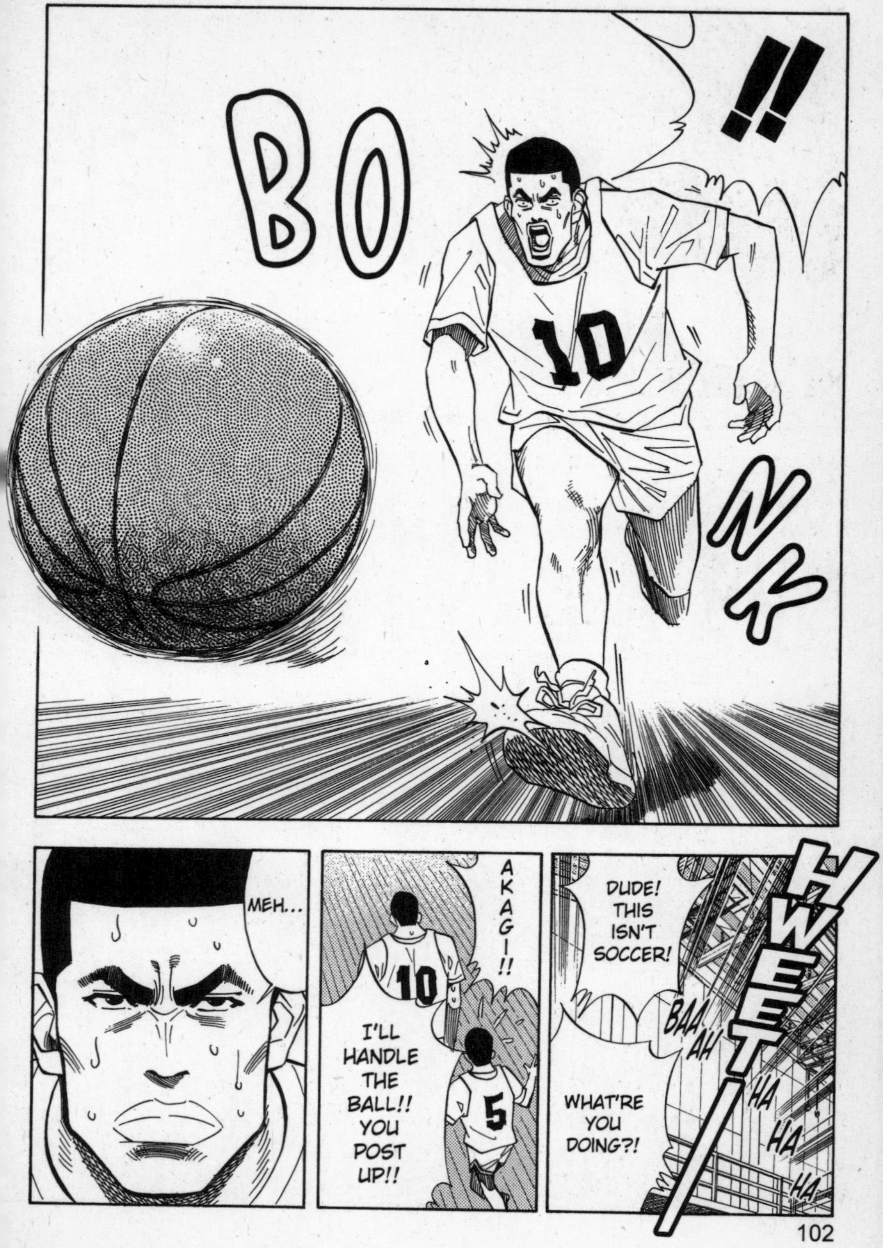
BONK
!!
HWEET!
DUDE! THIS ISN'T SOCCER!
BAAAH
HA HA HA HA
WHAT'RE YOU DOING?!
AKAGI!!
I'LL HANDLE THE BALL!! YOU POST UP!!
MEH...

READ THIS WAY

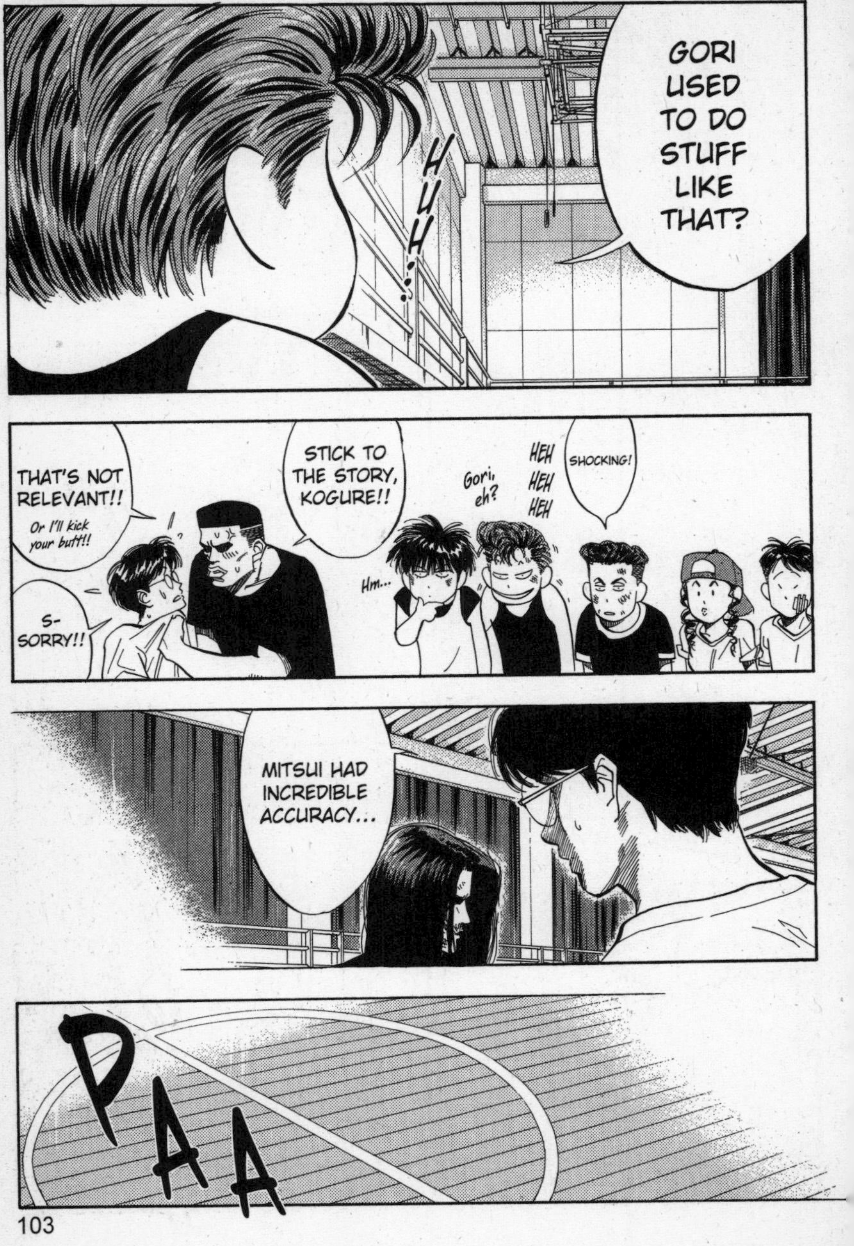
GORI USED TO DO STUFF LIKE THAT?
HUH!?
SHOCKING!
HEH HEH HEH
Gori, eh?
Hm...
STICK TO THE STORY, KOGURE!!
THAT'S NOT RELEVANT!!
Or I'll kick your butt!!
S-SORRY!!
MITSUI HAD INCREDIBLE ACCURACY...
PAA

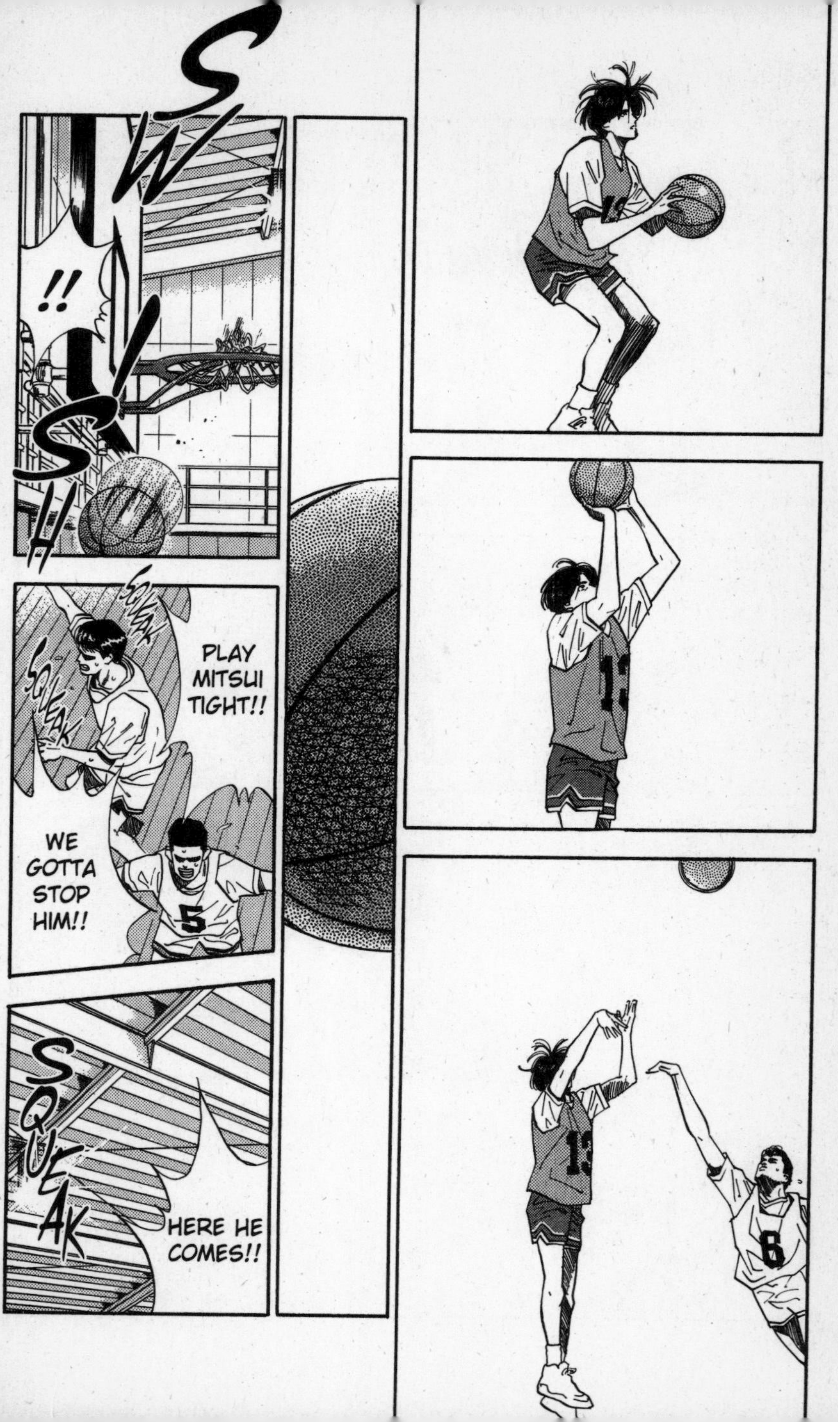
SWISH
!!
SQUEAK
SQUEAK
PLAY MITSUI TIGHT!!
WE GOTTA STOP HIM!!
SQUEAK
HERE HE COMES!!

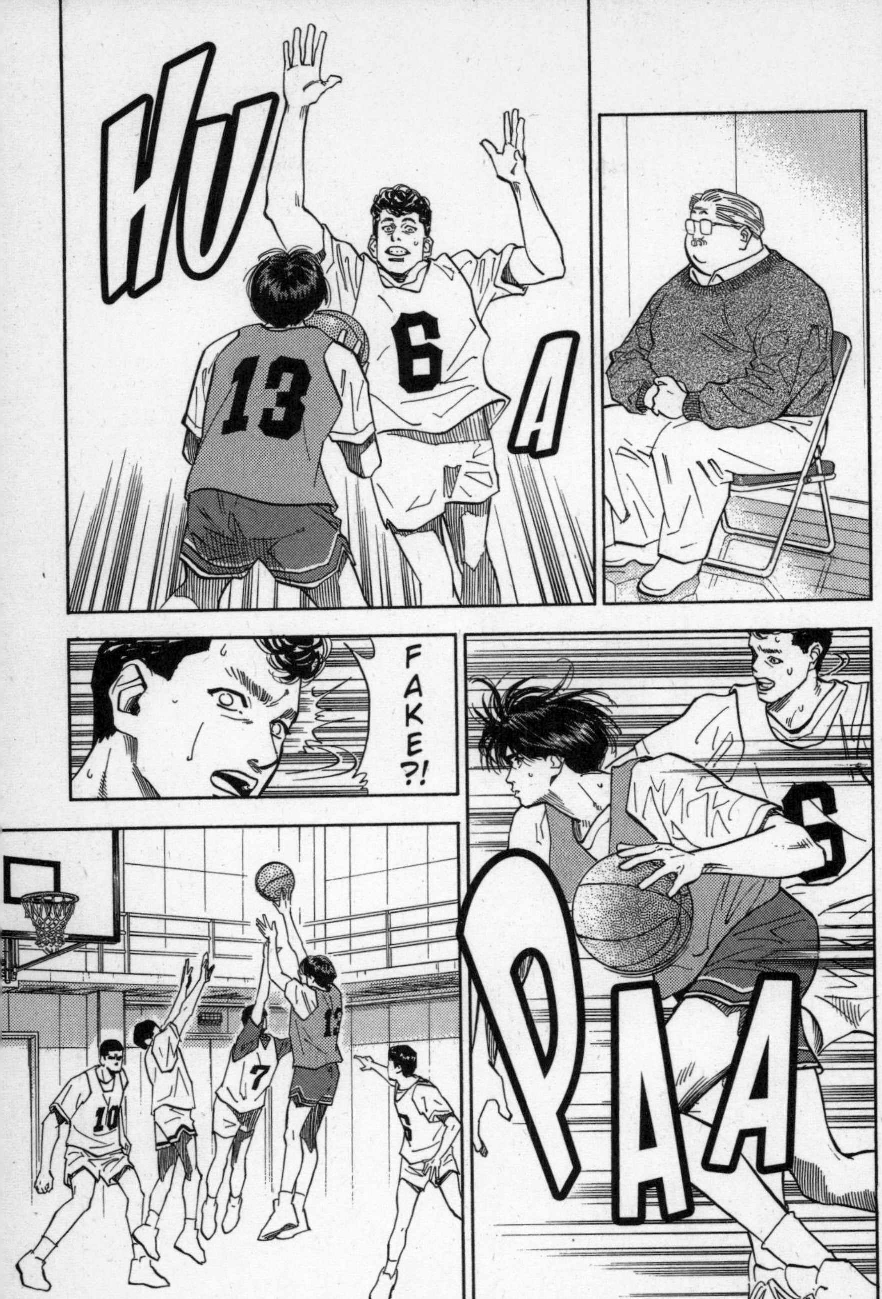
HUA
PAAA
FAKE?!

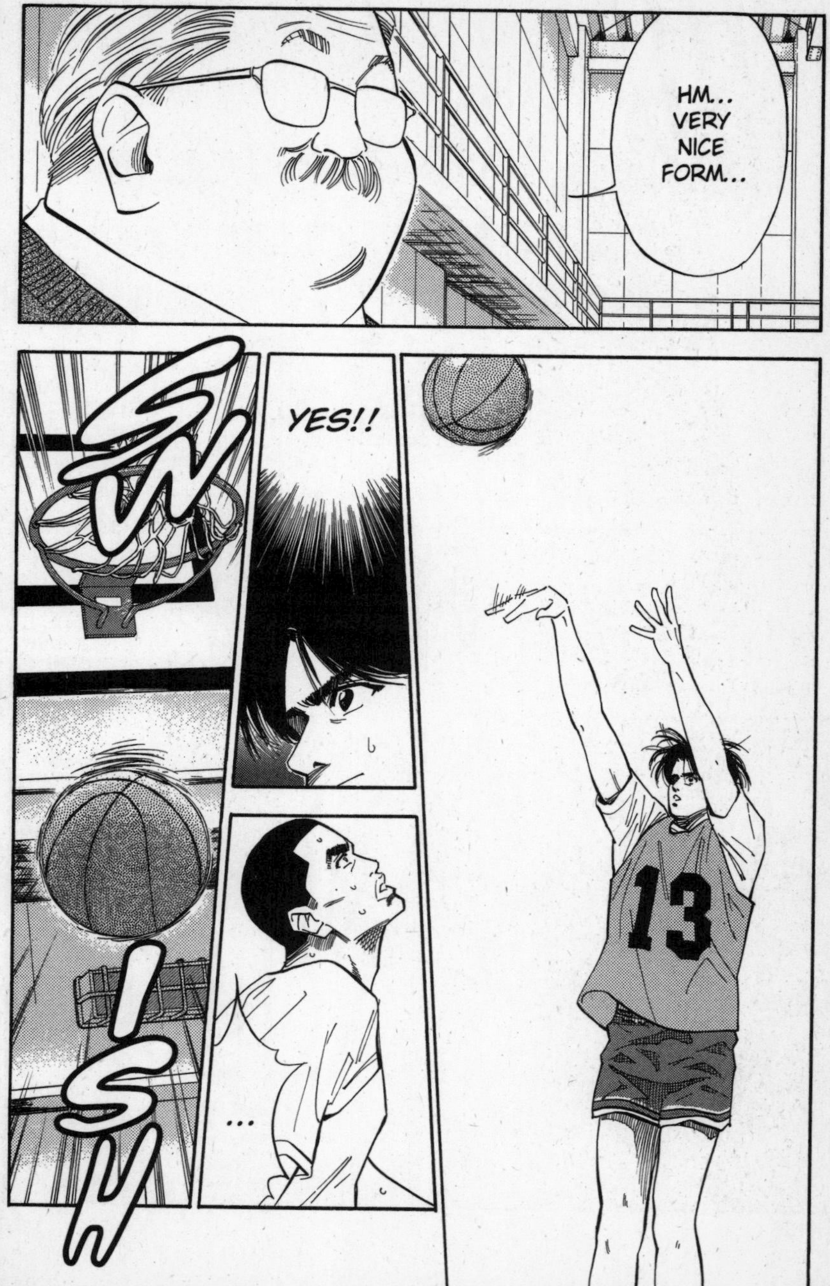
HM... VERY NICE FORM...
YES!!
...
SW
ISH

READ THIS WAY

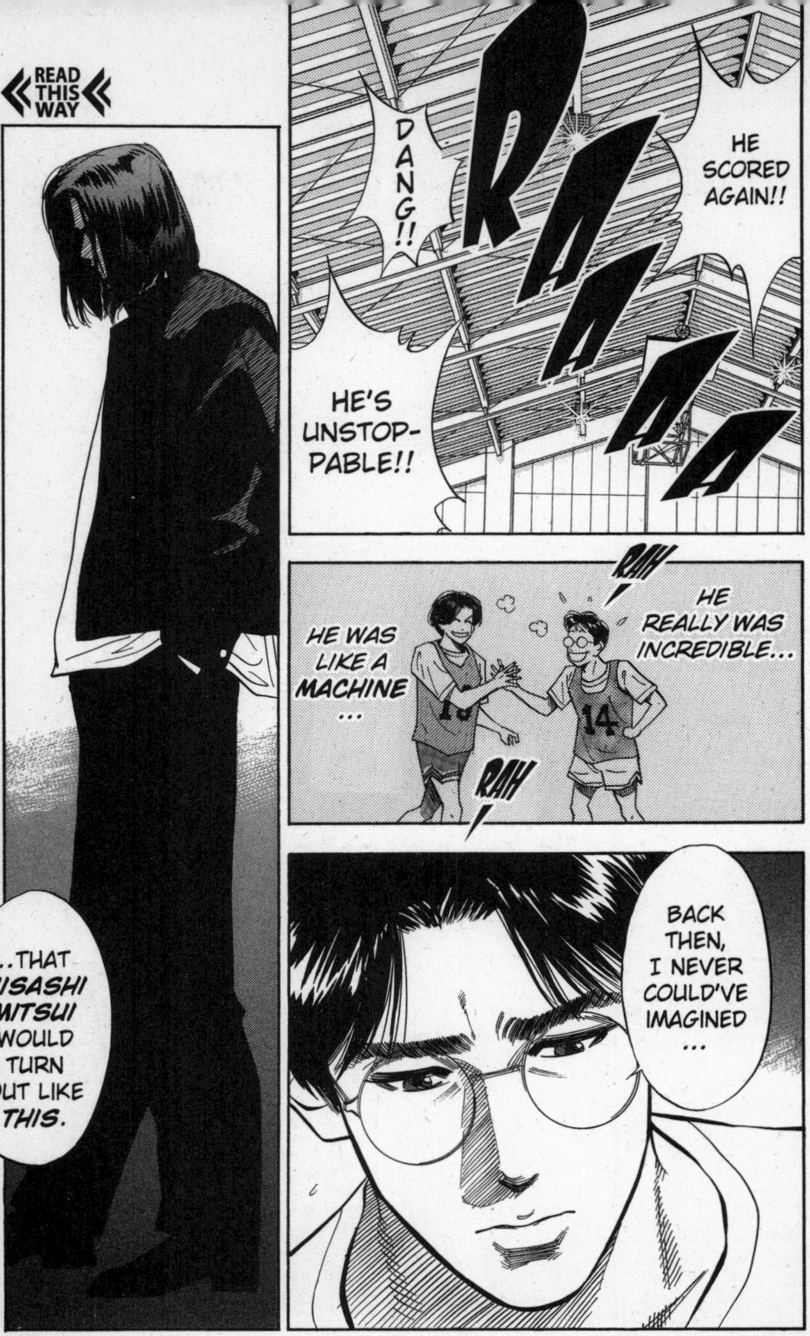
HE SCORED AGAIN!!
DANG!!
HE'S UNSTOPPABLE!!
HE REALLY WAS INCREDIBLE...
RAH
HE WAS LIKE A MACHINE...
RAH
BACK THEN, I NEVER COULD'VE IMAGINED...
...THAT HISASHI MITSUI WOULD TURN OUT LIKE THIS.

Yo...

SLAM DUNK

#68 HISASHI MITSUI AT 15

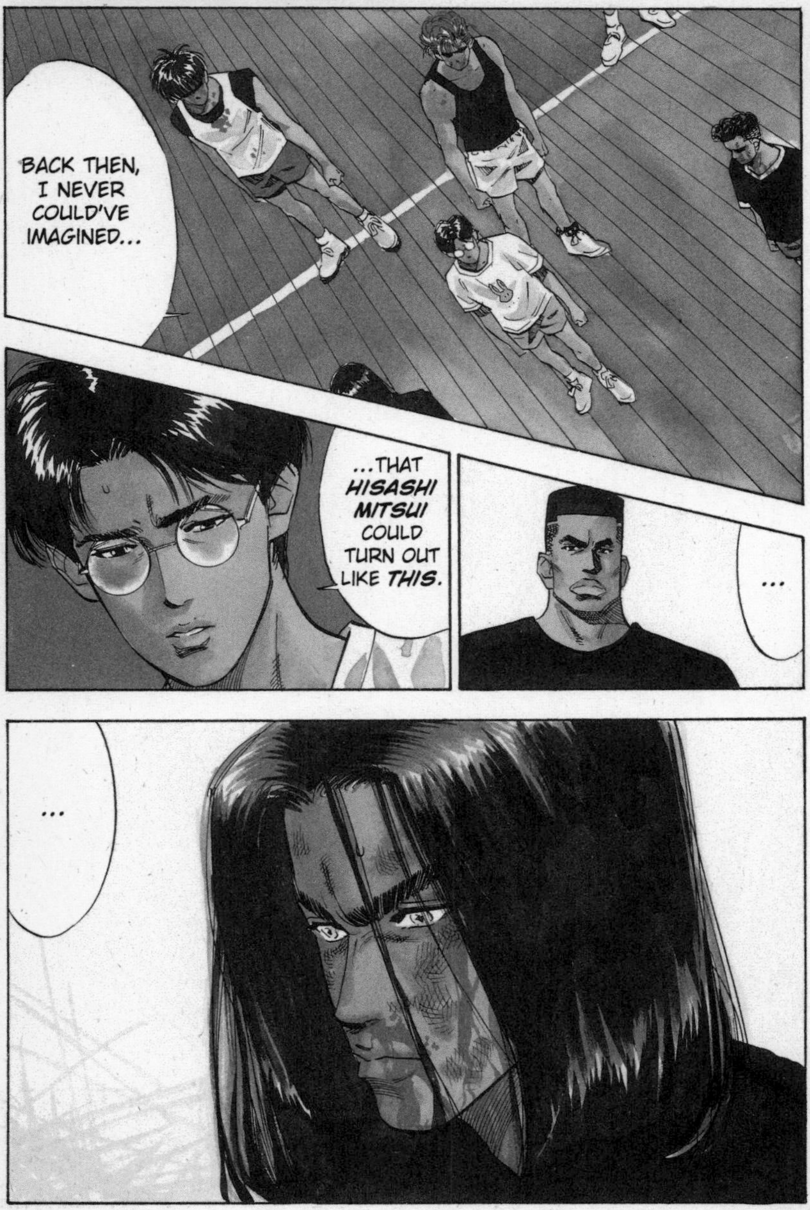
BACK THEN, I NEVER COULD'VE IMAGINED...
...THAT *HISASHI MITSUI* COULD TURN OUT LIKE *THIS*.
...
...

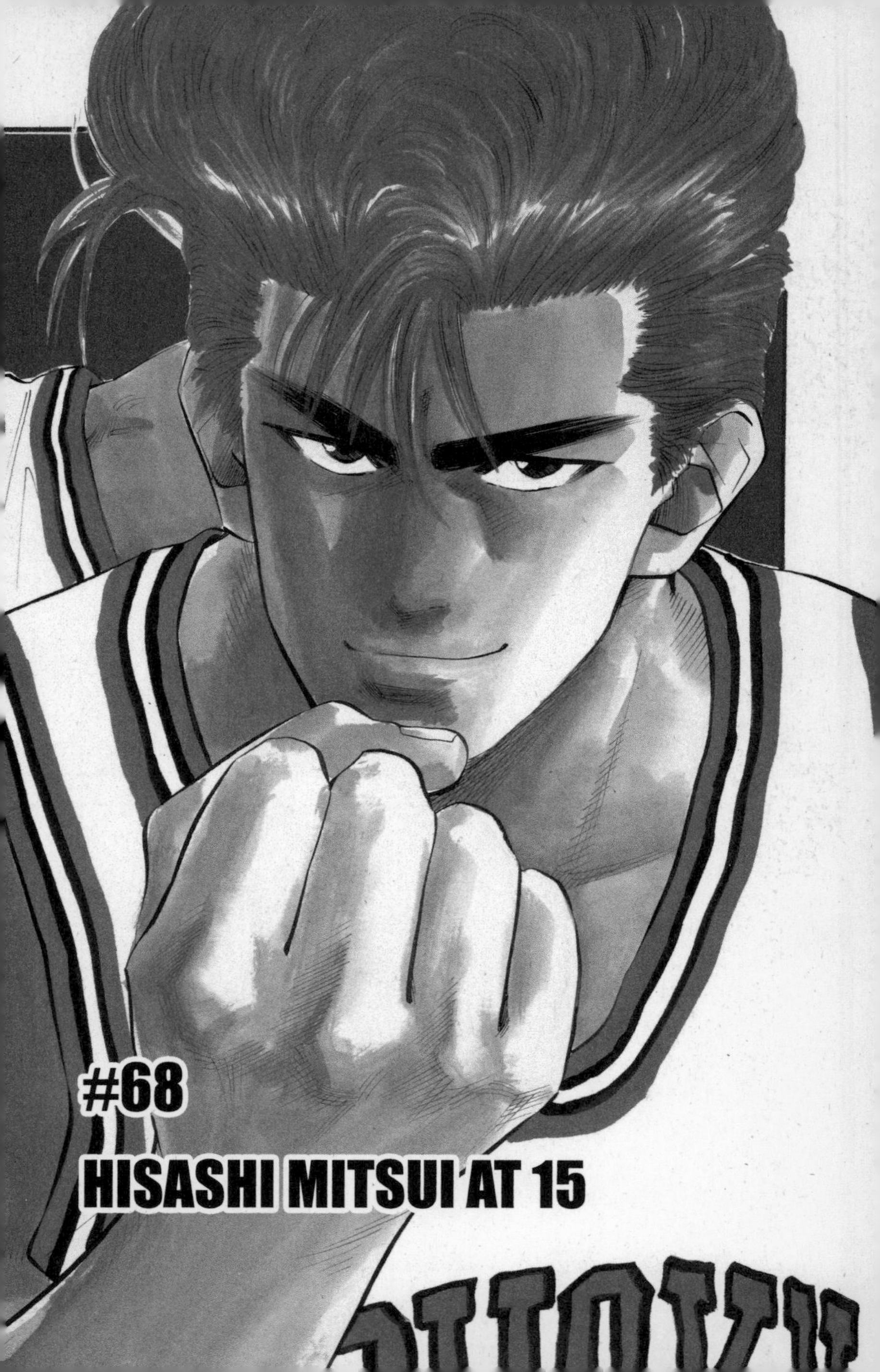

#68 HISASHI MITSUI AT 15

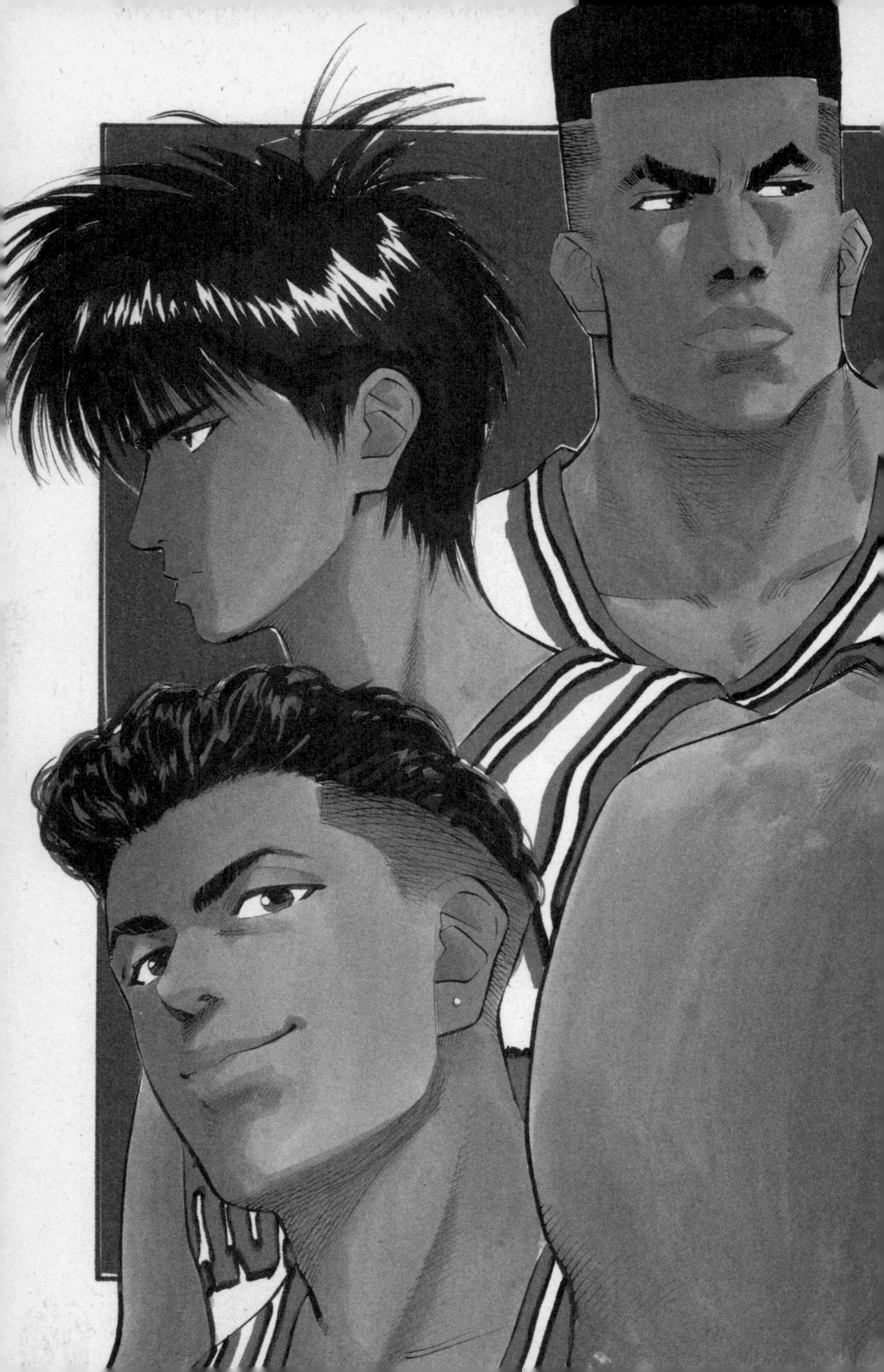

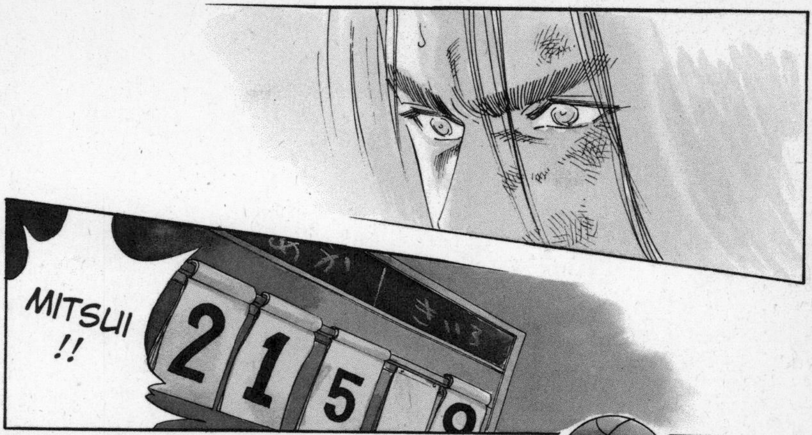
MITSUI !!

Scoreboard: Red Yellow

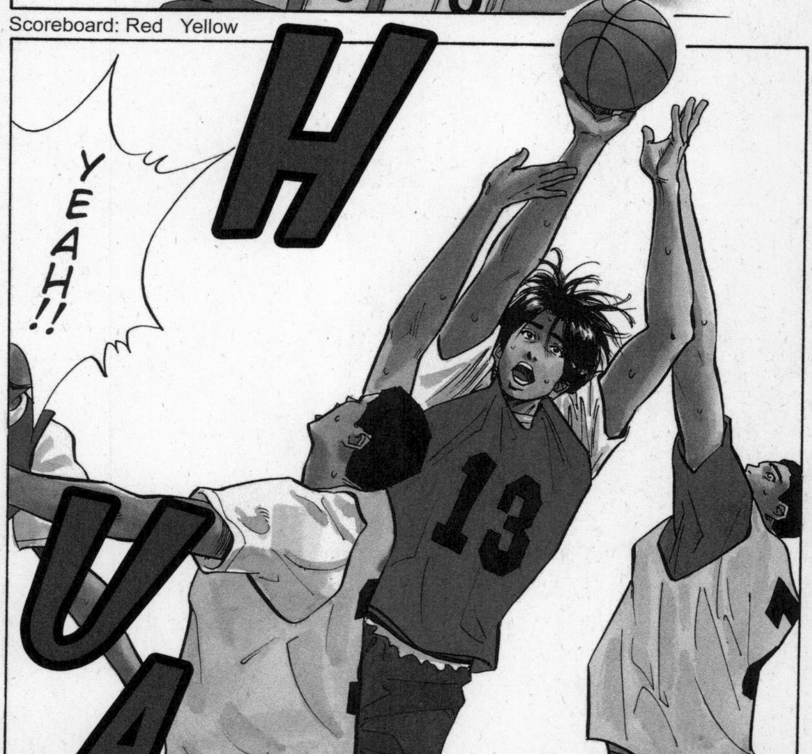
YEAH!!
HUA

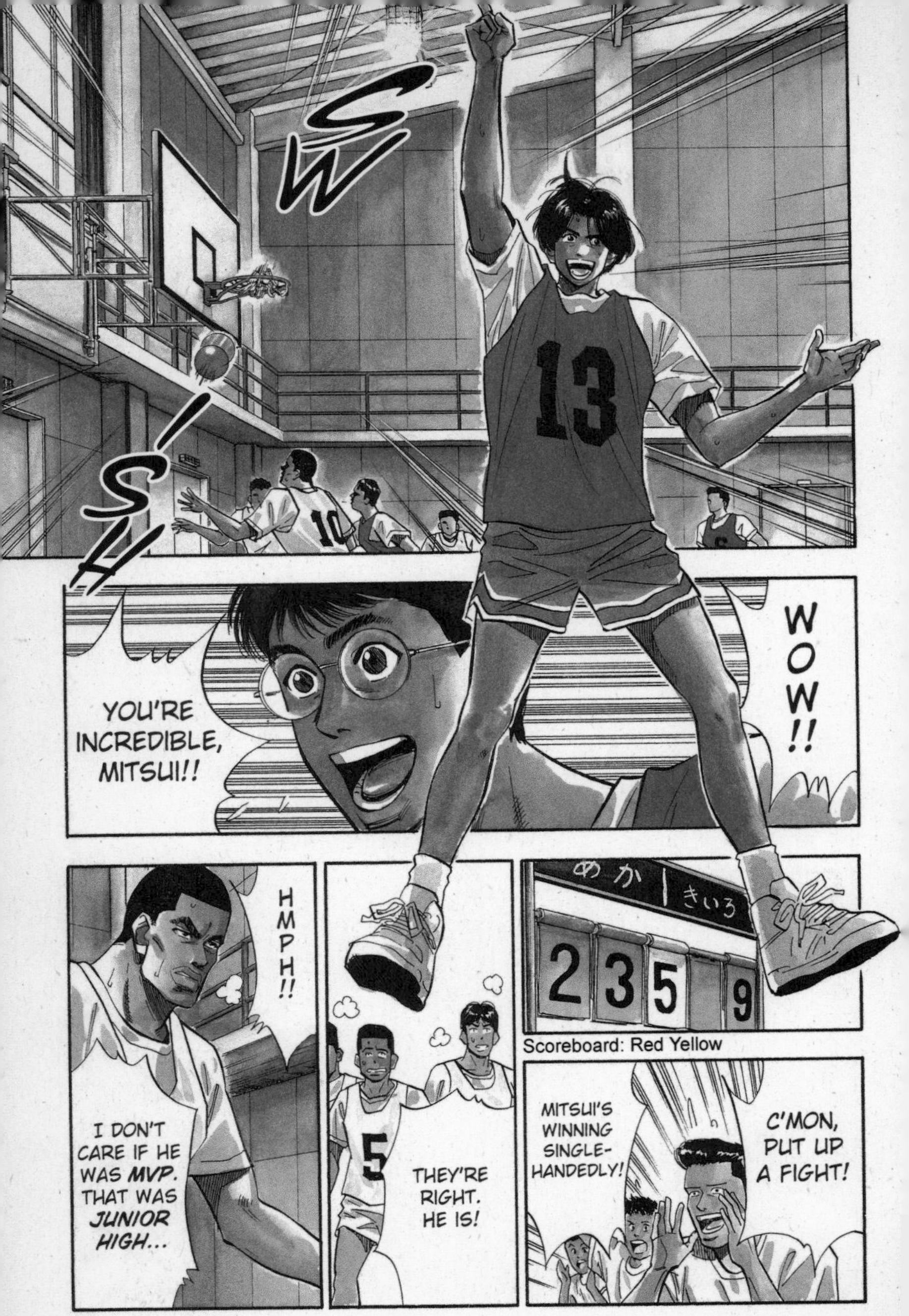
SWISH
WOW!!
YOU'RE INCREDIBLE, MITSUI!!
めか
きいろ
2 3 5 9
Scoreboard: Red Yellow
C'MON, PUT UP A FIGHT!
MITSUI'S WINNING SINGLE-HANDEDLY!
THEY'RE RIGHT. HE IS!
HMPH!!
I DON'T CARE IF HE WAS ***MVP***. THAT WAS ***JUNIOR HIGH***...

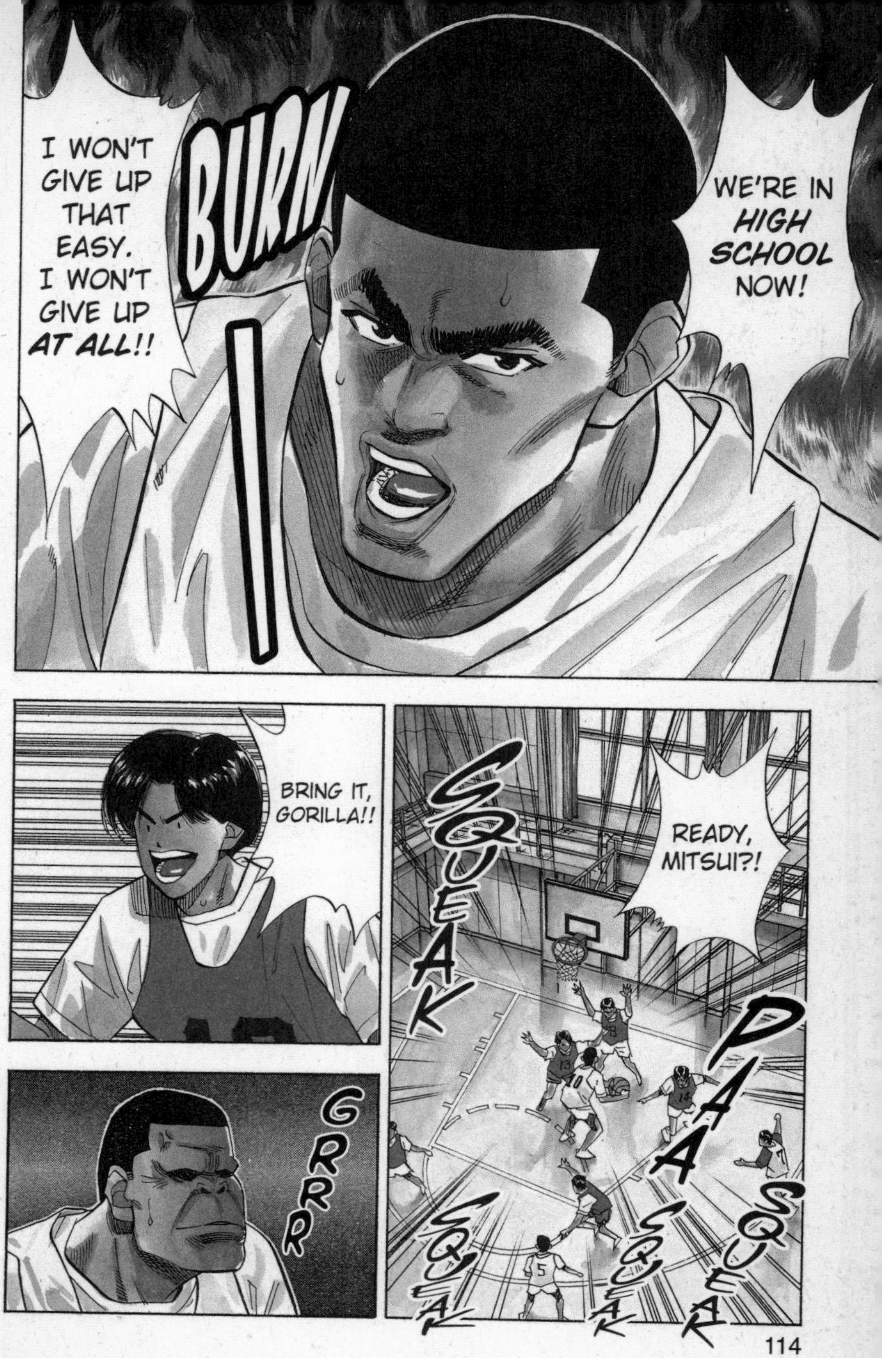
WE'RE IN HIGH SCHOOL NOW!
BURN
I WON'T GIVE UP THAT EASY. I WON'T GIVE UP AT ALL!!
READY, MITSUI?!
SQUEAK
PAAA
SQUEAK
SQUEAK
SQUEAK
BRING IT, GORILLA!!
GRRR

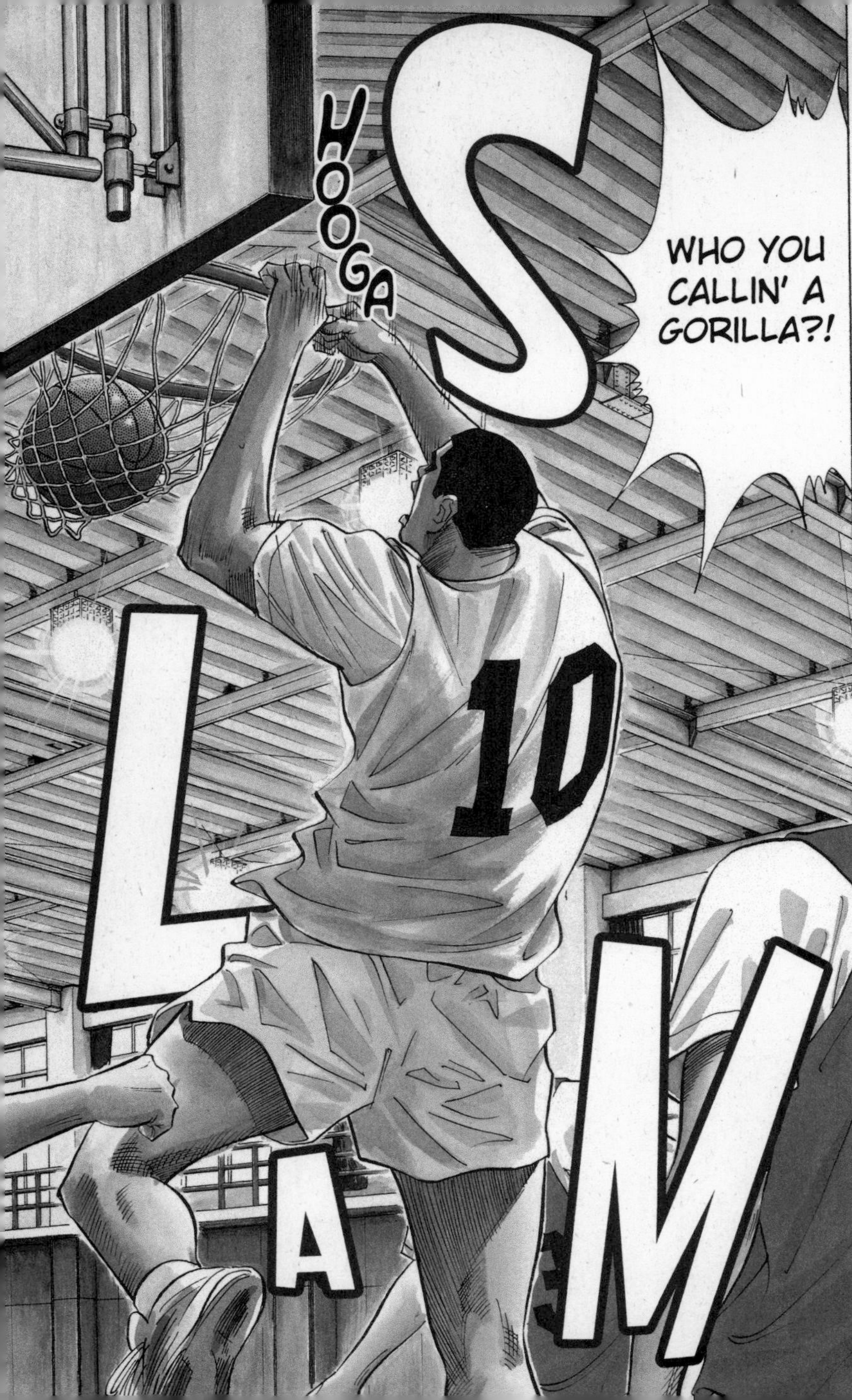
WHO YOU CALLIN' A GORILLA?!
HOOGA
SLAM

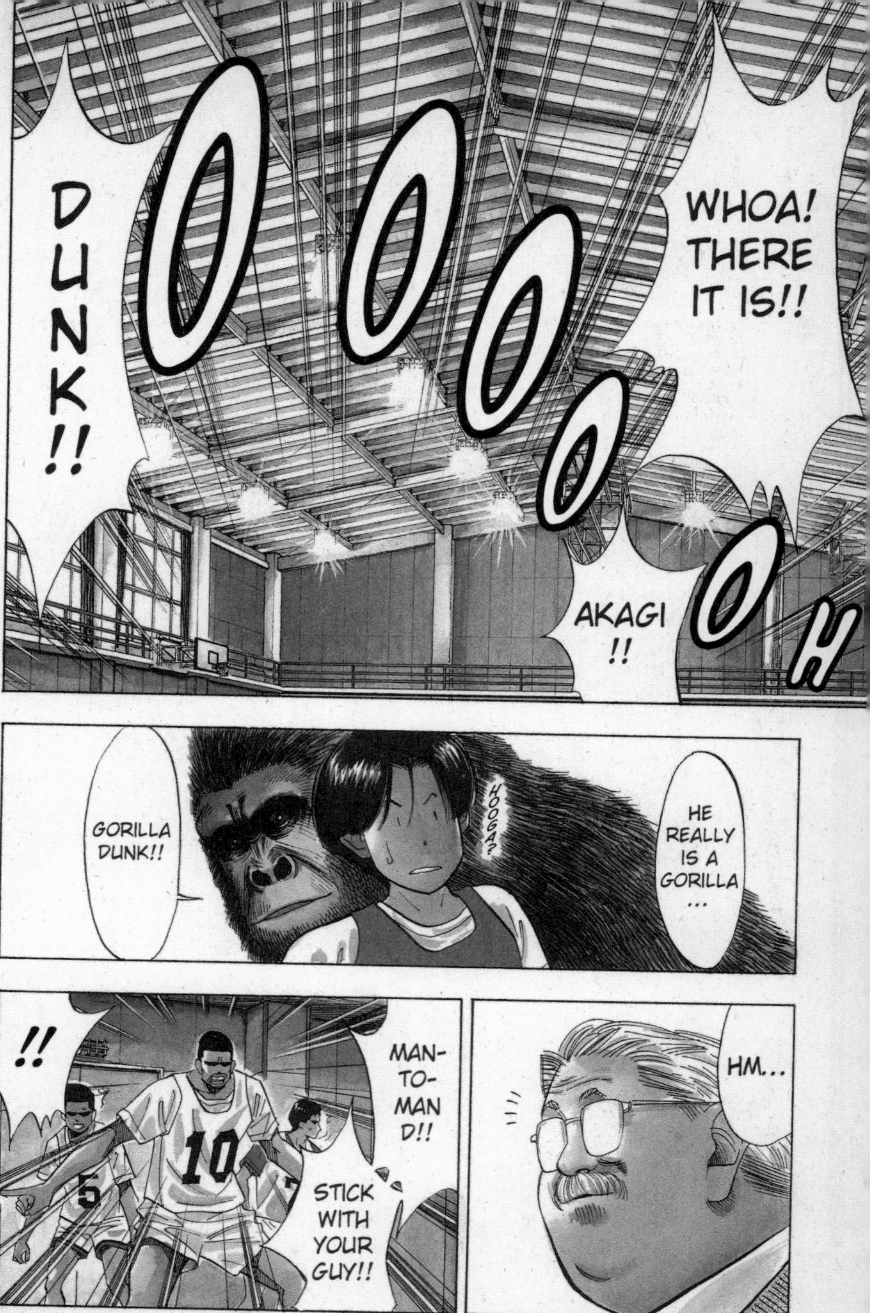
WHOA! THERE IT IS!!
OOOOOOH
AKAGI!!
DUNK!!
HE REALLY IS A GORILLA...
HOOGA?
GORILLA DUNK!!
HM...
MAN-TO-MAN D!!
STICK WITH YOUR GUY!!
!!

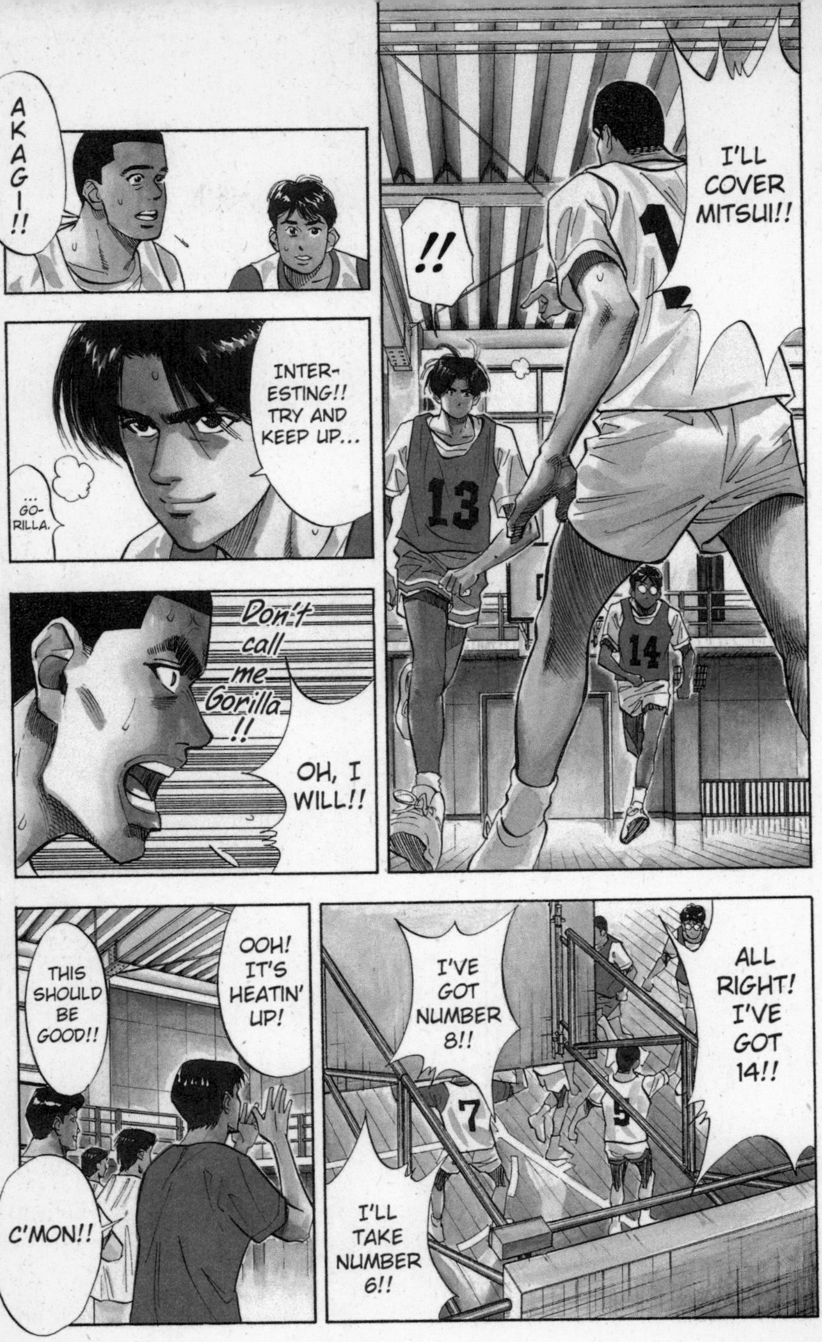
I'LL COVER MITSUI!!
!!
AKAGI!!
INTER-ESTING!! TRY AND KEEP UP...
...GO-RILLA.
Don't call me Gorilla!!
OH, I WILL!!
ALL RIGHT! I'VE GOT 14!!
I'VE GOT NUMBER 8!!
I'LL TAKE NUMBER 6!!
OOH! IT'S HEATIN' UP!
THIS SHOULD BE GOOD!!
C'MON!!

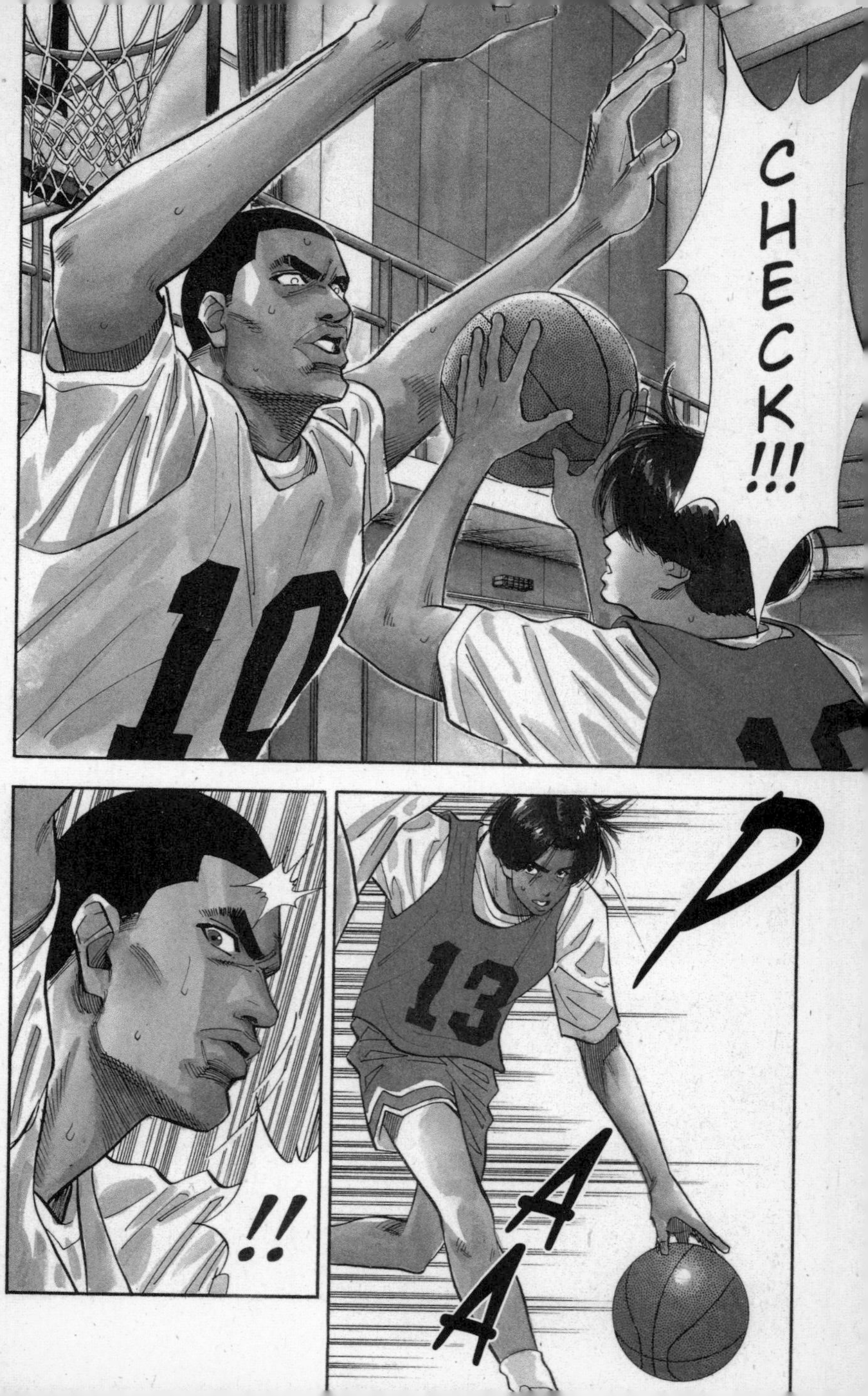
CHECK!!!
PAA
!!

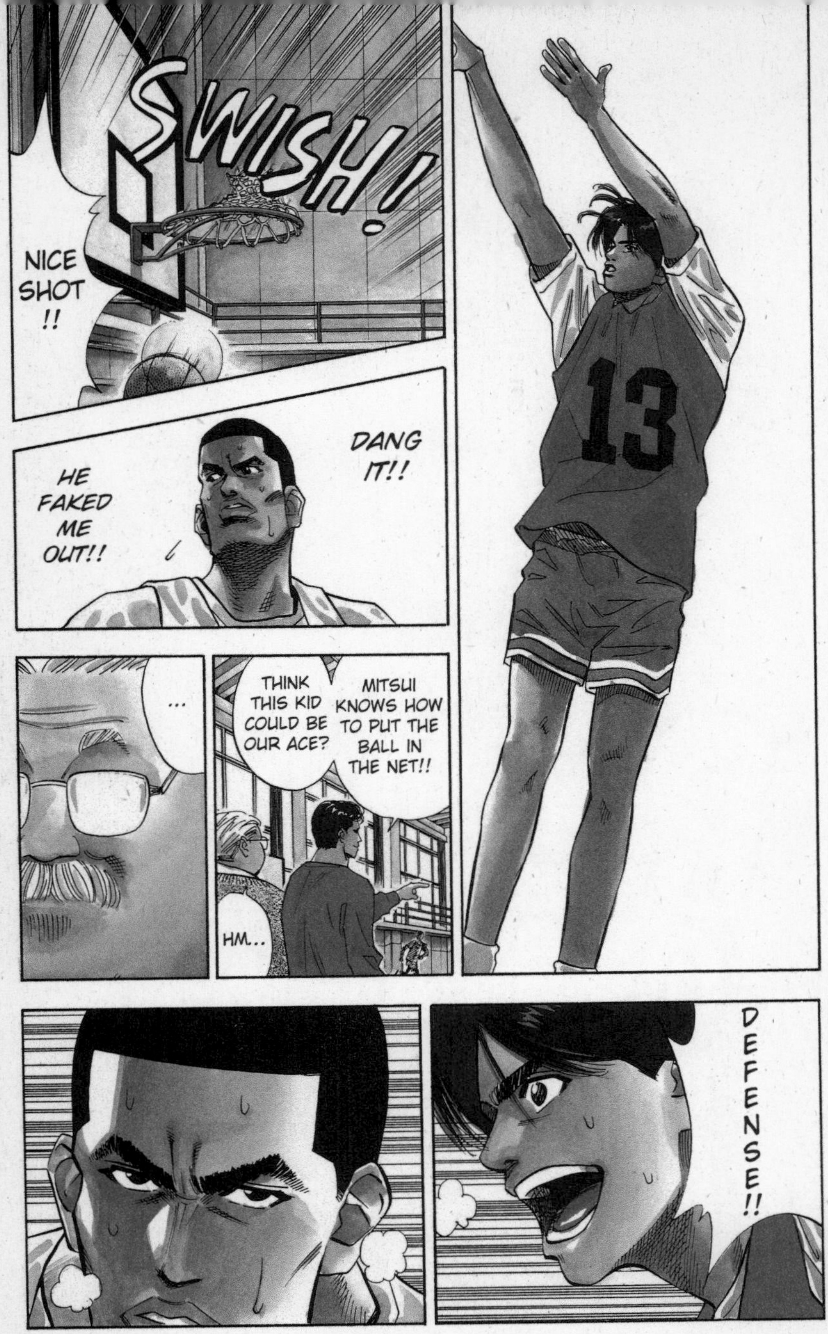
SWISH!
NICE SHOT!!
DANG IT!!
HE FAKED ME OUT!!
MITSUI KNOWS HOW TO PUT THE BALL IN THE NET!!
THINK THIS KID COULD BE OUR ACE?
HM...
...
DEFENSE!!

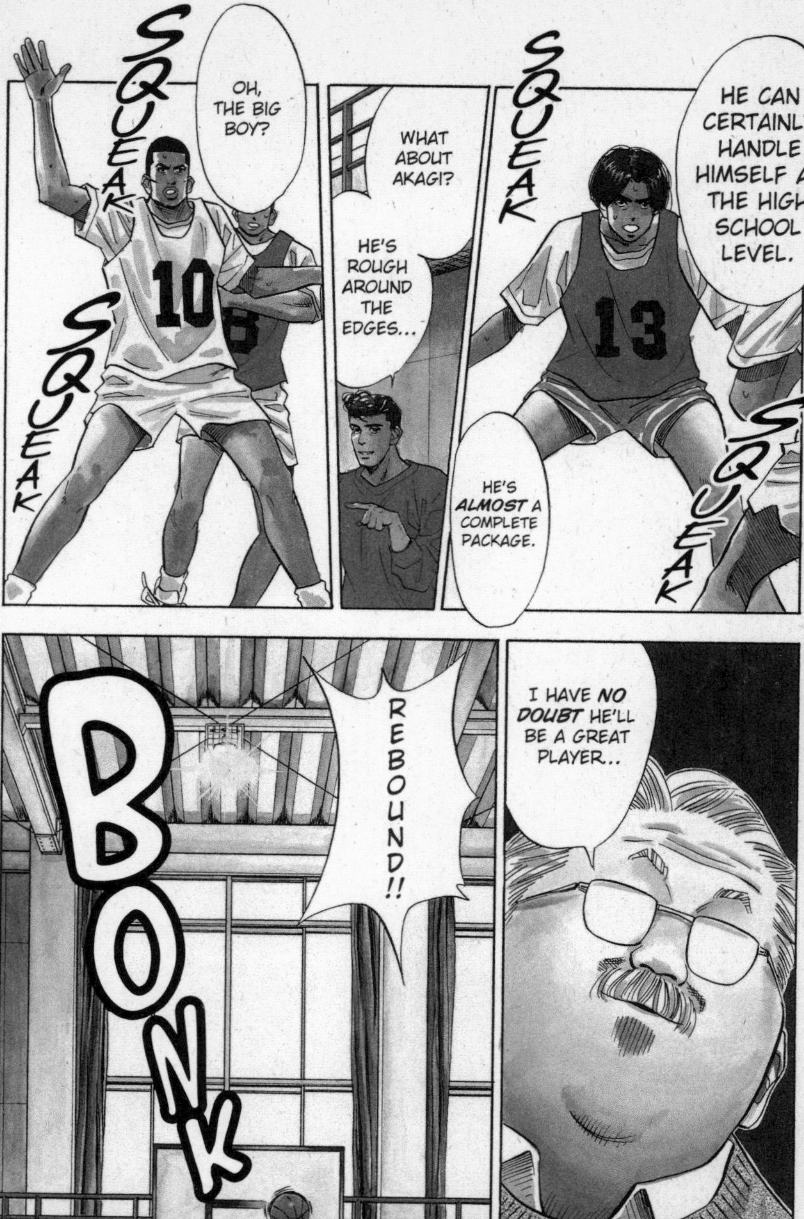
SQUEAK
HE CAN CERTAINLY HANDLE HIMSELF AT THE HIGH SCHOOL LEVEL.
HE'S *ALMOST* A COMPLETE PACKAGE.
SQUEAK
WHAT ABOUT AKAGI?
HE'S ROUGH AROUND THE EDGES...
OH, THE BIG BOY?
SQUEAK
SQUEAK
I HAVE *NO DOUBT* HE'LL BE A GREAT PLAYER...
REBOUND!!
BONK

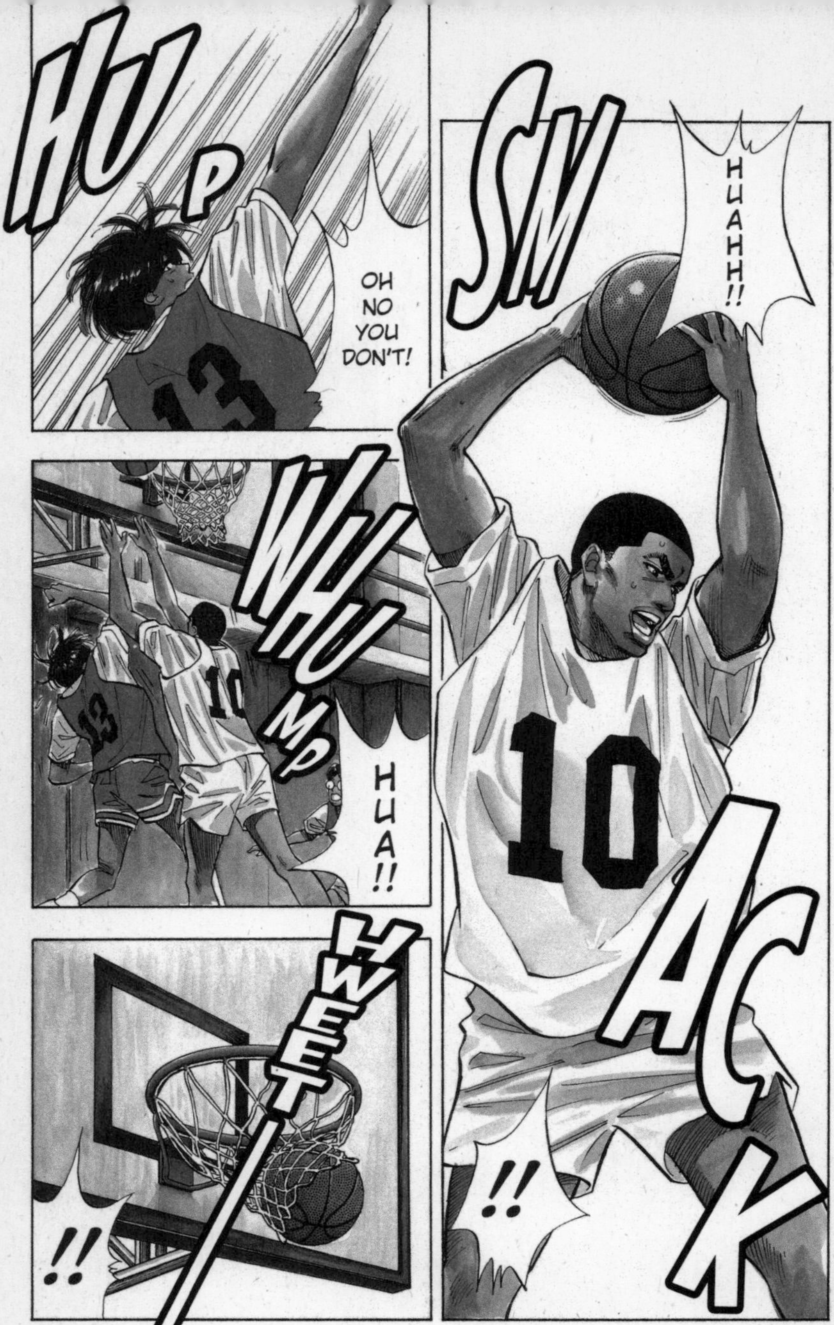
SM
HUAHH!!
ACK
!!
HUP
OH NO YOU DON'T!
WHUMP
HUA!!
HWEET
!!

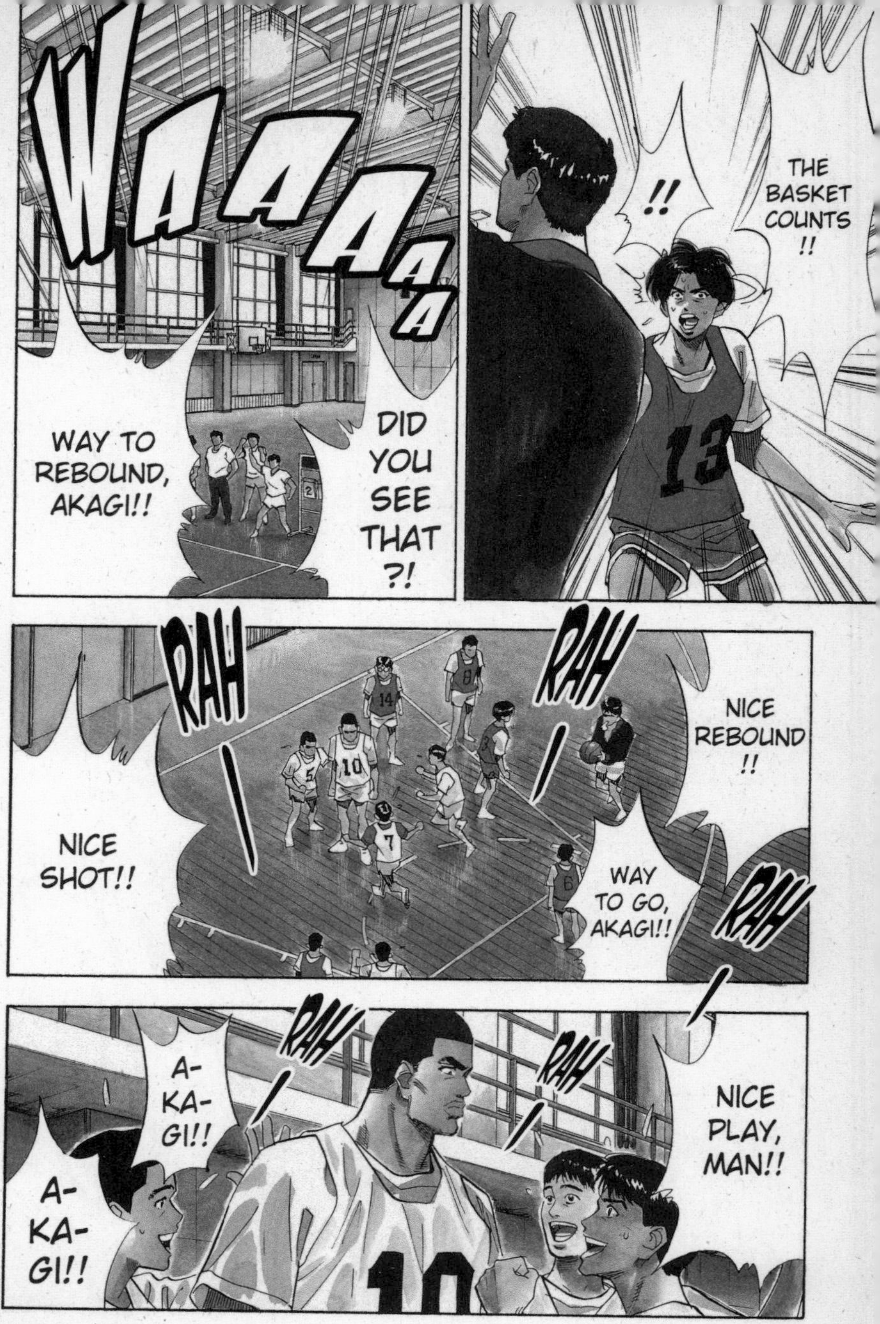
!!
THE BASKET COUNTS!!
WAAAAAA
DID YOU SEE THAT?!
WAY TO REBOUND, AKAGI!!
RAH
NICE REBOUND!!
RAH
WAY TO GO, AKAGI!!
RAH
NICE SHOT!!
NICE PLAY, MAN!!
RAH
RAH
A-KA-GI!!
A-KA-GI!!

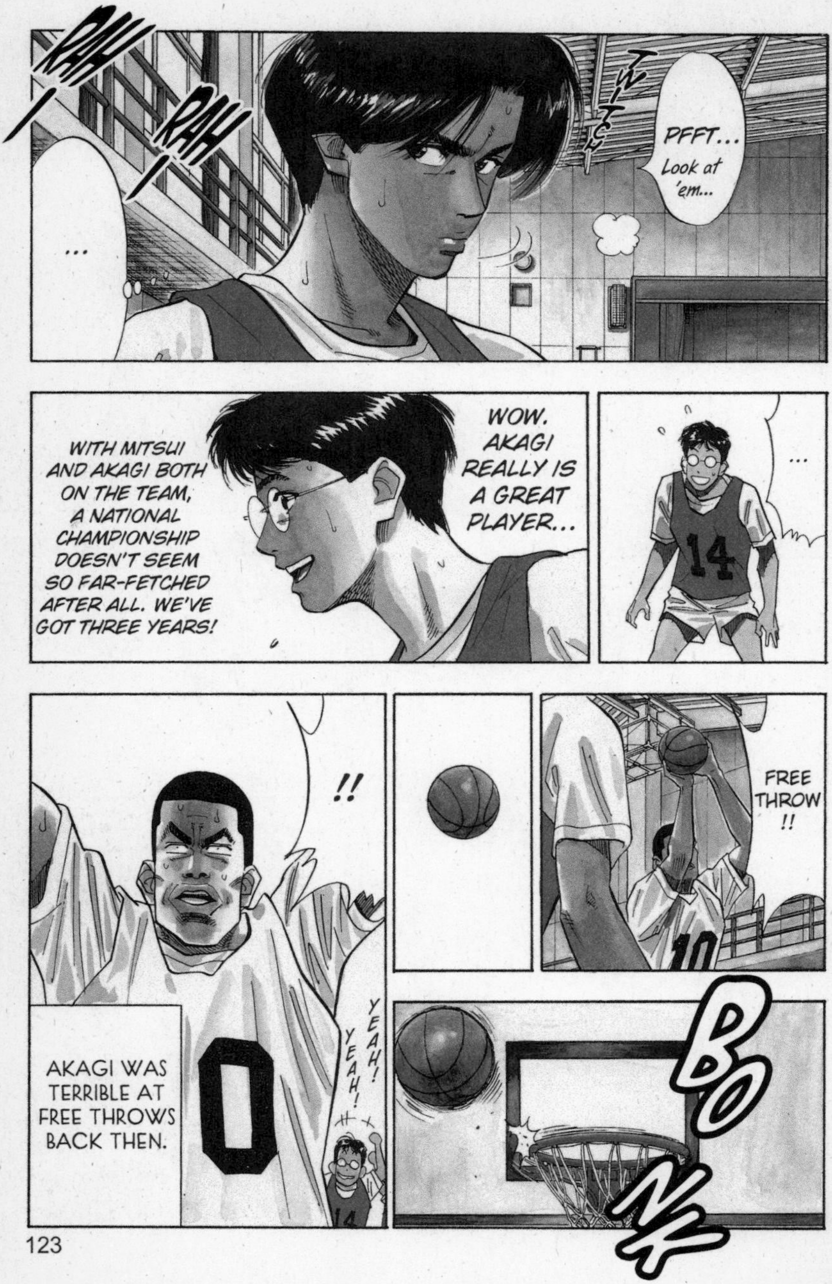
PFFT... Look at 'em...
TWITCH
RAH RAH
...
...
WOW. AKAGI REALLY IS A GREAT PLAYER...
WITH MITSUI AND AKAGI BOTH ON THE TEAM, A NATIONAL CHAMPIONSHIP DOESN'T SEEM SO FAR-FETCHED AFTER ALL. WE'VE GOT THREE YEARS!
FREE THROW !!
BONK
!!
YEAH! YEAH!
AKAGI WAS TERRIBLE AT FREE THROWS BACK THEN.

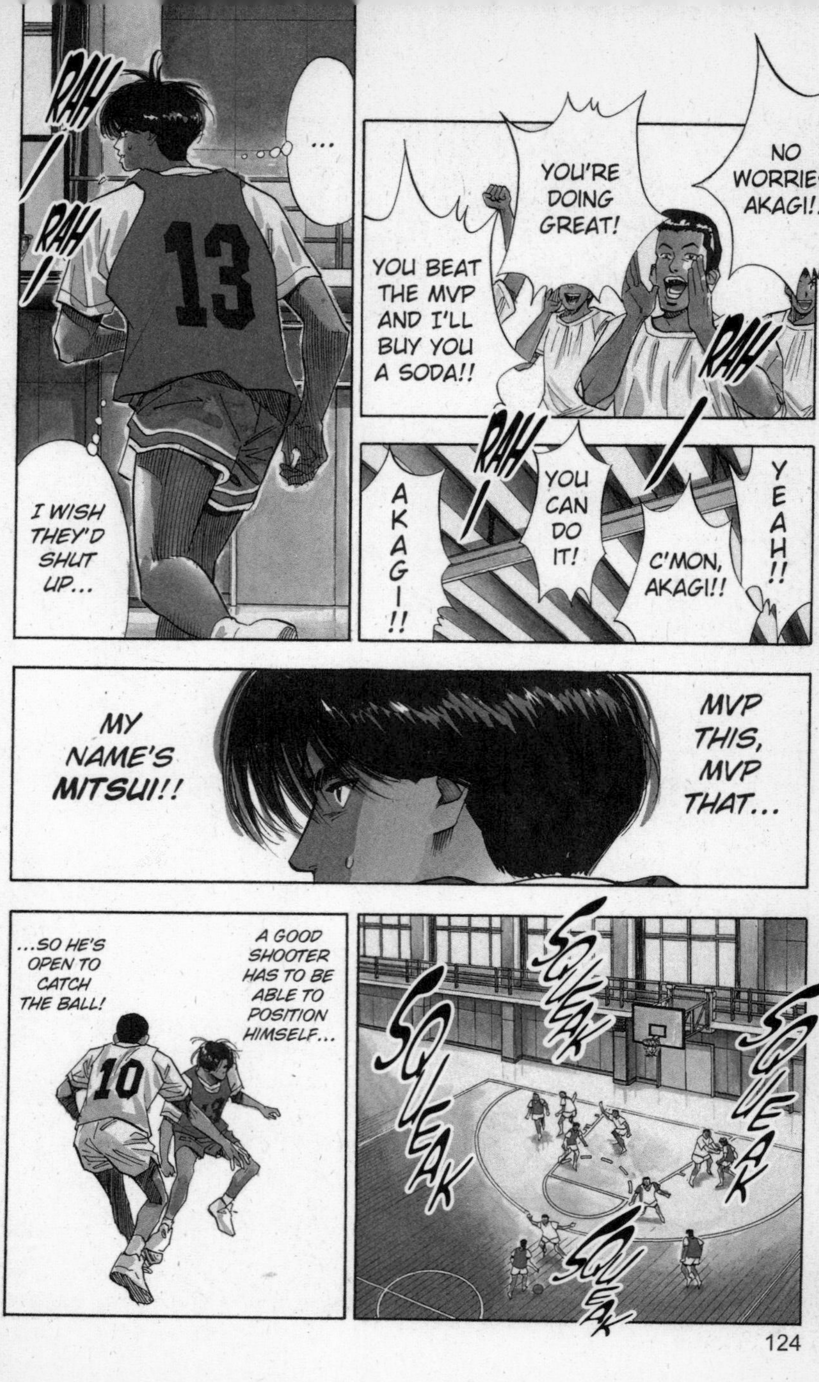
NO WORRIES, AKAGI!!
YOU'RE DOING GREAT!
YOU BEAT THE MVP AND I'LL BUY YOU A SODA!!
RAH-
YEAH!!
C'MON, AKAGI!!
YOU CAN DO IT!
RAH-
AKAGI!!
...
RAH-RAH-
I WISH THEY'D SHUT UP...
MVP THIS, MVP THAT...
MY NAME'S MITSUI!!
SQUEAK
SQUEAK
SQUEAK
SQUEAK
A GOOD SHOOTER HAS TO BE ABLE TO POSITION HIMSELF...
...SO HE'S OPEN TO CATCH THE BALL!

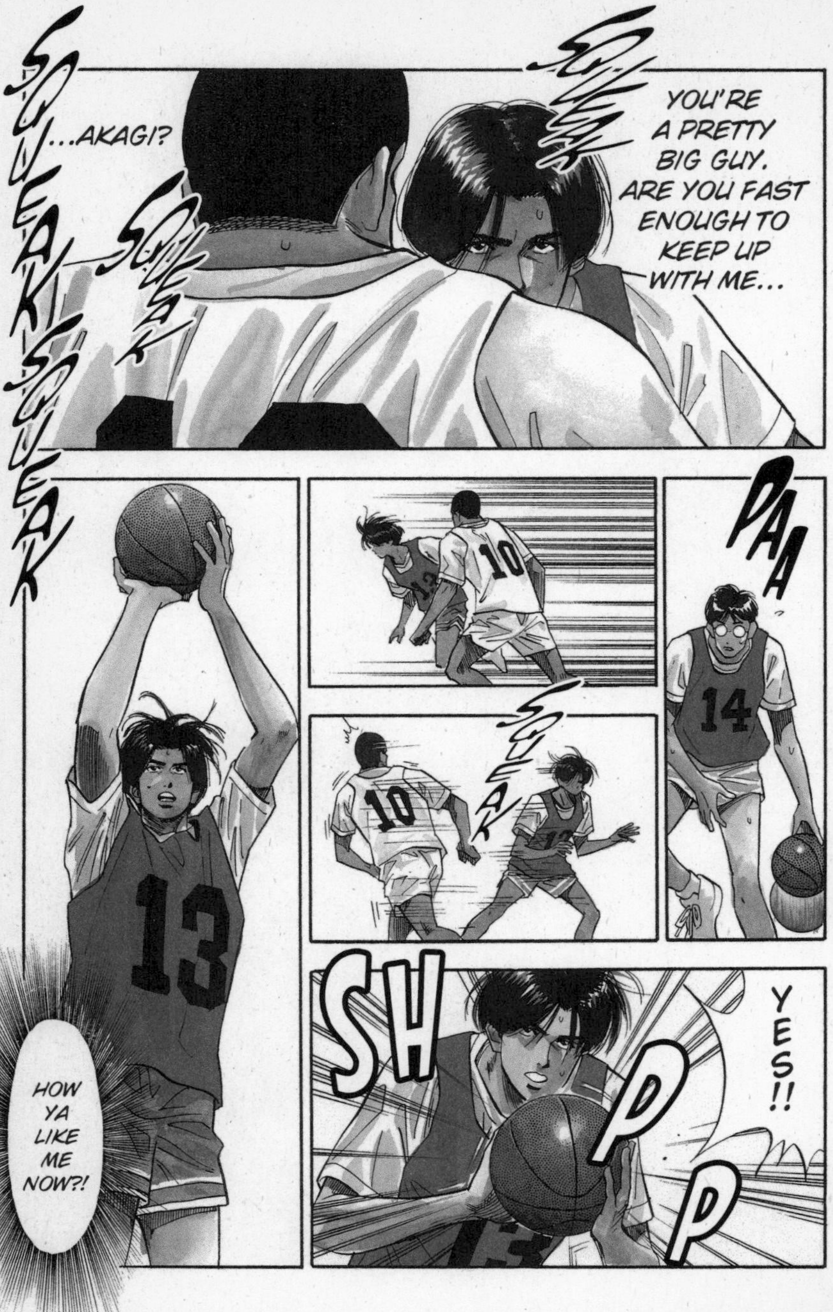
SQUEAK
YOU'RE A PRETTY BIG GUY. ARE YOU FAST ENOUGH TO KEEP UP WITH ME...
SQUEAK
...AKAGI?
SQUEAK SQUEAK
PAA
SQUEAK
SHPP
YES!!
HOW YA LIKE ME NOW?!

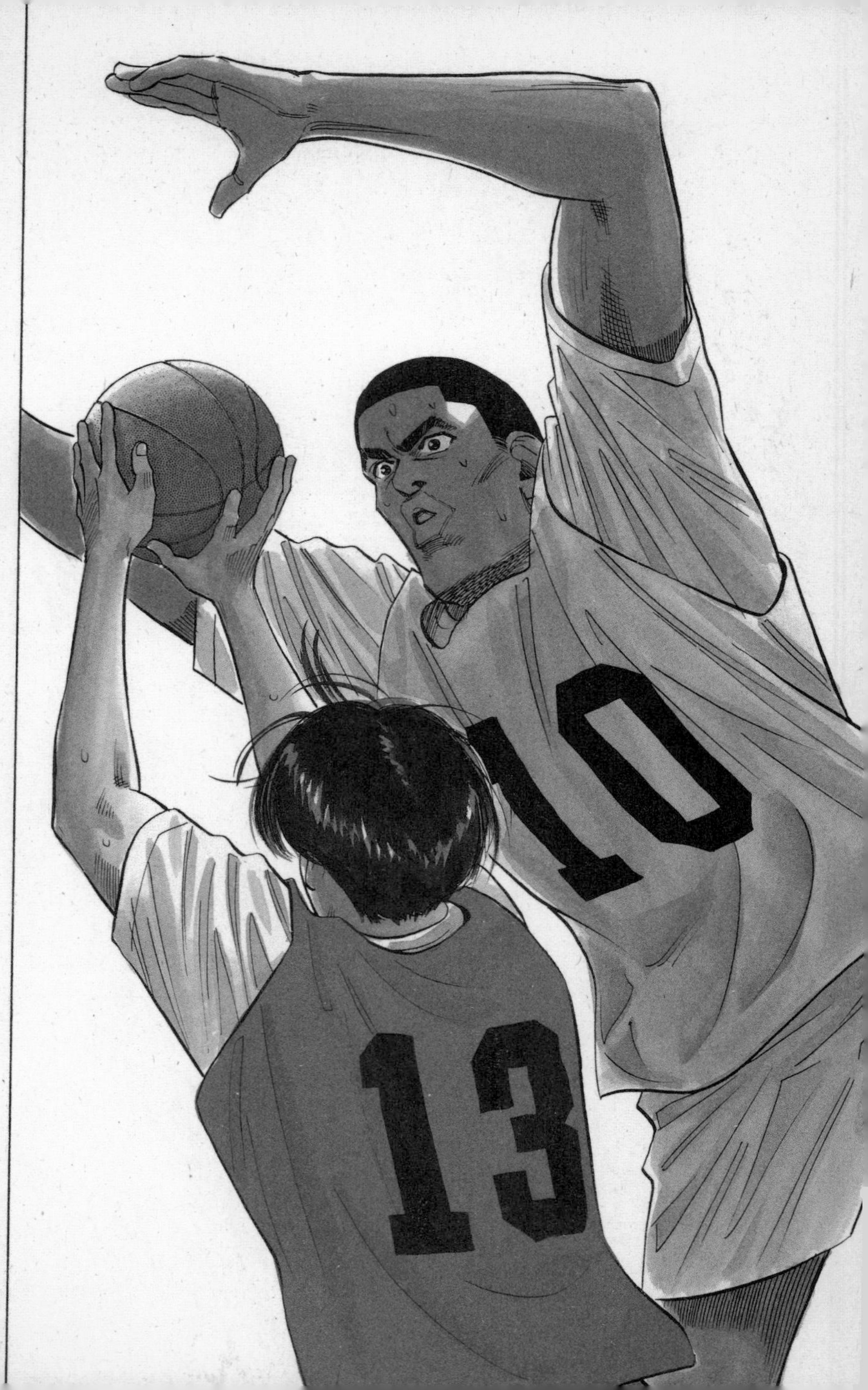

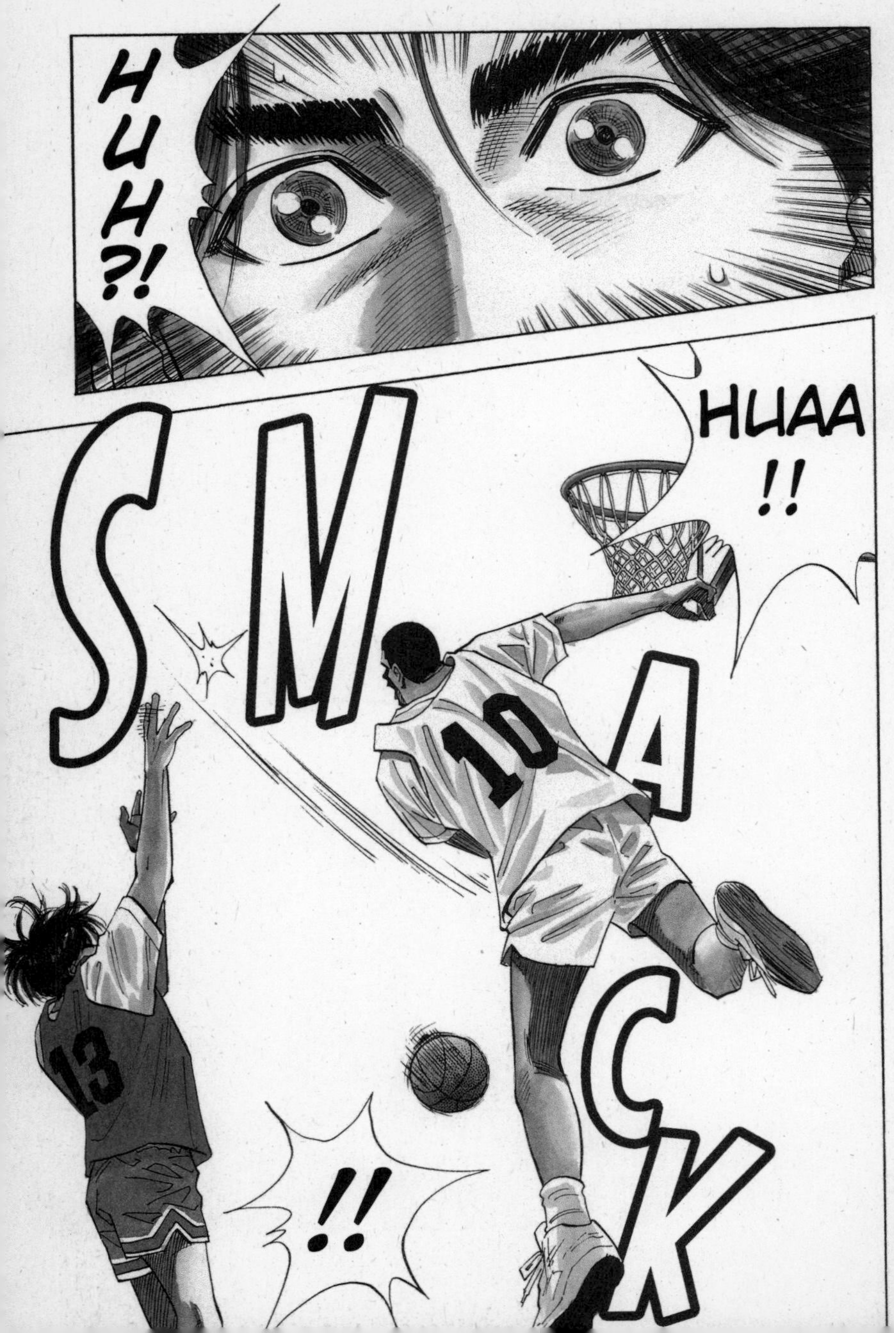
HUH?!
HUAA !!
SMACK
!!

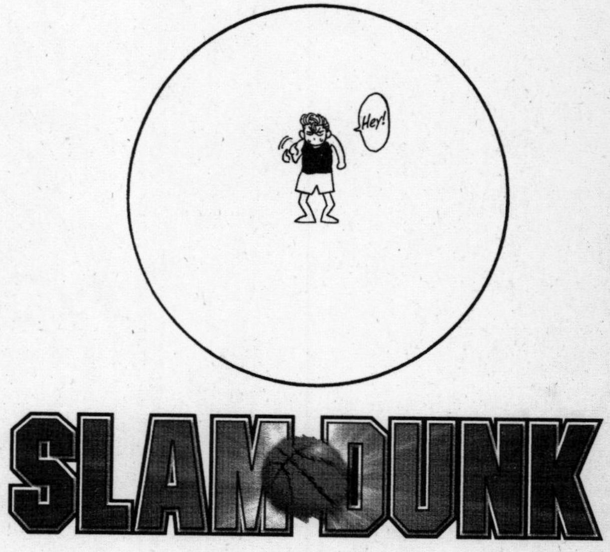
Hey!

SLAM DUNK

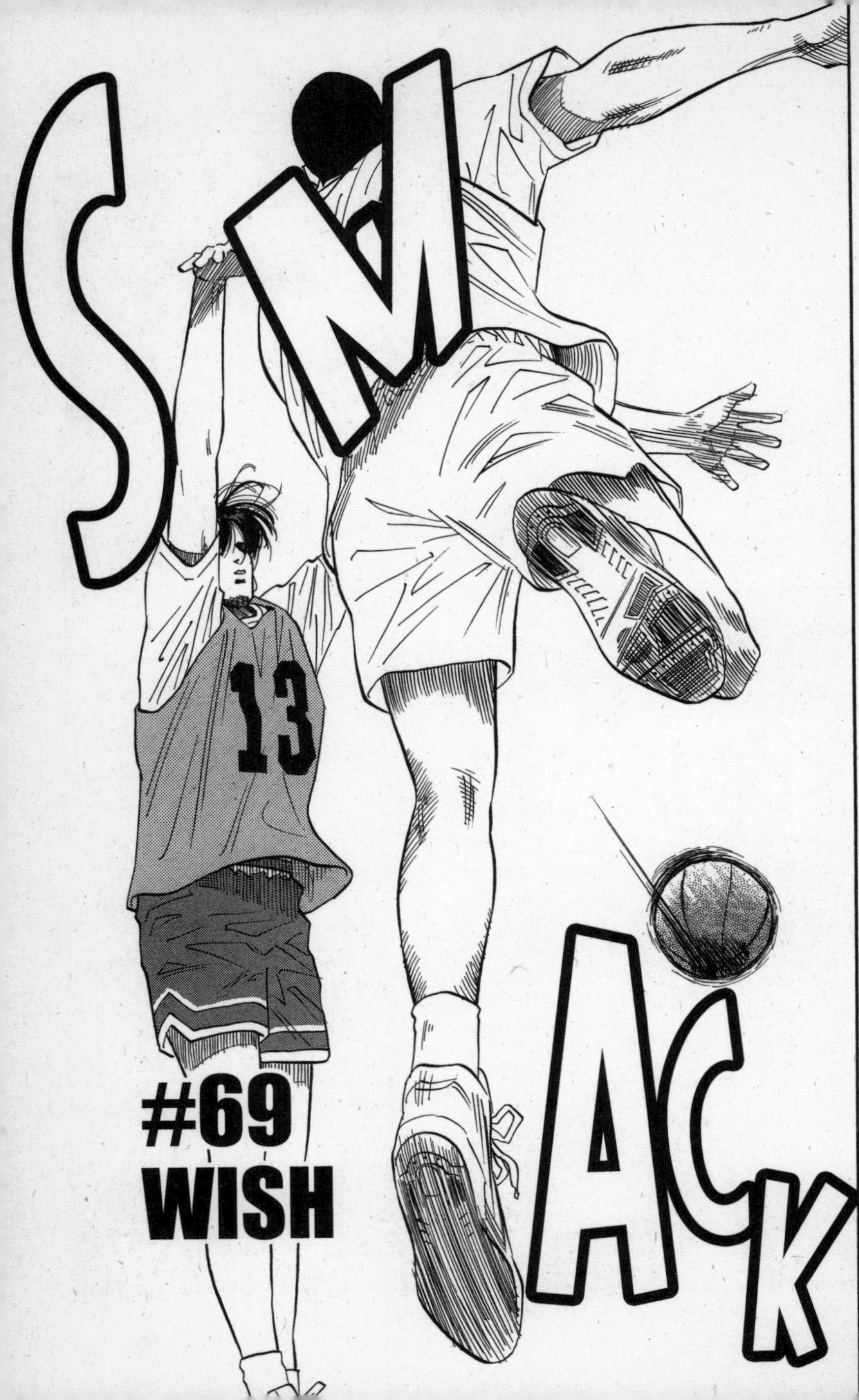
SMACK
#69
WISH

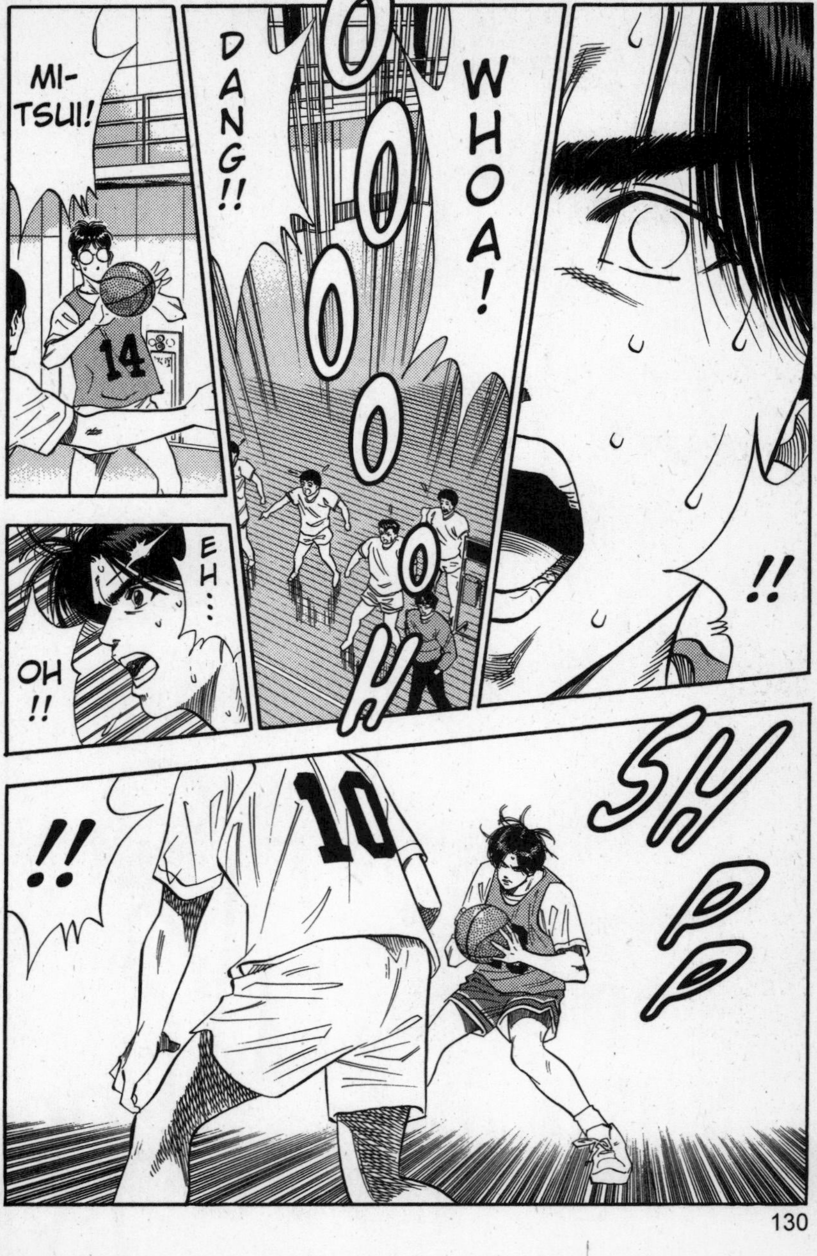
!!
WHOA!
DANG!!
OOOOOOH
MI-TSUI!
EH... OH!!
SHPP
!!

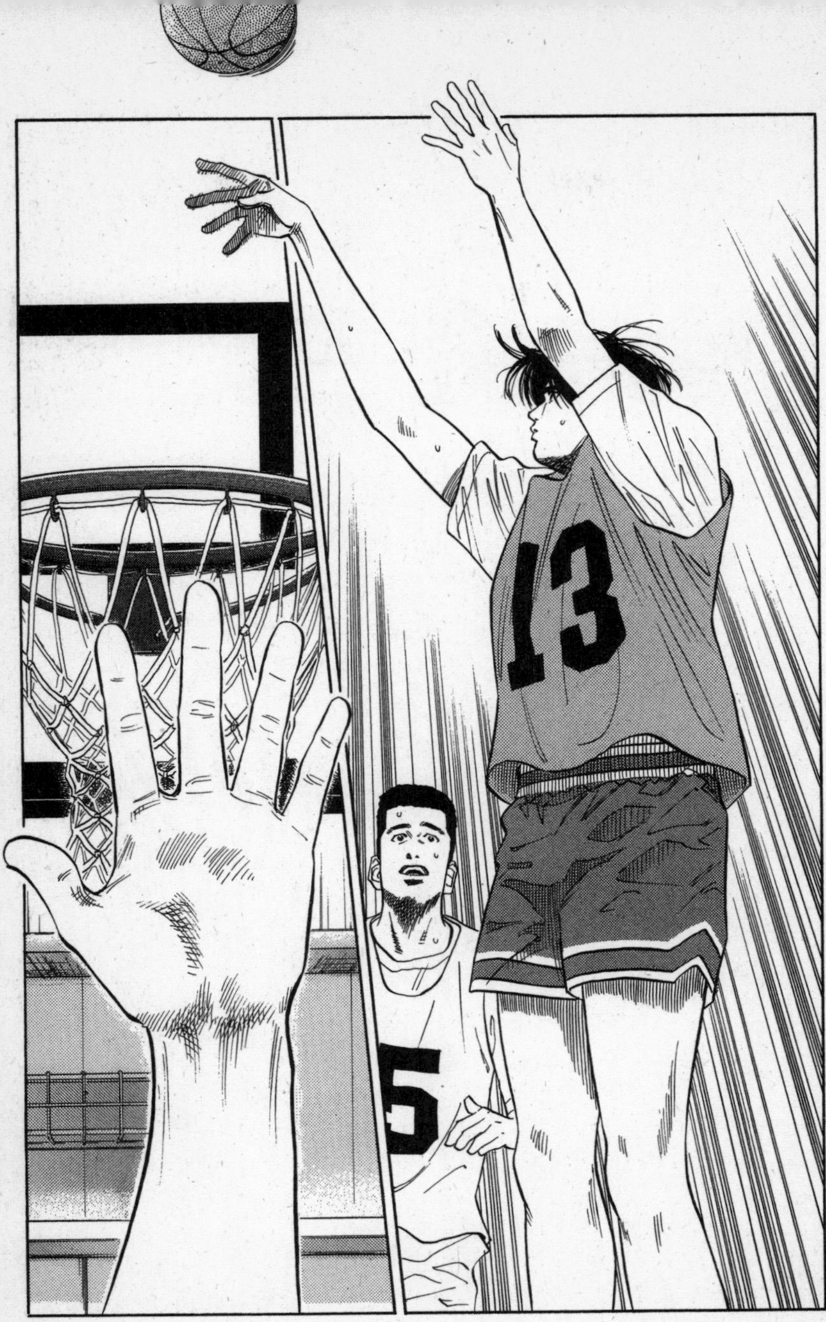
13
5

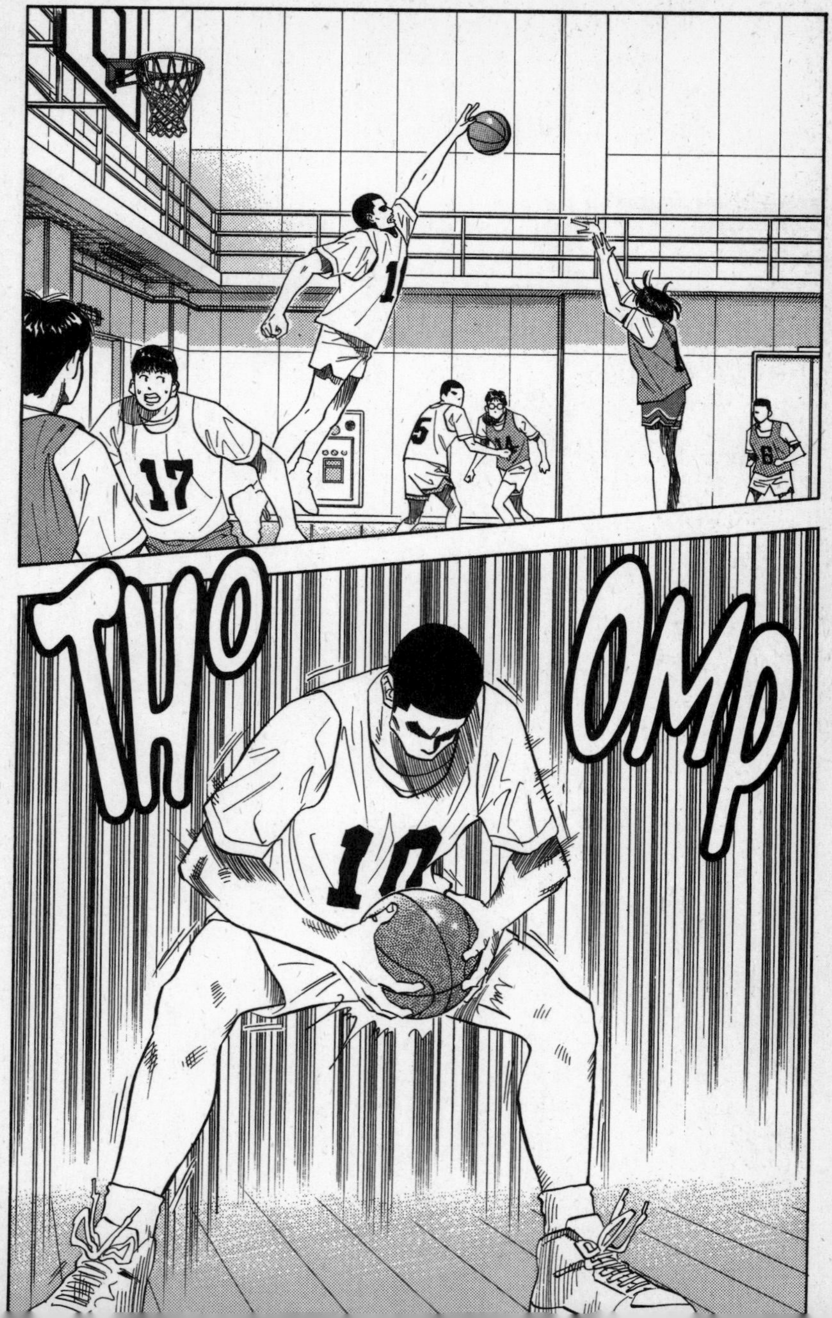
THOMP

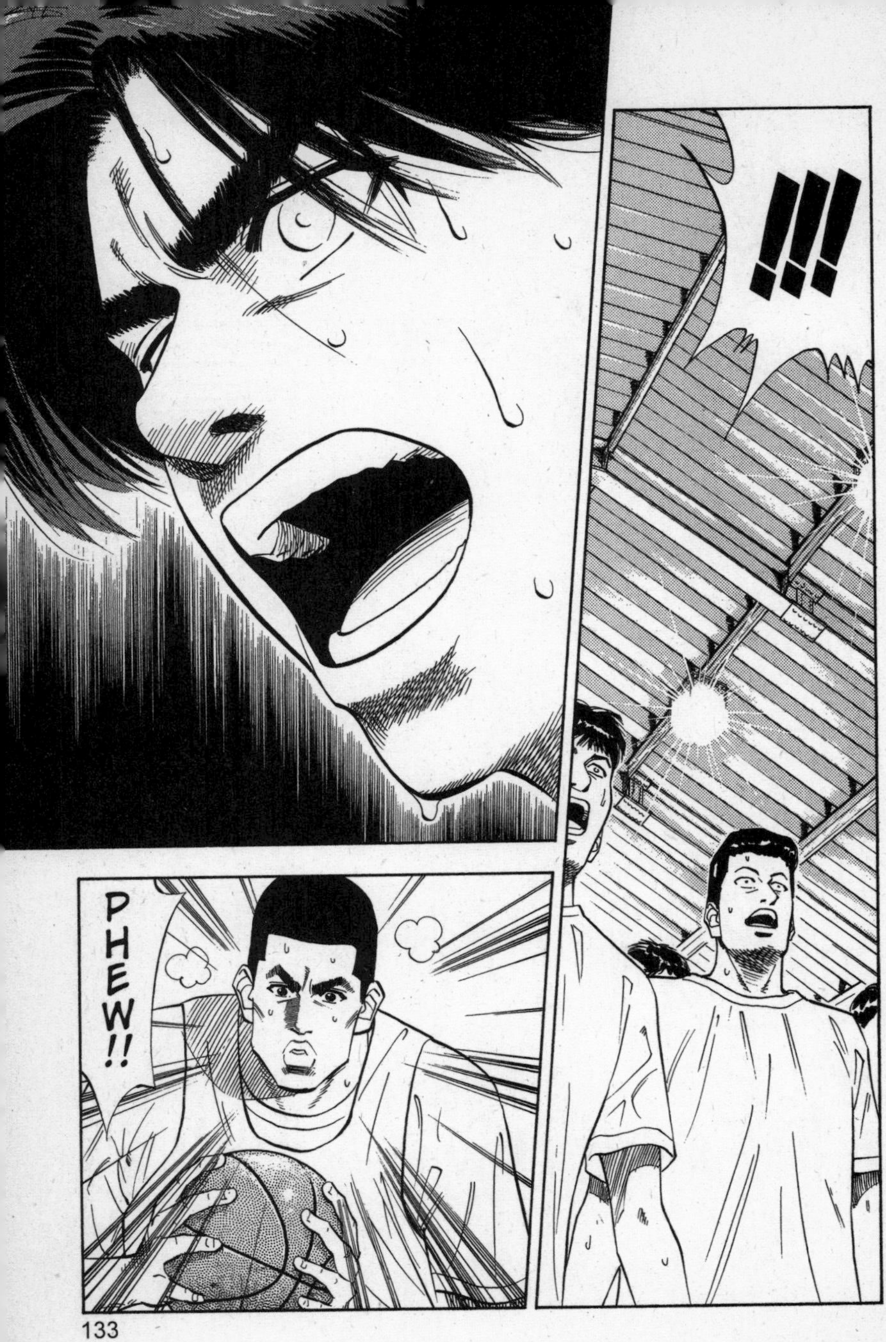
!!!
PHEW!!

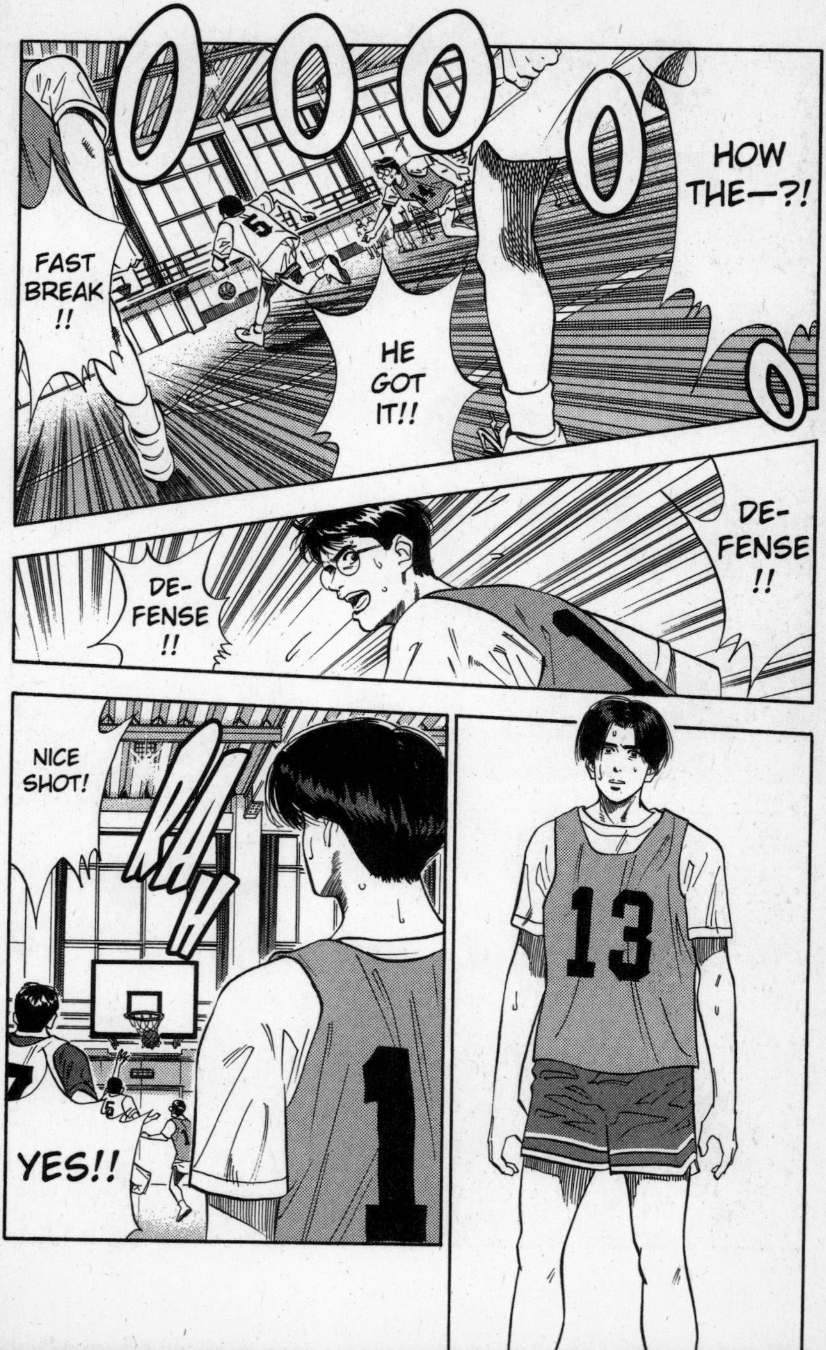
OOOOO
HOW THE—?!
HE GOT IT!!
FAST BREAK !!
DE-FENSE !!
DE-FENSE !!
NICE SHOT!
YES!!

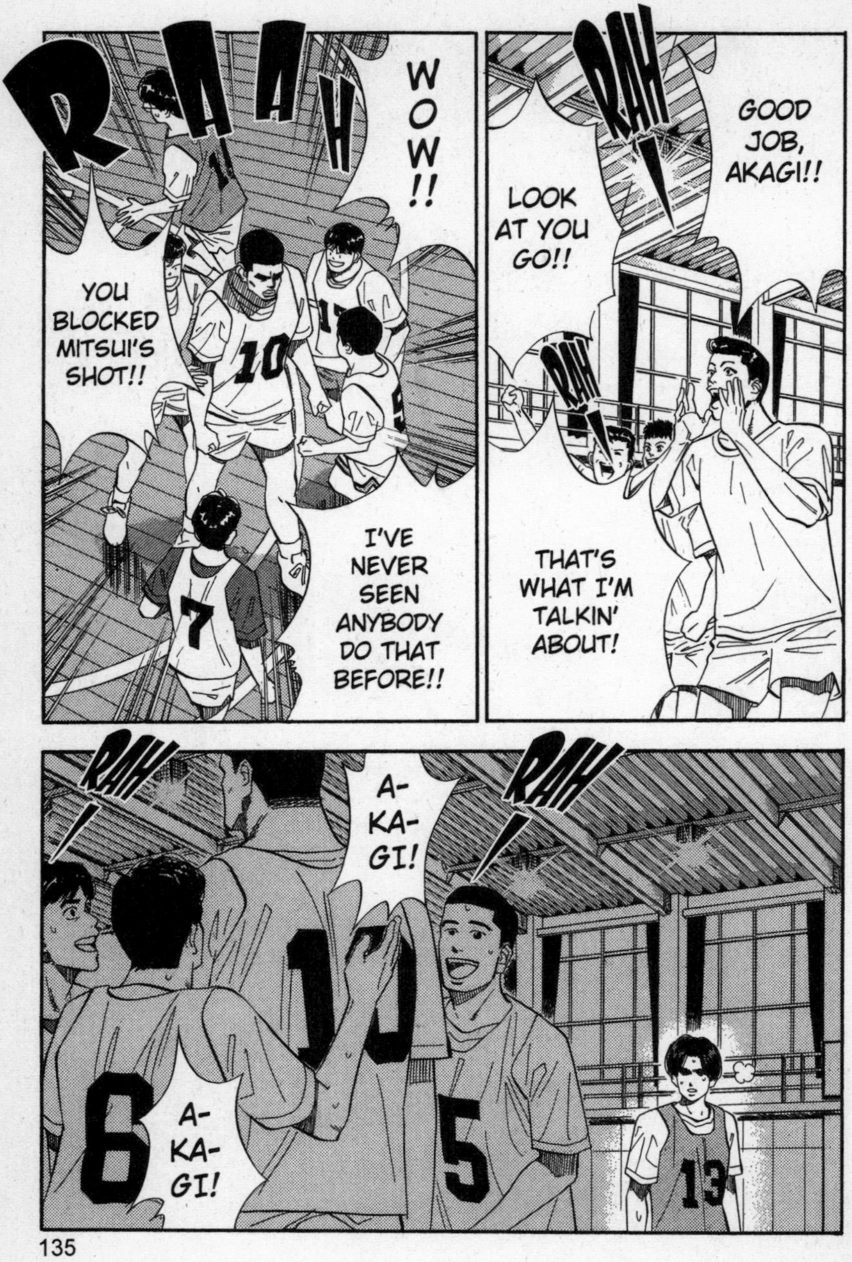
RAH
GOOD JOB, AKAGI!!
LOOK AT YOU GO!!
RAH
THAT'S WHAT I'M TALKIN' ABOUT!
RAAH
WOW!!
YOU BLOCKED MITSUI'S SHOT!!
I'VE NEVER SEEN ANYBODY DO THAT BEFORE!!
RAH
A-KA-GI!
RAH
A-KA-GI!

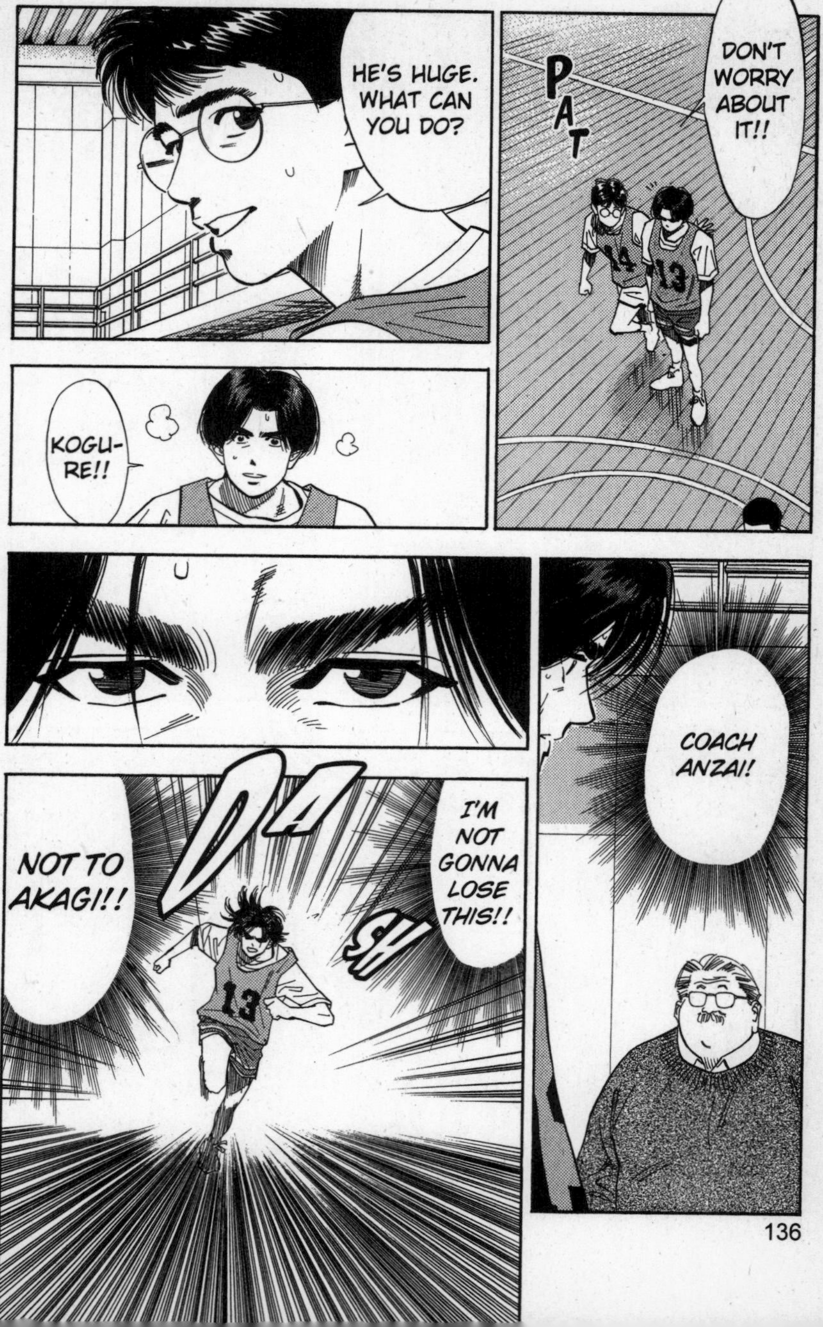
PAT
DON'T WORRY ABOUT IT!!
HE'S HUGE. WHAT CAN YOU DO?
KOGU-RE!!
COACH ANZAI!
I'M NOT GONNA LOSE THIS!!
DASH
NOT TO AKAGI!!

READ THIS WAY

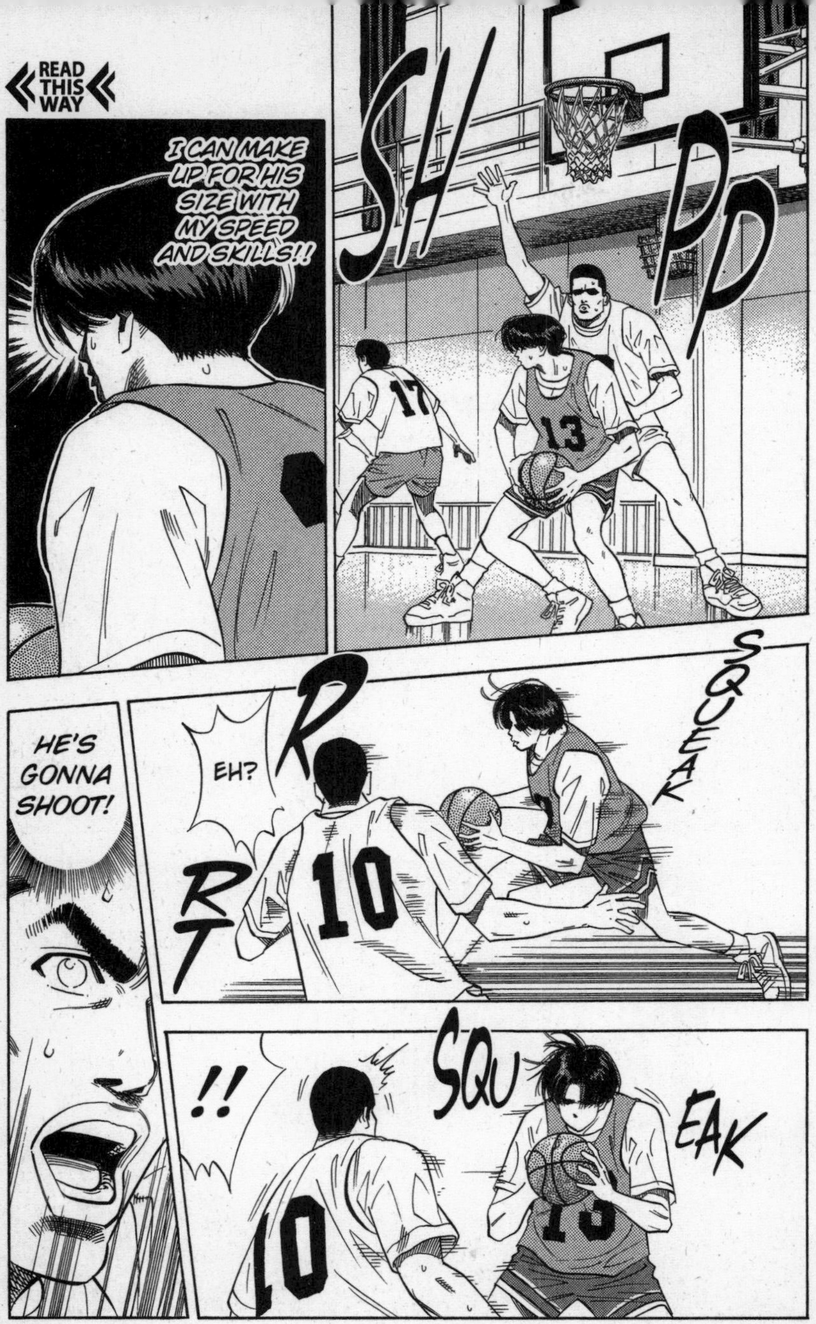

SHPP
I CAN MAKE UP FOR HIS SIZE WITH MY SPEED AND SKILLS!!
SQUEAK
R
EH?
RT
SQUEAK
!!
HE'S GONNA SHOOT!

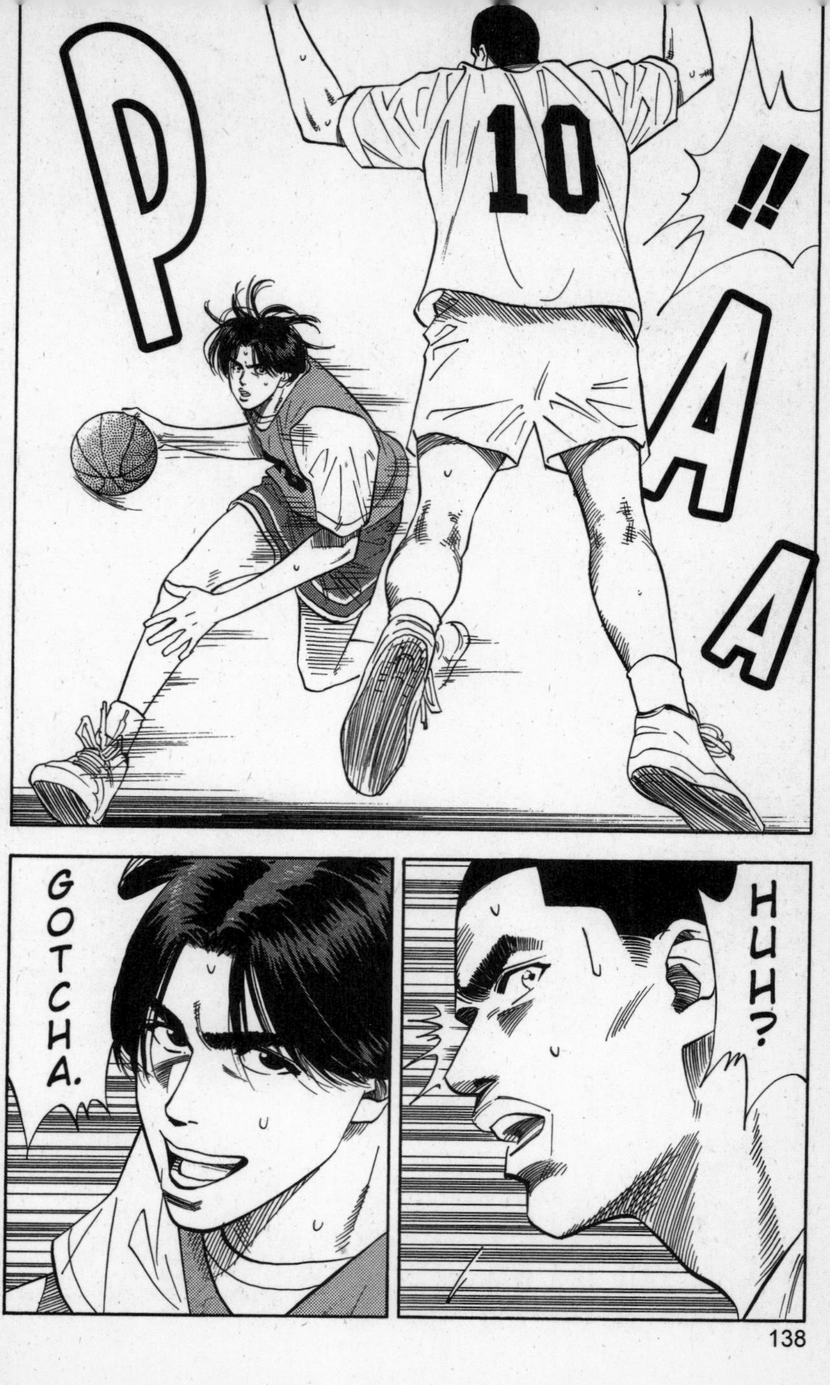
PAA!!
HUH?
GOTCHA.

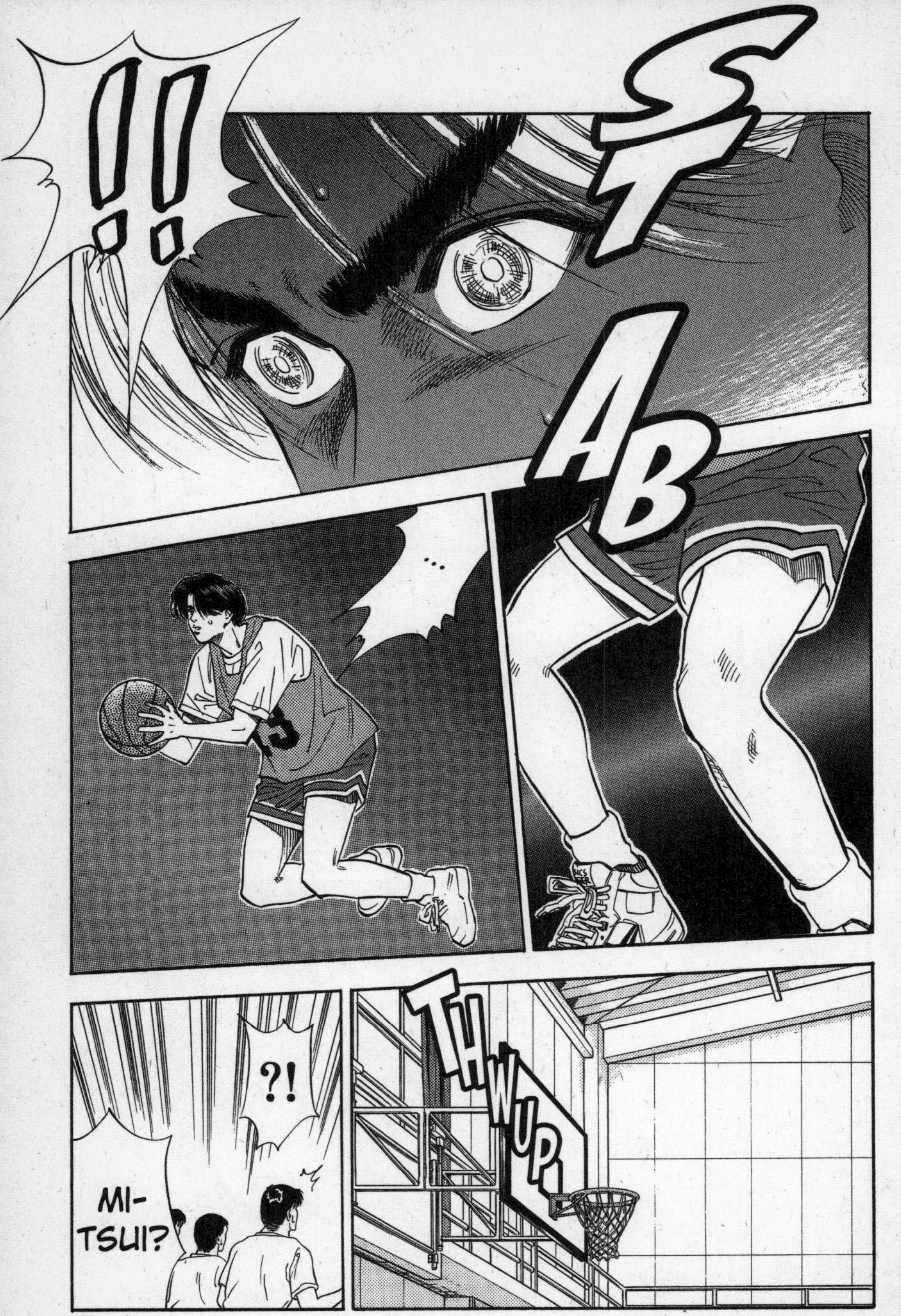
STAB
!!
...
THWUP!
?!
MI-TSUI?

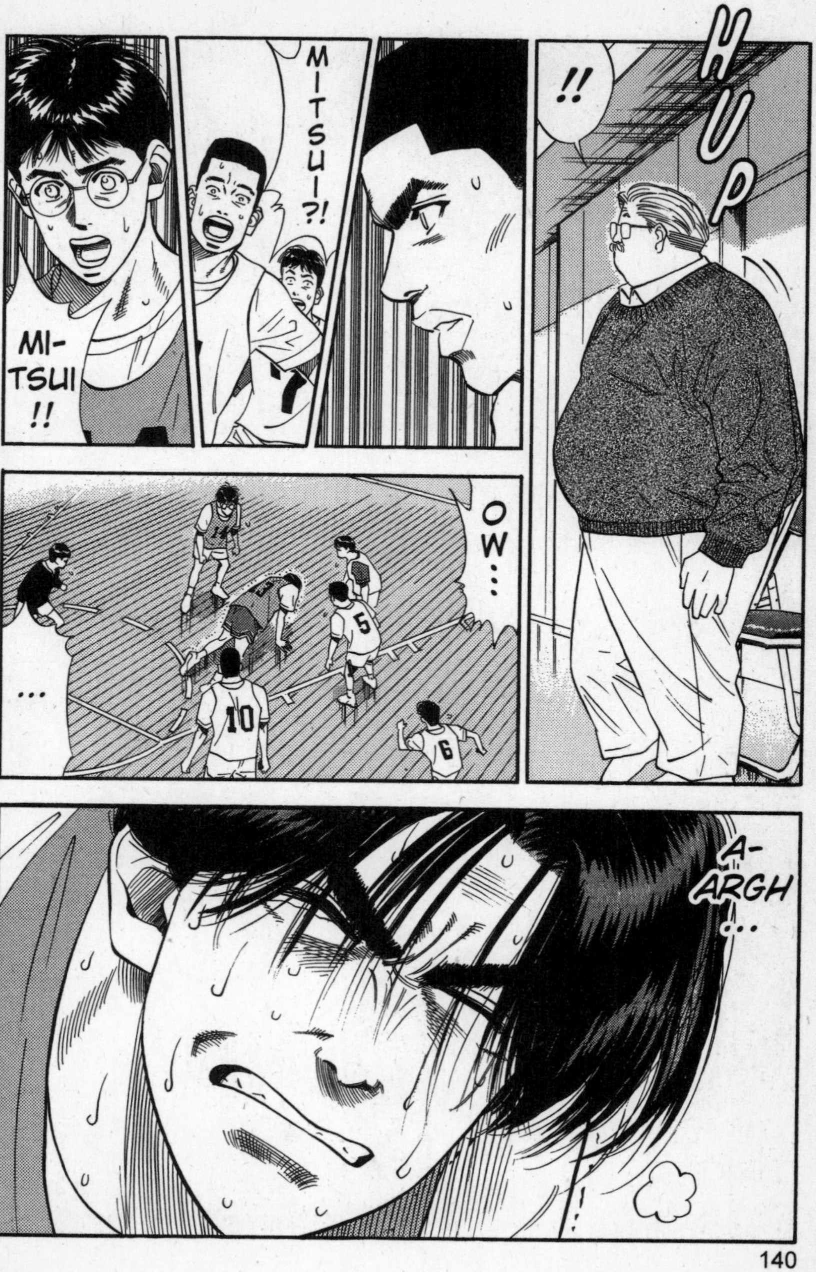
HUP
!!
MITSUI?!
MI-TSUI!!
OW...
...
A-ARGH...

READ THIS WAY

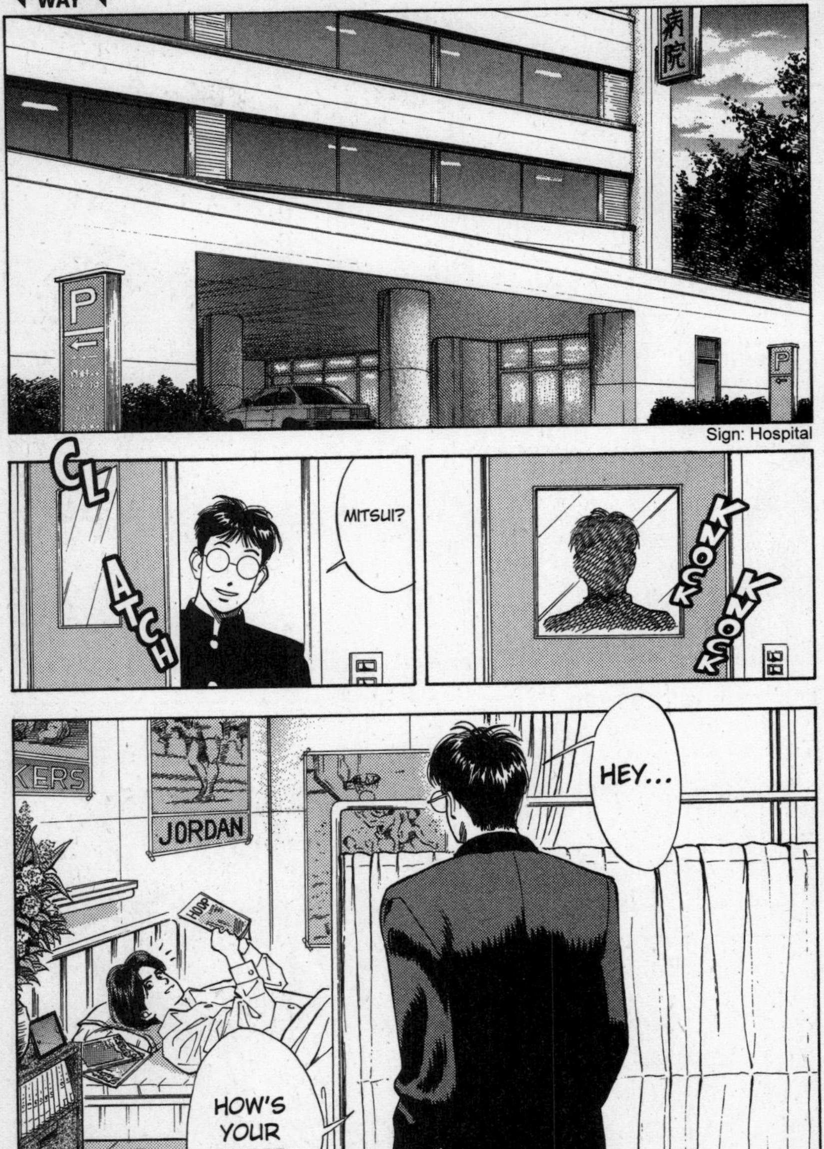
KNOCK
KNOCK
CLATCH
MITSUI?
KERS
JORDAN
HEY...
HOW'S YOUR KNEE?

Sign: Hospital

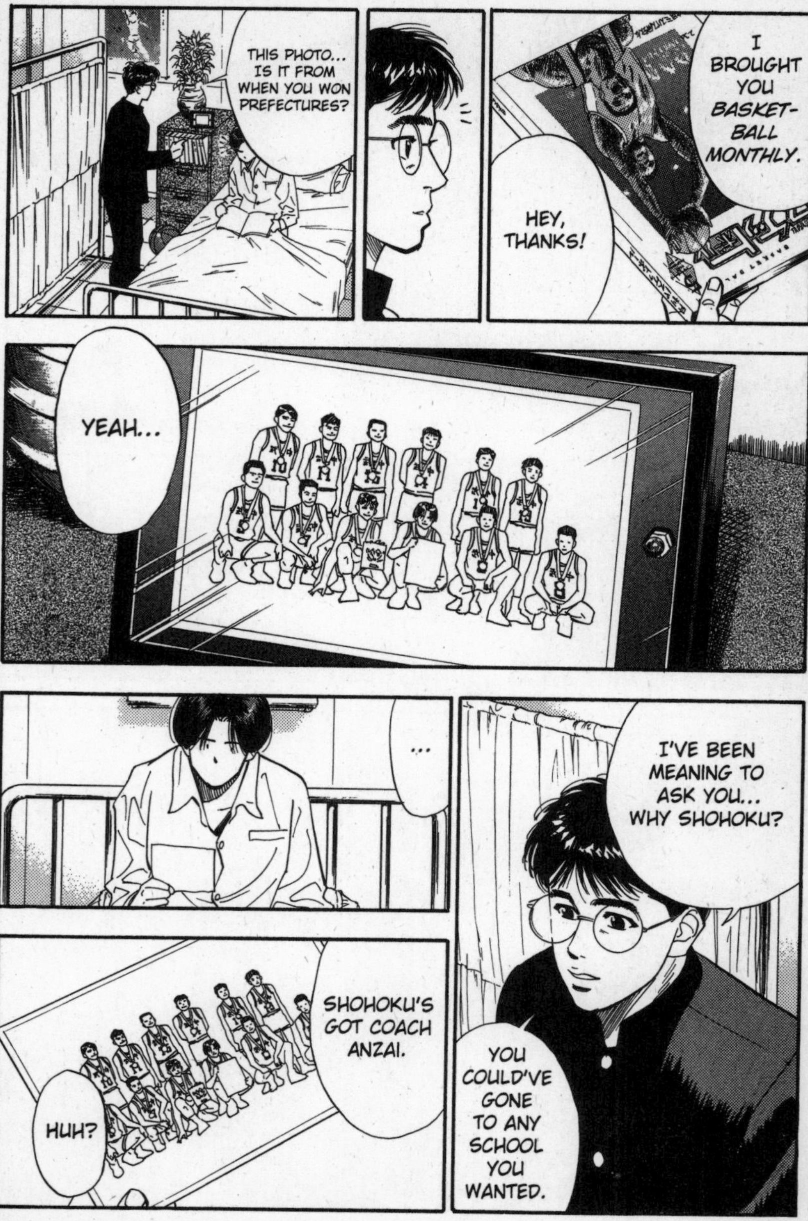
I BROUGHT YOU BASKET-BALL MONTHLY.
HEY, THANKS!
THIS PHOTO... IS IT FROM WHEN YOU WON PREFECTURES?
YEAH...
I'VE BEEN MEANING TO ASK YOU... WHY SHOHOKU?
YOU COULD'VE GONE TO ANY SCHOOL YOU WANTED.
...
SHOHOKU'S GOT COACH ANZAI.
HUH?

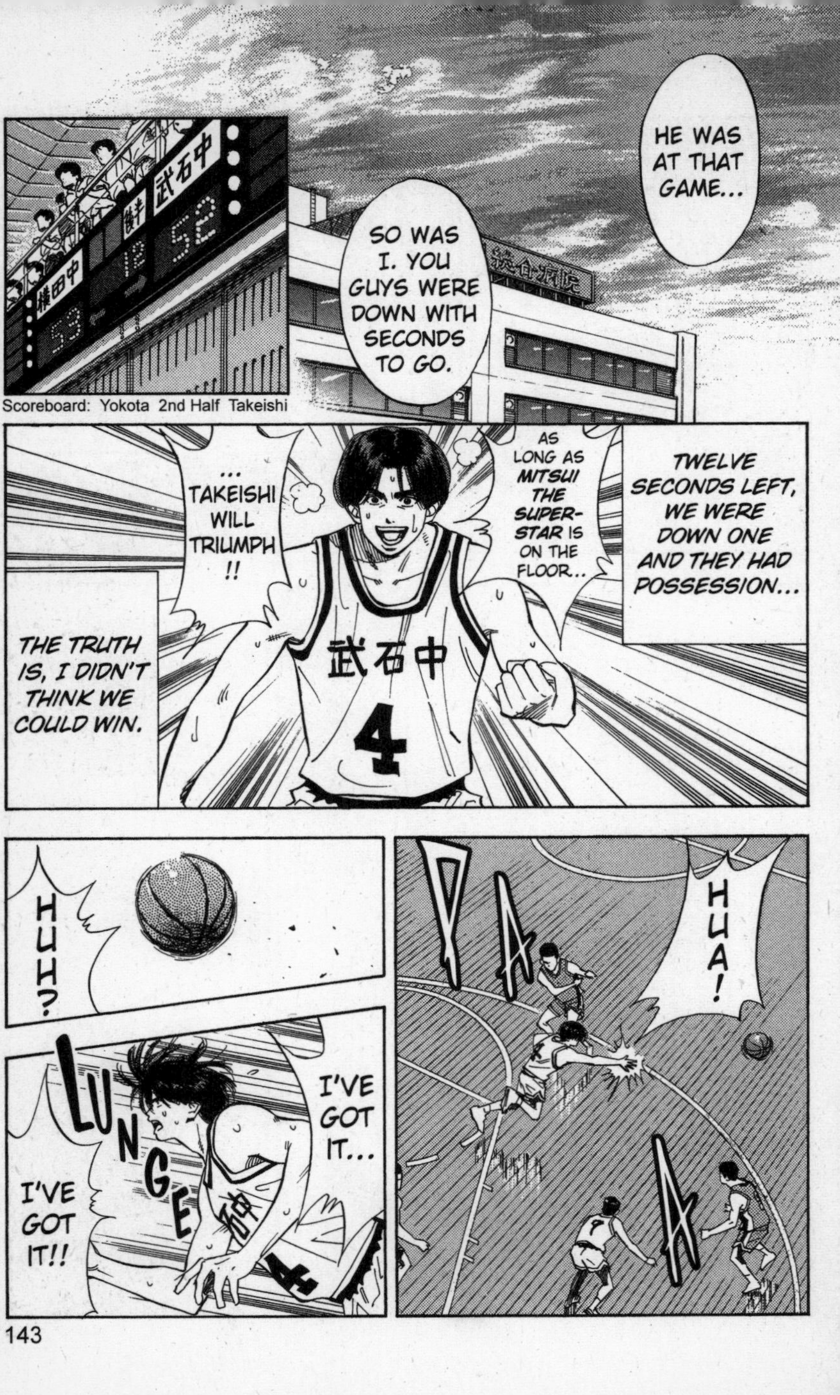
HE WAS AT THAT GAME...
SO WAS I. YOU GUYS WERE DOWN WITH SECONDS TO GO.
Scoreboard: Yokota 2nd Half Takeishi
TWELVE SECONDS LEFT, WE WERE DOWN ONE AND THEY HAD POSSESSION...
AS LONG AS MITSUI THE SUPER-STAR IS ON THE FLOOR...
... TAKEISHI WILL TRIUMPH !!
THE TRUTH IS, I DIDN'T THINK WE COULD WIN.
HUA!
DA
DA
HUH?
LUNGE
I'VE GOT IT...
I'VE GOT IT!!

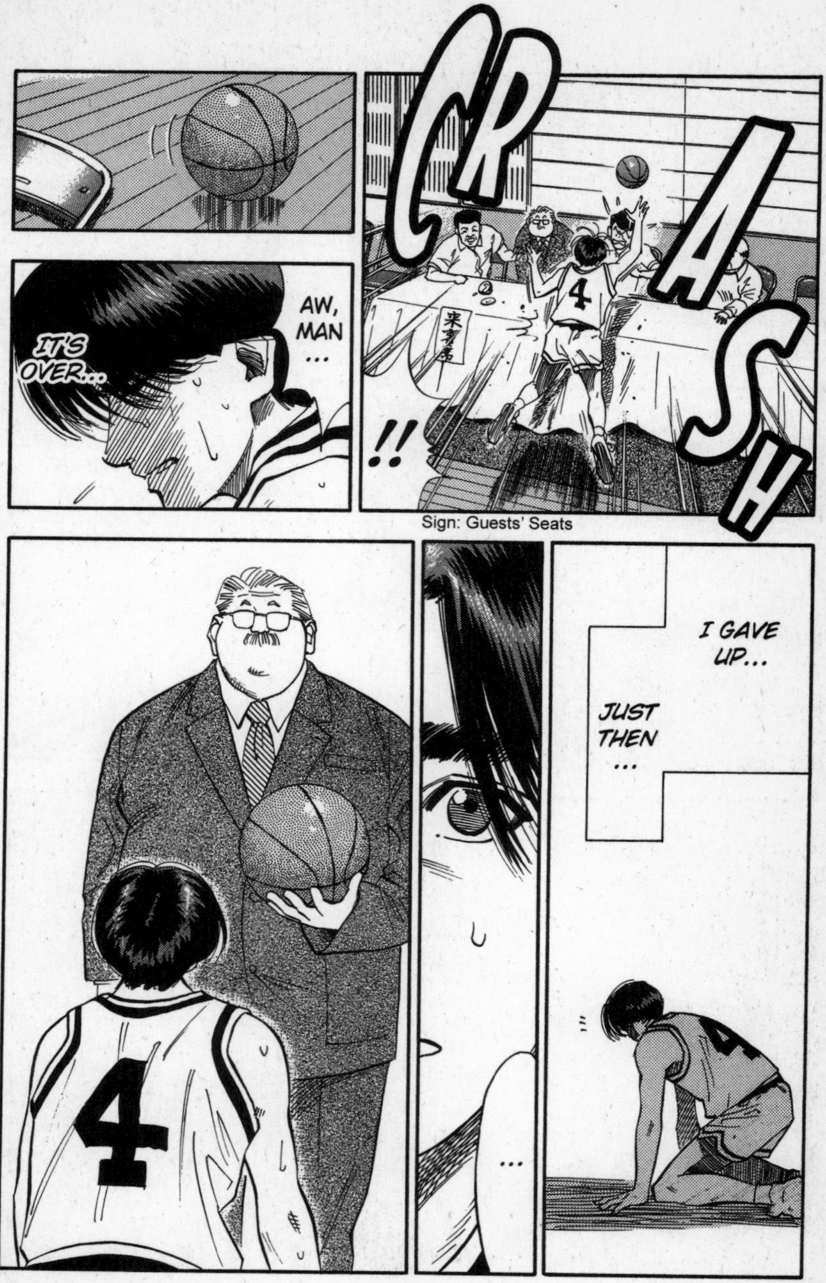
CRASH
!!
AW, MAN ...
IT'S OVER...
I GAVE UP...
JUST THEN ...
...
Sign: Guests' Seats

READ THIS WAY

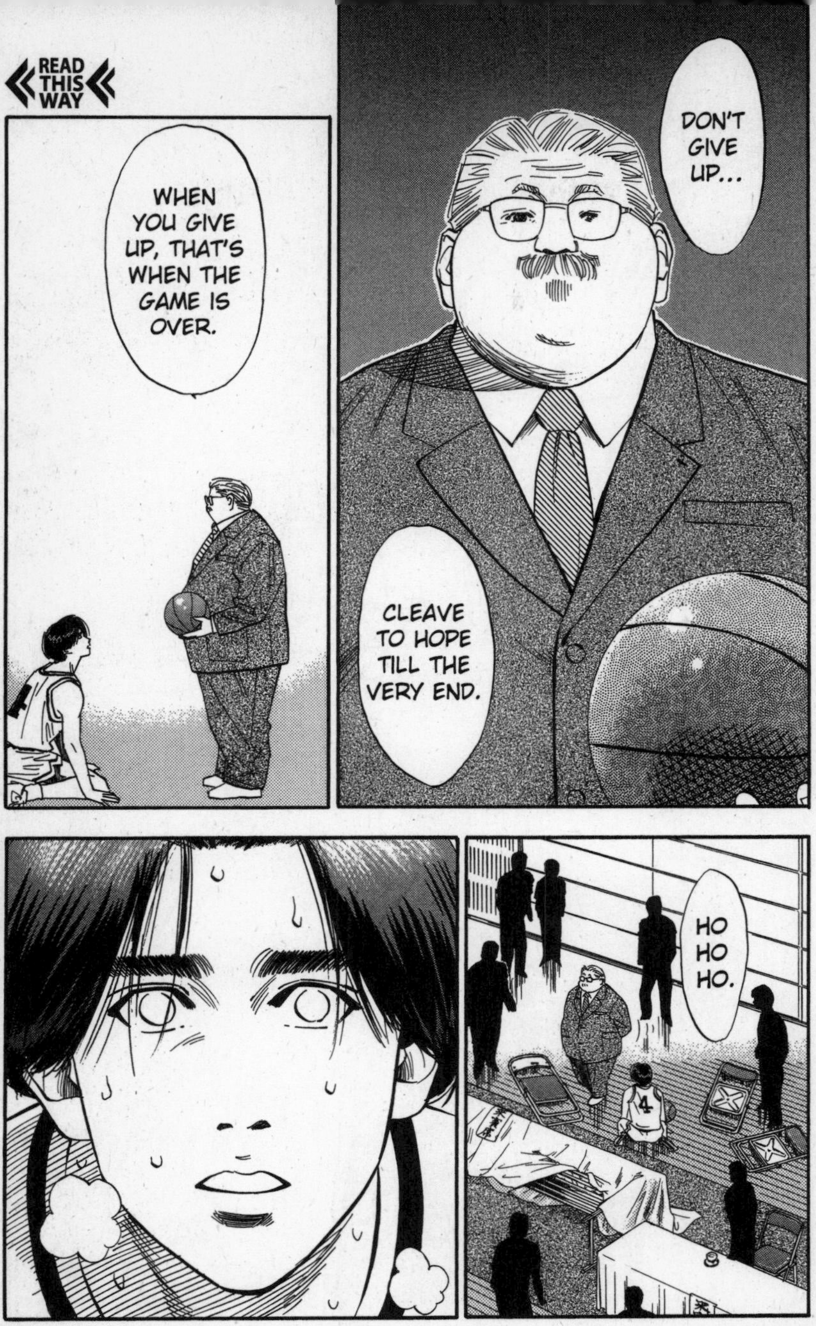
DON'T GIVE UP...
CLEAVE TO HOPE TILL THE VERY END.
WHEN YOU GIVE UP, THAT'S WHEN THE GAME IS OVER.
HO HO HO.

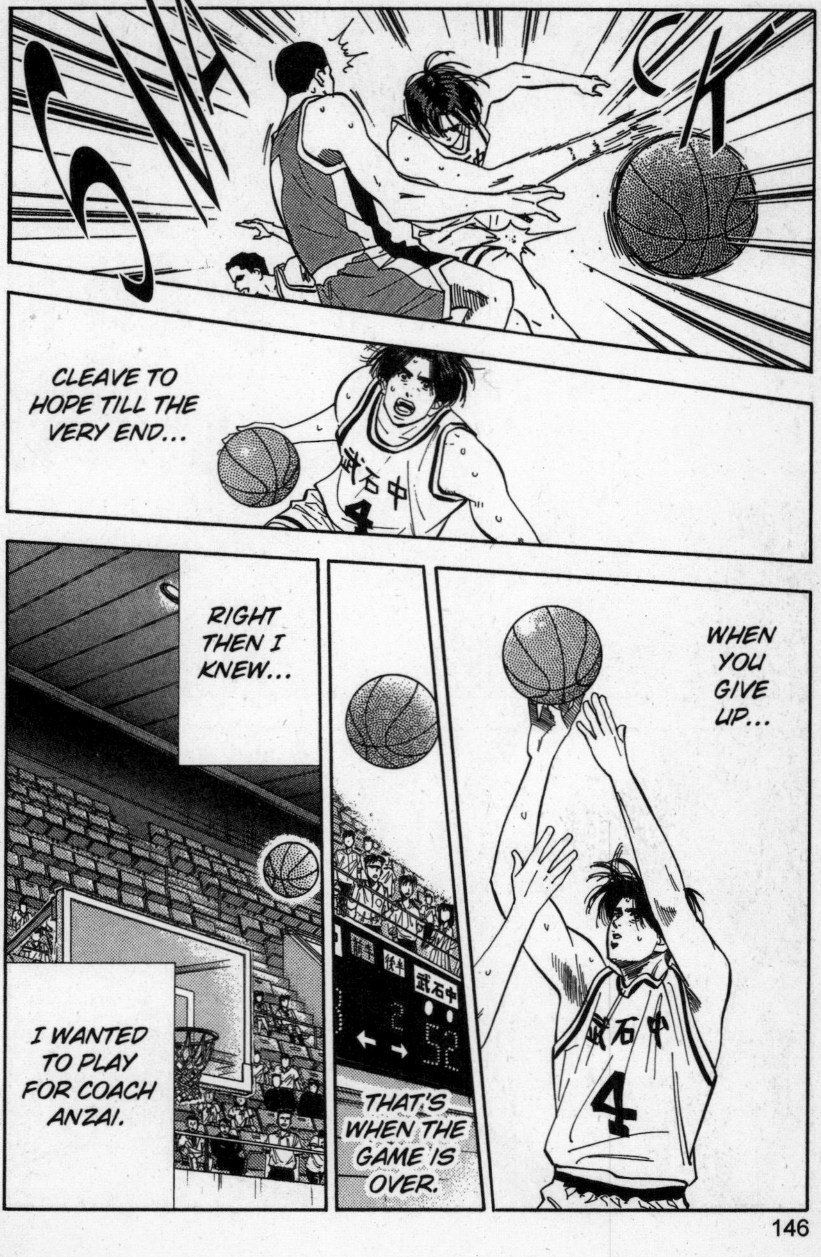
SMACK
CLEAVE TO HOPE TILL THE VERY END...
WHEN YOU GIVE UP...
THAT'S WHEN THE GAME IS OVER.
RIGHT THEN I KNEW...
I WANTED TO PLAY FOR COACH ANZAI.

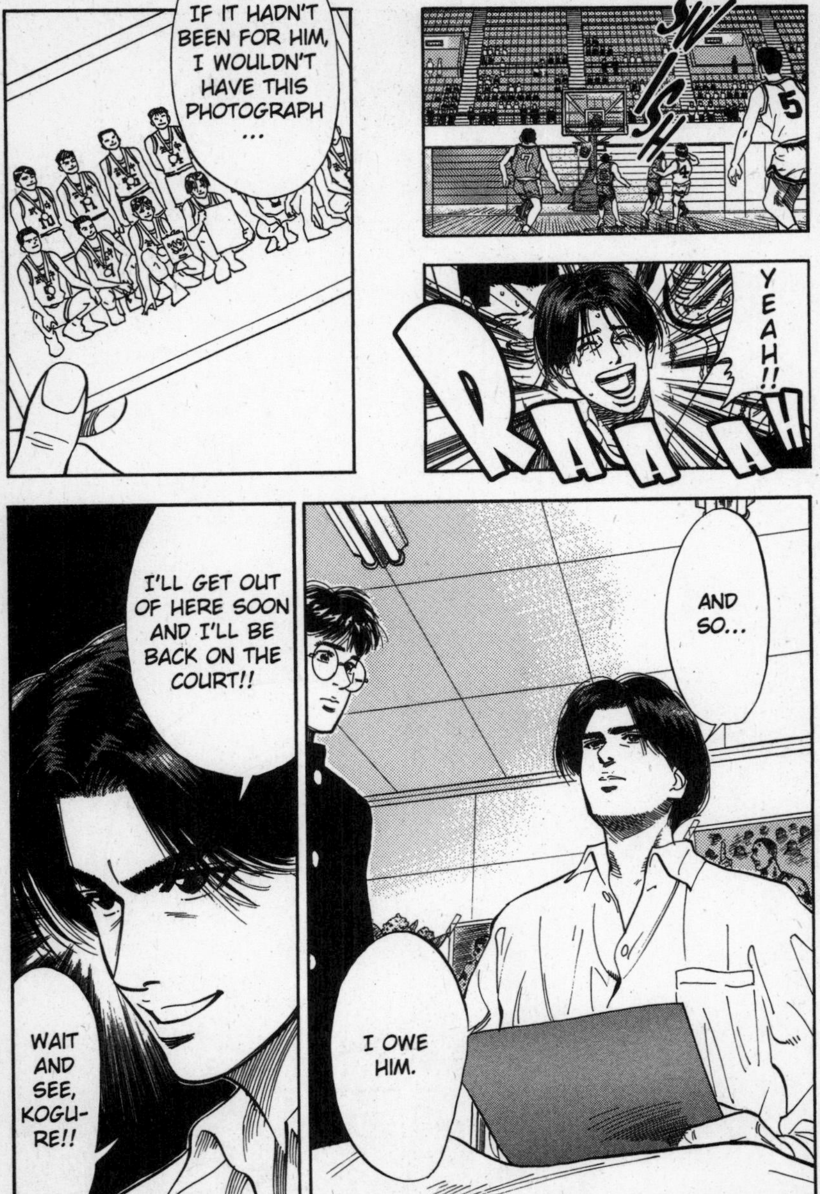
SWISH
YEAH!!
RAAAH
IF IT HADN'T BEEN FOR HIM, I WOULDN'T HAVE THIS PHOTOGRAPH ...
AND SO...
I OWE HIM.
I'LL GET OUT OF HERE SOON AND I'LL BE BACK ON THE COURT!!
WAIT AND SEE, KOGU-RE!!

Hey !!

SLAM DUNK

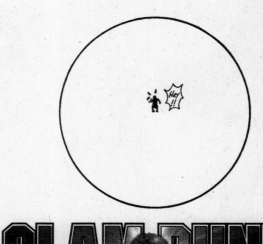

#70 IT DOESN'T HURT

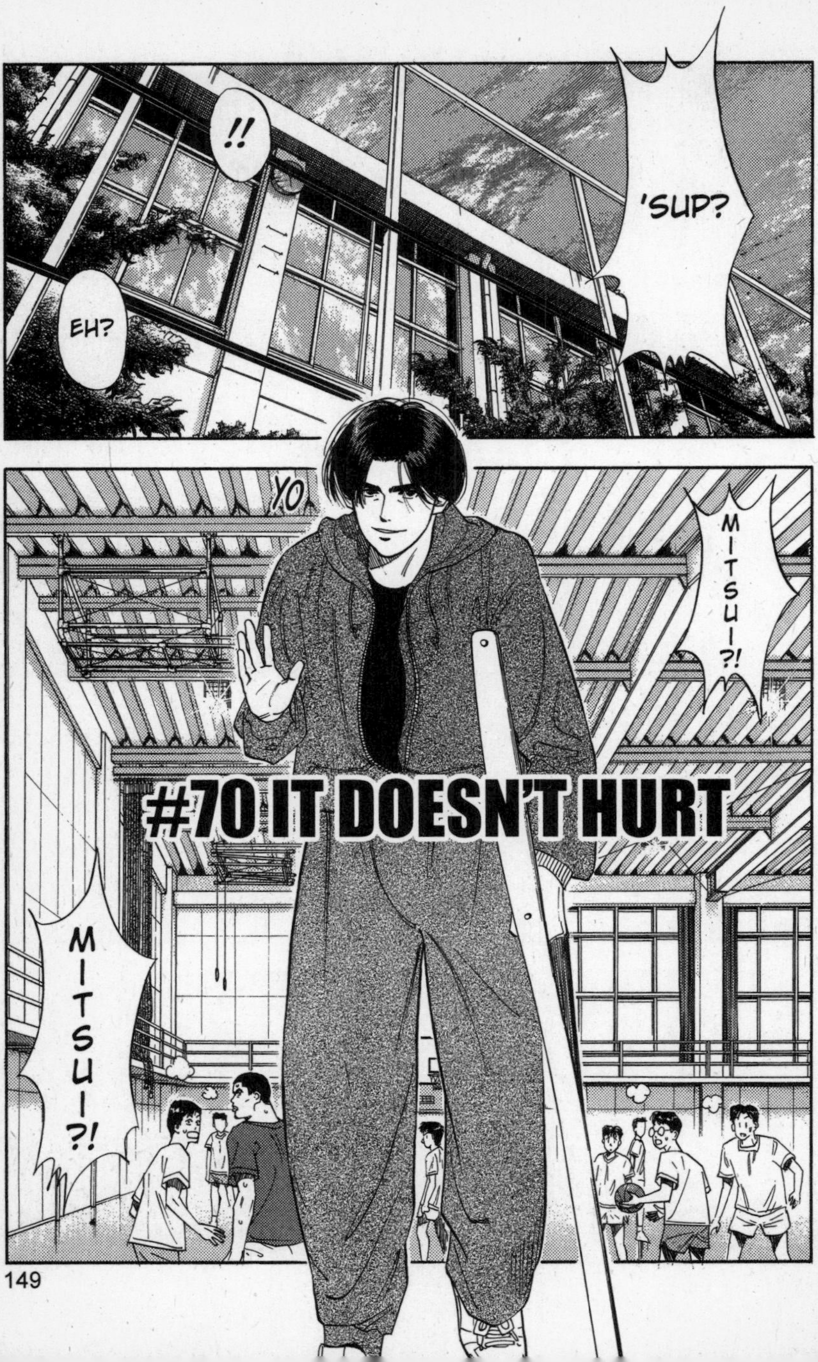
'SUP?
!!
EH?
MITSUI?!
YO
MITSUI?!

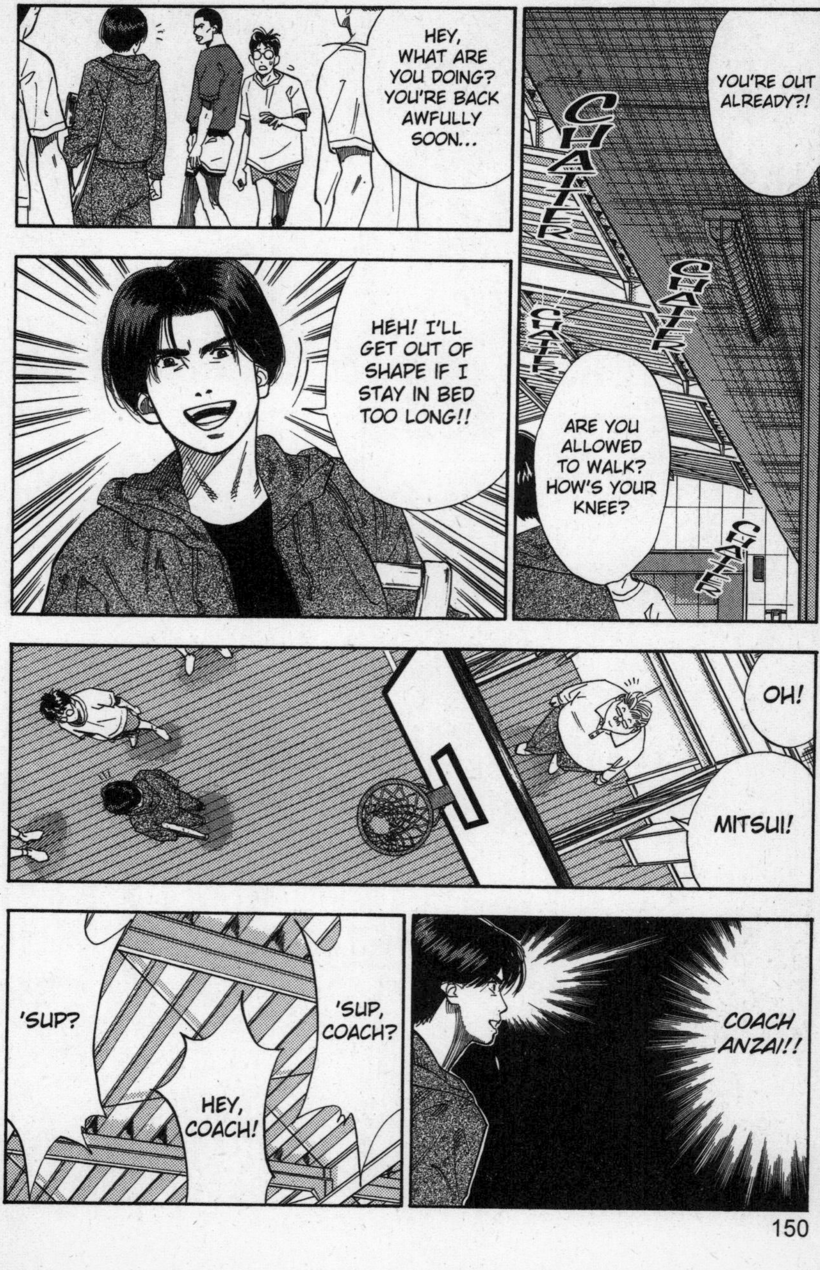
YOU'RE OUT ALREADY?!
CHATTER
CHATTER
CHATTER
ARE YOU ALLOWED TO WALK? HOW'S YOUR KNEE?
CHATTER
HEY, WHAT ARE YOU DOING? YOU'RE BACK AWFULLY SOON...
HEH! I'LL GET OUT OF SHAPE IF I STAY IN BED TOO LONG!!
OH!
MITSUI!
COACH ANZAI!!
'SUP, COACH?
'SUP?
HEY, COACH!

READ THIS WAY

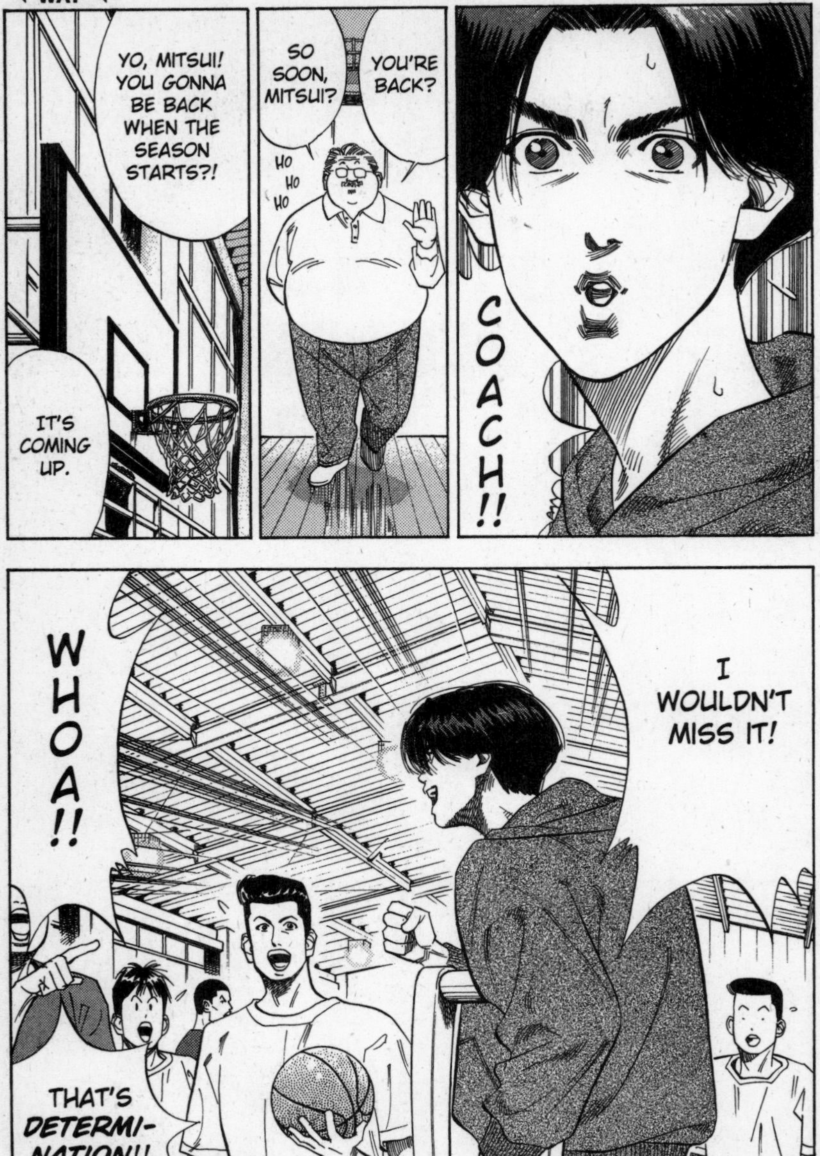
COACH!!
YOU'RE BACK?
SO SOON, MITSUI?
HO HO HO
YO, MITSUI! YOU GONNA BE BACK WHEN THE SEASON STARTS?!
IT'S COMING UP.
I WOULDN'T MISS IT!
WHOA!!
THAT'S DETERMINATION!!

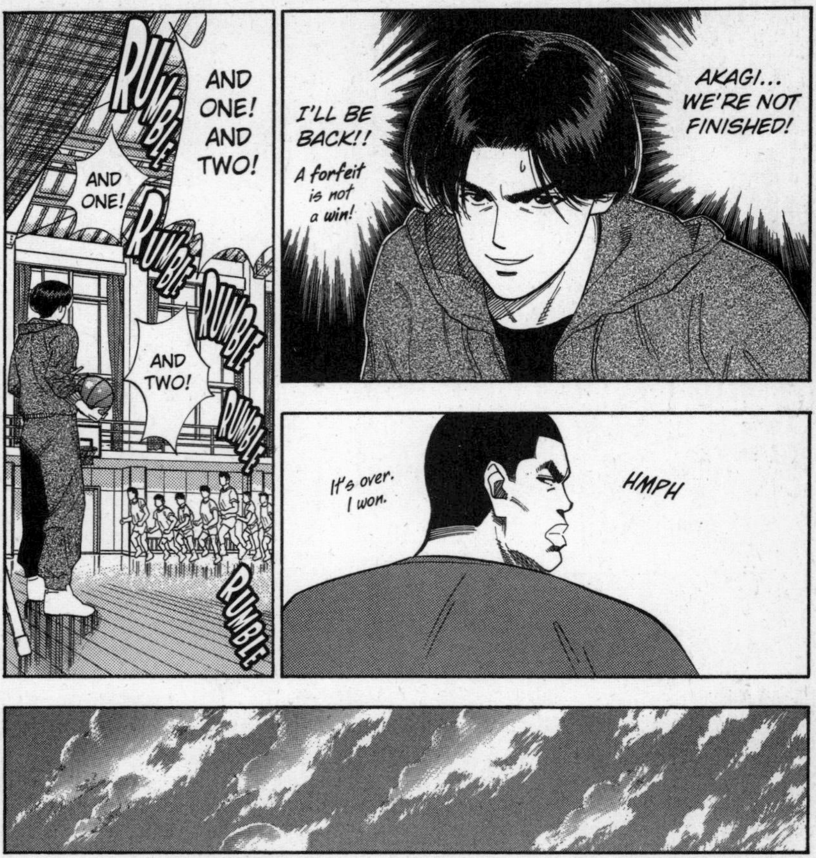
AKAGI... WE'RE NOT FINISHED!
I'LL BE BACK!!
A forfeit is not a win!
HMPH
It's over. I won.
AND ONE! AND TWO!
AND ONE!
AND TWO!
RUMBLE
RUMBLE
RUMBLE
RUMBLE
RUMBLE

Sign: Hisashi Mitsui

Sign: Noguchi General Hospital

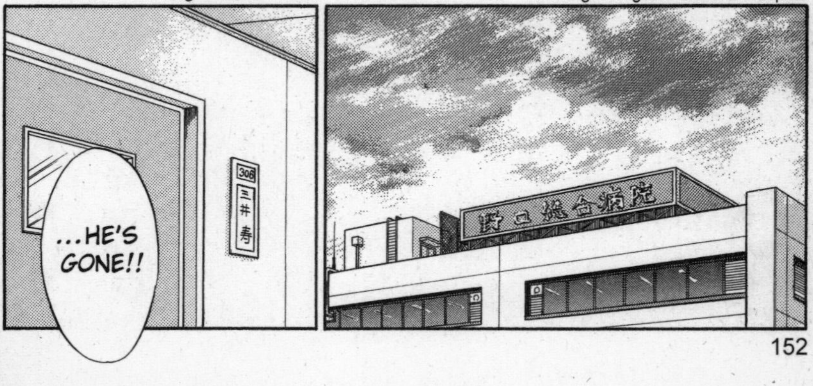
...HE'S GONE!!

READ THIS WAY

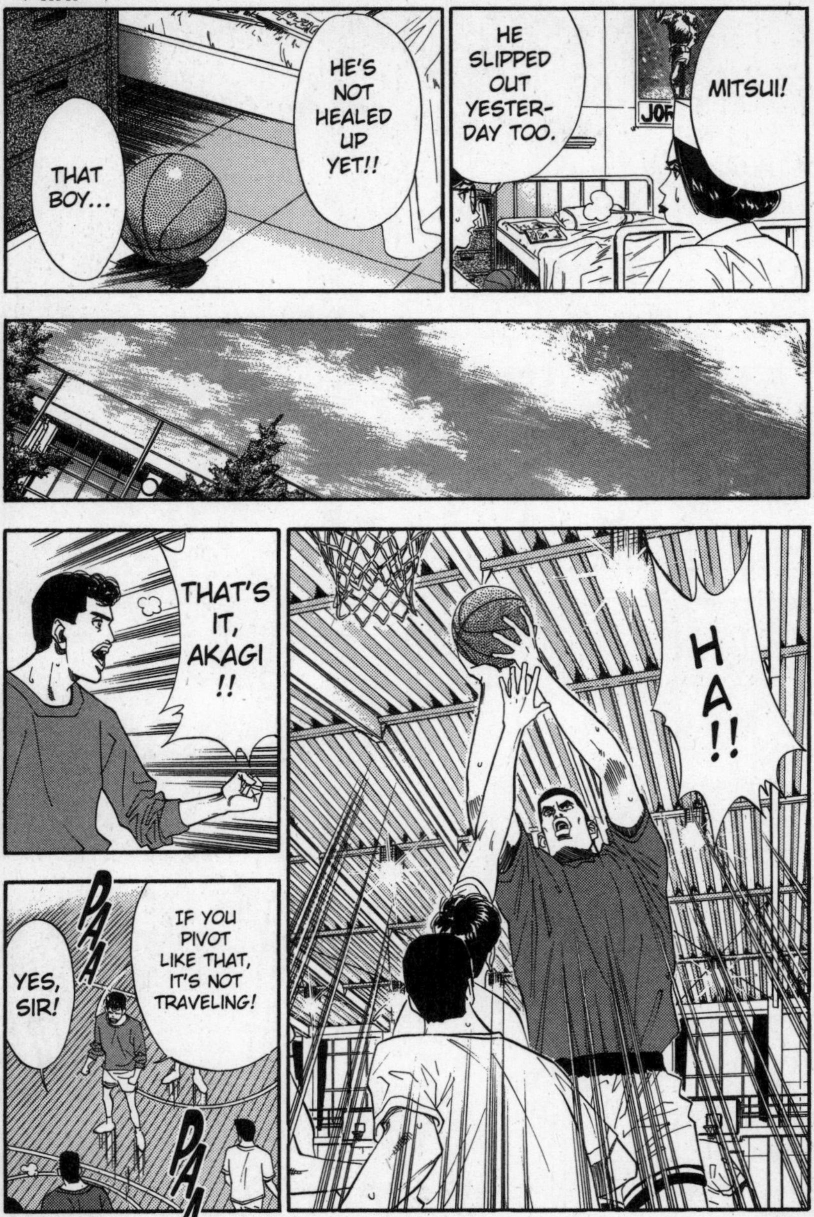
MITSUI!
HE SLIPPED OUT YESTER-DAY TOO.
HE'S NOT HEALED UP YET!!
THAT BOY...
HA!!
THAT'S IT, AKAGI!!
IF YOU PIVOT LIKE THAT, IT'S NOT TRAVELING!
YES, SIR!
PAA
PAA

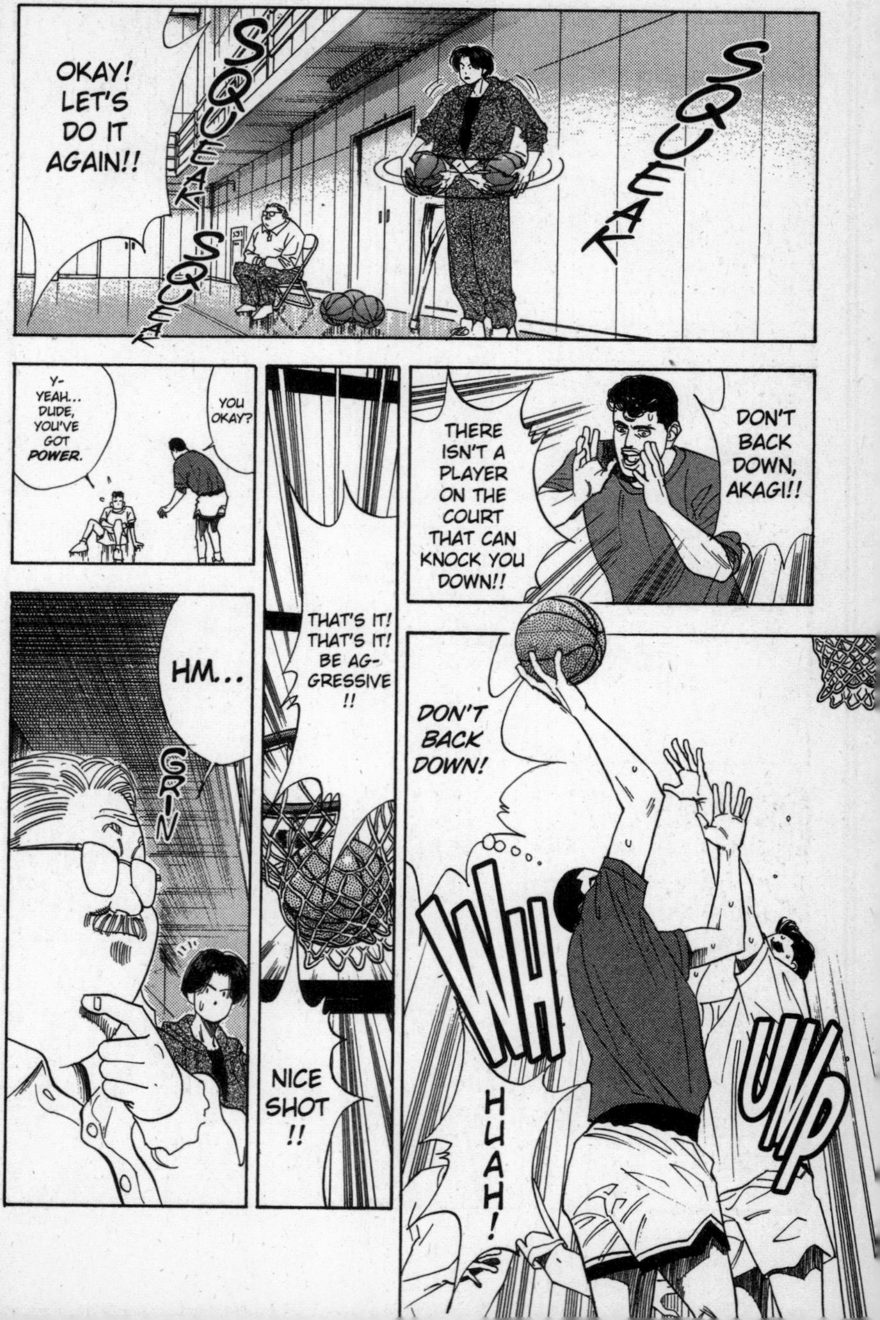
SQUEAK
OKAY! LET'S DO IT AGAIN!!
SQUEAK
SQUEAK
DON'T BACK DOWN, AKAGI!!
THERE ISN'T A PLAYER ON THE COURT THAT CAN KNOCK YOU DOWN!!
DON'T BACK DOWN!
WHUP
HUAH!
THAT'S IT! THAT'S IT! BE AG-GRESSIVE!!
NICE SHOT!!
YOU OKAY?
Y-YEAH... DUDE, YOU'VE GOT POWER.
HM...
GRIN

READ THIS WAY

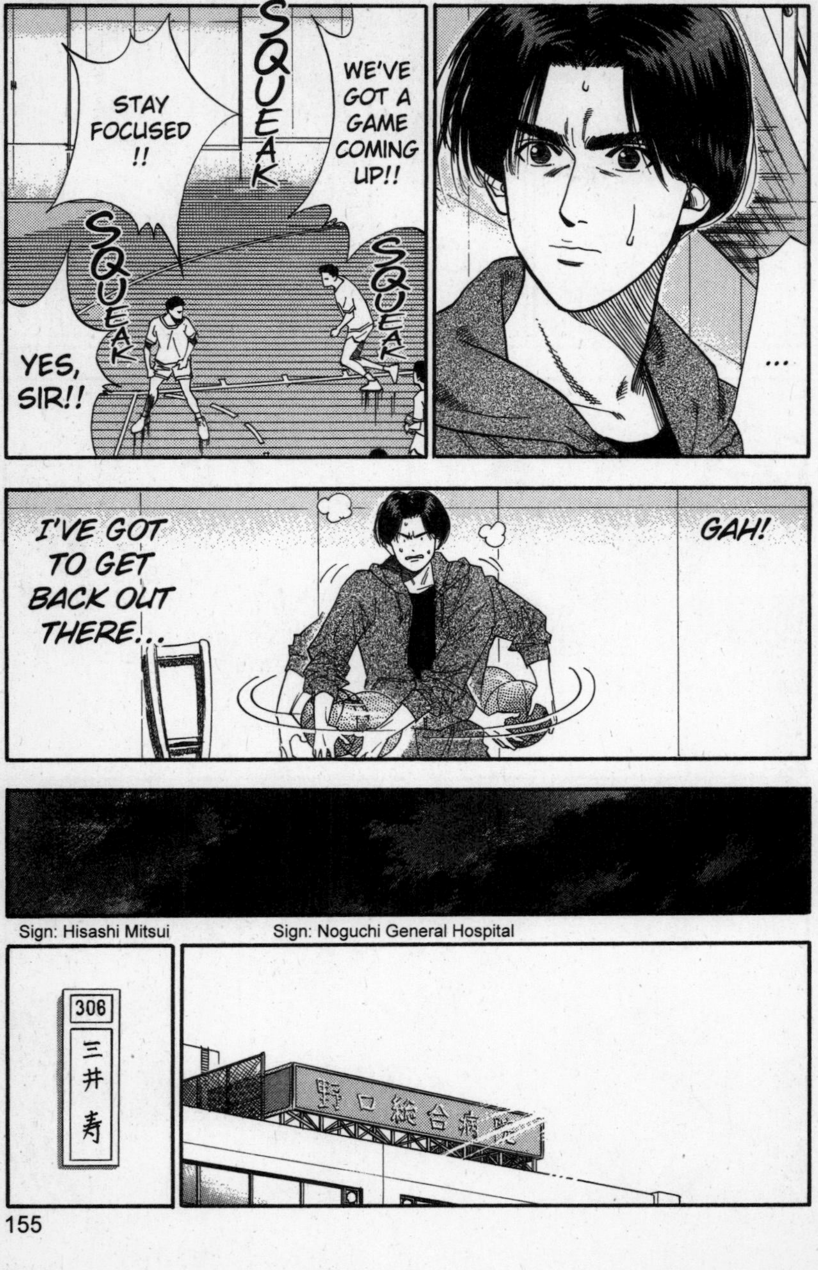
...
WE'VE GOT A GAME COMING UP!!
SQUEAK
STAY FOCUSED!!
SQUEAK
SQUEAK
YES, SIR!!
GAH!
I'VE GOT TO GET BACK OUT THERE...
Sign: Noguchi General Hospital
野口総合病
Sign: Hisashi Mitsui
306
三井 寿

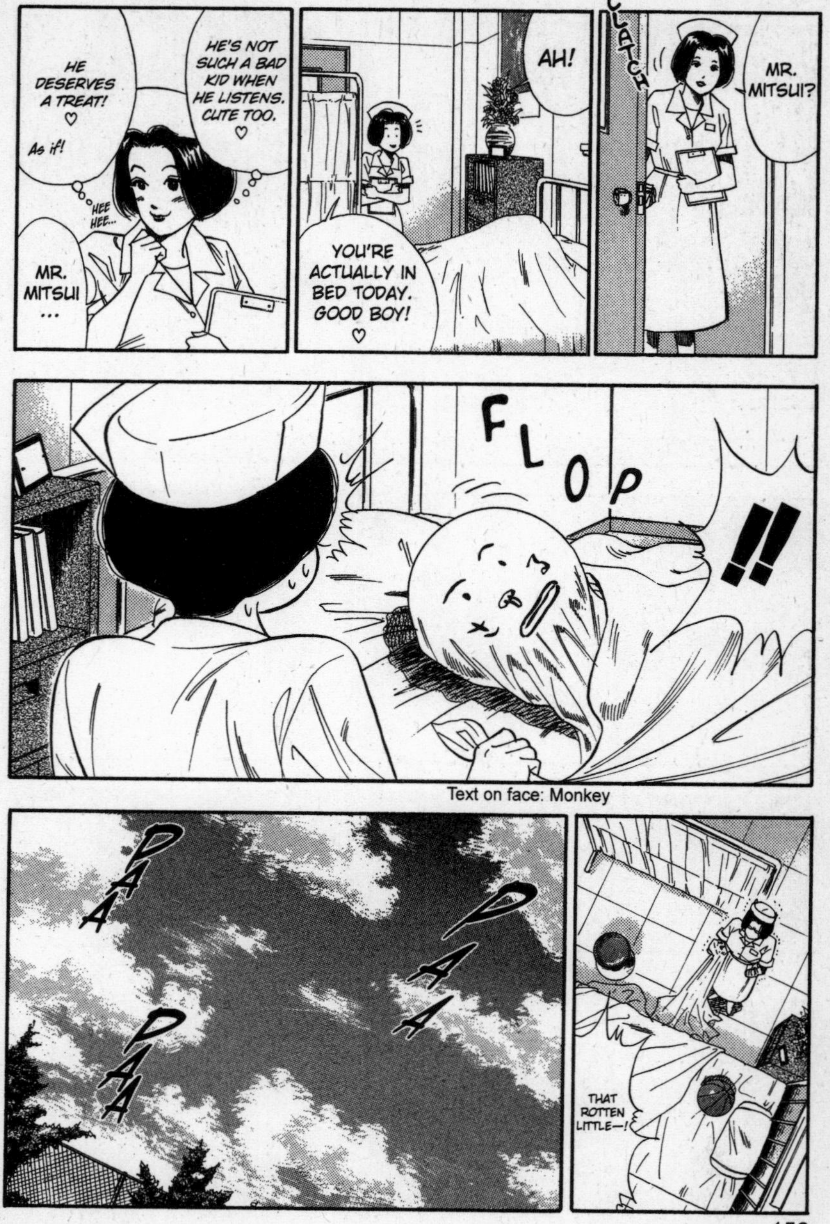
CLATCH
MR. MITSUI?
AH!
YOU'RE ACTUALLY IN BED TODAY. GOOD BOY! ♡
HE'S NOT SUCH A BAD KID WHEN HE LISTENS. CUTE TOO. ♡
HE DESERVES A TREAT! ♡
As if!
HEE HEE...
MR. MITSUI ...
FLOP
!!
THAT ROTTEN LITTLE—!
PAA
PAA
PAA

Text on face: Monkey

READ THIS WAY

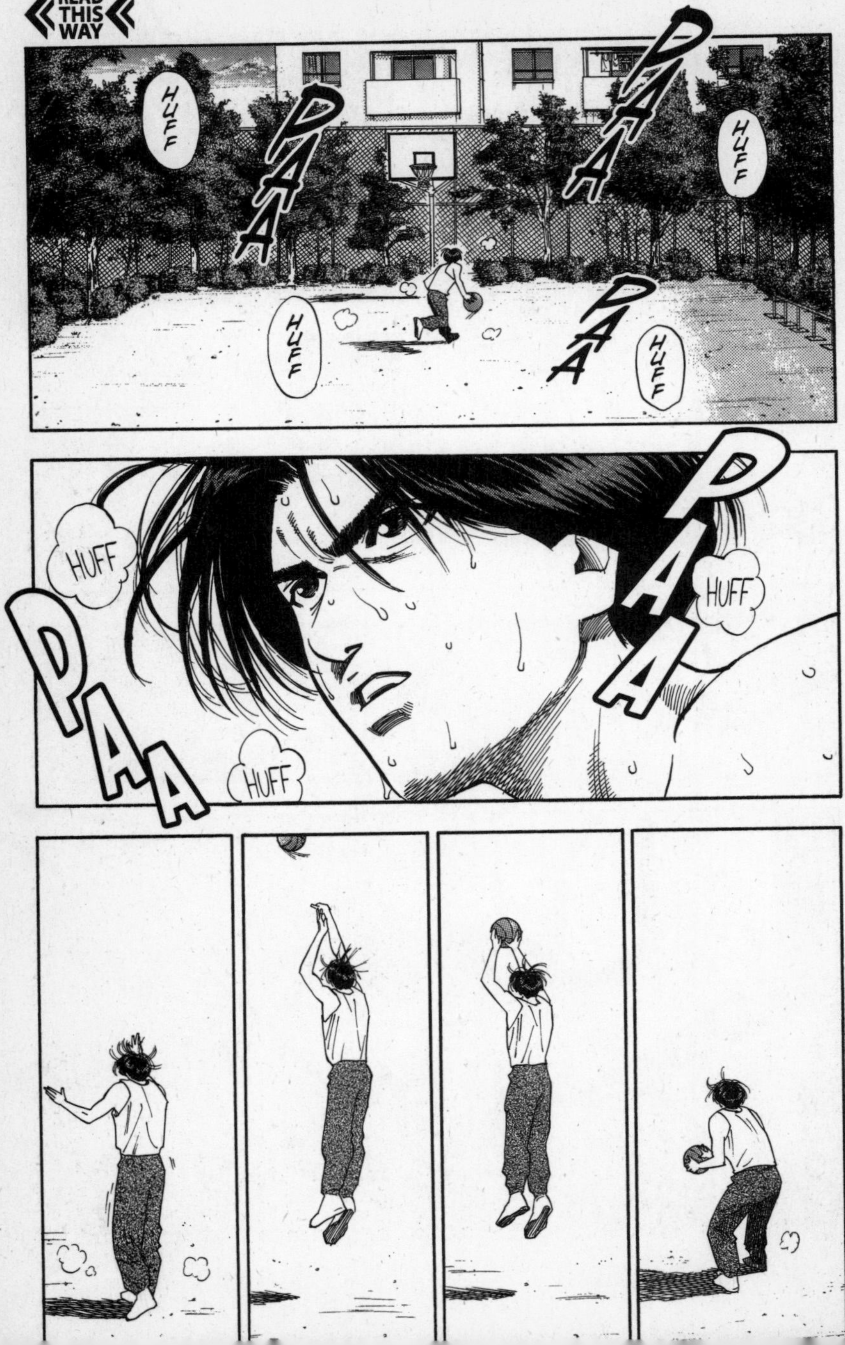
PAAA
HUFF
PAA
HUFF
HUFF
PAAA
HUFF
PAAA
HUFF
HUFF
PAAA
HUFF

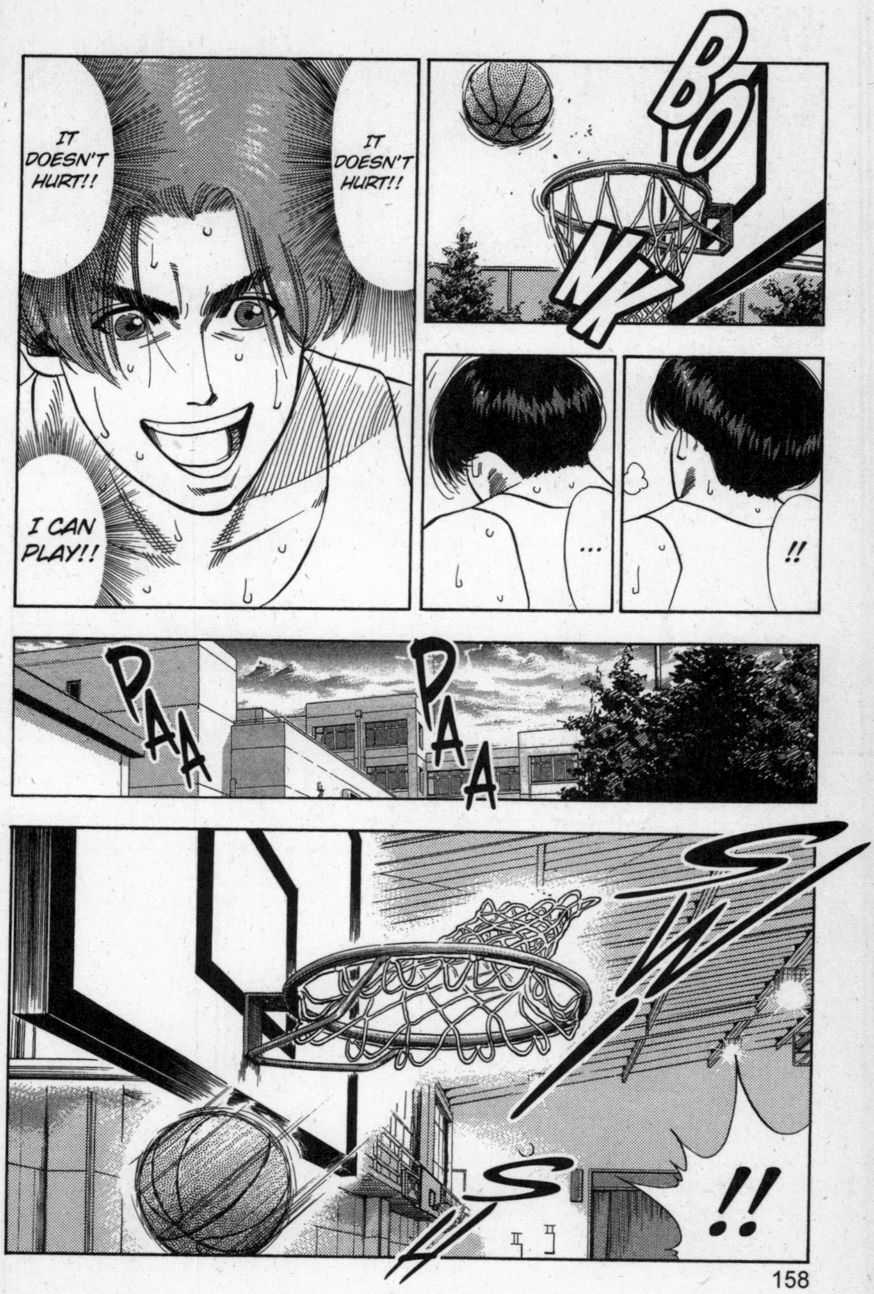
BONK
!!
...
IT DOESN'T HURT!!
IT DOESN'T HURT!!
I CAN PLAY!!
PAA
PAA
SWISH
!!

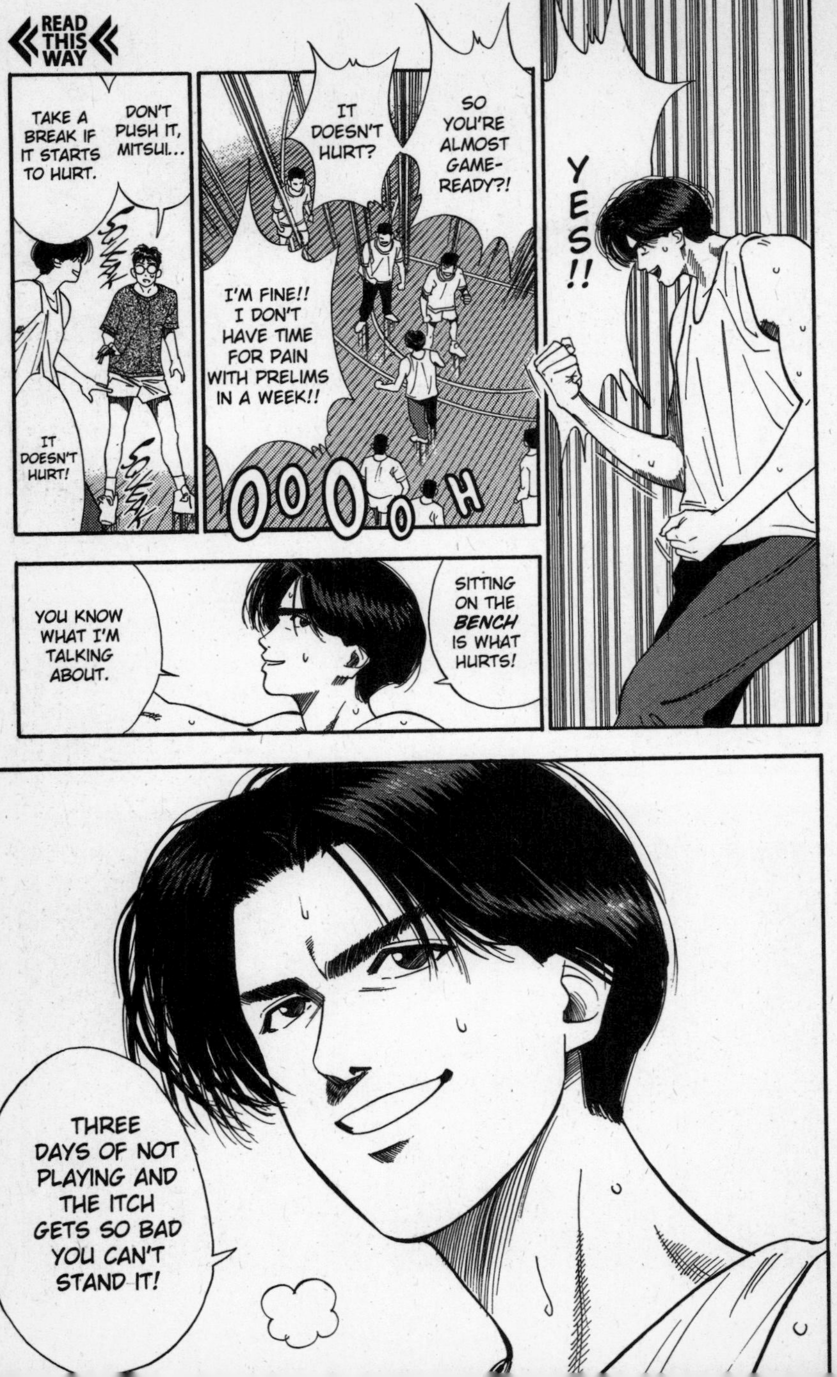
READ THIS WAY
YES!!
SO YOU'RE ALMOST GAME-READY?!
IT DOESN'T HURT?
I'M FINE!! I DON'T HAVE TIME FOR PAIN WITH PRELIMS IN A WEEK!!
OOOOoH
DON'T PUSH IT, MITSUI...
TAKE A BREAK IF IT STARTS TO HURT.
IT DOESN'T HURT!
SITTING ON THE *BENCH* IS WHAT HURTS!
YOU KNOW WHAT I'M TALKING ABOUT.
THREE DAYS OF NOT PLAYING AND THE ITCH GETS SO BAD YOU CAN'T STAND IT!

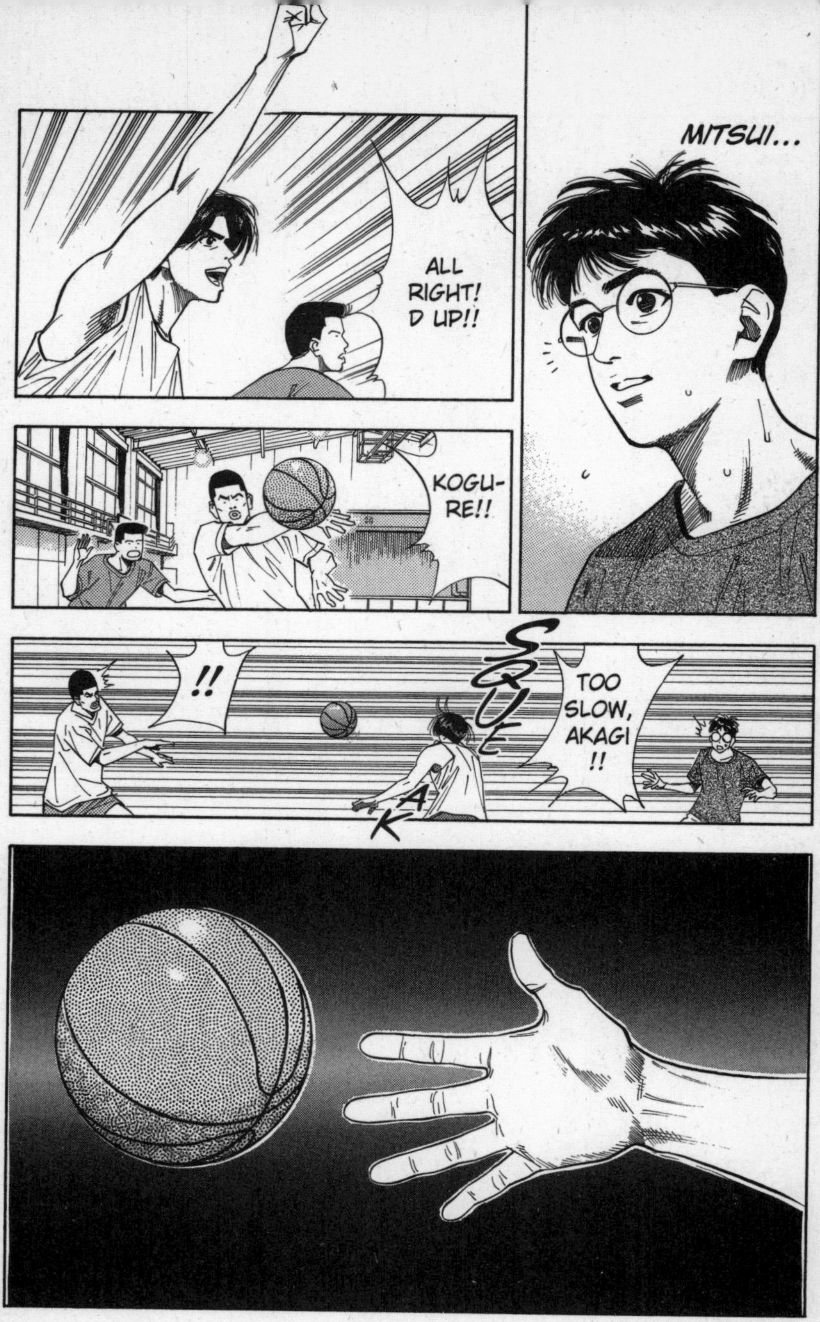
MITSUI...
ALL RIGHT! D UP!!
KOGURE!!
TOO SLOW, AKAGI!!
SQUEAK
!!

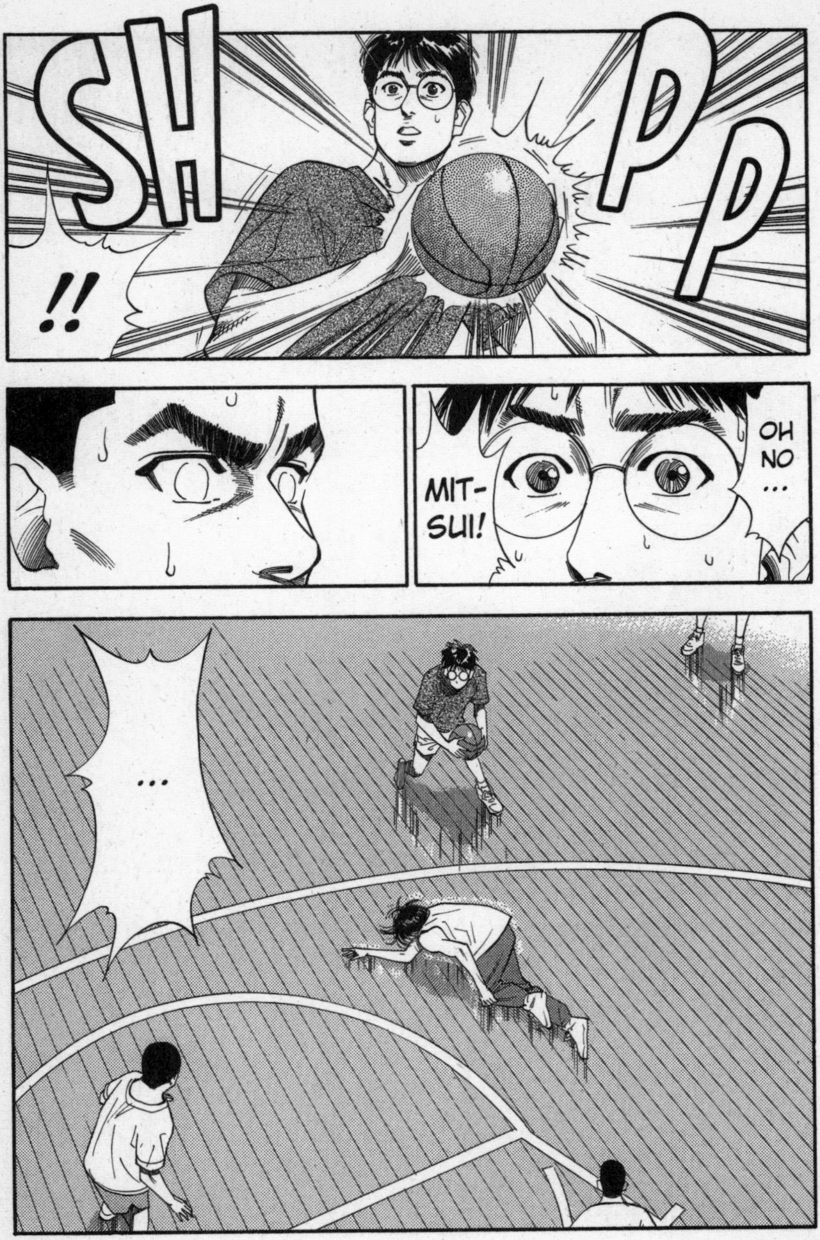
SHPP
!!
OH NO ...
MIT-SUI!
...

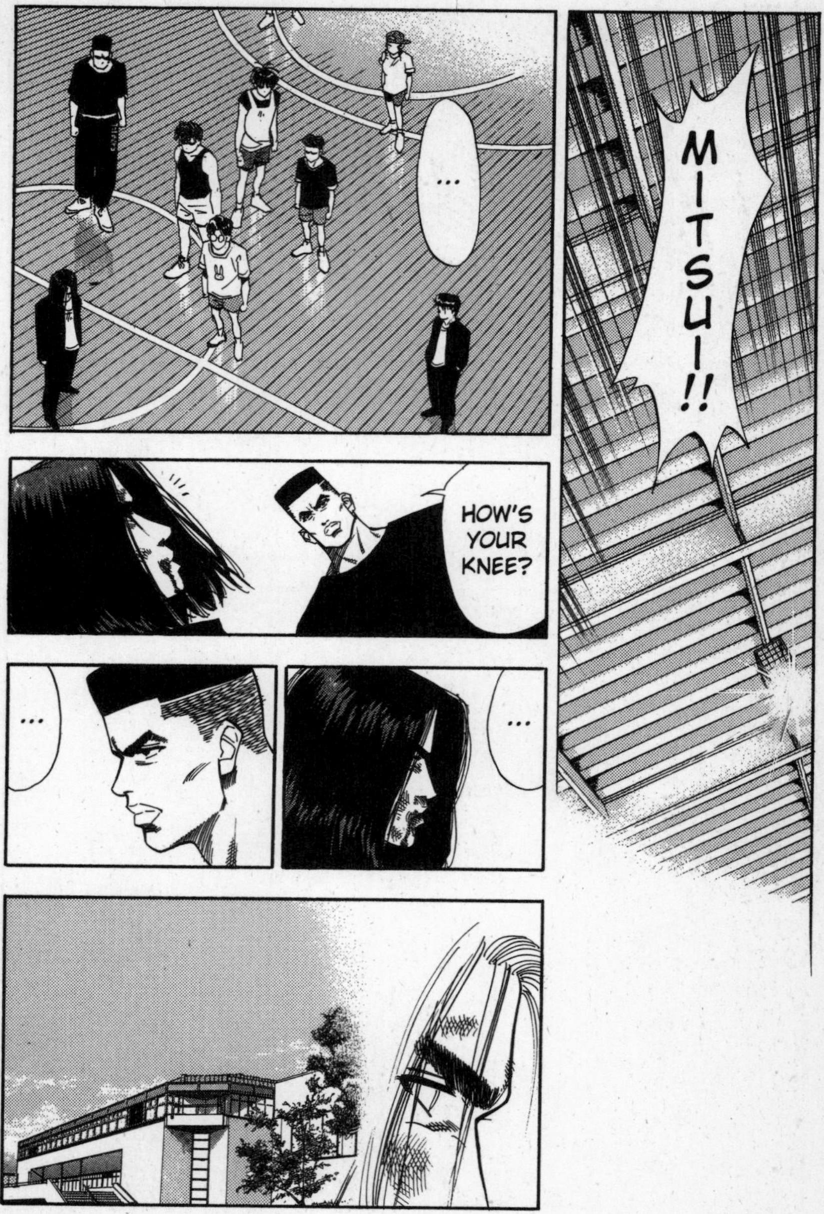
MITSUI!!
...
HOW'S YOUR KNEE?
...
...

READ THIS WAY

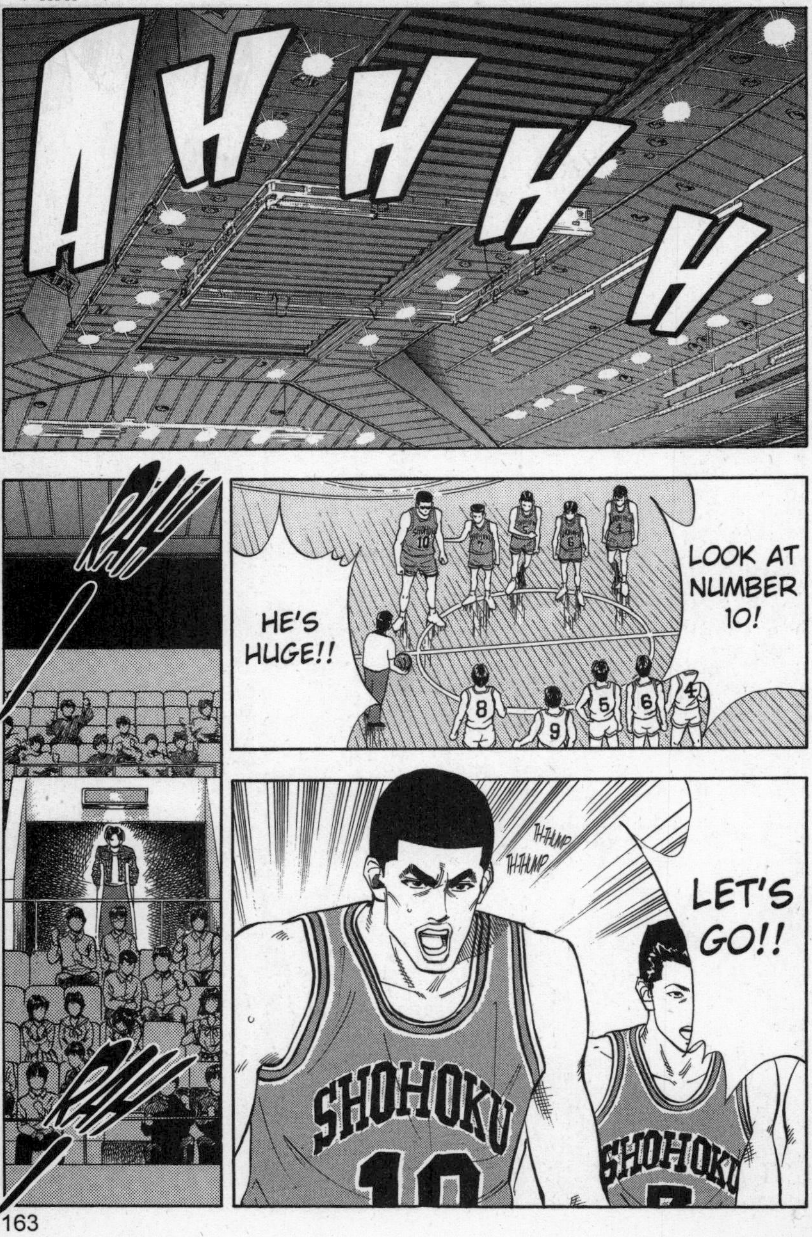

AHHHHH
LOOK AT NUMBER 10!
HE'S HUGE!!
RAH
TH-THUMP
TH-THUMP
LET'S GO!!
RAH

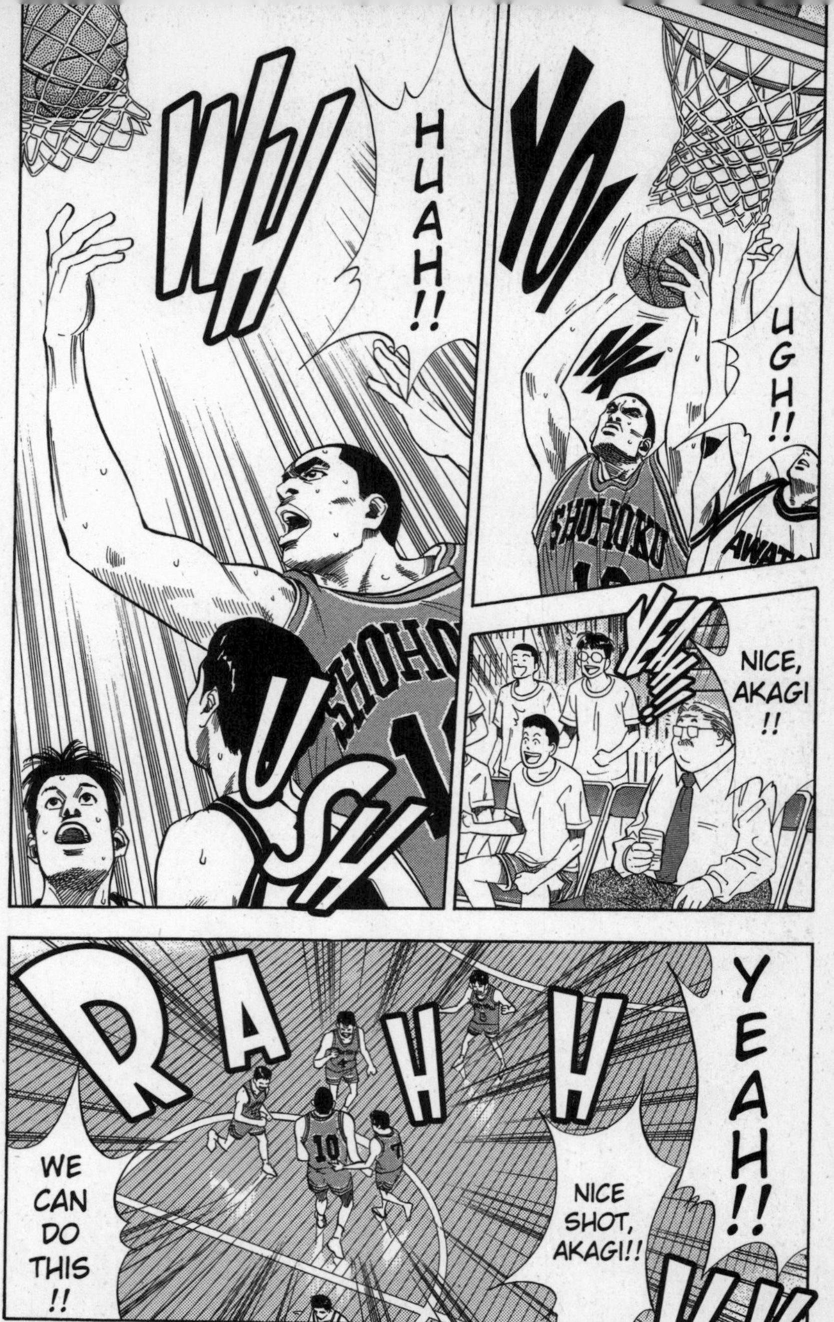
UGH!!
NICE, AKAGI !!
HUAH!!
YEAH!!
NICE SHOT, AKAGI!!
WE CAN DO THIS !!

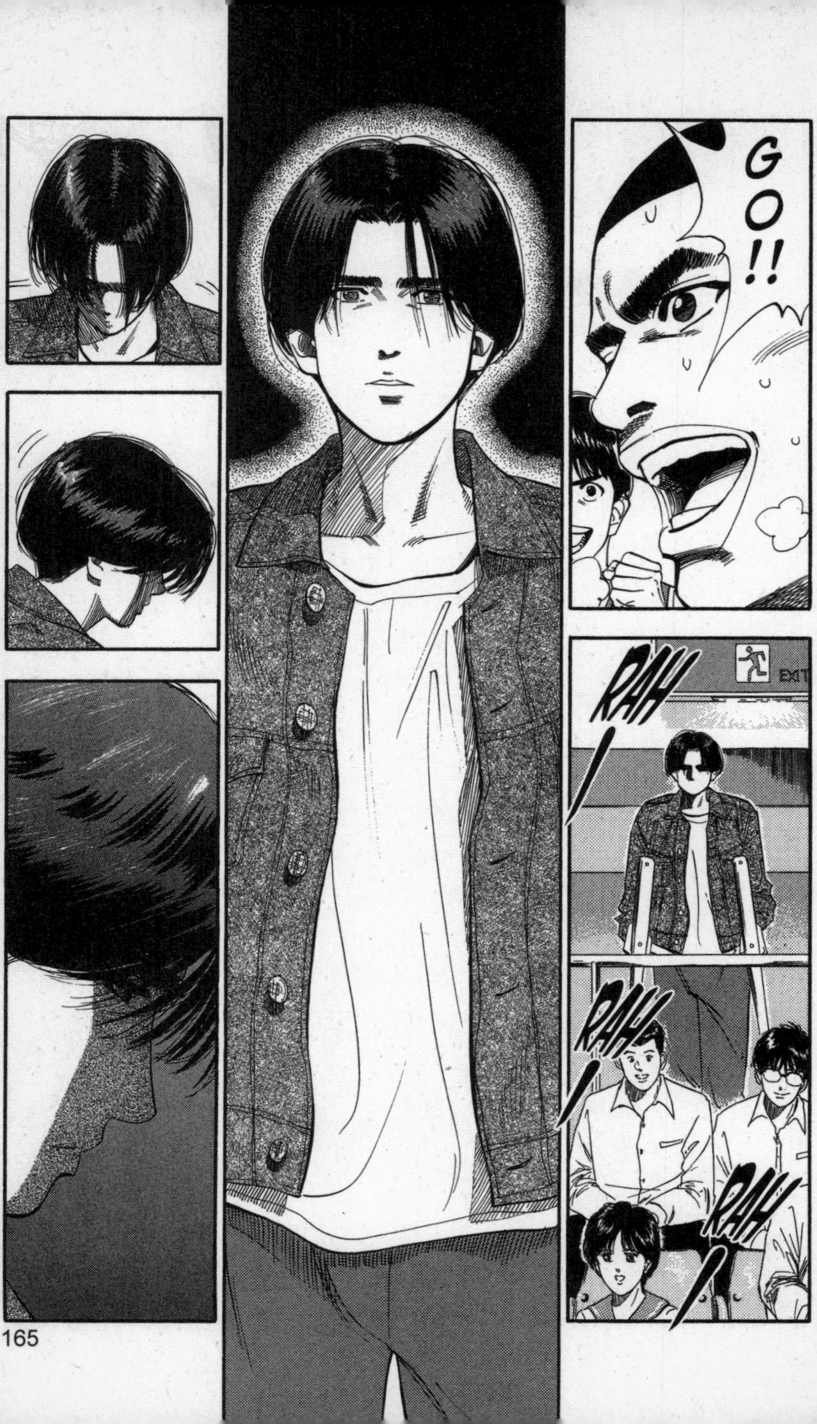
GO!!
RAH
RAH
RAH

RAH

RAH

RAH

RAH

THAT'S WHERE THE STORY ENDS...

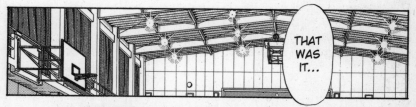

THAT WAS IT...

MITSUI...

...

HE NEVER CAME BACK.

READ THIS WAY

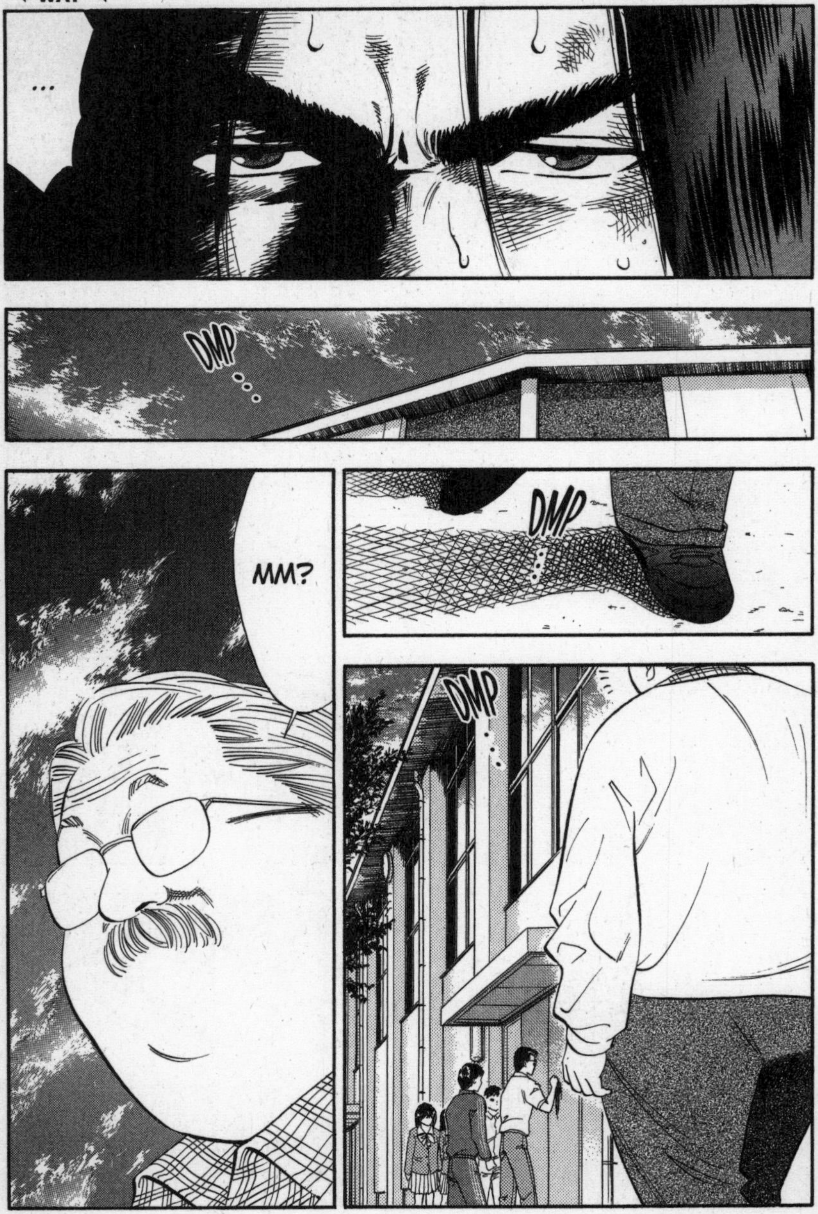
...
DMP...
DMP
DMP
MM?

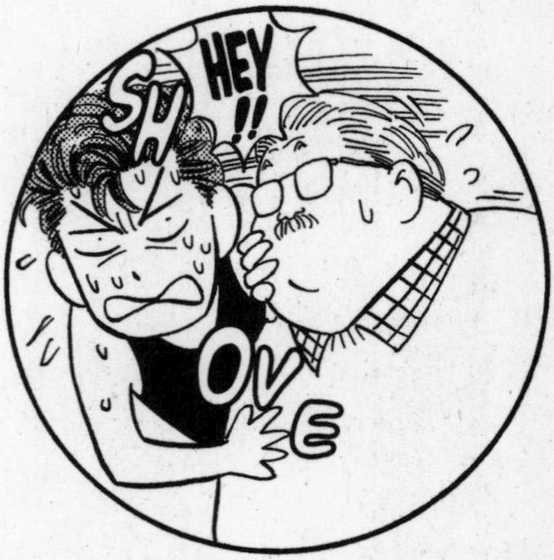
HEY !!
SHOVE

SLAM DUNK

#71 BASKETBALL

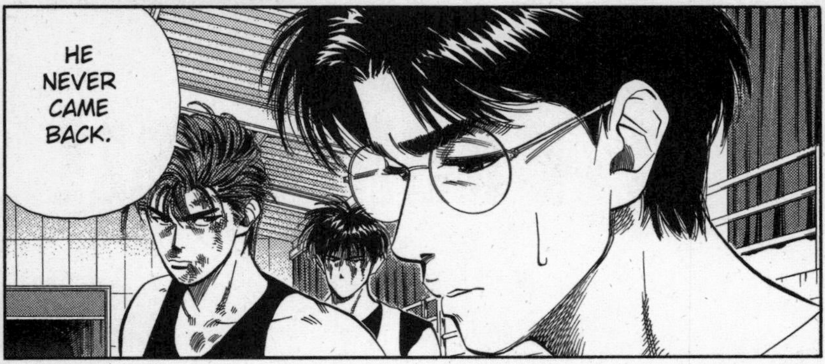
HE NEVER CAME BACK.

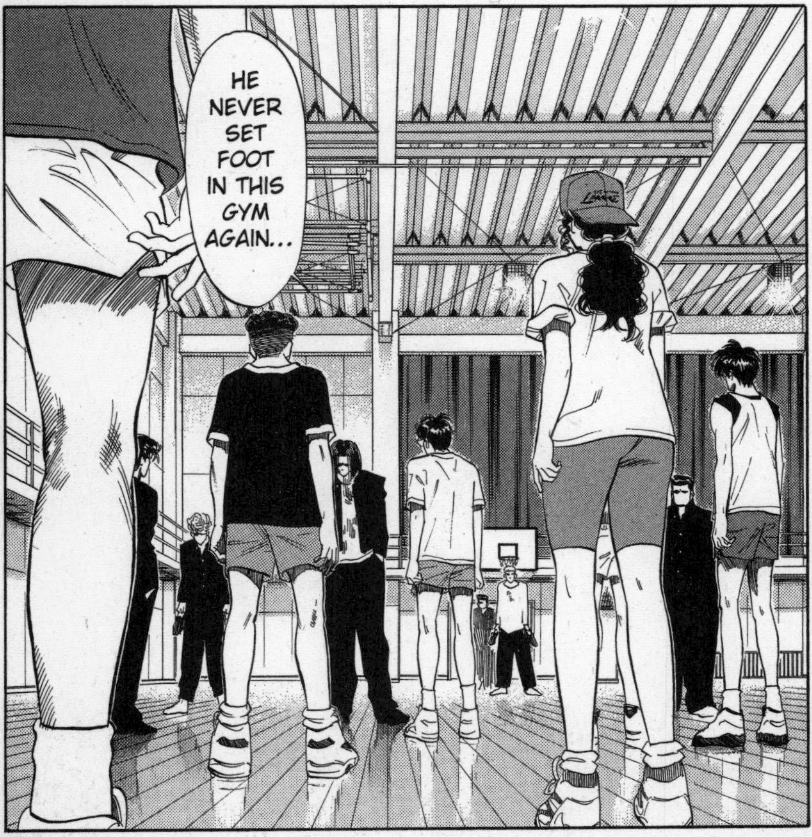
HE NEVER SET FOOT IN THIS GYM AGAIN...

#71 BASKETBALL

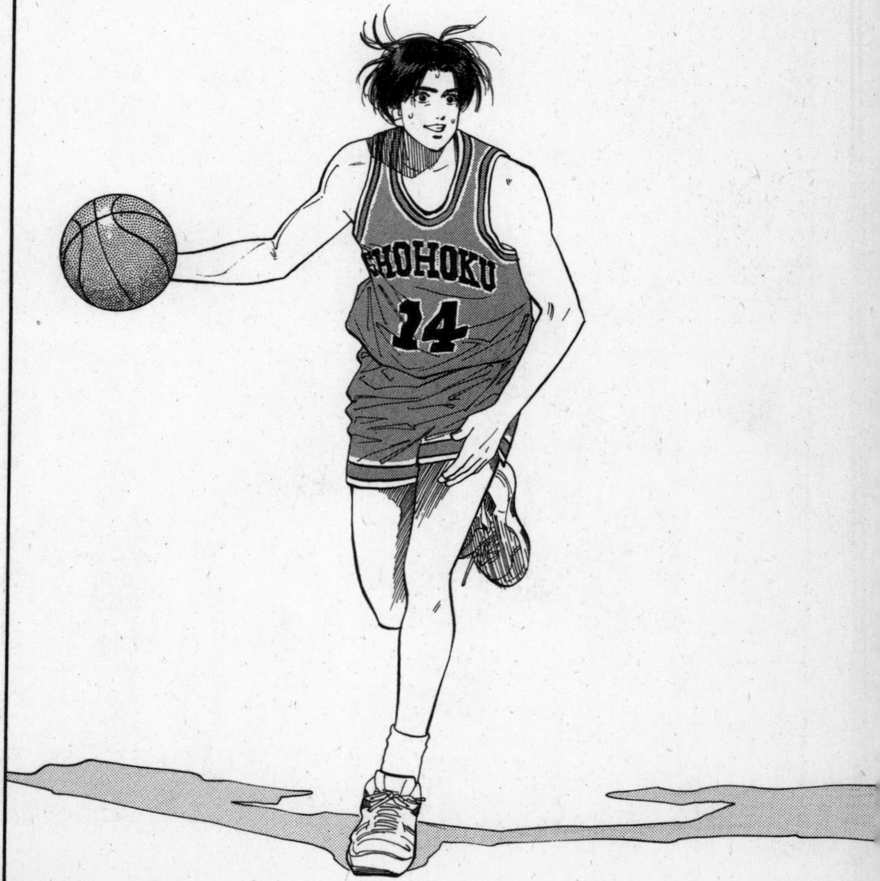

READ THIS WAY

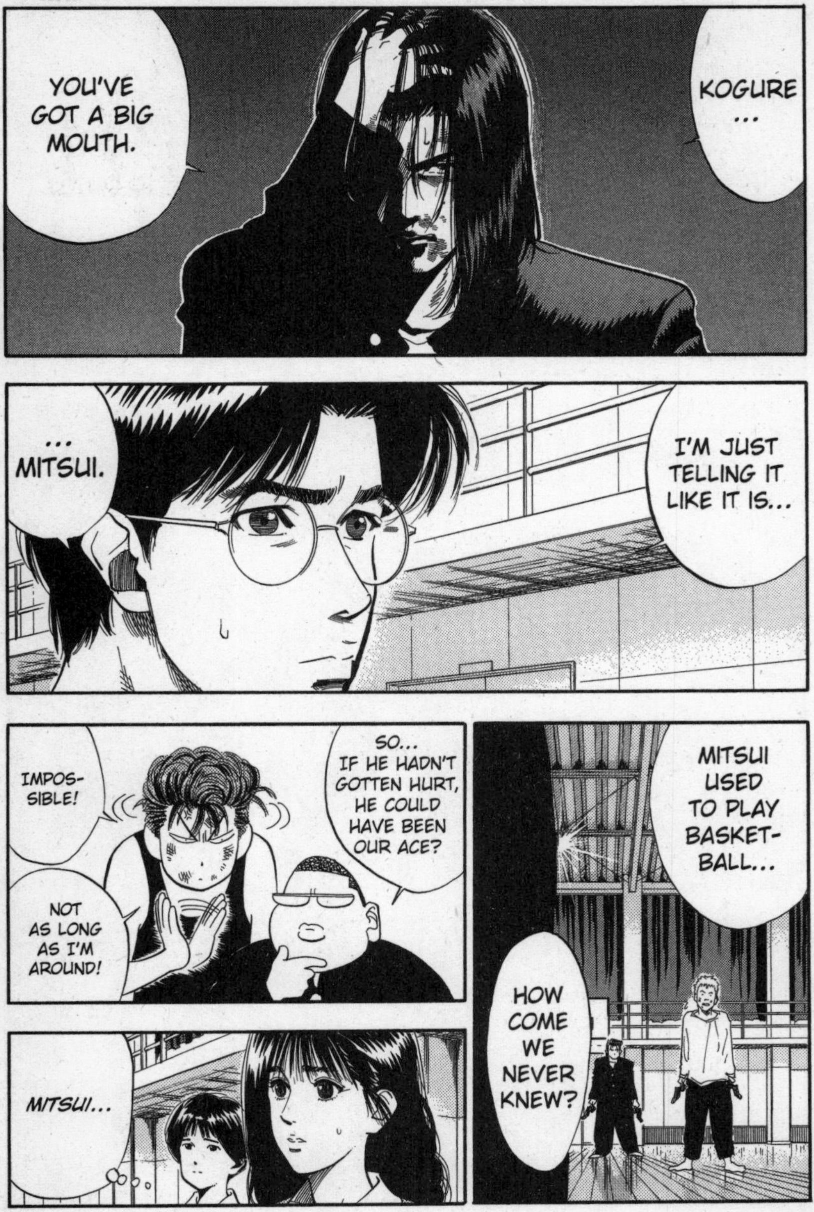
KOGURE ...
YOU'VE GOT A BIG MOUTH.
I'M JUST TELLING IT LIKE IT IS...
... MITSUI.
MITSUI USED TO PLAY BASKET-BALL...
HOW COME WE NEVER KNEW?
SO... IF HE HADN'T GOTTEN HURT, HE COULD HAVE BEEN OUR ACE?
IMPOS-SIBLE!
NOT AS LONG AS I'M AROUND!
MITSUI...

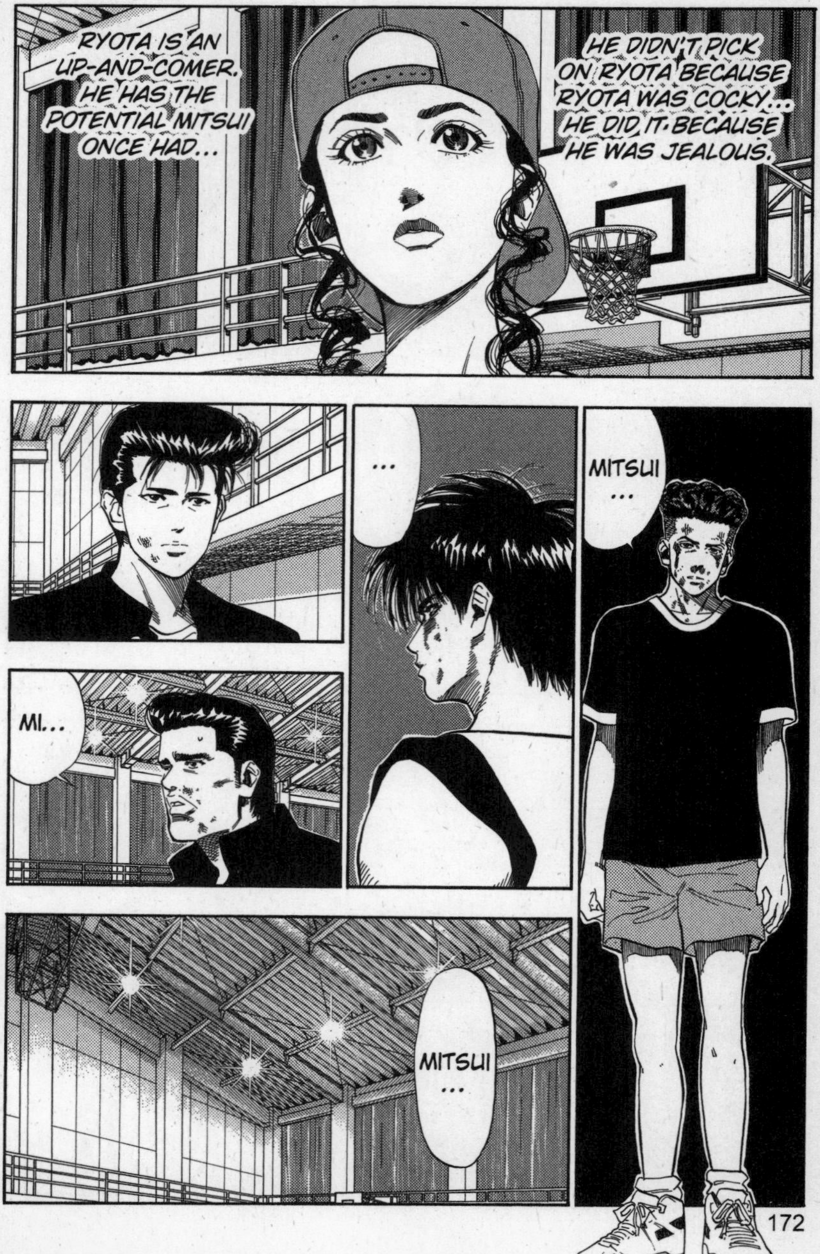
HE DIDN'T PICK ON RYOTA BECAUSE RYOTA WAS COCKY... HE DID IT BECAUSE HE WAS JEALOUS.
RYOTA IS AN UP-AND-COMER. HE HAS THE POTENTIAL MITSUI ONCE HAD...
MITSUI ...
...
MI...
MITSUI ...

READ THIS WAY

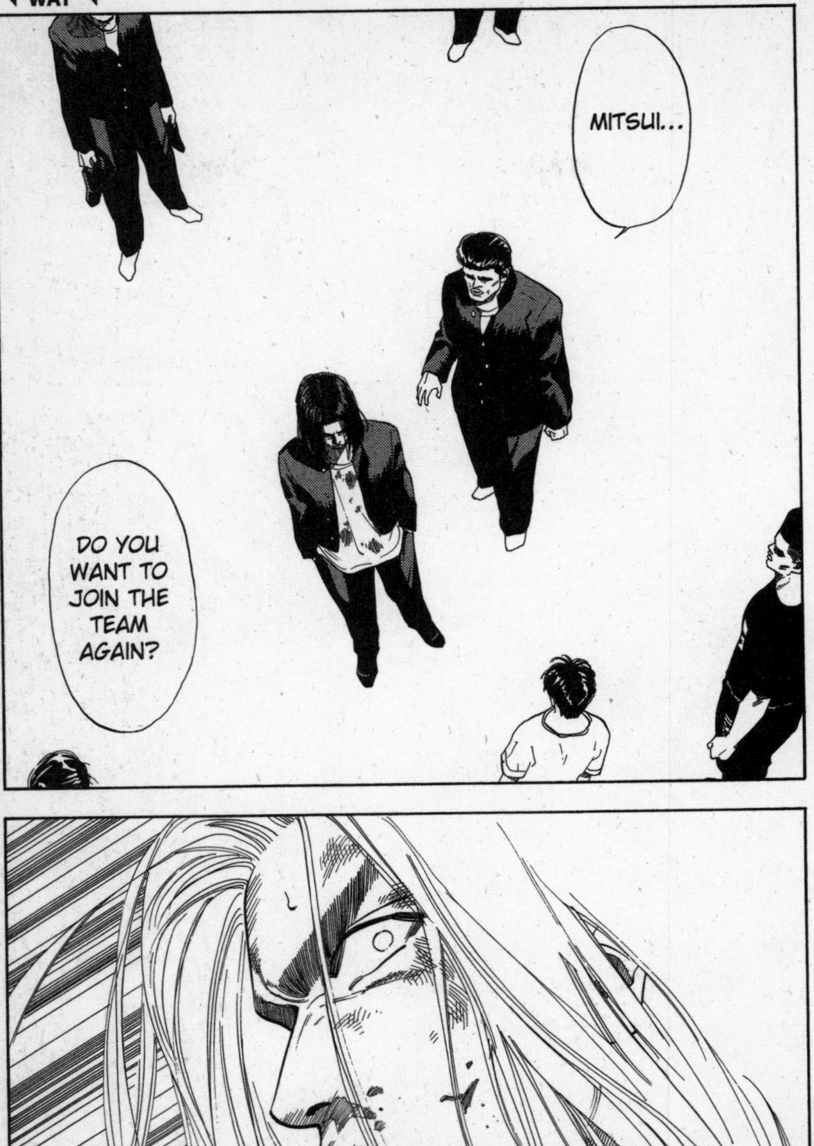
MITSUI...
DO YOU WANT TO JOIN THE TEAM AGAIN?

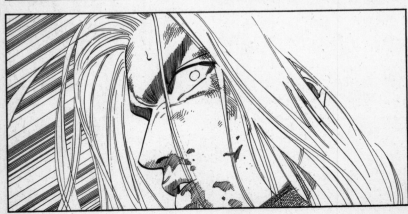

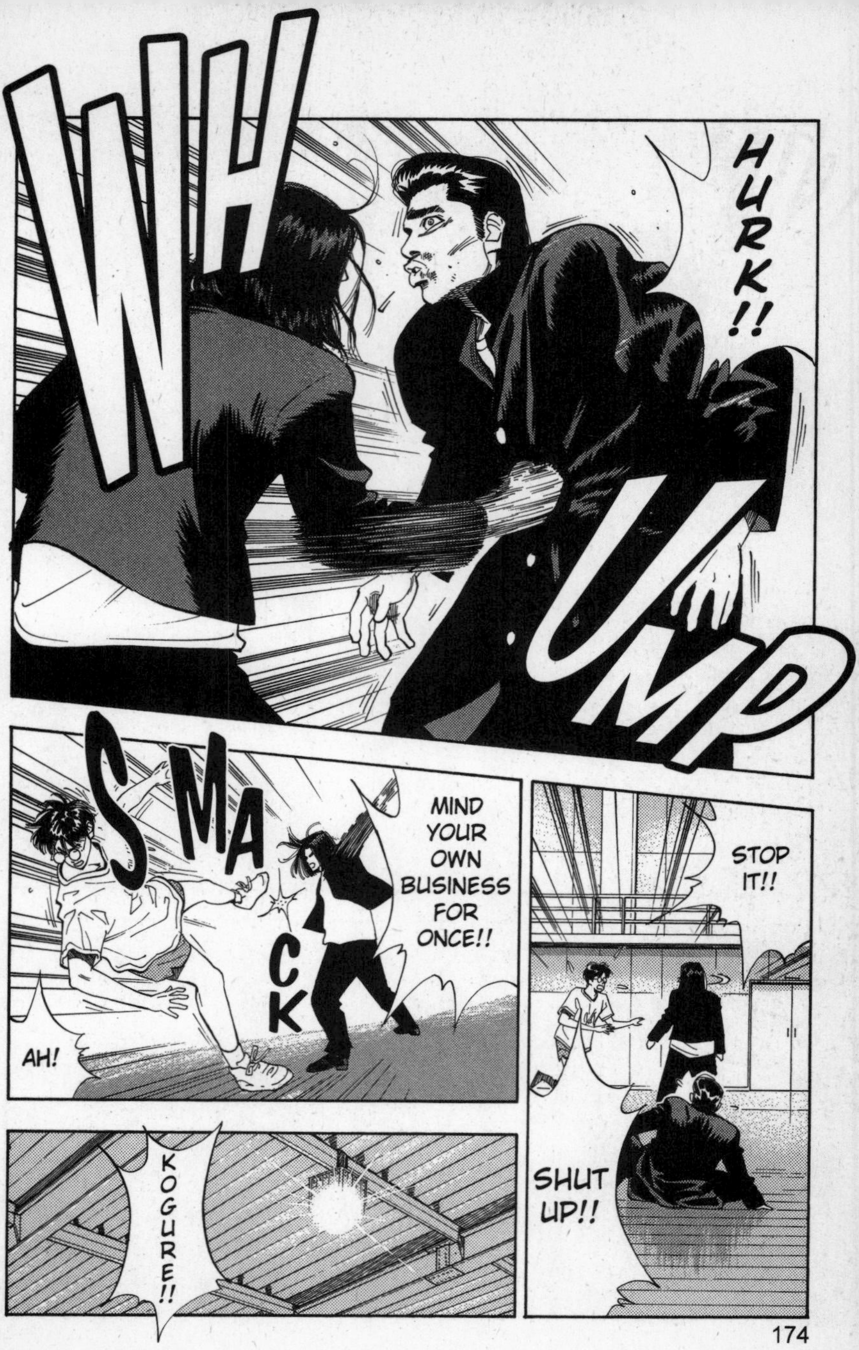
HURK!!
WHUMP
STOP IT!!
SHUT UP!!
MIND YOUR OWN BUSINESS FOR ONCE!!
SMACK
AH!
KOGURE!!

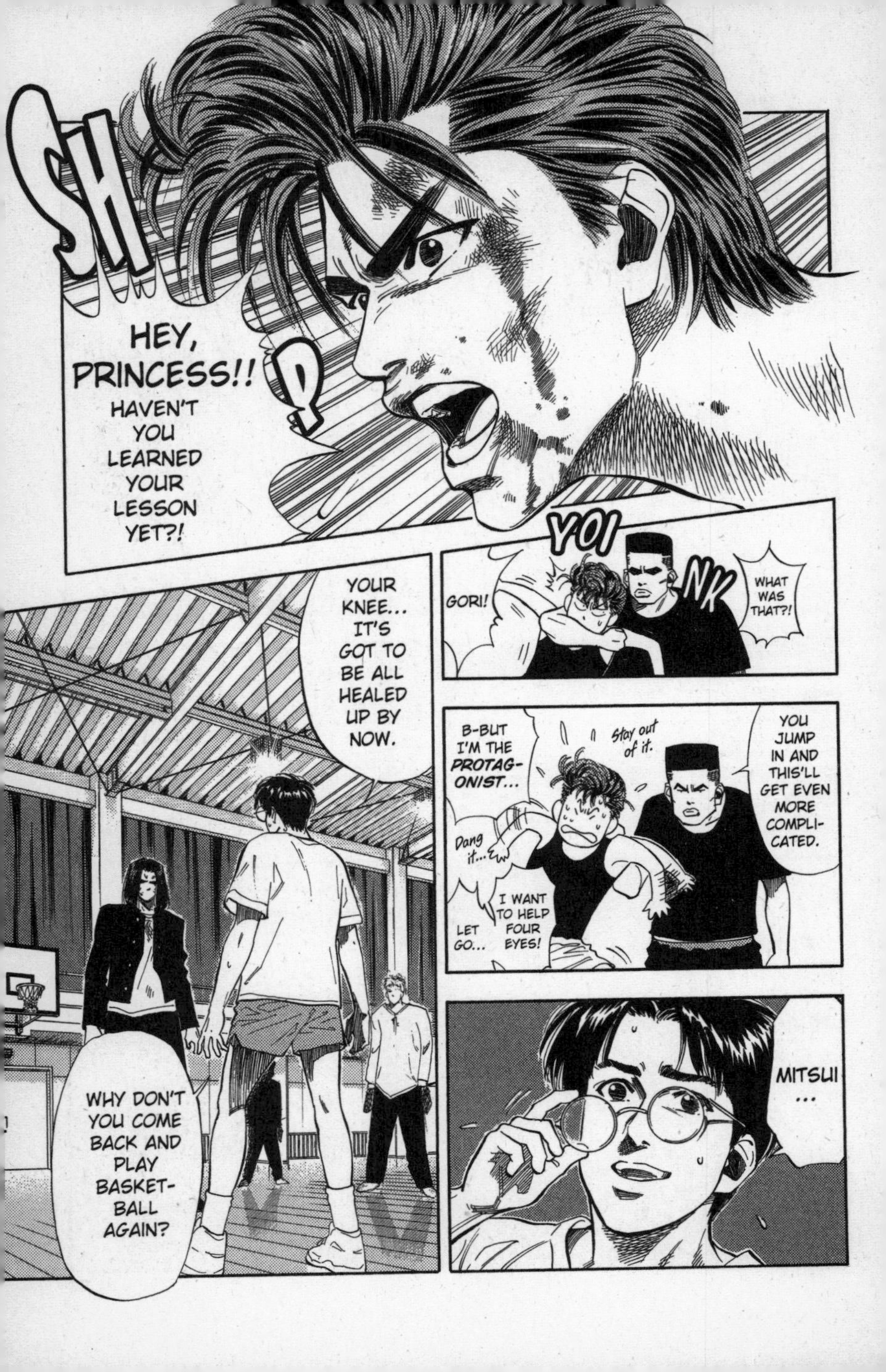
SH
HEY, PRINCESS!! HAVEN'T YOU LEARNED YOUR LESSON YET?!
YOINK
WHAT WAS THAT?!
GORI!
YOU JUMP IN AND THIS'LL GET EVEN MORE COMPLICATED.
Stay out of it.
B-BUT I'M THE PROTAGONIST...
Dang it...
I WANT TO HELP FOUR EYES!
LET GO...
MITSUI...
YOUR KNEE... IT'S GOT TO BE ALL HEALED UP BY NOW.
WHY DON'T YOU COME BACK AND PLAY BASKETBALL AGAIN?

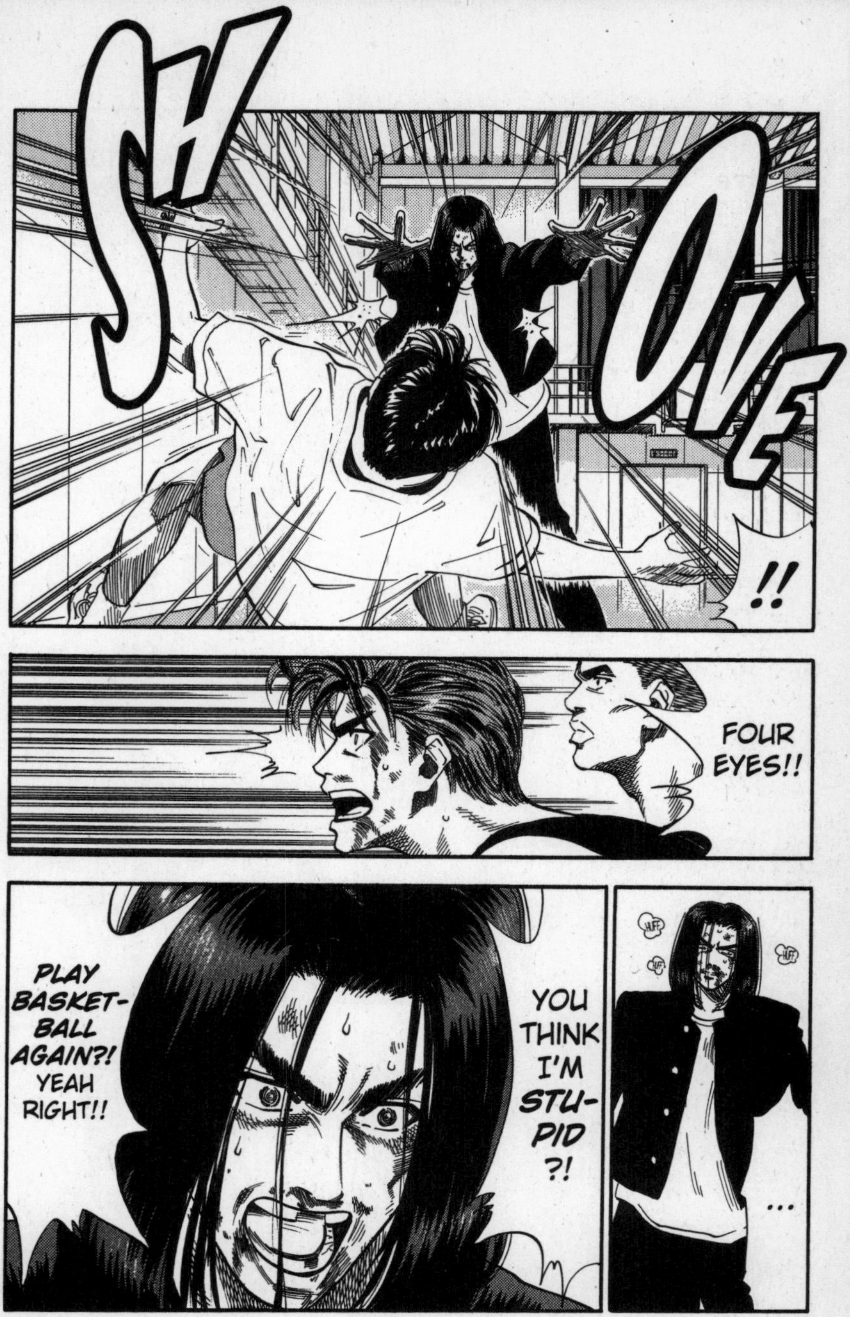
SHOVE
!!
FOUR EYES!!
HUFF
HUFF
HUFF
...
YOU THINK I'M STUPID?!
PLAY BASKETBALL AGAIN?! YEAH RIGHT!!

READ THIS WAY

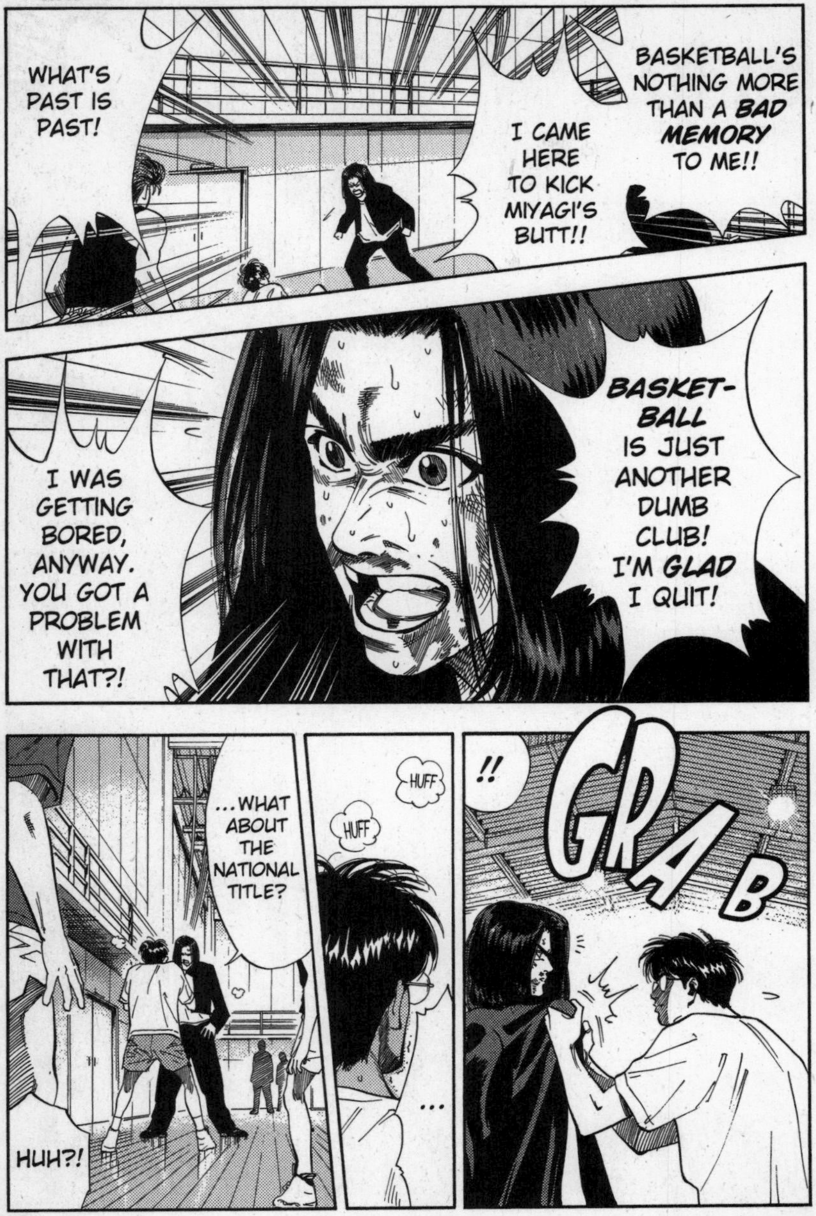

BASKETBALL'S NOTHING MORE THAN A BAD MEMORY TO ME!!
I CAME HERE TO KICK MIYAGI'S BUTT!!
WHAT'S PAST IS PAST!
BASKET-BALL IS JUST ANOTHER DUMB CLUB! I'M GLAD I QUIT!
I WAS GETTING BORED, ANYWAY. YOU GOT A PROBLEM WITH THAT?!
GRAB
!!
HUFF
HUFF
...
...WHAT ABOUT THE NATIONAL TITLE?
HUH?!

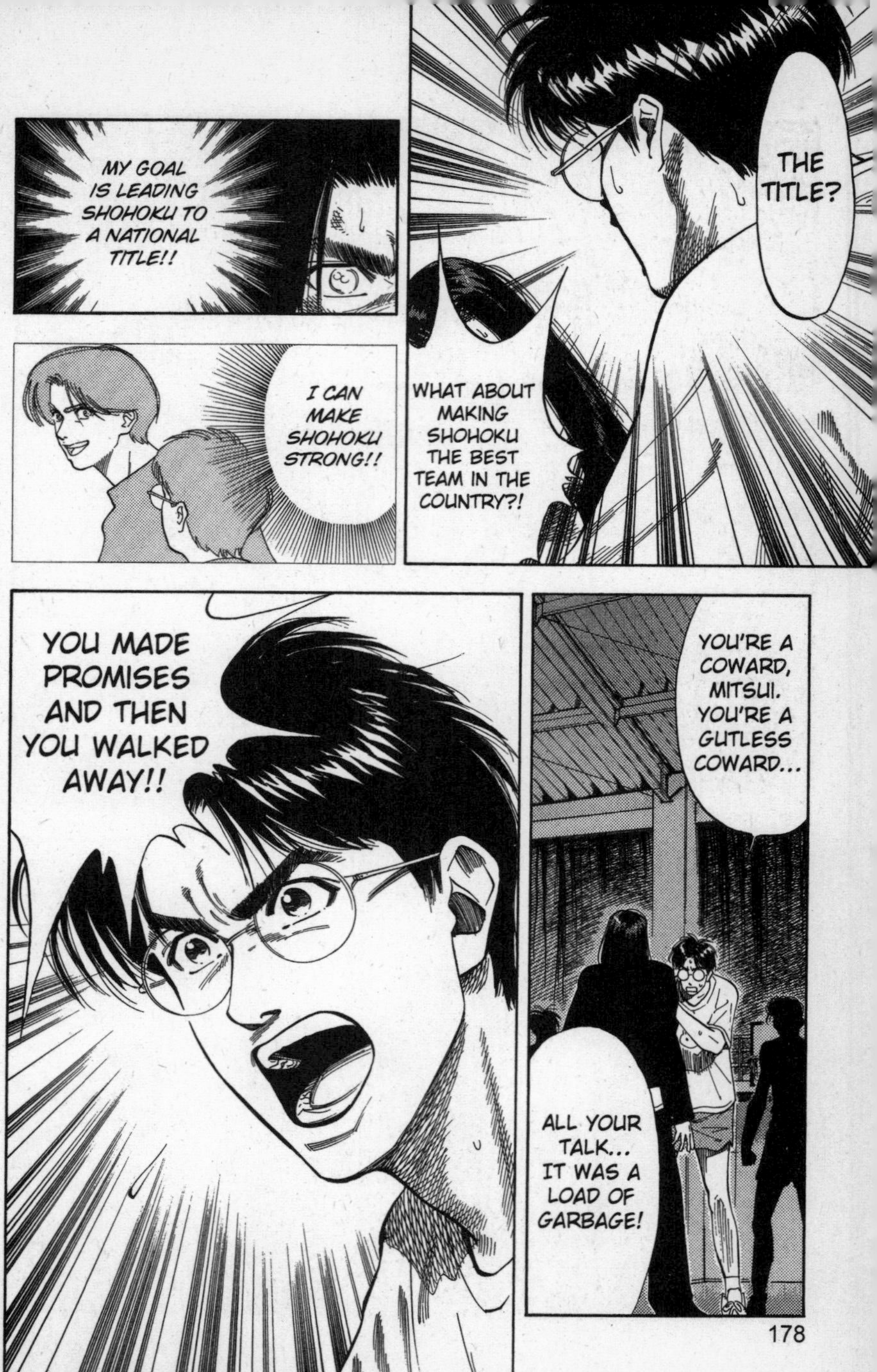
THE TITLE?
WHAT ABOUT MAKING SHOHOKU THE BEST TEAM IN THE COUNTRY?!
MY GOAL IS LEADING SHOHOKU TO A NATIONAL TITLE!!
I CAN MAKE SHOHOKU STRONG!!
YOU'RE A COWARD, MITSUI. YOU'RE A GUTLESS COWARD...
ALL YOUR TALK... IT WAS A LOAD OF GARBAGE!
YOU MADE PROMISES AND THEN YOU WALKED AWAY!!

READ THIS WAY

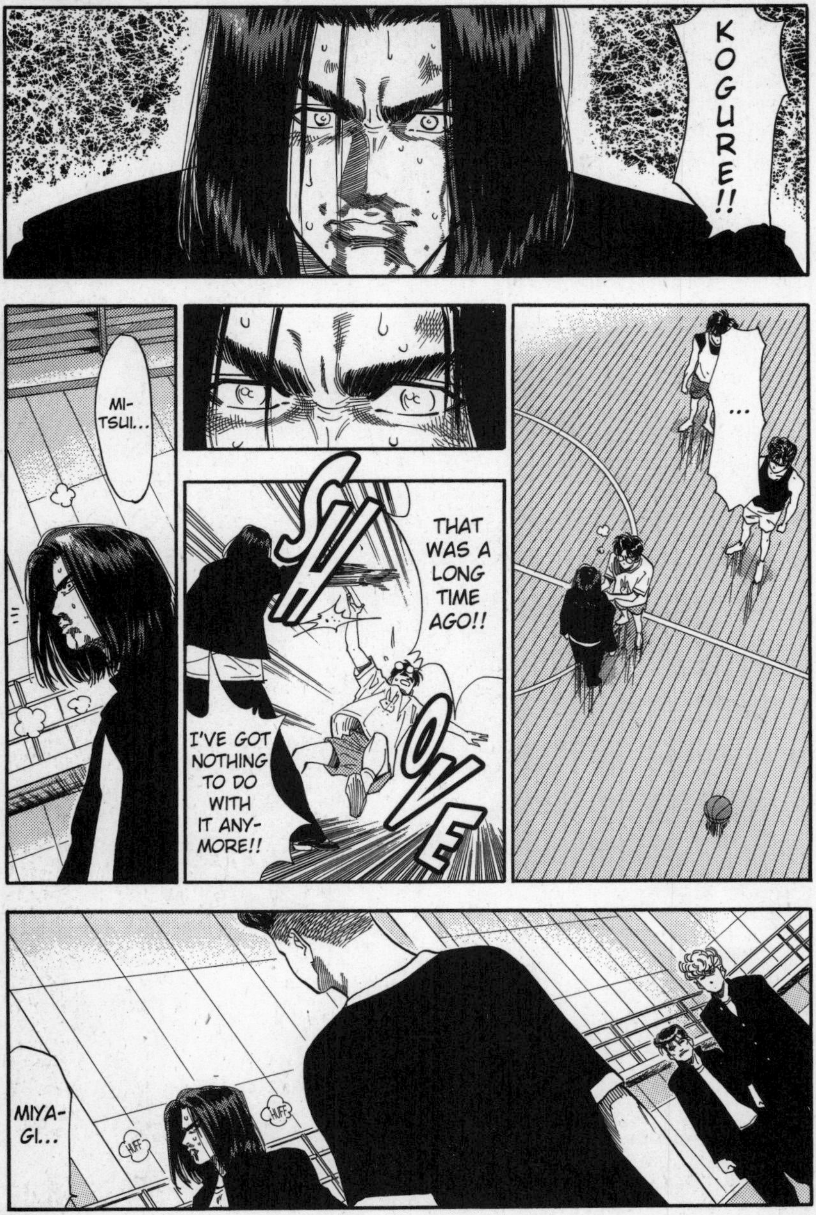
KOGURE!!
...
THAT WAS A LONG TIME AGO!!
I'VE GOT NOTHING TO DO WITH IT ANYMORE!!
SHOVE
MI-TSUI...
HUFF
HUFF
MIYA-GI...

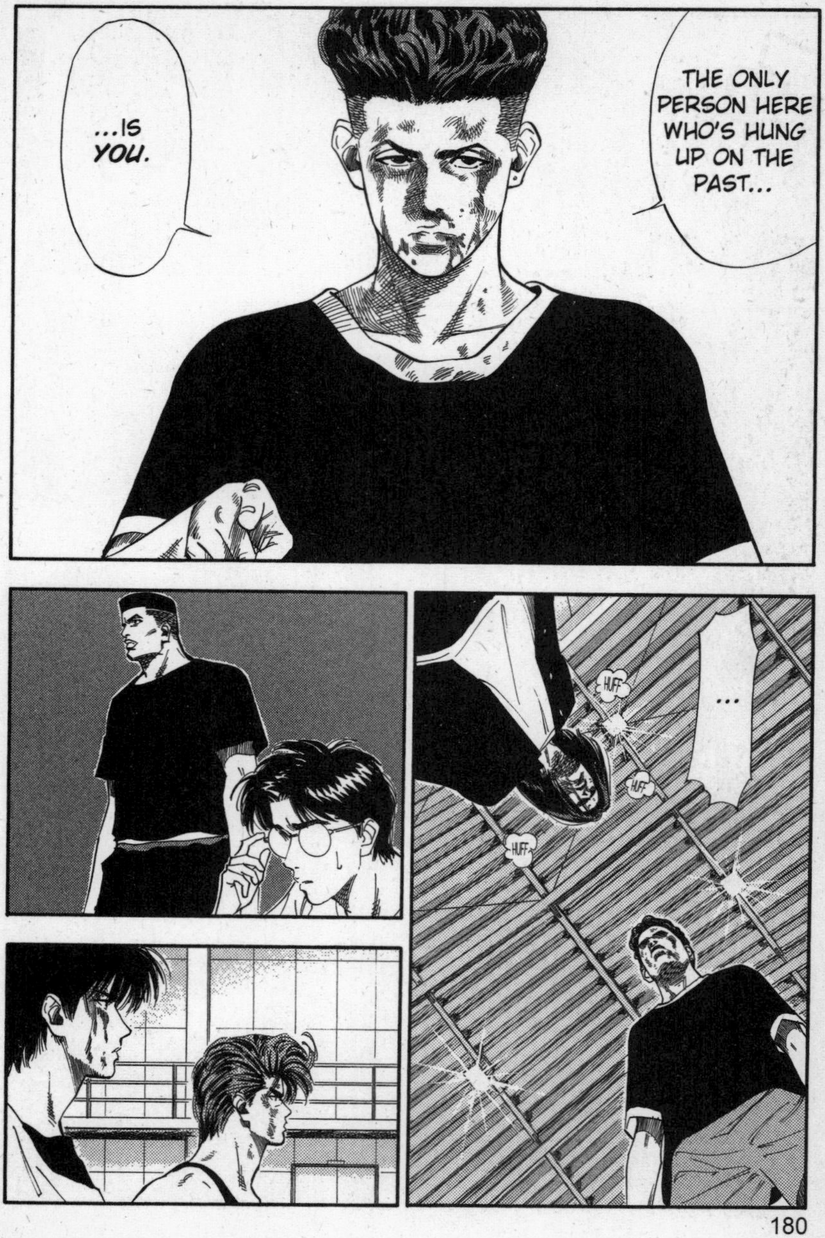
THE ONLY PERSON HERE WHO'S HUNG UP ON THE PAST...
...IS YOU.
HUFF
...
HUFF
HUFF

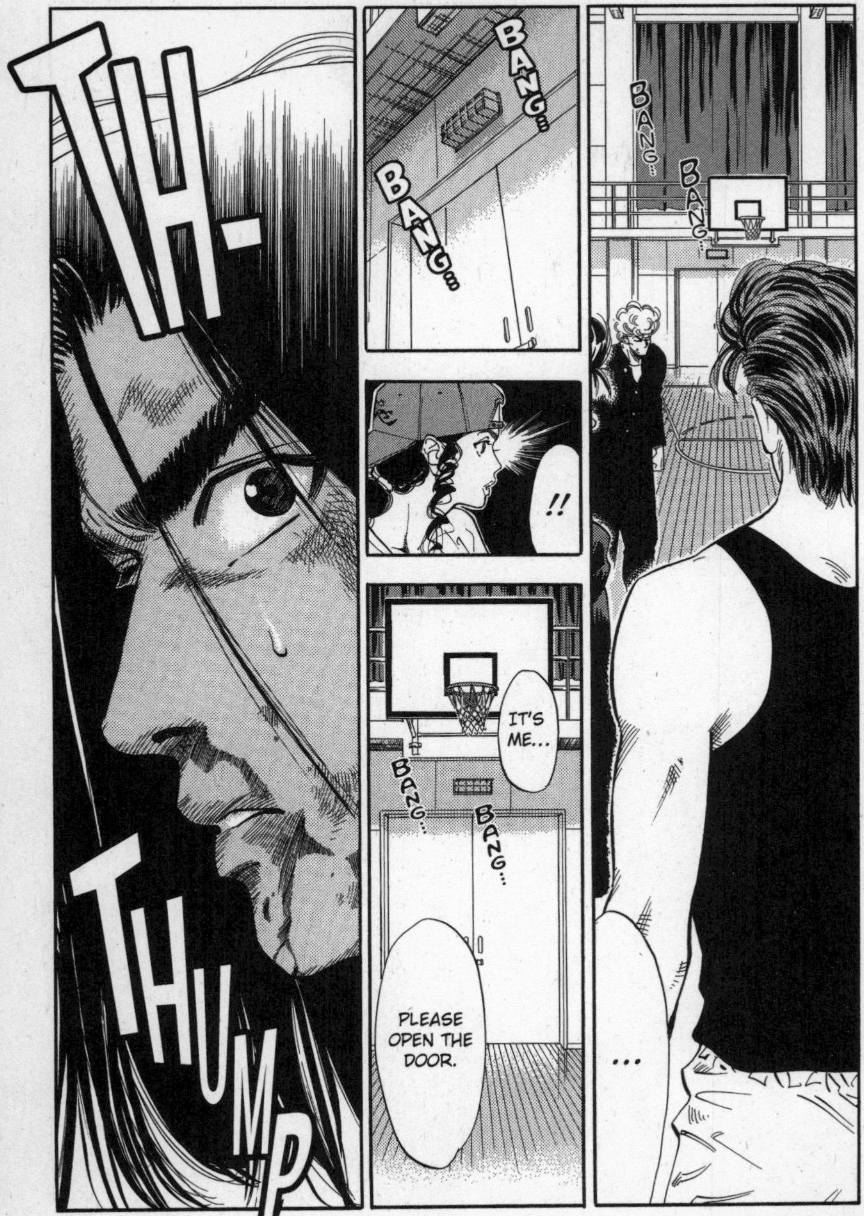
BANG...
BANG...
...
BANG...
BANG...
!!
IT'S ME...
BANG...
BANG...
PLEASE OPEN THE DOOR.
TH-
THUMP

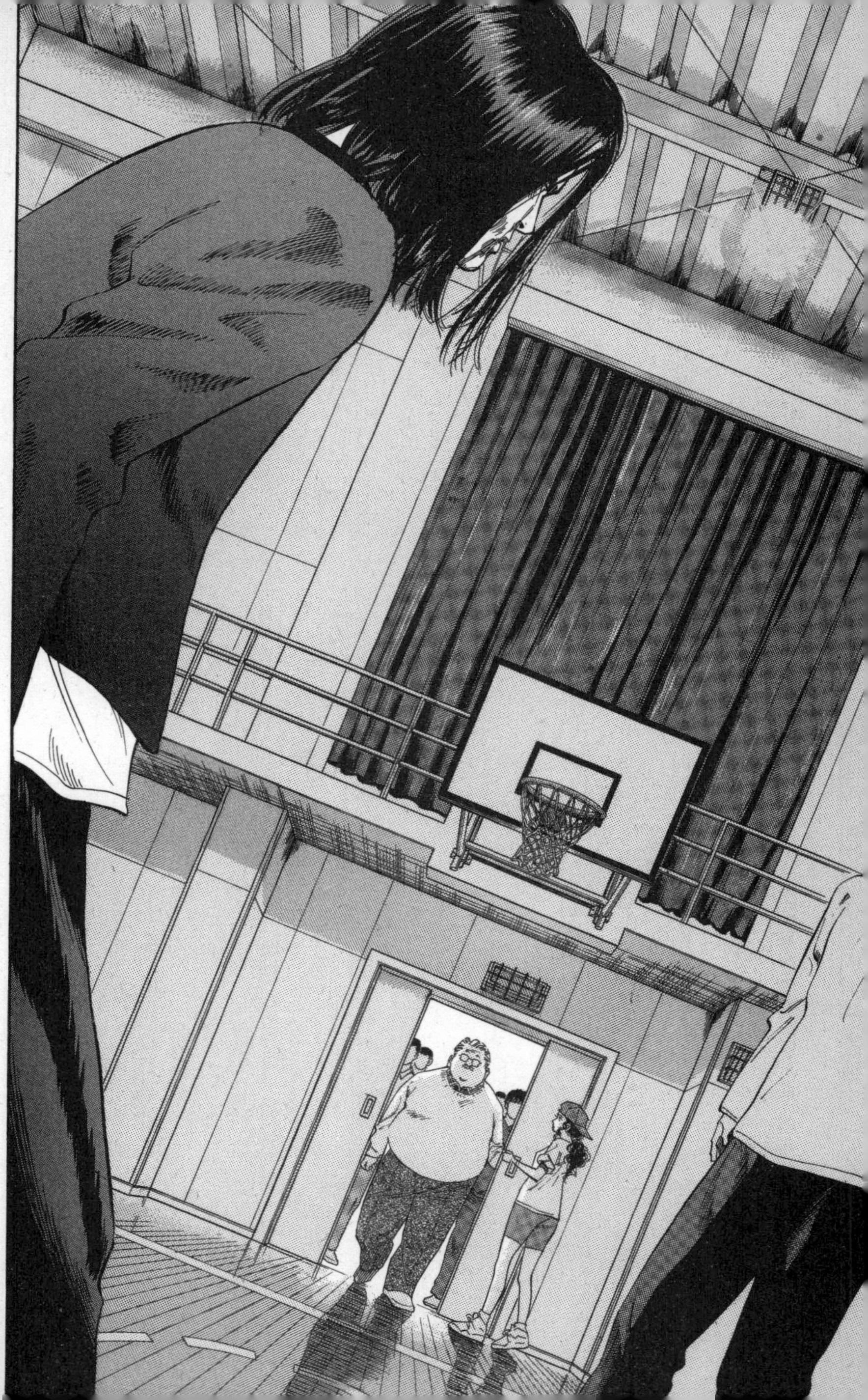

OH!

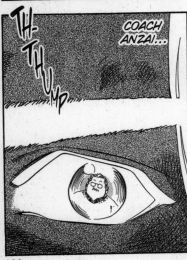

TH-TH-THUMP

COACH ANZAI...

TH-TH-THUMP

COACH...

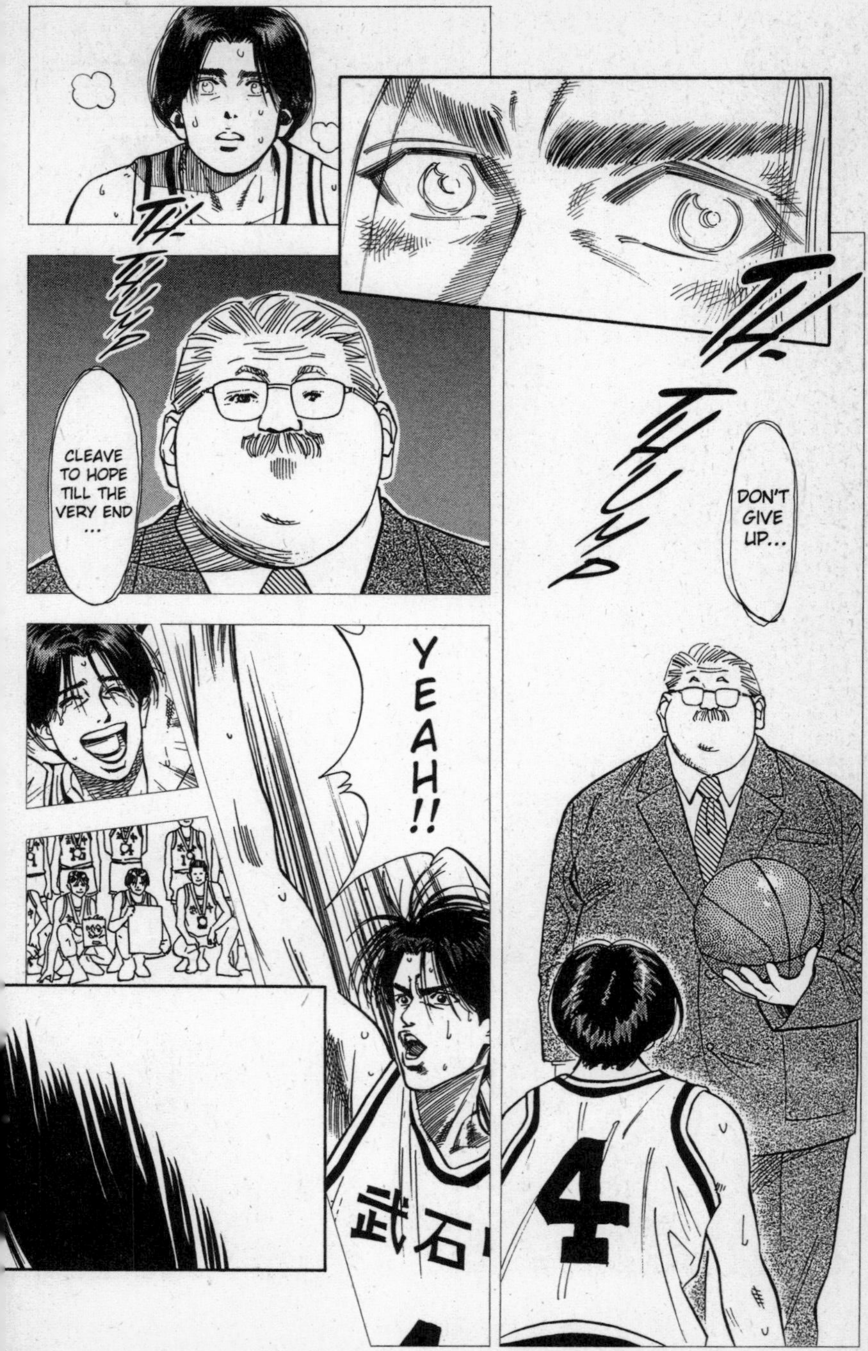
TH-THUMP
DON'T GIVE UP...
TH-THUMP
CLEAVE TO HOPE TILL THE VERY END ...
YEAH!!

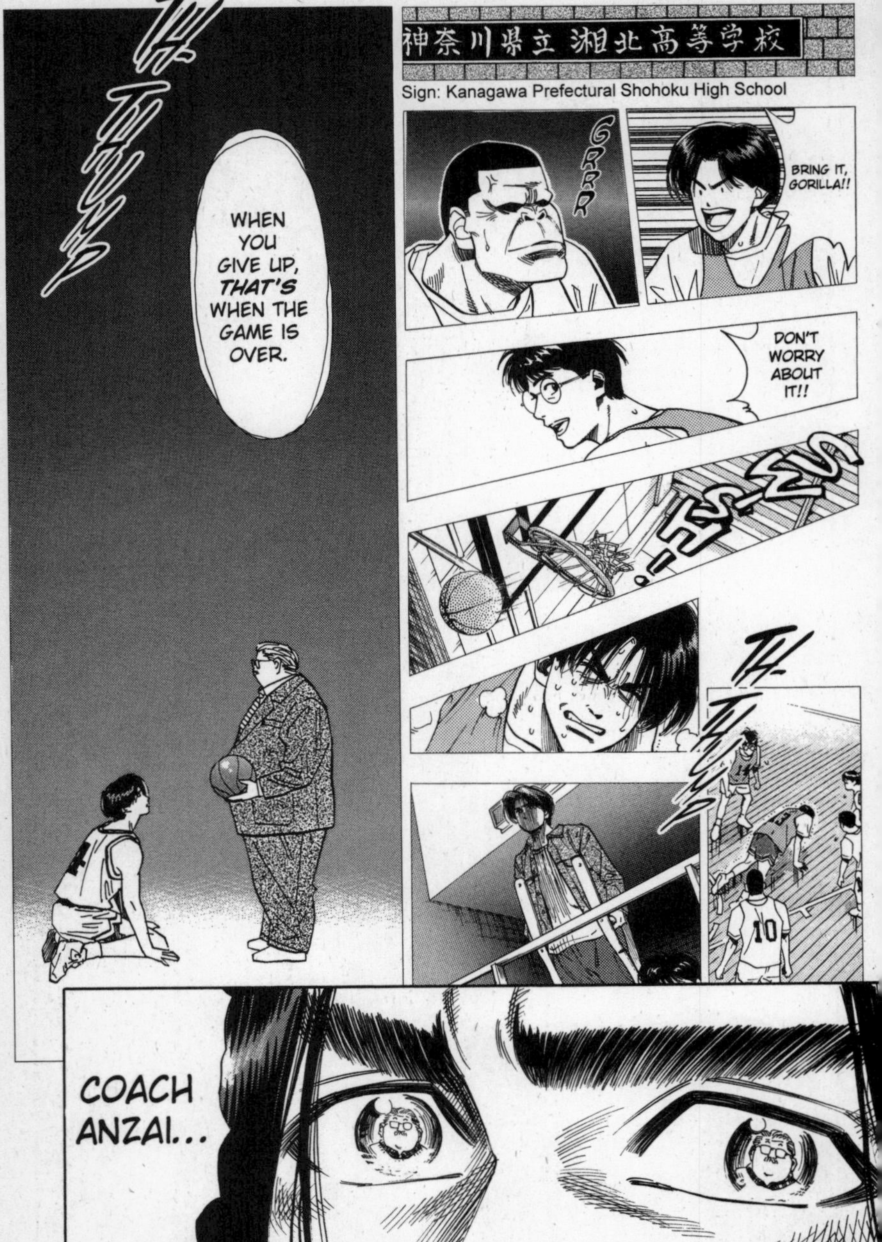

神奈川県立 湘北高等学校
Sign: Kanagawa Prefectural Shohoku High School
BRING IT, GORILLA!!
GRRRR
DON'T WORRY ABOUT IT!!
WHEN YOU GIVE UP, *THAT'S* WHEN THE GAME IS OVER.
COACH ANZAI...

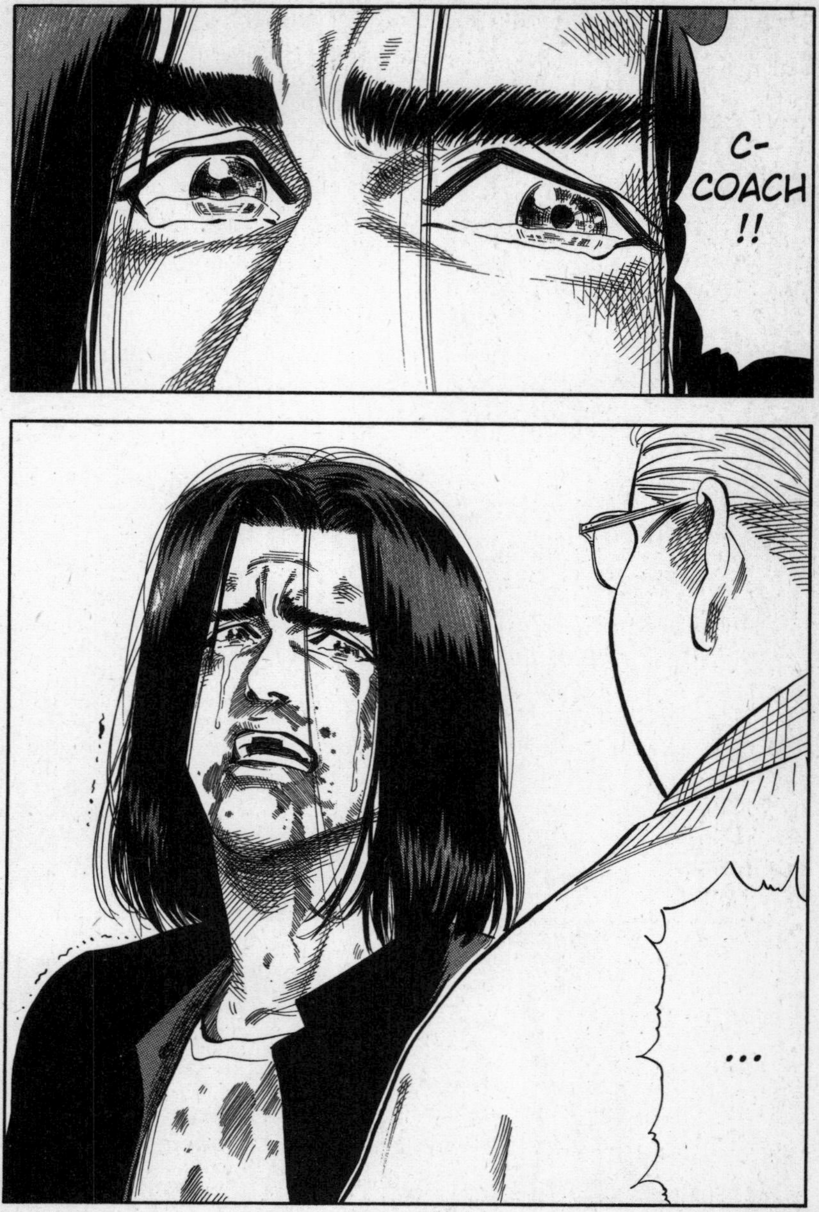
C-
COACH
!!
...

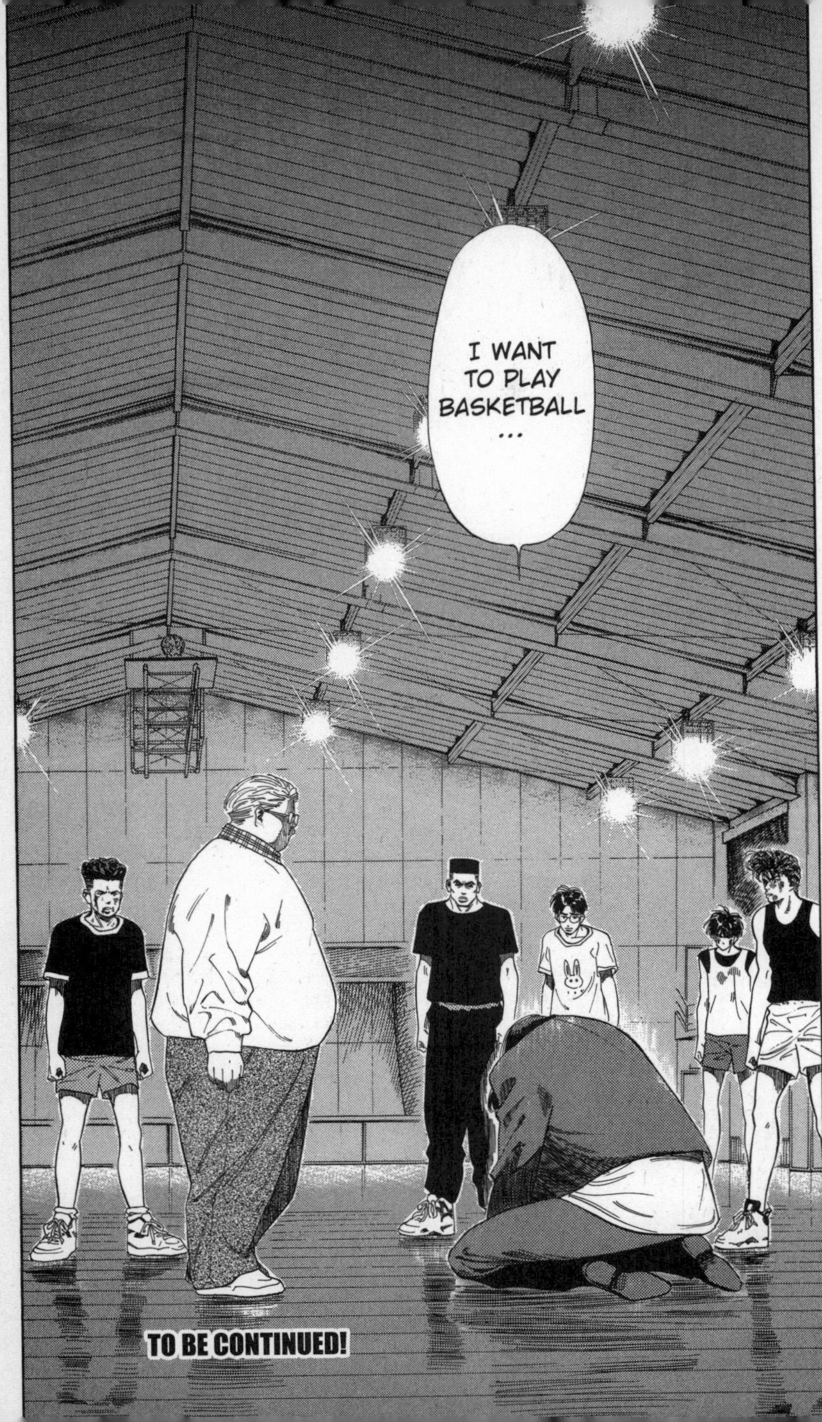
I WANT TO PLAY BASKETBALL ...
TO BE CONTINUED!

Coming Next Volume

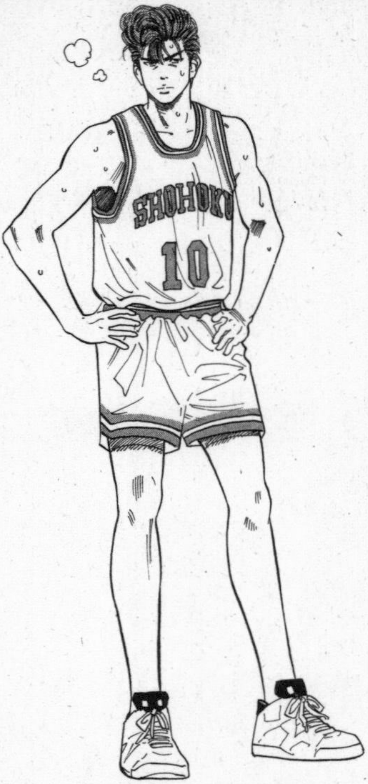
SHOHOKU
10

The players avoid getting in trouble over their raucous fistfight and quickly get back to practice. However, as punishment for their actions, Coach Anzai forces some of Shohoku's best players (and biggest problems) to sit out the match against the team from Miuradai. Because of this, though, Miuradai takes a commanding lead in the first half. If Hanamichi gets to hit the floor, will he be able to keep his cool, or will he only succeed in getting ejected in record time?

ON SALE APRIL 2010

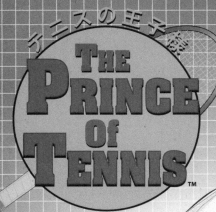

THE PRINCE OF TENNIS™

Action! Intrigue! Espionage! High School tennis has never been this exciting!

$7.95

SHONEN JUMP GRAPHIC NOVEL

THE PRINCE OF TENNIS

Story & Art by Takeshi Konomi

volume 1

Manga on sale now!

Join the Cast of Three's Company

All right, kiddos—Coach O's aiming to put you in league with the greatest NBA three-point shooters all time: Bird, Ellis, Hodges and Hornacek. So to honor the old school, throw on your John Stockton short-shorts and let's get cracking!

Do Sweat the Technique

First things first: the three-point arc. Know your arc like Noah knew his. The arc consists of two parallel lines extending from underneath each basket, which then converge near center court to form a semicircle. Any shot taken from anywhere behind this line is worth three points.

1. Be sure to find an opening. As your point guard is running the offense, move without the ball and find a weak spot in the defense. Situate yourself somewhere behind the arc—wherever you're most comfortable—be it the left or right wing or the top of the key. It's important to remember that both feet must be completely behind the line as you're taking the shot. After the shot has left your hands, however, it is permissible for your feet to land on or inside the line.

2. Once you receive the ball, hold your dribble. Keep your knees bent and your feet solidly on the ground. Be ready to shoot—keeping your arms raised at 90-degree angles. This gives you the advantage of the "triple-threat" position. Coach Omake doesn't mean to say you can sing, dance and act all in one go—no, triple threat means you are a threat to dribble, shoot or pass. This will keep the defense honest and create a small window of space between you and your defender.

3. Hold the ball correctly! The fingertips of your strong hand should be directly in front of your face and centered on the ball. Your weak hand should merely offer support on the side of the ball. Keep the ball held high—but not too high! You still want to be able to view your defender over the ball. Your strong shooting hand should be cocked and ready to shoot. How do you know it's cocked? You should be able to see wrinkles on the back of your wrist.

4. If you're in the right spot and in the ready position (keep in mind this should all take place within a fraction of a second), you've got the green light to shoot the ball! Spring yourself upward off the floor—your jump should be directly up and down to increase your accuracy—and release the ball on your way up into the air, not at the apex of your jump. As the ball is released from your hands, your shooting arm should be straight and the wrist of your shooting hand should drop downward. This follow-through will give the ball a nice reverse-spin as it travels toward the basket. Watch the shot fall through the basket and then watch the referee—if both arms are raised with three fingers held up on each hand, you've scored a three-pointer!

Advanced Training

You may be thinking, "But Coach Omake, what if I can't get open and my opponent is playing me too tightly? How can I shoot the ball?" In that case, you may want to employ some deceptive tactics—a well-rehearsed jab-step or a pump-fake can keep your opponent at bay and give you an open shot. Or have one of your teammates set a screen for you.

Congratulations, *S-Dunkers*—you've just received your certificate of completion from the SDOT Sharpshooters Academy! So hit the showers and don't forget to celebrate—you've earned it!

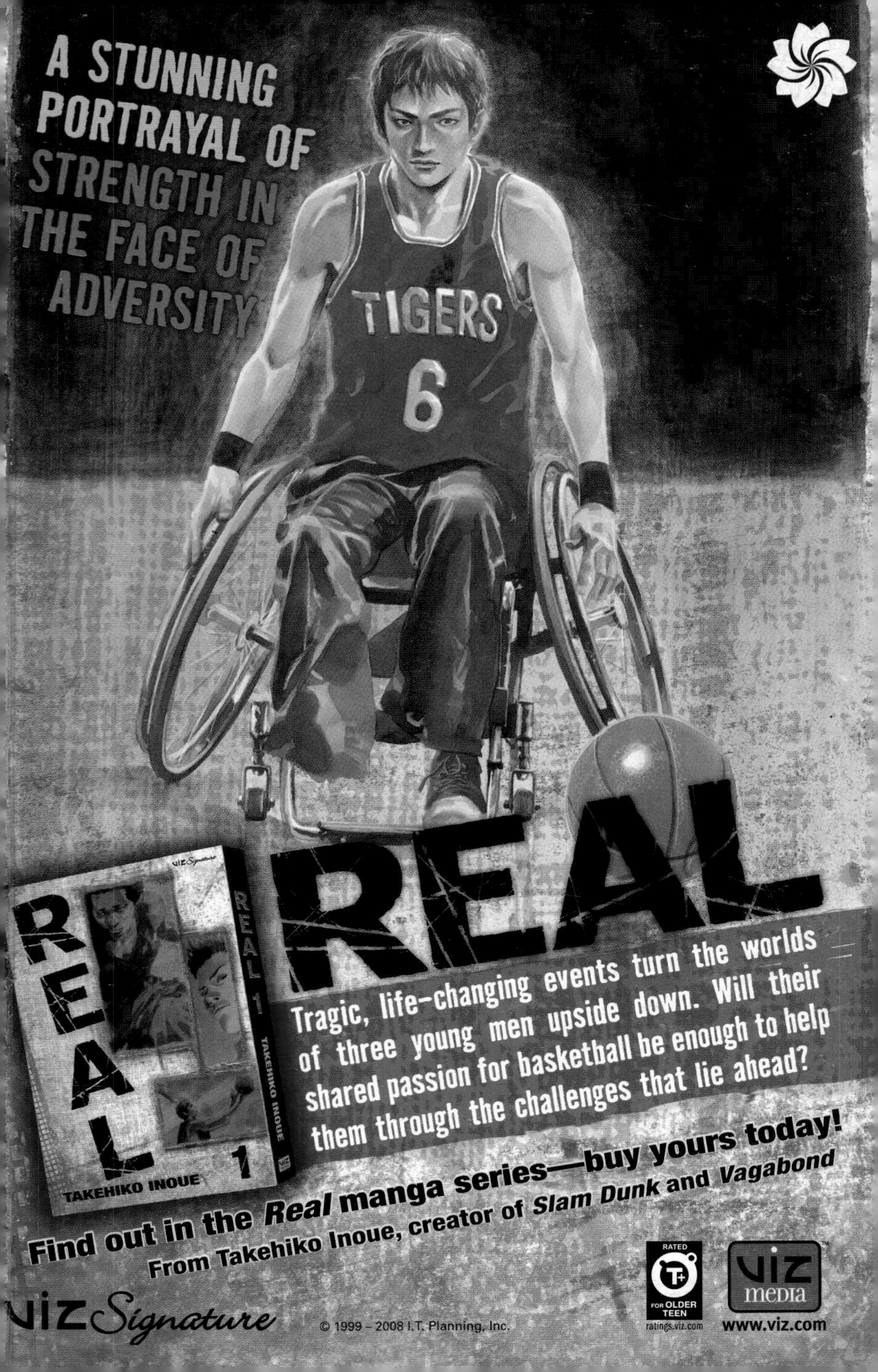
A STUNNING PORTRAYAL OF STRENGTH IN THE FACE OF ADVERSITY
TIGERS
6
REAL
REAL 1 TAKEHIKO INOUE
REAL 1
TAKEHIKO INOUE
Tragic, life-changing events turn the worlds of three young men upside down. Will their shared passion for basketball be enough to help them through the challenges that lie ahead?
Find out in the Real manga series—buy yours today!
From Takehiko Inoue, creator of Slam Dunk and Vagabond
VIZ Signature
© 1999 – 2008 I.T. Planning, Inc.
RATED T+ FOR OLDER TEEN
ratings.viz.com
VIZ media
www.viz.com